Extension of Coastal State Jurisdiction in Enclosed and Semi-enclosed Seas

The current jurisdictional status of the Mediterranean Sea is remarkable. Nearly 50 per cent of the Mediterranean waters are high seas and therefore beyond the jurisdiction of coastal States. This situation means that there are no points in the Mediterranean Sea where the coasts of two States would be more than 400 nautical miles apart. Such a legal situation generally prevents coastal States from adopting and enforcing their laws on the Mediterranean high seas, in respect of many important fields such as the protection and preservation of the marine environment, as well as the conservation of marine living resources.

The jurisdictional landscape of the Adriatic Sea as a sub-sea and sub-region of the Mediterranean is even more interesting. Croatia has proclaimed an Ecological and Fisheries Protection Zone, Slovenia has proclaimed a Zone of Ecological Protection, while Italy has adopted a framework law for the proclamation of its Zone of Ecological Protection without proclaiming its regime in the Adriatic. It is noteworthy that if all Mediterranean and Adriatic States would proclaim an Exclusive Economic Zone (EEZ), there would not be a single stretch of high seas left in the entire Mediterranean Sea. Both the Adriatic and Mediterranean fall into the category of enclosed or semi-enclosed seas regulated by Part IX of the United Nations Convention on the Law of the Sea (UNCLOS).

This book assesses the legal nature of Part IX of UNCLOS and discusses potential benefits of the extension of coastal State jurisdiction (proclamation of EEZs and/or similar *sui generis* zones), particularly in light of the recent calls for an integrated and holistic approach to the management of different activities in the Mediterranean Sea. It examines the actual or potential extension of coastal State jurisdiction in the Adriatic Sea, against the background of similar extensions elsewhere in the Mediterranean and against the background of relevant EU policies. It additionally explores whether Part IX of UNCLOS imposes any duties of co-operation in relation to the extension of coastal State jurisdiction in enclosed or semi-enclosed seas, and puts forward practical suggestions as to how the issue of extension of coastal State jurisdiction could be approached in a way which would enhance States' existing co-operation and improve the overall governance in the Mediterranean and Adriatic seas.

This book will be of interest to policymakers and academics, and students of international law and the law of the sea.

Mitja Grbec is the President of the Maritime Law Association of Slovenia, senior lecturer at the University of Ljubljana, Faculty of Maritime Studies and Transportation, and visiting lecturer at the IMO International Maritime Law Institute in Malta. He read law at the University of Ljubljana, Faculty of Law and completed his LL.M. and Ph.D. studies in international maritime law at the IMO International Maritime Law Institute (IMO IMLI) in Malta.

IMLI Studies in International Maritime Law
Series Editor: Professor David Joseph Attard
Director of the IMO International Maritime Law Institute

The IMO International Maritime Law Institute (IMLI) was established under the auspices of the International Maritime Organization, a specialised agency of the United Nations.

The Institute is an international centre for the training of specialists in international maritime law. It contributes to the development and dissemination of knowledge and expertise in the international regime of merchant shipping and related areas of maritime law and the general law of the sea, with special reference to the international regulations and procedures for safety and efficiency of shipping and the prevention of marine pollution. For further information on the Institute please visit its website at: www.imli.org.

The series is dedicated to publishing original, scholarly contributions which analyse key issues in international maritime law. The works published in the series will be of interest to an audience of students and scholars in maritime law, maritime lawyers and barristers, and professionals in the shipping industry.

Available Titles:

Limitation of Liability in International Maritime Conventions
The Relationship between Global Limitation Conventions and Particular Liability Regimes
Norman A. Martínez Gutiérrez

Serving the Rule of International Maritime Law
Essays in Honour of Professor David Joseph Attard
Edited by A. Martínez Gutiérrez

Extension of Coastal State Jurisdiction in Enclosed or Semi-enclosed Seas
A Mediterranean and Adriatic Perspective
Mitja Grbec

Extension of Coastal State Jurisdiction in Enclosed and Semi-enclosed Seas

A Mediterranean and Adriatic Perspective

Mitja Grbec

LONDON AND NEW YORK

First published 2014
by Routledge
2 Park Square, Milton Park, Abingdon, Oxon, OX14 4RN

Simultaneously published in the USA and Canada
by Routledge
711 Third Avenue, New York, NY 10017

Routledge is an imprint of the Taylor & Francis Group, an informa business

© 2014 Mitja Grbec

The right of Mitja Grbec to be identified as author of this work has been asserted by him in accordance with sections 77 and 78 of the Copyright, Designs and Patents Act 1988.

All rights reserved. No part of this book may be reprinted or reproduced or utilised in any form or by any electronic, mechanical, or other means, now known or hereafter invented, including photocopying and recording, or in any information storage or retrieval system, without permission in writing from the publishers.

Trademark notice: Product or corporate names may be trademarks or registered trademarks, and are used only for identification and explanation without intent to infringe.
British Library Cataloguing in Publication

British Library Cataloguing in Publication Data
A catalogue record for this book is available from the British Library

Library of Congress Cataloging-in-Publication Data
A catalog record has been requested for this book

ISBN: 978-0-415-64044-2 (hbk)
ISBN: 978-0-203-07472-5 (ebk)

Typeset in Baskerville
by Keystroke, Station Road, Codsall, Wolverhampton

Printed and bound in Great Britain by
TJ International Ltd, Padstow, Cornwall

**This book is dedicated to the memory of Jan Guzej,
a dear friend and excellent lawyer**

Contents

Foreword	xiii
Preface	xv
Acknowledgements	xvii
Table of cases	xix
Table of treaties	xxi
Table of selected legal instruments	xxix
Table of statutes and other national legislation	xxxv
List of figures	xxxix
List of abbreviations	xli

Introduction   1

I   *Current jurisdictional landscape of the Mediterranean and Adriatic Seas 1*
II *Part IX of UNCLOS 2*
III *Aims of the work 3*
IV *Methodology and contents 3*

1 The Mediterranean and Adriatic as enclosed or semi-enclosed seas   6

1.1 The Mediterranean Sea 6
1.2 The Adriatic Sea 9
1.3 The Mediterranean and/or Adriatic: Enclosed or semi-enclosed seas? 13
1.4 Concluding remarks 15

2 Development of the concept of enclosed or semi-enclosed seas at UNCLOS III and its reflection in the contemporary law of the sea   17

2.1 UNCLOS III 17
    2.1.1 The pre-UNCLOS III period 18
    2.1.2 Position of states at UNCLOS III 19

viii *Extension of Coastal State Jurisdiction in Enclosed or Semi-enclosed Seas*

    2.1.3 Main reasons for the inclusion of specific rules
        on enclosed or semi-enclosed seas in UNCLOS 20

2.2 *A legal definition of an enclosed or semi-enclosed sea 22*
    2.2.1 Evolution of Article 122 at UNCLOS III 22
        2.2.1.1 *ISNT* and *RSNT* 24
    2.2.2 Article 122 of UNCLOS 25
        2.2.2.1 The two State requirements 25
        2.2.2.2 Connection to another sea or the ocean by a narrow
            outlet 26
        2.2.2.3 Consisting entirely or primarily of the territorial seas and
            EEZs of two or more coastal States 28
        2.2.2.4 Should there be a proclaimed EEZ? 29

2.3 *Rights and duties of states bordering an enclosed or semi-enclosed sea 30*
    2.3.1 The Iranian proposal 31
    2.3.2 ISNT 33
    2.3.3 RSNT 34
    2.3.4 Article 123 of UNCLOS 35
        2.3.4.1 An obligation or just an exhortation to co-operate? 36
            2.3.4.1.1 Relevance of the chairman's statement 37
        2.3.4.2 Areas of co-operation 38
        2.3.4.3 The introductory statement of Article 123 and its
            influence on the application of the general rules of
            UNCLOS 39
        2.3.4.4 Interrelation between the introductory and the second
            element of Article 123 42
        2.3.4.5 Institutional or non-institutional co-operation? 44
        2.3.4.6 Does Article 123 affect other users of enclosed or
            semi-enclosed seas? 45

2.4 *Influence of Part IX of UNCLOS on the extension of coastal
State jurisdiction in enclosed or semi-enclosed seas 46*
    2.4.1 Extension of the breadth of the territorial sea in
        enclosed or semi-enclosed seas 47
        2.4.1.1 Proposals by states at UNCLOS III and within the
            SBC 47
        2.4.1.2 Extension of the territorial sea up to the maximum extent
            permitted by international law: A right or a duty? 48
        2.4.1.3 Practice of states bordering enclosed or semi-enclosed
            seas 50
    2.4.2 Proclamation of EEZs and similar zones in enclosed or
        semi-enclosed seas 51
        2.4.2.1 Positions of States at UNCLOS III 51
            2.4.2.1.1 A right to proclaim an EEZ 52

Contents ix

2.4.2.1.2 Delimitation of EEZs 52
2.4.2.1.3 Conservation of living resources and
preservation of historic fishing rights 53
2.4.2.1.4 Navigation 54
2.4.2.2 Proclamation of EEZs 55
2.4.2.3 Fixing external limits of EEZs 56
2.4.2.4 Delimitation of EEZs 58
2.4.2.5 Conclusion of provisional arrangements of a practical
nature pending delimitation (Article 74(3)) 61
2.4.2.5.1 2002 Tunisia/Algeria Agreement: Application
of Article 74(3) and 83(3) of UNCLOS in the
light of Part IX of UNCLOS? 64
2.5 Concluding remarks 67

**3 Extension of coastal State jurisdiction in the
Mediterranean: An Adriatic and EU perspective**   **68**

3.1 The continental shelf and the Mediterranean 68
3.1.1 Delimitation of the Mediterranean continental shelf 71
3.2 The Mediterranean status quo (jurisdictional landscape) 74
*3.3 Extension of coastal state jurisdiction in the Mediterranean and
Adriatic: sui generis zones or quasi EEZs? 76*
3.3.1 Fisheries protection zone (Spain) 76
3.3.2 Zone of ecological protection (France) 80
3.3.3 The Mediterranean (Pelagos) sanctuary: The first
Mediterranean *sui generis* zone? 83
3.3.4 Ecological and fisheries protection zone (Croatia) 87
3.3.5 Zone(s) of ecological protection (Italy): An *in plus
stat minus* or a real *sui generis* zone? 94
3.3.6 Zone of ecological protection (Slovenia) 101
*3.4 Recently proclaimed EEZs in the Mediterranean: de facto or
just virtual EEZs? 105*
3.4.1 Cyprus 105
3.4.2 Syria 112
3.4.3 Libya: In transition from a *sui generis* zone to a full EEZ? 114
3.4.3.1 The limits of the Libyan FPZ 116
3.4.3.2 The Libyan EEZ (2009) 118
3.4.4 Tunisia 119
3.4.5 Malta 121
3.4.6 French and Lebanese EEZs: The end of a '*sui generis* zones
era' in the Mediterranean? 122
*3.5 Recent positions of the EU regarding the extension of coastal
state jurisdiction in the Mediterranean 124*

x *Extension of Coastal State Jurisdiction in Enclosed or Semi-enclosed Seas*

      3.5.1 Extension of coastal state jurisdiction and delimitation
         of maritime zones by EU Member States 125
      3.5.2 Recent initiatives and positions of the EU (European
         Commission) on the extension of coastal state
         jurisdiction in the Mediterranean 126
         3.5.2.1 Venice Declaration (2003) 127
         3.5.2.2 Towards an integrated maritime policy for better
            governance of the Mediterranean? 130
   3.6 Concluding remarks 133

4 Delimitation of maritime boundaries in the (Eastern) Adriatic Sea: Border bays, *uti possidetis* and an enclosed or semi-enclosed sea   134

4.1 Uti possidetis *134*
4.2 Uti possidetis *and the dissolution of the former SFRY 135*
4.3 Uti Possidetis *and maritime delimitations 139*
      4.3.1 Pre-2007 jurisprudence on *uti possidetis 140*
      4.3.2 The applicability of the doctrine of 'effective control'
         (*effectivités*) to cases of maritime delimitation 141
      4.3.3 Application of the principle of *uti possidetis* (and/
         or doctrine of *effectivités*) in cases where it conflicts with
         generally recognized rules and principles of
         international law (law of the sea) 144
4.4 Border bays in international law 148
      4.4.1 State practice regarding bays bordered by more than one
         state (border bays) 148
         4.4.1.1 The Sea of Azov and the Strait of Kerch 150
         4.4.1.2 Delimitation of historic waters (India-Sri Lanka
            and the Mozambique-Tanzania Agreement) 151
*4.5 Croatia/Bosnia and Herzegovina: Is a solution in line with Part IX
of UNCLOS possible? 153*
      4.5.1 The legality of the enclosure of the maritime zone(s)
         of Bosnia Herzegovina within the Croatian system
         of straight baselines 155
      4.5.2 Treaty on the state border between the Republic of
         Croatia and the Republic of Bosnia and Herzegovina 158
      4.5.3 Access of Bosnia and Herzegovina to the Adriatic's
         high seas/EEZs 160
*4.6 Delimitation of the maritime (and land) boundary between
Croatia and Montenegro 162*
      4.6.1 The 2002 Protocol: Provisional arrangements of a practical
         nature applicable to internal waters and territorial sea? 163

Contents xi

4.7 Slovenia-Croatia maritime delimitation dispute: Looking for solutions in the spirit of Part IX of UNCLOS? 166

    4.7.1 Geographical characteristics and general historical background 167

    4.7.2 Delimitation of the (maritime) boundary between the Republic of Croatia and the Republic of Slovenia 168

        4.7.2.1 Border Bay of Piran 169

        4.7.2.2 Territorial contact of Slovenia with the high seas: A reflection of the Slovenian claim to its own continental shelf and EEZ? 172

    4.7.3 Drnovšek-Račan Treaty (2001) 174

    4.7.4 Joint fishing zone (SOPS): Preservation of historic fishing rights in the Northern Adriatic? 177

4.8 2009 Arbitral Agreement between Slovenia and Croatia: Reflecting the spirit of Part IX of UNCLOS? 181

    4.8.1 EU element 183

    4.8.2 Bay of Piran 185

    4.8.3 Applicable law and the principle of *uti possidetis 186*

    4.8.4 Territorial contact of Slovenia with the high seas and zones of sovereign rights and jurisdictions 186

4.9 Concluding remarks 189

5 Present and future co-operation of Adriatic States: Has Part IX of UNCLOS been implemented in the Adriatic?   **190**

5.1 Existing forms of co-operation at Mediterranean level: an Adriatic Sea perspective 190

    5.1.1 Protection and preservation of the marine environment 190

    5.1.2 The Barcelona System 192

        5.1.2.1 Enforcement of the Barcelona system on the high seas: How much added value would bring the extension of coastal State jurisdiction? 193

        5.1.2.2 EEZs or ZEPs? 196

        5.1.2.3 Compliance with the Barcelona Convention 198

    5.1.3 Implementation of the Barcelona System by Adriatic States 200

        5.1.3.1 The Biodiversity Protocol 200

        5.1.3.2 The Prevention and Emergency Protocol 204

        5.1.3.3 The Land-Based Protocol 206

        5.1.3.4 The Offshore Protocol 208

        5.1.3.5 The ICZM Protocol 213

xii *Extension of Coastal State Jurisdiction in Enclosed or Semi-enclosed Seas*

5.2 Management and conservation of living resources 217

5.3 Co-operation in the field of marine scientific research 220

5.4 Other co-operative arrangements between Adriatic States 222

    5.4.1 Agreements concluded within the AII framework 225

        5.4.1.1 Safety of navigation 226

5.5 Adriatic PSSA: Added value to the protection of the Adriatic marine environment? 229

    5.5.1 Work undertaken in relation to the proclamation of an Adriatic PSSA 230

5.6 The role of the EU in the protection and preservation of the Adriatic marine environment 232

5.7 Other areas of co-operation 235

5.8 Concluding remarks 237

6 Current state and possible way forward　　　　　　**239**

6.1 Extension of coastal State jurisdiction in the Adriatic: 'Mini EEZs' or real sui generis *zones? 240*

    6.1.1 *In plus stat minus?* 240

    6.1.2 Real *sui generis* zones or mini EEZs? 243

    6.1.3 The rights of third States and the relation of *sui generis* zones with the high seas 244

6.2 Delimitation of zones of sovereign rights and jurisdiction 246

6.3 A possible way forward in the Adriatic Sea 247

Select bibliography　　　　　　251
Index　　　　　　261

Foreword

The establishment and implementation of maritime jurisdictional claims under the new law of the sea in the Mediterranean Sea are often problematic. There are hardly any points where the coasts of neighbouring States are more than 400 nmi apart. In practical terms, this means that Mediterranean coastal States are not in a position to extend their continental shelf or EEZ up to the maximum extent permitted by international law. Furthermore, in most cases the extension of maritime jurisdiction creates new neighbours and triggers a greater need for the delimitation of maritime boundaries. Indeed, given the 'proximity' between Mediterranean States, the extension of jurisdiction by one coastal State generally affects the interests of more than one State. The ensuing overlapping jurisdictional claims of the littoral States, often facing already tense relations, may produce a conflict potential which frequently leads Mediterranean States not to exercise fully their jurisdictional rights. In this regard, this book written by Dr Mitja Grbec represents an important and scholarly contribution as it provides a valuable analysis which assists in the understanding of the delimitation challenges which Mediterranean States face.

Particularly interesting are the author's views on the linkage between the Adriatic jurisdictional claims and Part IX of UNCLOS on 'Enclosed or Semi-Enclosed Seas'. He provides in this respect a concise examination of the drafting history of the enclosed or semi-enclosed seas provisions at UNCLOS III, which were first proposed by the Government of Italy; an analysis of the legal regime of Part IX of UNCLOS; and an examination of the relevance of the said regime to the extension of coastal State maritime jurisdiction and delimitation of maritime boundaries in the Adriatic and the Mediterranean more generally.

The author in his study focuses on the identification of – at times unique – recent jurisdictional trends in the Mediterranean. He analyses the complex legal nature of the maritime jurisdictional zones claimed by Mediterranean States, and the sensitive problems related to the definition of their external limits. Particularly noteworthy is the author's useful analysis of the maritime jurisdictional practice of the Adriatic States and his emphasis on the multitude of maritime delimitation disputes which arose as a result of the dissolution of the former SFRY.

Given the complexity of delimitation disputes, the author wisely discusses existing co-operative arrangements and the prospects for increased co-operation

xiv *Extension of Coastal State Jurisdiction in Enclosed or Semi-enclosed Seas*

among Adriatic States, emphasising the EU dimension which exerts an important influence in this respect. His proposed possible alternatives to the current process of extension of maritime jurisdiction in the Adriatic and more generally in the Mediterranean are noteworthy. One must support the conclusions of the author that the role of the EU in fostering co-operation in the Mediterranean is crucial.

The author must be complemented for tackling a complex and intricate subject which is of vital importance to littoral States of enclosed and semi-enclosed seas. His conclusions constitute a valuable contribution to the law of maritime delimitation generally, and in particular as it is applied in the Mediterranean Sea. Indeed, his study provides valuable tool to negotiators in their quest to agree on maritime boundaries which achieve an equitable solution.

This monograph, the second in the series 'IMLI Studies in International Maritime Law' follows the highly successful study by N. Martinez on the Limitation of Liability in International Maritime Conventions. Given the high standard of Dr Grbec's work, I am confident that it too will receive a positive response, and contribute to the development of the law of the sea.

D.J. Attard
Director
IMO International Maritime Law Institute

Preface

The aim of this book is to assess the legal nature of Part IX of UNCLOS on enclosed or semi-enclosed seas and to provide a concise study on the recent process of the extension of coastal State jurisdiction (proclamation of EEZs and/ or similar *sui generis* zones) in the Adriatic and the Mediterranean Seas. The analysis is undertaken in the light of the recent trends which advocate for an integrated and holistic approach to the management of the different activities in the two seas. Reference is made in this regard to applicable EU laws and policies and to various problems and possible solutions regarding the delimitation of maritime zones. The main goal is to examine the actual or potential extension of coastal State jurisdiction in the Adriatic, against the background of similar extensions elsewhere in the Mediterranean. This book ultimately attempts to identify solutions in the light of Part IX of UNCLOS, which would overcome the absence of a final delimitation agreement and enhance the existing co-operation among Adriatic and Mediterranean States.

This book is an updated version of a research undertaken within the framework of a Ph.D. Programme in International Maritime Law at the IMO International Maritime Law Institute in Malta (IMO IMLI). The thesis was submitted in December 2010 and the need was accordingly felt to update the original text with the most important developments which occurred in the discussed areas since then. Some notable examples are the transformation of the French Mediterranean ZEP into a full EEZ in October 2012 and the specific situation in the Eastern Mediterranean where the discoveries of significant quantities of oil and gas at the end of the first decade of the millennium triggered the proclamation of a new EEZ (e.g. Lebanon) and the conclusion of new delimitation agreements relating to actual or potential zones of sovereign rights and jurisdiction (Cyprus-Lebanon, Cyprus-Israel). In the field of Mediterranean and Adriatic co-operation the most important developments seemed to be the entry into force of the ICZM and Offshore Protocols to the Barcelona Convention in March 2011. Nonetheless, reference should be made to the fact that the main body of this book was written in the period between 2008 and 2010, therefore before the turbulent events that have since marked international life in the Mediterranean region, particularly on its southern shores.

xvi *Extension of Coastal State Jurisdiction in Enclosed or Semi-enclosed Seas*

The present manuscript is based on materials available to the author as at 1 December 2012. The discussion and views contained in this book represent exclusively the views of the author developed within the framework of academic research. They shall not be in any way associated with the past, present or future positions of any State or institution. The figures included in the main text are for illustrative purposes only.

Mitja Grbec
Slovenia, January 2013

Acknowledgements

During the course of my Ph.D. research I had the honour of working under the supervision of Professor Robin Churchill, Professor of International Law (Dundee School of Law, UK), widely recognized as one of the leading authorities in the field of the law of the sea and international law in general. His dedication to my work was impressive and his commitment to detail admirable. I am indebted to him for his academic and professional support and guidance.

I am also indebted to Professors David J. Attard and Marko Pavliha, two international maritime law experts who I greatly admire and with whom I have had the pleasure of working and learning in different periods and forms during the last decade or so. I also wish to acknowledge the collaboration of the staff at all levels at IMO IMLI. A special thanks goes to Dr Norman A. Martínez Gutiérrez (Senior Lecturer, IMO IMLI) and Mrs Josephine Aquilina (Head of Personnel, IMO IMLI). Their unconditional help in the final editing and their understanding of the different problems along the way helped me rediscover the true meaning of the term 'friendship'.

The finalization of this book would have not been possible without the precious guidance and support of the staff at Routledge. I am particularly indebted to Ms Katherine Carpenter, Mr Mark Sapwell and Mr Stephen Gutierrez. The various figures included in this book were diligently prepared by Mr Aleksander Rovan.

I also wish to thank the representatives of Titus Group, Mr Robert H. Appleby and Mr Klavdij Metlika, for their understanding and support in the finalization of this work.

There were also many other eminent scholars whom I had the honour to meet and who at some stage of my research provided me with documents, opinions and support, amongst whom I cannot fail to mention Professor Borut Bohte, Professor Umberto Leanza, Professor Mirjam Škrk, Professor Tullio Scovazzi, Professor Tullio Treves and Professor Davor Vidas.

Lastly, I wish to express my deepest gratitude to my wife, Matejka, who not only supported me unconditionally during the preparation of this book, but also helped me in the editing and in the preparation of the bibliography to this work. I am, furthermore, grateful to my little son Val who had to cope with the fact that his daddy had to spend most of his available time at home 'reading and writing'.

A special thanks goes also to my mother, Rozana, for her uninterrupted support, continuous prayers and understanding.

I dedicate this book to the memory of the late Jan Guzej, a faithful friend and excellent lawyer, whose young life and promising career were tragically interrupted by a car accident in July 2012.

Table of cases

International Court of Justice (ICJ)

Accordance with International Law of the Unilateral Declaration of Independence in Respect of Kosovo, Advisory Opinion, ICJ Reports 2010, p. 453

Anglo-Norwegian Fisheries Case, ICJ Reports 1951, p. 132

Arbitral Award of 31 July 1989 (Guinea Bissau v Senegal), ICJ Reports 1991, p. 53

Case Concerning Maritime Delimitation in the Black Sea (Romania v Ukraine), ICJ Reports 2009, p. 1

Continental Shelf (Libyan Arab Jamahiriya/Malta), ICJ Reports 1985, p. 13

Continental Shelf (Tunisia/Libyan Arab Jamahiriya), ICJ Reports 1982, p. 18

Frontier Dispute (Burkina Faso/Republic of Mali), ICJ Reports 1986, p. 554

Land and Maritime Boundary between Cameroon and Nigeria (Cameroon v Nigeria: Equatorial Guinea intervening), ICJ Reports 1998, p. 275 and ICJ Reports 2002, p. 303

Land, Island and Maritime Frontier Dispute (El Salvador/Honduras: Nicaragua intervening), ICJ Reports 1992, p. 351

Maritime Delimitation and Territorial Questions between Qatar and Bahrain (Qatar v Bahrain), ICJ Reports 2001, p. 40

North Sea Continental Shelf Cases, Judgment, ICJ Reports 1969, p. 3

Sovereignty over Pulau Ligitan and Pulau Sipadan (Indonesia/Malaysia), Application by the Philippines for Permission to Intervene, ICJ Reports 2001, p. 575

Territorial and Maritime Dispute between Nicaragua and Honduras in the Caribbean Sea (Nicaragua v Honduras), ICJ Reports 2007, p. 659

Territorial and Maritime Dispute (Nicaragua v Colombia), Judgment, 19 November 2012

Arbitral Tribunals

Arbitration Between The Republic of Croatia and The Republic of Slovenia (ongoing)

Arbitration between Barbados and the Republic of Trinidad and Tobago, relating to the delimitation of the exclusive economic zone and the continental shelf between them, Decision of 11 April 2006, RIAA, Vol. XXVII, 2006, pp. 147–251

Argentina-Chile Frontier Case, Award of Her Majesty Queen Elisabeth II, RIAA, Volume XVI, 1966, pp. 109–182 (Palena Case)

Beagle Channel Arbitration (Chile/Argentina), (1977; Holy See, 1984), RIAA, Vol. XXI, 1977, pp. 53–264

Delimitation of Maritime Areas Arbitration (Canada/France) (1992), 31 ILM 1145 (1992)

Guinea Bissau/Senegal Case, (1989) (1990), RGDIP, pp. 204–257

Guyana v Suriname, Award of the Arbitral Tribunal, 17 September 2007
Ireland v United Kingdom (MOX Plant Case), PCA, 2008 (without award on the merits)
Territorial Sovereignty and Scope of the Dispute (Eritrea and Yemen), RIAA, Volume XXII, 1998, pp. 209–332

International Tribunal for the Law of the Sea (ITLOS)

Dispute concerning delimitation of the maritime boundary between Bangladesh and Myanmar in the Bay of Bengal (Bangladesh/Myanmar), Case No. 16, Judgment, 14 March 2012
The MOX Plant Case (Ireland v United Kingdom), Provisional Measures, Case No. 10, Order, 3 December 2001
The M/V 'SAIGA' Case (Saint Vincent and the Grenadines v Guinea), Case No. 2, Judgment, 1 July 1999

Conference on Yugoslavia Arbitration Committee (Badinter Commission)

Opinion No. 2, 31 ILM 1497, 11 January 1992
Opinion No. 3, 31 ILM 1499, 11 January 1992

Court of Justice of the European Union

Case C-91/03, Spain v Council, Judgment of 17 March 2005 [2005] ECR I-2267
Case C-6/04, Commission v UK, Judgment of 20 October 2005 [2005] ECR I-9017

Other International Courts

Gulf of Fonseca Case (El Salvador/Nicaragua), Central American Court of Justice, 1917, 11 AJIL (1917), pp. 674–730
Legal Status of Eastern Greenland, Permanent Court of International Justice, PCIJ Series A/B No. 53 (1933)

Constitutional Court of the Republic of Slovenia

Opinion on the Compatibility of the Agreement between the Republic of Slovenia and the Republic of Croatia on Border Traffic and Co-operation [SOPS] with the Constitution of the Republic of Slovenia, Opinion Rm-1/00-29, 19 April 2001, OGRS No. 43/2001
Opinion on the Compatibility of the Arbitration Agreement between the Government of the Republic of Slovenia and the Government of the Republic of Croatia with the Constitution of the Republic of Slovenia, Opinion No. Rm-1/09-26, 18 March 2010, OGRS No. 25/2010

Table of treaties

Multilateral

1919 Agreement Establishing the Mediterranean Science Commission, Madrid, November 1919, as amended on 8 April 2007 (CIESM Agreement)

1949 Agreement for the Establishment of the General Fisheries Commission for the Mediterranean (as amended), Rome, 24 September 1949, entry into force of the current version: 29 April 2004 (GFCM Agreement)

1958 Convention on the Continental Shelf, Geneva, 29 April 1958, entry into force: 10 June 1964, 499 UNTS 311 (CSC)

Convention on Fishing and Conservation of the Living Resources of the High Seas, Geneva, 29 April 1958, entry into force: 20 March 1966, 559 UNTS 285

Convention on the High Seas, Geneva, 29 April 1958, entry into force: 30 September 1962, 450 UNTS 11 (CHS)

Convention on the Territorial Sea and the Contiguous Zone, Geneva, 29 April 1958, entry into force: 10 September 1964, 516 UNTS 205 (TSC)

1960 Treaty between the United Kingdom of Great Britain and Northern Ireland, the Hellenic Republic, the Republic of Turkey and the Republic of Cyprus concerning the Establishment of the Republic of Cyprus, 16 August 1960. Entry into force: 16 August 1960, 382 UNTS 10

1969 Vienna Convention on the Law of Treaties, done at Vienna on 23 May 1969, entry into force: 27 January 1980, 1155 UNTS 331 (VCLT)

International Convention on Civil Liability for Oil Pollution Damage, Brussels, 29 November 1969, entry into force: 19 June 1975, 973 UNTS 3; 9 ILM 45; RMC I.7.30, II.7.30 (CLC)

1972 Convention on the Prevention of Marine Pollution by Dumping of Wastes and Other Matter, London, Mexico City, Moscow and Washington, 29 December 1972, 1046 UNTS 120, entry into force: 30 August 1975 (London Convention)

1973 International Convention for the Prevention of Pollution from Ships, London, 4 November 1973, entry into force: not intended to enter into force without the 1978 Protocol, 1340 UNTS 184; 12 ILM 1319, as

xxii *Extension of Coastal State Jurisdiction in Enclosed or Semi-enclosed Seas*

modified by the Protocol of 1978 relating to the International Convention for the Prevention of Pollution from Ships, 1973, London, 17 February 1978, entry into force: 2 October 1983, 1340 UNTS 61, 62; 17 ILM 546 (MARPOL)

1974 International Convention for the Safety of Life at Sea, London, 1 November 1974, entry into force: 25 May 1980, 1184 UNTS 277; 14 ILM 959; RMC I.3.20, II.3.20 (SOLAS)

1976 Convention for the Protection of the Marine Environment and the Coastal Region of the Mediterranean, Barcelona, 16 February 1976 (as Convention for the Protection of the Mediterranean Sea against Pollution), 15 ILM 290 (1976), entry into force: 12 February 1978, as amended: Barcelona, 10 June 1995, in force on 9 July 2004 (Barcelona Convention)

Protocol for the Prevention of Pollution in the Mediterranean Sea by Dumping from Ships and Aircraft [Barcelona Convention], Barcelona, 16 February 1976, entry into force: 12 February 1978 (Dumping Protocol). The Dumping Protocol was amended and recorded as: Protocol for the Prevention and Elimination of Pollution in the Mediterranean Sea by Dumping from Ships and Aircraft or Incineration at Sea, Barcelona, 10 June 1995, not yet in force

Protocol Concerning Cooperation in Combating Pollution of the Mediterranean Sea by Oil and other Harmful Substances in Cases of Emergency [Barcelona Convention], Barcelona, 16 February 1976, entry into force: 12 February 1978

1978 Vienna Convention on Succession of States in respect of Treaties, Vienna, 23 August 1978, entry into force: 6 November 1996, 1946 UNTS 3 (1978 Vienna Convention)

1980 Protocol on the Protection of the Mediterranean Sea against Pollution from Land-Based Sources [Barcelona Convention], Athens, 17 May 1980, entry into force: 17 June 1983. The Protocol was amended and recorded as: Protocol for the Protection of the Mediterranean Sea against Pollution from Land-Based Sources and Activities, Siracuse, 7 March 1996, entry into force: 11 May 2008, UNEP(OCA)/MED IG.7 (Land-Based Protocol)

1982 Protocol concerning Mediterranean Specially Protected Areas [Barcelona Convention], Geneva, 3 April 1982, entry into force: 23 March 1986

Memorandum of Understanding on Port State Control, Paris, 26 January 1982, entry into force: 6 August 1982, RMC I.3.100, II.3.100 (Paris MOU)

United Nations Convention on the Law of the Sea, Montego Bay, 10 December 1982, entry into force: 16 November 1994, 1833 UNTS 3, 397; 21 ILM 1261; RMC I.1.170, RMC II.1.170 (UNCLOS)

1989 Basel Convention on the Control of Transboundary Movements of Hazardous Wastes and their Disposal, Basel, 22 March 1989, 1673 UNTS 126; entry into force: 5 May 1992. Amended by the Amendment to the Convention on the Control of Transboundary Movements of Hazardous Wastes and their Disposal, Geneva, 22 September 1995, UNEP/CHW.3/35 (Basel Convention)

1992 Protocol of 1992 to amend the International Convention on Civil Liability for Oil Pollution Damage of 29 November 1969, London, 27 November 1992, entry into force: 30 May 1996, 1956 UNTS 255, RMC I.7.51, II.7.51 (1992 CLC)

Protocol of 1992 to amend International Convention on the Establishment of an International Fund for Compensation for Oil Pollution Damage, 1971, London, 27 November 1992, entry into force: 30 May 1996, replaces the Fund Convention, 1953 UNTS 330; RMC I.7.111, II.7.111 (1992 Fund)

Convention on Biological Diversity, Rio de Janeiro, 5 June 1992, entry into force: 29 December 1993, 31 ILM 818 (CBD Convention)

1993 Agreement to Promote Compliance with International Conservation and Management Measures by Fishing Vessels on the High Seas (FAO). Adopted: 24 November 1993; entry into force: 11 September 2003, 33 ILM 968 (Compliance Agreement)

Protocol for the Protection of the Mediterranean Sea against Pollution Resulting from Exploration and Exploitation of the Continental Shelf and the Sea-Bed and its Subsoil [Barcelona Convention], Madrid, 14 October 1994, entry into force: 24 March 2011, UNEP(OCA)/MED IG.4/4 (Offshore Protocol)

1995 Action Plan for the Protection of the Marine Environment and the Sustainable Development of the Coastal Areas of the Mediterranean (Mediterranean Action Plan or MAP Phase II), Barcelona, 10 June 1995, entry into force: 9 July 2004 (replacing the Mediterranean Action Plan (MAP) adopted in 1975)

Protocol Concerning Specially Protected Areas and Biological Diversity in the Mediterranean [Barcelona Convention], Barcelona, 10 June 1995, entry into force: 12 December 1999, UNEP(OCA)/MED IG.6/7 (Biodiversity Protocol)

Agreement for the implementation of the provisions of the United Nations Convention on the Law of the Sea of 10 December 1982 relating to the conservation and management of straddling fish stocks and highly migratory fish stocks, 4 August 1995, entry into force: 11 December 2001, 34 ILM 1542 (Fish Stocks Agreement)

General Framework Peace Accord for Bosnia and Herzegovina (The Republic of Bosnia and Herzegovina, the Federation of Bosnia and Herzegovina, and the Republika Srpska; endorsed by Croatia and the Federal Republic of Yugoslavia), Dayton, 21 November 1995, signature and entry into force: 14 December 1995 (Dayton Agreement)

1996 International Convention on Liability and Compensation for Damage in Connection with the Carriage of Hazardous and Noxious Substances by Sea, London, 3 May 1996, not yet in force, IMO Doc.:

LEG/CONF.10/8/2 of 9 May 1996; 35 ILM 1406; RMC I.7.125, II.7.125 (HNS Convention)

Protocol to the Convention on the Prevention of Marine Pollution by Dumping of Wastes and Other Matter, London, 7 November 1996, entry into force: 24 March 2006, as amended on 2 November 2006, in force on 10 February 2007 (1996 Protocol to the London Convention)

Protocol on the Prevention of Pollution of the Mediterranean Sea by Transboundary Movements of Hazardous Wastes and their Disposal (Barcelona Convention), Izmir, 1 October 1996, not yet in force (Waste Protocol)

1999 Agreement concerning the Creation of a Marine Mammal Sanctuary in the Mediterranean (France, Italy, Monaco), Rome, 25 November 1999, entry into force: 21 February 2002, 2176 UNTS 249 (The Sanctuary Agreement)

2000 Memorandum of Understanding between the Government of the Republic of Slovenia, the Government of the Republic of Croatia and the Government of the Italian Republic on Mandatory Ship Reporting System in the Adriatic Sea, Ancona, 19 May 2000, entry into force: 20 October 2000, OGRS 96/2000 (Adriatic Traffic)

Memorandum of Understanding between the Government of the Republic of Slovenia, the Government of the Republic of Croatia and the Government of the Italian Republic on the Establishment of a Common Routeing System and Traffic Separation Scheme in the Northern Part of the Northern Adriatic, Ancona, 19 May 2000, entry into force: 20 October 2000, OGRS 96/2000

2001 International Convention on Civil Liability for Bunker Oil Pollution Damage, London, 23 March 2001, entry into force: 21 November 2008, IMO Doc.: LEG/CONF.12/19 of 27 March 2001; RMC I.7.130, II.7.130 (Bunkers Convention)

Convention on the Protection of the Underwater Cultural Heritage, Paris, 2 November 2001, UNESCO, entry into force: 2 January 2009, 41 ILM 40 (2002) (UNESCO Convention)

2002 Protocol Concerning Co-operation in Preventing Pollution from Ships and, in Cases of Emergency, Combating Pollution of the Mediterranean Sea (Barcelona Convention), Valletta, 25 January 2002, entry into force: 17 March 2004, UNEP(OCA)/MED IG.14 (Prevention and Emergency Protocol)

2003 Protocol of 2003 to the International Convention on the Establishment of an International Fund for Compensation for Oil Pollution Damage, 1992, London, 16 May 2003, entry into force: 3 March 2005, IMO Doc.: LEG/CONF.14/20 of 27 May 2003; RMC I.7.115, II.7.115 (Supplementary Fund Protocol)

2004 International Convention for the Control and Management of Ships' Ballast Water and Sediments, London, 13 February 2004, not yet in force, IMO Doc. BWM/CONF/36 (Ballast Water Convention)

Table of treaties xxv

2005 Sub-Regional Contingency Plan for Prevention off, Preparedness, for and Response to Major Marine Pollution Incidents in the Adriatic Sea (Italy, Slovenia, Croatia), Portorož, 9 November 2005, entry into force: 30 May 2008, OGRS No. 61/2008

2007 Nairobi International Convention on the Removal of Wrecks, Nairobi, 18 May 2007, not yet in force, IMO Doc.: LEG/CONF.16/21 of 22 May 2007

2008 Protocol on Integrated Coastal Zone Management, Madrid, 21 January 2008, entry into force: 24 March 2011, UNEP(OCA)/MED IG. 18/4 UNEP(OCA)/MED IG. 18/4 (ICZM Protocol)

2010 International Convention on Liability and Compensation for Damage in Connection with the Carriage of Hazardous and Noxious Substances by Sea, 2010: The Consolidated Text of the HNS Convention 1996 and the 2010 HNS Protocol (HNS Convention, 2010)

Bilateral

1968 Agreement between Italy and Yugoslavia Concerning the Delimitation of the Continental Shelf between the two Countries in the Adriatic Sea, 8 January 1968, entry into force: 21 January 1970 (1968 Shelf Agreement)

1971 Agreement between the Government of the Republic of Tunisia and the Government of the Italian Republic Concerning the Delimitation of the Continental Shelf between the Two Countries, 20 August 1971, entry into force: 6 December 1978 (1971 Shelf Agreement)

1974 Agreement on Cooperation and Prevention of Pollution of the Adriatic Waters and its Coastal Zones (Italy-SFRY), Belgrade, 14 February 1974, entry into force: 20 April 1977, OGRI of 22 February 1977 (Belgrade Agreement)

Convention between Spain and Italy on the Delimitation of the Continental Shelf between the Two States, 19 February 1974, entry into force: 16 November 1978 (1974 Shelf Agreement)

Agreement between Sri Lanka and India on the Boundary in Historic Waters between the Two Countries and Related Matters, 26 and 28 June, 1974, entry into force: 8 July 1974

1975 Treaty between the Italian Republic and the SFRY, Osimo, 10 November 1975, entry into force: 3 April 1977 (Treaty of Osimo)

1978 Agreement on Delimitation of Marine and Submarine Areas and Maritime Cooperation between the Republic of Colombia and the Dominican Republic, 13 January 1978, entry into force: 15 February 1979

1983 Exchange of Notes between Italy and the SFRY Regarding the Creation of a Joint Fishing Zone in the Gulf of Trieste, 18 February 1983, entry into force: 16 June 1987

1985 Convention on Maritime Delimitation Agreement between the Government of His Most Serene Highness the Prince of Monaco and the Government of the French Republic, 16 February 1984, entry into force: 22 August 1985

1986 Agreement between the Great Socialist People's Libyan Arab Jamahiriya and the Republic of Malta implementing Article III of the Special Agreement and the Judgment of the International Court of Justice, 10 November 1986, entry into force: 11 December 1987

1988 Agreement between the Libyan Arab Socialist People's Jamahariya and the Republic of Tunisia to Implement the Judgment of the International Court of Justice in the Tunisia/Libya Continental Shelf Case, 8 August 1988, entry into force: 11 April 1989

Agreement between the Government of the United Republic of Tanzania and the Government of the People's Republic of Mozambique regarding the Tanzania/Mozambique Boundary, 28 December 1988, entry into force: 18 September 1989

1992 Agreement between Albania and Italy for the Determination of the Continental Shelf of each of the Two Countries, 18 December 1992, entry into force: 26 February 1999 (1992 Shelf Agreement)

1993 Maritime Delimitation Treaty between Jamaica and the Republic of Colombia, 12 November 1993, entry into force: 14 March 1994

1994 Exchange of Notes Constituting an Agreement on the Procedure to be followed in the Modification of the Limits of the Territorial Waters in the Gulf of Finland (Finland-Estonia), 6 April and 4 May 1994, entry into force: 30 July 1995

Agreement between Israel and the Palestine Liberation Organization on the Gaza Strip and the Jericho Area, Cairo, 4 May 1994, entry into force: 1 January 1995

1997 Agreement between the Republic of Slovenia and the Republic of Croatia on Border Traffic and Co-operation (SOPS), 28 April 1997, entry into force: 31 July 2001

1998 The Northern Ireland Peace Agreement, 10 April 1998, entry into force: 2 December 1999 (Belfast Agreement)

Agreement on Free Transit through the Territory of Croatia to and from the Port of Ploče and through the Territory of Bosnia and Herzegovina at Neum, 22 November 1998, not yet in force

1999 Treaty on the State Border between the Republic of Croatia and Bosnia and Herzegovina, 30 July 1999, not yet in force

2001 Treaty between the Republic of Slovenia and the Republic of Croatia on the Common State Border (Draft Treaty), initialled by the Heads of the two delegations, not yet in force (Drnovšek-Račan Treaty)

2002 Agreement on Provisional Arrangements for the Delimitation of the Maritime Boundaries between the Republic of Tunisia and the People's Democratic Republic of Algeria (with annex of 7 August 2002), 11 February 2002, entry into force: 23 November 2003

Protocol on the Interim Regime along the Southern Border between the Republic of Croatia and Serbia Montenegro, 10 December 2002 (2002 Protocol)

Table of treaties xxvii

2003 Agreement between the Republic of Cyprus and the Arab Republic of Egypt on the Delimitation of the Exclusive Economic Zone, 17 February 2003, entry into force: 7 April 2004

2007 Agreement between Cyprus and Lebanon to delimit their Exclusive Economic Zones, 17 January 2007, not yet in force

2009 Agreement on the Delimitation of their Respective Continental Shelf Areas and other Maritime Zones to which they are entitled under International Law (Albania/Greece), 27 April 2009, not yet in force

Arbitration Agreement between the Government of the Republic of Slovenia and the Government of the Republic of Croatia, 4 November 2009, entry into force: 29 November 2010 (2009 Arbitration Agreement)

2011 Agreement between the Government of the State of Israel and the Government of the Republic of Cyprus on the Delimitation of the Exclusive Economic Zone, 17 December 2010, entry into force: 25 February 2011

Table of selected legal documents

EU

Treaties

Treaty between the EU Member States and the Republic of Croatia concerning the accession of the Republic of Croatia to the European Union, 9 December 2011, OJ EU L112, 24.4.2012 (2011 Accession Treaty)

Consolidated versions of the Treaty on European Union and the Treaty on the Functioning of the European Union (TFEU), OJ C 83, 30.3.2010

Treaty of Lisbon amending the Treaty on European Union and the Treaty establishing the European Community, signed at Lisbon, 13 December 2007, entry into force: 1 December 2009, OJ C306, 17.12.2007 (Lisbon Treaty)

Regulations and Directives

Regulation of the European Parliament and of the Council Amending Council Regulation (EC) No. 2371/2002 on the Conservation and Sustainable Exploitation of Fisheries Resources under the Common Fisheries Policy, COM(2012)277 final, Brussels, 7.6.2012

Regulation No. 1255/2011 of the European Parliament and of the Council of 30 November 2011 establishing a Programme to support the further development of an Integrated Maritime Policy, OJ L 321, 5.11.2011

Directive 2008/56/EC of the European Parliament and of the Council of 17 June 2008 establishing a framework for community action in the field of marine environmental policy, OJ L 164, 25.6.2008 (Marine Strategy Directive)

Council Regulation (EC) No. 1967/2006 of 21 December 2006 concerning management measures for the sustainable exploitation of fishery resources in the Mediterranean Sea, amending Regulation (EEC) No. 2847/93 and repealing Regulation (EC) No 1626/94, OJ L 409, 30.12.2006

Directive 2004/35/CE of the European Parliament and of the Council of 21 April 2004 on environmental liability with regard to the prevention and remedying of environmental damage, OJ EU L 143, 30.4.2004 (Environmental Liability Directive)

Council Regulation (EC) No. 2371/2002 on the conservation and sustainable exploitation of fisheries resources under the Common Fisheries Policy, defined as waters under the sovereignty and jurisdiction of the Member States, OJ L 358, 31.12.2002

Directive 2000/60/EC of the European Parliament and of the Council of 23 October 2000 establishing a framework for Community action in the field of water policy, OJ L 327, 22.12.2000 (Water Framework Directive)

Council Directive 92/43/EEC of 21 May 1992 on the conservation of natural habitats and of wild fauna and flora (as amended), OJ L 206, 22.7.1992 (Habitats Directive)

Council Resolutions

Council Resolution of 3 November 1976 on certain external aspects of the creation of 200-mile fishing zone in the Community with effect from 1 January 1977, OJ C 105 of 07.05.1981

European Commission

Communication from the Commission: A Maritime Strategy for the Adriatic and Ionian Seas', COM(2012)713 final, Brussels, 30.11.2012

Report from the Commission to the European Parliament and the Council on the Implementation of the Water Framework Directive (2000/60/EC), River Basin Management Plans, COM(2012)670 final, Brussels, 14.11.2012

Progress of the EU's Integrated Maritime Policy (Report from the Commission), COM(2012)491 final, Brussels, 11.9.2012

Marine Knowledge 2020 from seabed mapping to ocean forecasting (Green Paper), COM(2012)473 final, Brussels, 29.8.2012

Commission Decision of 19 January 2012 on the setting up of the European Union Offshore Oil and Gas Authorities Group, OJ C 18, 21.1.2012

Proposal for a Council Decision on the accession of the European Union to the Protocol for the Protection of the Mediterranean Sea against pollution resulting from exploration and exploitation of the continental shelf and the seabed and its subsoil, 27.10.2011

Proposal for a Regulation of the European Parliament and of the Council on safety of offshore oil and gas prospection, exploration and production activities, COM(2011)688 final, 2011/0309(COD), 27.10.2011

Communication from the Commission: Reform of the Common Fisheries Policy, COM(2011)417 final, Brussels, 13.7.2011

Proposal for a Regulation of the European Parliament and of the Council on the Common Fisheries Policy, COM(2011) 425 final , Brussels, 13.7.2011

Maritime Spatial Planning in the EU: Achievements and Future Development, COM (2010)771 final, Brussels, 17.12.2010

Communication from the Commission: Facing the challenge of the safety of offshore oil and gas activities, COM(2010)560 final, Brussels, 12.10.2010

Developing the International dimension of the EU's Integrated Maritime Policy, COM (2009)536 final, Brussels, 11.11.2009

Progress Report on the EU's Integrated Maritime Policy, COM (2009)540 final, Brussels, 15.10.2009

Towards an Integrated Maritime Policy for better governance in the Mediterranean, COM (2009)466 final, Brussels, 11.09.2009

Roadmap for Maritime Spatial Planning: Achieving common principles in the EU, COM (2008)791 final, Brussels, 25.11.2008

An Integrated Marine Policy for the EU (Blue Paper), COM(2007)575 final, Brussels, 10.10.2007

An Evaluation of Integrated Coastal Zone Management, COM(2007)308 final, Brussels, 7.6.2007

Communication from the Commission to the Council and the European Parliament Establishing an Environmental Strategy for the Mediterranean, COM(2006)475 final, Brussels, 5.9.2006

Opinion on Croatia's Application for Membership of the European Union, COM(2004)257 final, Brussels, 20.4.2004

Communication laying down a Community Action Plan for the conservation and sustainable exploitation of fisheries resources in the Mediterranean Sea under the Common Fisheries Policy, COM(2002)535 final, Brussels, 09.10.2002

Recommendations

Recommendation of the European Parliament and of the Council of 30 May 2002 concerning the implementation of Integrated Coastal Zone Management in Europe (2002/413/EC), OJ L 148, 6.6.2002

GFCM

Recommendations

REC.CM-GFCM/30/2006/3	Establishment of fisheries restricted areas in order to protect the deep sea sensitive habitats
REC.CM-GFCM/29/2005/1	Management of certain fisheries exploiting demersal and deepwater species

Resolutions

RES-GFCM/33/2009/2	Establishment of Geographical Sub-Areas in the GFCM area amending the resolution GFCM/31/2007/2

IMO

2011 International Convention for the Control and Management of Ship's Ballast Water and Sediments (Harmonized Voluntary Arrangements for Ballast Water Management in the Mediterranean Region), Communication received from REMPEC, BWM.2/Circ.35, 15 August 2011, Annex 1

2005 Revised Guidelines for the Identification and Designation of Particularly Sensitive Sea Area, IMO Assembly Resolution A.982(24), 1 December 2005

2004 Report of the Maritime Safety Committee on its Seventy-Eight Session, MSC 78/26 of 28 May 2004, p. 86 and Annex 21

2004 New and Amended Traffic Separation Schemes, COLREG.2/Circ. 54, 28 May 2004

2003 Establishment of new Recommended Traffic Separation Schemes and other new Routing Measures in the Adriatic Sea, submitted by Albania, Croatia, Italy, Slovenia and Serbia and Montenegro, IMO Doc. NAV 49/3/7, 27 March 2003

xxxii *Extension of Coastal State Jurisdiction in Enclosed or Semi-enclosed Seas*

Designation of a Western European Particularly Sensitive Sea Area, submitted by Belgium, France, Ireland, Portugal, Spain and the United Kingdom, IMO Doc. MEPC 49/8/1, 11 April 2003
Designation of the Baltic Sea as a Particularly Sensitive Sea Area, submitted by Denmark, Estonia, Finland, Germany, Latvia, Lithuania, Poland and Sweden, IMO Doc. MEPC 51/8/1, 19 December 2003

2002 Mandatory Ship Reporting Systems, Resolution MSC.139(76), 5 December 2002

2001 Establishment of a Mandatory Ship Reporting System in the Adriatic Sea known as 'ADRIATIC TRAFFIC': Submitted by Albania, Croatia, Italy, Slovenia and Yugoslavia, NAV 47/3/4, 30 March 2001

UNCLOS III documents

Working Papers of the Plenary

A/CONF.62/L.8/REV.1, 17 October 1974, Statement of activities of the Conference during its first and second sessions, Allocation of Work to Main Committees
A/CONF.62/WP.8/Part I-III, 7 May 1975, Informal single negotiating text (ISNT)
A/CONF.62/WP.8/REV.1/Part I-III, 6 May 1976, Revised single negotiating text (RSNT)
A/CONF.62/WP.10, 15 July 1977, Informal Composite Negotiating Text (ICNT)

Summary Records (Second Committee)

A/CONF.62/C.2/SR.5, 16 July 1974. Second Committee, 5th meeting, Tuesday 16 July 1974, Mr Andrés Aguilar (Chairman), Territorial sea (continued) [Agenda item 2]
A/CONF.62/C.2/SR.6, 17 July 1974. Second Committee, 6th meeting, Wednesday 17 July 1974, Mr Andrés Aguilar (Chairman), Organization of work
A/CONF.62/C.2/SR.17, 26 July 1974. Second Committee, 17th meeting, Friday 26 July 1974, Mr Andrés Aguilar (Chairman), Continental shelf (continued) [Agenda item 5]
A/CONF. 62/C.2/SR.22, 31 July 1974. Second Committee, 22nd meeting, Wednesday 31 July 1974, Mr Andrés Aguilar (Chairman), Continental shelf (concluded) [Agenda item 5]
A/CONF.62/C.2/SR.28, 6 August 1974. Second Committee, 28th meeting, Tuesday 6 August 1974, Mr Andrés Aguilar (Chairman), Exclusive economic zone beyond the territorial sea (continued) [Agenda item 6]
A/CONF.62/C.2/SR.38, 13 August 1974. Second Committee, 38th meeting, Tuesday 13 August 1974, Mr Andrés Aguilar (Chairman), Enclosed and semi-enclosed seas [Agenda item 17]
A/CONF. 62/C.2/SR.43, 23 August 1974. Second Committee, 43rd meeting, Friday 23 August 1974, Mr Andrés Aguilar (Chairman), Organization of work
A/CONF.62/C.2/SR.127, 3 April 1980. Second Committee, 127th meeting, Thursday 3 April 1980, Mr H. S. Amerasinghe (President), Statements on the second revision of the informal composite negotiating text (continued)

Proposals by States (Second Committee)

A/CONF.62/C.2/L.8, 15 July 1974. Turkey: draft article on the breadth of the territorial sea; global or regional criteria, open seas and oceans, semi-enclosed or enclosed seas.

Table of selected legal documents xxxiii

A/CONF.62/C.2/L.56, 13 August 1974. Turkey: draft article on enclosed and semi-enclosed seas

A/CONF.62/C.2/L.71 and ADD.1 and ADD. 2, 21 August 1974. Iraq: draft articles on enclosed and semi-enclosed seas

A/CONF.62/C.2/L.72, 21 August 1974. Iran: draft articles on enclosed or semi-enclosed seas

Chairman (Second Committee)

Document A/CONF.62/WP.8/Part II (ISNT, 1975), articles 134 and 135 (Chairman, Second Committee)

Document A/CONF.62/WP.8/Part II (ISNT, 1975), article 133 (Chairman, Second Committee)

Document CONF.62/WP.8/Rev.1/Part II (RSNT, 1976), Article 130, V Off. Rec. 151, 172 (Chairman, Second Committee), Introductory Note

Sea-bed Committee

A/AC.138/SC.II/L.16, Sea-bed Committee, 2 August 1973, III SBC Report 1973 at 2 (Turkey)

A/AC.138/SC.II/L.24, article 2, paragraph 2, reproduced in III SBC Report 1973 at 23, 25 (Uruguay)

UNEP-MAP

UNEP(DEPI)/MED IG.20/8, 14 February 2012 (Report of the 17th ordinary meeting of the contracting parties to the Barcelona Convention and its protocols)

UNEP(DEPI)/MED WG.348/5, 1 June 2010 (Report of the Extraordinary Meeting of the Focal Points for SPAs)

UNEP(DEPI)/MED IG.19/8, Annex I, p. 4, 24 November 2009 (Marrakesh Declaration)

UNEP(DEPI)/MED IG 19/7, 24 October 2009 (Report of the Compliance Committee to the 16th Meeting of the Contracting Parties)

UNEP(DEPI)/MED.IG.17/10, 18 January 2008 (Guidelines for the Determination of Liability and Compensation for Damage Resulting from Pollution of the Marine Environment in the Mediterranean Sea Area)

UNEP(DEC)/MED IG. 17/13, 15–18 January 2008 (Report by the Coordinator for the 15th Meeting of the Contracting Parties)

UNEP(DEC)/MED IG.17/10, 15–18 January 2008

UNEP(DEC)/MED IG. 16/7, 8–11 November 2005 (Mediterranean Strategy for Sustainable Development: A framework for Environmental Sustainability and Shared Prosperity)

UNEP(DEC)/MED IG. 16/11, 8–11 November 2005 (Principles for the Development and Respect of the Marine Environment by Pleasure Craft Activities in the Mediterranean Sea)

UNEP(DEC)/MED IG. 16/10, 8–11 November 2005 (Regional Strategy for Prevention of and Response to Marine Pollution from Ships)

Table of statutes and other national legislation

Albania

Law on the Coast Guard, 4 April 2002

Algeria

Legislative Decree No. 94-13 of 17 Dhu'lhijjah 1414, corresponding to 28 May 1994, establishing the general rules relating to fisheries, 22 June 1994

Canada

1867 Canada Constitution Act

Croatia

Constitutional Decision on the Sovereignty and Independence of the Republic of Croatia, 25 June 1991
Maritime Code of the Republic of Croatia, 27 January 1994 (not in force)
Decision on the Extension of the Jurisdiction of the Republic of Croatia in the Adriatic Sea, 3 October 2003
Decision on Amending the Decision on the Extension of the Jurisdiction of the Republic of Croatia in the Adriatic Sea of 3 October 2003, 3 June 2004
Maritime Code of the Republic of Croatia (as amended), 8 December 2004
List of geographical coordinates defining the outer limit of the Ecological and Fisheries Protection Zone, 2 September 2005
Decision on Modifying and Amending the Decision on the Extension of the Jurisdiction of the Republic of Croatia in the Adriatic Sea, 15 December 2006

Cyprus

Law to provide for the Proclamation of the EEZ by the Republic of Cyprus, 2 April 2004

France

Act No. 68-1181 of 30 December 1968 relating to the exploration of the Continental Shelf and to the exploitation of its natural resources

Law No. 76-655 of 16 July 1976 relating to the Economic Zone off the coasts of the territory of the Republic

Decree No. 77-130 of 11 February 1977 on the establishment, pursuant to the law of 16 July 1976, of an Economic Zone off the coasts of the territory of the Republic bordering the North Sea, the English Channel and the Atlantic, from the Franco-Belgian border to the Franco-Spanish border

Act No. 2003-346 of 15 April 2003 on the establishment of a zone of ecological protection off the coast of the territories of the Republic

Decree No. 2004-33 of 8 January 2004 on the establishment of a zone of ecological protection off the coasts of the territories of the Republic in the Mediterranean

Decree No. 2012-1148 of 12 October 2012 on the establishment of an exclusive economic zone off the coasts of the territories of the Republic in the Mediterranean

Ireland

Constitution of Ireland (as amended), 1 July 1937

Nineteenth Amendment of the Constitution Act, 3 June 1998

Italy

Legislative Decree No. 41 of 22 January 2004 (archeological zone)

Law No. 61 on the establishment of an ecological protection zone beyond the outer limit of the territorial sea, 8 February 2006

Law No. 157 on the ratification and implementation of the Convention on the Protection of the Underwater Cultural Heritage (and Annexes) adopted in Paris on 2 November 2001, 23 October 2009

Presidential Decree No. 209 on the proclamation of a zone of ecological protection in the North-West Mediterranean, Ligurian and Tyrrhenian Sea, 27 October 2011

Lebanon

Law No. 163 dated 18 August 2011 concerning the delineation and declaration of the maritime regions of the Republic of Lebanon

Decree No. 6433 concerning delineation of the boundaries of the exclusive economic zone of Lebanon, 16 November 2011

Libya

General People's Committee Decision No. 37 concerning the declaration of a Libyan Fisheries Protection Zone in the Mediterranean Sea, 24 February 2005

General's People's Committee Decision No. 104 of the year 1373 D.P. (2005) concerning straight baselines for measuring the breadth of the territorial sea and maritime zones of the Libyan Arab Jamahiriya

General's People's Committee Decision No. 105 of the year 1373 D.P. (2005) concerning the delimitation of the Libyan Fisheries Protection Zone in the Mediterranean Sea.

General People's Committee Decision No. 260 of A.J. 1377 (2009) concerning the declaration of the exclusive economic zone of the Great Socialist People's Libyan Arab Jamahiriya, 31 May 2009

Table of statutes and other national legislation xxxvii

Malta

Territorial Waters and Contiguous Zone Act, No. XXXII of 1971, as amended by Acts XLVI of 1975, XXIV of 1978, XXVIII of 1981 and I of 2002
Fishing Waters (Designation) and Extended Maritime Jurisdiction Act, Chapter 479 of the Laws of Malta, 26 July 2005

Morocco

Act No. 1-81 of 18 December 1980, Promulgated by Dahir No. 1-81-179 of 8 April 1981, establishing a 200-nautical-mile Exclusive Economic Zone off the Moroccan coasts

Slovenia

Basic Constitutional Charter on the Independence and Sovereignty of the Republic of Slovenia, 25 June 1991
Constitution of the Republic of Slovenia (as amended), 23 December 1991
Memorandum on the Bay of Piran, 26 May 1993
Act on the Ratification of the Agreement between the Republic of Slovenia and the Republic of Croatia on border traffic and cooperation (SOPS), 19 July 2001
Ecological Protection Zone and Continental Shelf of the Republic of Slovenia Act, 22 October 2005
Decree on the Determination of Fisheries Areas of the Republic of Slovenia, 5 January 2006
Resolution by the Slovenian Parliament on the Strategy for the Adriatic Sea, 22 December 2009
Act ratifying the Arbitration Agreement between the Government of the Republic of Slovenia and the Government of the Republic of Croatia, 19 April 2010

SFRY

Constitution of the Socialist Federal Republic of Yugoslavia, 21 February 1974
Act concerning the Coastal Sea and the Continental Shelf, 23 July 1987

Spain

Act No. 15/1978 on the Economic Zone of 20 February 1978
Royal Decree 1315/1997, of 1 August 1997, establishing a Fisheries Protection Zone in the Mediterranean Sea
List of geographical coordinates of points constituting the delimitation made by Spain of the Fisheries Protection Zone in the Mediterranean Sea, established by Royal Decree 1313/1997 of 1 August 1997, 13 April 2000

Syria

Law No. 28 dated 19 November 2003: Definition Act of Internal Waters and Territorial Sea Limits of the Syrian Arab Republic

Tunisia

Decree of 26 July 1951 as modified by Law No. 63-49 of 30 December 1963
Act No. 50/2005 dated 27 June 2005 concerning the exclusive economic zone off the
Tunisian coast

List of figures

Figure 1.1	The Mediterranean Sea and its sub-seas	8
Figure 1.2	Overlapping claims in the Central Mediterranean	10
Figure 1.3	Adriatic Sea: Coastal States and main ports	12
Figure 2.1	Algeria-Tunisia: provisional delimitation	66
Figure 3.1	Outer limits of the Spanish FPZ	78
Figure 3.2	External limits of the French ZEP	82
Figure 3.3	Mediterranean Sanctuary (1999 Sanctuary Agreement)	84
Figure 3.4	Croatian EFPZ	89
Figure 3.5	Italian ZEP in the North-West Mediterranean, Ligurian and Tyrrhenian Seas and its relation with the French zone	96
Figure 3.6	Provisional limits of the Slovenian ZEP	104
Figure 3.7	The territorial sea of the (UK) sovereign bases on Cyprus	107
Figure 3.8	Cyprus-Lebanon delimitation agreement (unratified)	110
Figure 3.9	Baseline and external limits of the Libyan FPZ	117
Figure 4.1	Relationship between the coastlines of Croatia and Bosnia and Herzegovina	154
Figure 4.2	'Bosnian' maritime zones (1999 Border Treaty)	156
Figure 4.3	Disputed area and provisional delimitation in the Bay of Boka Kotorska	164
Figure 4.4	The Bay of Piran and the territorial sea boundary within the Gulf of Trieste	170
Figure 4.5	'Drnovšek-Račan' Treaty (envisaged solutions)	176
Figure 4.6	Joint fishing zone (SOPS)	178
Figure 5.1	Traffic separation schemes in the Northern Adriatic (Port of Koper)	228

List of abbreviations

1954 London Agreement	Memorandum of Understanding Regarding the Free Territory of Trieste
1968 Shelf Agreement	Agreement between Italy and Yugoslavia concerning the Delimitation of the Continental Shelf between the two Countries in the Adriatic Sea
1978 Vienna Convention	Vienna Convention on Succession of States in respect of Treaties
1992 CLC	Protocol of 1992 to amend the International Convention on Civil Liability for Oil Pollution Damage of 29 November 1969
1992 FUND	Protocol of 1992 to amend International Convention on the Establishment of an International Fund for Compensation for Oil Pollution Damage of 1971
2010 HNS Convention	International Convention on Liability and Compensation for Damage in Connection with the Carriage of Hazardous and Noxious Substances by Sea as amended with the 2010 HNS Protocol
ACCOBAMS	Agreement on the Conservation of Cetaceans of the Black Sea, Mediterranean Sea and Contiguous Atlantic
ADRIACOMS	Adriatic Sea Integrated Coastal Areas and River Basin Management System Pilot Project
ADRIAMED	Scientific Cooperation to Support Responsible Fisheries in the Adriatic Sea
AFDI	Annuaire français de droit international
AII	Adriatic – Ionian Initiative
AJIL	American Journal of International Law
ASIL	American Society of International Law
Ballast Water Convention	International Convention for the Control and Management of Ships' Ballast Water and Sediments
Barcelona Convention	Convention for the Protection of the Marine Environment and the Coastal Region of the Mediterranean

Basel Convention	Basel Convention on the Control of Transboundary Movements of Hazardous Wastes and their Disposal
Belfast Agreement	The Northern Ireland Peace Agreement
Belgrade Agreement	Agreement on Cooperation and Prevention of Pollution of the Adriatic Waters and its Coastal Zones
Biodiversity Protocol	Protocol Concerning Specially Protected Areas and Biological Diversity in the Mediterranean (Barcelona Convention)
BOD	Biochemical Oxygen Demand
Bunkers Convention	International Convention on Civil Liability for Bunker Oil Pollution Damage
Can. Y.B. Int'l L.	Canadian Yearbook of International Law
CBD Convention	Convention on Biological Diversity
CFP	Common Fisheries Policy (EU)
CHS	Convention on the High Seas
CIESM	Commission for the Scientific Exploration of the Mediterranean Sea
CJIL	Chinese Journal of International Law
Compliance Agreement	Agreement to Promote Compliance with International Conservation and Management Measures by Fishing Vessels on the High Seas (FAO)
CSC	Convention on the Continental Shelf, Geneva
CYIL	Canadian Yearbook of International Law
Dayton Agreement	General Framework Peace Accord for Bosnia and Herzegovina
DOALOS	United Nations, Division for Ocean Affairs and the Law of the Sea (UN)
Dumping Protocol	Protocol for the Prevention and Elimination of Pollution in the Mediterranean Sea by Dumping from Ships and Aircraft or Incineration at Sea (Barcelona Convention)
EC	European Community
ECJ	European Court of Justice
EEZ	Exclusive Economic Zone
EFPZ	Ecological and Fisheries Protection Zone
EFZ	Exclusive Fishery Zone
EJIL	European Journal of International Law
ENPI	European Neighbourhood Policy
EPZCSA	Ecological Protection Zone and Continental Shelf of the Republic of Slovenia Act
EU	European Union
FAO	Food and Agriculture Organization
Fish Stocks Agreement	Agreement for the Implementation of the Provisions of the United Nations Convention on the Law of

List of abbreviations xliii

	the Sea of 10 December 1982 relating to the Conservation and Management of Straddling Fish Stocks and Highly Migratory Fish Stocks
FPZ	Fisheries Protection Zone
FRY	Federal Republic of Yugoslavia
FTT	Free Territory of Trieste
GDS	Geographically Disadvantaged State
GFCM	General Fisheries Commission for the Mediterranean
GJIL	German Journal of International Law
Habitats Directive	Council Directive 92/43/EEC of 21 May 1992 on the Conservation of Natural Habitats and of wild Fauna and Flora (as amended)
HSMPA	High Seas Marine Protected Area
IBRU	International Boundaries Research Unit, University of Durham
ICES	International Council for the Exploration of the Sea
ICCAT	International Commission for the Conservation of Atlantic Tunas
ICJ	International Court of Justice
ICLQ	International & Comparative Law Quarterly
ICNT	Informal Composite Negotiating Text
ICZM Protocol	Protocol on Integrated Coastal Zone Management (Barcelona Convention)
IFIMES	International Institute for Middle-East and Balkan Studies
IJMCL	International Journal of Marine and Coastal Law
ILC	International Law Commission
ILM	International Legal Materials
ILR	International Law Reports
IMO	International Maritime Organization
ISNT	Informal Single Negotiating Text
ITLOS	International Tribunal for the Law of the Sea
IUCN	International Union for Conservation of Nature
IUU	Illegal, Unreported and Unregulated Fishing
IYIL	Italian Yearbook of International Law
km	Kilometre
Land-Based Protocol	Protocol for the Protection of the Mediterranean Sea against Pollution from Land-Based Sources and Activities (Barcelona Convention)
LLS	Land Locked State
LNG	Liquefied Natural Gas
London Convention	Convention on the Prevention of Marine Pollution by Dumping of Wastes and Other Matter

London Protocol	Protocol to the Convention on the Prevention of Marine Pollution by Dumping of Wastes and other Matter
m	Metre
MAP	Mediterranean Action Plan
MAP Phase II	Action Plan for the Protection of the Marine Environment and the Sustainable Development of the Coastal Areas of the Mediterranean
Marine Strategy Directive	Directive 2008/56/EC of the European Parliament and of the Council of 17 June 2008 establishing a framework for community action in the field of marine environmental policy
MARPOL	International Convention for the Prevention of Pollution from Ships
MEPC	Marine Environment Protection Committee (IMO)
MSC	Marine Safety Committee (IMO)
MSP	Maritime Spatial Planning
MPA	Marine Protected Area
NAV	Sub-Committee on Safety of Navigation (IMO)
nmi	Nautical Mile
OAU	Organization of African Unity
op. cit.	*opus citatum* – from the cited work
ODIL	Ocean Development and International Law
Offshore Protocol	Protocol for the Protection of the Mediterranean Sea against Pollution Resulting from Exploration and Exploitation of the Continental Shelf and the Sea-Bed and its Subsoil (Barcelona Convention)
OGFR	Official Gazette of the French Republic
OGKS	Official Gazette of the Kingdom of Spain
OGRC	Official Gazette of the Republic of Croatia
OGRS	Official Gazette of the Republic of Slovenia
OJ	Official Journal of the European Union
Osimo Treaty	Treaty between the Italian Republic and the SFRY
Paris MOU	Memorandum of Understanding on Port State Control
PCA	Permanent Court of Arbitration
PCIJ	Permanent Court of International Justice
PPP	*Poredbeno pomorsko pravo* (Comparative Maritime Law)
Prevention and Emergency Protocol	Protocol Concerning Co-operation in Preventing Pollution from Ships and, in Cases of Emergency, Combating Pollution of the Mediterranean Sea (Barcelona Convention)
PSSA	Particularly Sensitive Sea Area

RAC/SPA	Regional Activity Centre for Specially Protected Areas (UNEP)
REMPEC	Regional Marine Pollution Emergency Centre for the Mediterranean Sea
RGDIP	Revue Générale de Droit International Public
RIAA	Reports of International Arbitral Awards
RSNT	Revised Single Negotiating Text
Sanctuary Agreement	Agreement concerning the Creation of a Marine Mammal Sanctuary in the Mediterranean (France, Italy, Monaco)
SBA	Sovereign Base Area
SBC	Sea-bed Committee
SFRY	Socialist Federal Republic of Yugoslavia
SOLAS	International Convention for the Safety of Life at Sea
SOPS	Agreement between the Republic of Slovenia and the Republic of Croatia on Border Traffic and Co-operation
SPA	Specially Protected Area
SPAMI	Specially Protected Area of Mediterranean Importance
SPAMI List	List of Specially Protected Areas of Mediterranean Importance
Sub-Regional Contingency Plan	Sub-Regional Contingency Plan for Prevention of, Preparedness, for and Response to Major Marine Pollution Incidents in the Adriatic Sea
Supplementary Fund Protocol	Protocol of 2003 to the International Convention on the Establishment of an International Fund for Compensation for Oil Pollution Damage
TFEU	Treaty on the Functioning of the European Union
TSC	Convention on the Territorial Sea and the Contiguous Zone
UFM	Union for the Mediterranean
UK	The United Kingdom of Great Britain and Northern Ireland
UN	United Nations
UNCED	United Nations Conference on Environment and Development
UNCLOS	United Nations Convention on the Law of the Sea
UNCLOS I	First United Nations Conference on the Law of the Sea
UNCLOS II	Second United Nations Conference on the Law of the Sea
UNCLOS III	Third United Nations Conference on the Law of the Sea

UNEP	United Nations Environment Programme
UNESCO Convention	Convention on the Protection of the Underwater Cultural Heritage
UNPROFOR	United Nations Protection Force
UNTS	United Nations, Treaty Series
USA	United States of America
USSR	Union of Soviet Socialist Republics
VCLT	Vienna Convention on the Law of Treaties
Virginia Commentary	United Nations Convention on the Law of the Sea 1982: A Commentary (Vols I–VI)
Waste Protocol	Protocol on the Prevention of Pollution of the Mediterranean Sea by Transboundary Movements of Hazardous Wastes and their Disposal (Barcelona Convention)
ZEP	Zone of Ecological Protection

Introduction

I Current jurisdictional landscape of the Mediterranean and Adriatic Seas

The current jurisdictional status of the Mediterranean Sea is remarkable. Nearly 50 per cent of the Mediterranean waters are high seas and are therefore beyond the jurisdiction of coastal States.[1] The described situation is particularly interesting in the light of the fact that there are no points in the Mediterranean Sea where the coasts of two States would be more than 400 nmi apart. Such a legal situation generally prevents coastal States from adopting and enforcing their laws on the Mediterranean high seas in respect of many important fields such as the protection and preservation of the marine environment, as well as the conservation of marine living resources. Therefore, currently, the only available way of regulating the mentioned activities on that part of the sea is on the basis of flag State jurisdiction. This is, however, generally considered more restrictive and less effective than regulation by coastal States within zones of national jurisdiction. The described situation also differs from other enclosed or semi-enclosed seas (e.g. the Caribbean Sea, the Baltic Sea, the Black Sea, the Persian Gulf) where the bordering States have, despite similar problems (including delimitation problems), proceeded with the proclamation of EEZs.[2]

The jurisdictional landscape of the Adriatic Sea,[3] as a sub-sea and sub-region of the Mediterranean, is even more interesting. Croatia has proclaimed an EFPZ (whose regime is not applicable to EU Member States), Slovenia has proclaimed a ZEP (whose provisional limits completely overlap with the Croatian EFPZ), while Italy has adopted a framework law for the proclamation of its ZEP without actually proclaiming its regime in the Adriatic. Montenegro and Albania have

---

1 T. Treves, 'Potential Exclusive Economic Zones in the Mediterranean', paper delivered at the 11th Mediterranean Research Meeting, Florence and Montecatini Terme, 24–27 March 2010, p. 4.
2 Another enclosed or semi-enclosed sea where not all bordering States have proclaimed EEZs is the Red Sea. See M. Carleton, 'Red Sea/Persian Gulf Maritime Boundaries', in D.A. Colson and R.W. Smith (eds), *International Maritime Boundaries*, Vol. V, ASIL, 2005, pp. 3467–3475.
3 The border between the Adriatic and the Ionian Seas is located outside the Strait of Otranto. According to the suggestion of the International Hydrographic Organization, the border should follow the line linking the mouth of the Butrinto River (latitude 39°44'N) in Albania and Cape Santa Maria di Leuca in Italy (39°45'N). See, however, the discussion in section 1.2.

2 Extension of Coastal State Jurisdiction in Enclosed or Semi-enclosed Seas

not extended their jurisdiction beyond the limits of their territorial seas.[4] It is noteworthy that if all Mediterranean and Adriatic States would proclaim an EEZ, there would not be a single 'stretch' of high seas left in the entire Mediterranean Sea.[5]

II Part IX of UNCLOS

When discussing the governance of the Adriatic and Mediterranean Seas, including the actual or potential role of the proclamation of maritime zones (e.g. the EEZ), reference should be also made to the provisions of Part IX of UNCLOS on enclosed or semi-enclosed seas. It is noteworthy that Article 123 provides that:

> [...] States bordering an enclosed or semi-enclosed sea should cooperate with each other in the exercise of their rights and in the performance of their duties under this Convention. To this end they shall endeavour, directly or through an appropriate regional organization:
>
> (a) to coordinate the management, conservation, exploration and exploitation of the living resources of the sea;
> (b) to coordinate the implementation of their rights and duties with respect to the protection and preservation of the marine environment;
> (c) to coordinate their scientific research policies and undertake where appropriate joint programmes of scientific research in the area;
> (d) to invite, as appropriate, other interested States or international organizations to cooperate with them in furtherance of the provisions of this article.

Part IX of UNCLOS therefore calls for enhanced co-operation between States surrounding enclosed and semi-enclosed seas. As explained in Chapter 1, such group of seas includes both the Adriatic and Mediterranean. The need for such co-operation is, however, both emphasized and complicated by the current jurisdictional landscape of the Adriatic and the Mediterranean Seas. As pointed out by Treves:

> [...] the presence in the Mediterranean [including the Adriatic] of a wide area which lies outside the coastal States' powers, and the fact that coastal States' powers extend to different distances and have different contents, can be a source of difficulties for assuring a rational and environmentally friendly governance.[6]

4 See Chapter 3.
5 Treves, op. cit., p. 1.
6 Treves, op. cit., p. 4.

III Aims of the work

The main aim of this work is to assess the legal nature of Part IX of UNCLOS[7] and to discuss potential benefits of the extension of coastal State jurisdiction (proclamation of EEZs and/or similar *sui generis* zones) particularly in the light of the recent trends which advocate for an integrated and holistic approach to the management of the different activities in the Mediterranean and Adriatic Seas. The principal aim is to examine the actual or potential extension of coastal State jurisdiction in the Adriatic Sea, against the background of similar extensions elsewhere in the Mediterranean.[8] The work considers what the implications and benefits of the extension of coastal State jurisdiction would be, as well as some delimitation problems that would need to be resolved.[9] An important question addressed is also whether Part IX of UNCLOS imposes any duties of co-operation in relation to the extension of coastal State jurisdiction in enclosed or semi-enclosed seas.[10]

As there cannot be good governance of the Mediterranean and Adriatic without an enhanced level of co-operation between its bordering States, and taking into account that unresolved boundaries and/or overlapping claims generally hinder attempts at co-operation, this work *inter alia* attempts to identify solutions, reflecting the spirit of Part IX of UNCLOS which may help Adriatic and Mediterranean States to temporarily or permanently override the lack of final delimitation agreements.

This work also provides an assessment on how the provisions of Part IX of UNCLOS have been implemented in the Adriatic Sea and attempts to determine whether there is a need for some other forms of sub-regional co-operation in addition to those in existence and/or those contemplated at the regional (Mediterranean) level. The last goal is to advise Adriatic and generally Mediterranean States on how to approach the issue of extension of coastal State jurisdiction in a way which would enhance their existing co-operation and improve the overall governance of the two seas.

IV Methodology and contents

Bearing in mind that the Adriatic Sea is a sub-sea of the wider Mediterranean Sea,[11] and taking into account that the recent process of extension of coastal State jurisdiction in the Adriatic Sea has been influenced by similar moves by some other Mediterranean States (particularly Spain and France) and also by some EU proposals and policies (particularly those addressing sustainable fisheries and environmental governance in the Mediterranean),[12] it is deemed necessary to address

---

7 See Chapter 2.
8 See Chapter 3.
9 See Chapter 4.
10 See Chapter 2.
11 See Chapter 1.
12 See Chapter 3.

the current and future jurisdictional landscape of the Adriatic Sea from a wider Mediterranean perspective.[13]

Each chapter of this work sets out to discuss, through an analysis of primary and secondary sources, some specific problems relating to the extension of coastal State jurisdiction and/or the implementation of Part IX of UNCLOS in the Adriatic and Mediterranean which have proved to be controversial and are subject to debate by scholars and international courts alike. The work is divided into six chapters.

Chapter 1 focuses on the general geographical characteristics of both the Mediterranean and Adriatic Seas, on their interrelation and on the implications of their size and configuration on their legal status.

Chapter 2 discusses the emergence of the concept of enclosed or semi-enclosed seas at UNCLOS III and its codification in UNCLOS. Particular attention is paid to the question whether the provisions of Part IX of UNCLOS are mandatory or merely hortatory in nature. Reference is also made to the application of the concept of enclosed or semi-enclosed seas in the jurisprudence of international courts and tribunals, and to its potential relevance in the process of extension of coastal State jurisdiction and in the delimitation of maritime zones in the Adriatic and wider Mediterranean Sea.

Chapter 3 provides an overall discussion of the recent trends in the extension of coastal State jurisdiction in the Mediterranean, with special attention on the practice of Adriatic States regarding the proclamation of *sui generis* zones. The chapter seeks to determine whether the mentioned proclamations have created real *sui generis* zones or just *mini EEZs*, and to identify recent jurisdictional trends in the Mediterranean and Adriatic Seas. The discussion then turns to the legal nature of the proclaimed zones, the problems related with their external limits, and ultimately to the desirability of such proclamations from the standpoint of the overall governance of the Adriatic and/or Mediterranean Seas.[14] Lastly, reference is made to the recent positions of the EU regarding the extension of coastal State jurisdiction in the Mediterranean. This work, however, does not discuss in detail the general basis for such extension of jurisdiction (the concept of the EEZ and its historical development) as this has been amply covered in contemporary literature.[15]

Chapter 4 focuses on the three main maritime delimitation disputes and related legal questions which arose as a result of the dissolution of the former SFRY (Slovenia-Croatia, Croatia-Bosnia and Herzegovina and Croatia-Montenegro). Emphasis is added on the potential application of the principle of *uti possidetis* to maritime delimitations, to the status of border bays in international law, and to the various possible solutions to the problems of maritime delimitation in the Adriatic Sea in the spirit of Part IX of UNCLOS. The situation in the Adriatic Sea is particularly complicated by the fact that administrative (maritime) boundaries

---

13 Ibid.

14 See also the discussion in Chapter 6.

15 See for example D. Attard, *Exclusive Economic Zone in International Law*, Oxford: Clarendon Press, 1987 and M. Gavouneli, *Functional Jurisdiction in the Law of the Sea*, Publication on Ocean Development, Vol. 62, Leiden and Boston, MA: Martinus Nijhoff Publishers, 2007.

did not exist during the times of the former SFRY, and that this currently results in a situation where the maritime boundaries between the States' successors of the former SFRY have still to be finally delimited both with regard to zones of sovereign rights and jurisdiction (EEZs and/or *sui generis* zones) and zones of sovereignty (internal waters and/or territorial sea). Reference is made to the specifics of the Arbitration Agreement concluded between Slovenia and Croatia on 4 November 2009 (through the facilitation of the EU), with which the two States agreed to set up an *ad hoc* arbitral tribunal entrusted with the task to finally determine the maritime and land boundaries between them, Slovenia's junction to the high seas and the regime for the use of the relevant maritime areas; and on whether the said Agreement may represent a precedent also for other Adriatic and/or Mediterranean States.

Existing co-operative arrangements and the prospects for increased co-operation among Adriatic States, their EU dimension and the potential alternatives to the process of extension of coastal State jurisdiction in the Adriatic and/or Mediterranean are discussed in Chapter 5. It is suggested that the role of the EU is already important and will be potentially crucial in the future governance of the Adriatic Sea. Italy and Slovenia are already Member States of the EU, Croatia and Montenegro are candidate States (Croatia joined the EU on 1 July 2013), while Albania and Bosnia and Herzegovina are expected to acquire the candidate status in the years to come. Nonetheless, a comprehensive discussion of the competencies of the EU in the field of the law of the sea (including ECJ case law) and its application in the Mediterranean and Adriatic is beyond the scope of this work.

Chapter 6 sets forth general conclusions and recommendations containing *inter alia* possible solutions to the problems discussed.

It should be reiterated that this work approaches the various implications of the extension of coastal State jurisdiction in the Adriatic Sea from a wider Mediterranean and EU perspective, and is focused on the identification of solutions which would reflect the spirit of co-operation embodied in Part IX of UNCLOS. Although substantial emphasis is placed on the proclamation (or non-proclamation) of *sui generis* maritime zones and to questions related to the delimitation of maritime boundaries, this does not mean that these are the only two potential problems associated with the governance of the Adriatic and/or Mediterranean Seas. There are several other factors (e.g. political problems, questions related to enforcement of already existing international obligations) which are not addressed in detail but which are just as important (or even more) as those analyzed in this work. The author selected the particular topics discussed in this work considering that these were areas in which a contribution to the ongoing debate at the international, particularly Adriatic, Mediterranean and EU level, could be made.

Due to space concerns, the work is focused on the various issues arising from the proclamation of EEZs and/or *sui generis* zones and not specifically on the contiguous zone.[16] Data is generally adjusted *as per* 1 December 2012.

---

16 Reference is, however, made to the proclamation of archeological-contiguous zones. See the discussion in Chapters 3 and 5.

1 The Mediterranean and Adriatic as enclosed or semi-enclosed seas

This introductory chapter offers a basic discussion on the general geographic characteristics of the Mediterranean and Adriatic Seas, on the interrelation between the two seas, and on the influence of the size and configuration of the Mediterranean and Adriatic on their legal status. A tentative answer is provided at the end on whether the Mediterranean and/or the Adriatic qualify as a 'juridical' enclosed or semi-enclosed sea in line with the provisions of Part IX of UNCLOS.

1.1 The Mediterranean Sea[1]

Throughout history the Mediterranean Sea has been known by a number of alternative names. During Roman times it was commonly referred to as the *Mare Nostrum* and from this expression it may be implied that it was, to a certain extent, also a *Mare Clausum*. Noteworthy is the fact that its current name is derived from the Latin word *mediterraneous*, meaning 'in the middle of the earth' or 'between lands'.[2] The name Mediterranean, therefore, clearly emphasizes the 'enclosed' position of this sea between not less than three continents, Africa, Asia and Europe.

Nowadays, quite contrary from ancient times, the Mediterranean coastline, which extends to approximately 22,500 km, is shared by 21 States including the UK.[3] The overall surface of the Mediterranean Sea amounts to 2,500,000 km², while its average depth is approximately 1,500 m. The Mediterranean Sea stretches over a distance of 3,500 km (from Gibraltar to the east), although its maximum breadth amounts to 800 km measured from the Italian coast close to

---

1 For the purposes of this work, the Mediterranean Sea is defined *as per* Art. 1(1) of the Barcelona Convention (Mediterranean Sea proper). The Black Sea is excluded from the definition.
2 See Wikipedia (Mediterranean Sea).
3 The UK exercises sovereignty over Gibraltar and the two sovereign bases of Akrotiri and Dhekelia on the island of Cyprus. For a general discussion of the 'juridical' status of the Mediterranean, see U. Leanza, *Il regime giuridico internazionale del mare Mediterraneo*, Studi e documenti di diritto internazionale e comunitario, No. 44, Napoli: Editioriale Scientifica, 2008, and F.A. Anish, *The International Law of Maritime Boundaries and the Practice of States in the Mediterranean*, Oxford: Clarendon Press, 1993. For more information on the history of the Mediterranean, see E. Bradford, *Mediterranean: Portrait of a Sea*, London: Penguin Books, 2000.

Genoa, up to Tunisia.[4] It is generally divided into two main basins, Western and Eastern.[5] These two basins are then further sub-divided into 'sub-seas', one of them being the Adriatic.

It is noteworthy that States bordering the Mediterranean form part of three continents (Europe, Africa and Asia) with different cultures, religions and levels of economic development. States bordering the Northern Mediterranean (European) shore include UK (Gibraltar), Spain, France, Monaco, Italy, Slovenia, Croatia, Bosnia and Herzegovina, Montenegro, Greece and Turkey. Reference should be made in this regard to the island States of Malta and Cyprus (including 'Northern Cyprus' and the UK sovereign bases of Akrotiri and Dhekelia).[6] The Eastern Mediterranean shore, on the other hand, is bordered by Syria, Lebanon, Israel (and Palestine), while its southern shores are bordered by Morocco, Algeria, Tunisia, Libya and Egypt. The Mediterranean Sea is an international waterway linking the Atlantic and Indian Oceans through the Suez Canal, and both of them with the Black Sea, through the Turkish straits of Bosporus and Dardanelles. Due to the slow exchange of waters through the Strait of Gibraltar, the Mediterranean is at great risk of pollution.[7]

Another important characteristic of the Mediterranean Sea is, as mentioned, that it comprises a number of sub-seas[8] which are either indented inside the continent (e.g. the Adriatic Sea) or situated between a continent and a group of islands (e.g. the Tyrrhenian Sea). The main sub-seas in the Western Basin include the Alboran Sea (between Spain and Morocco), the Balearic Sea (between the Spanish coast and the Balearic Islands) and the Ligurian and Tyrrhenian Seas, lying between mainland Italy and the islands of Corsica, Sardinia and Sicily.[9] The sub-seas in the Eastern Mediterranean include the Ionian, Aegean and ultimately the Adriatic Sea. The common denominator of the mentioned sub-seas, both in the Western and Eastern Basins is restricted space, coupled in the majority of cases with narrow connections to other sub-seas (e.g. Strait of Otranto). The political and legal map of the Mediterranean region draws two important lines of demarcation (see Figure 1.1). The first is between the generally developed States on its northern shores (including EU Member States)[10] and the developing States on its southern shores.[11] The second is between the eight EU Member States and the remaining coastal States.

---

4 For more details see Leanza, op. cit., pp. 7–10.
5 Leanza, op. cit., pp. 7–10.
6 See the discussion on the specific position of Cyprus in section 3.4.1.
7 More than 80 years is the period needed for a single exchange of Mediterranean waters through the Strait if Gibraltar. See Leanza, op. cit., p. 8.
8 See Figure 1.
9 Cf fn 3.
10 Cyprus, France, Greece, Italy, Malta, Slovenia and Spain. Croatia, Montenegro and Turkey are candidate States.
11 Morocco, Algeria, Tunisia, Libya, Egypt, Israel (and Palestine), Lebanon and Syria.

8 *Extension of Coastal State Jurisdiction in Enclosed or Semi-enclosed Seas*

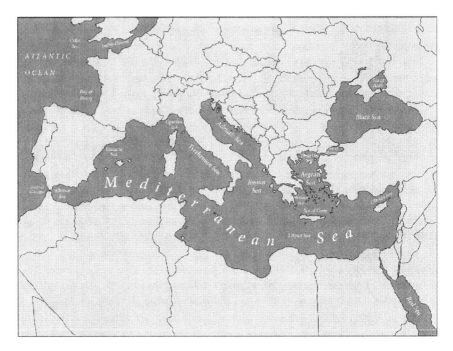

Figure 1.1 The Mediterranean Sea and its sub-seas[12]

It is noteworthy that the various Mediterranean sub-seas show different levels of autonomy, and this consideration may be important when trying to determine which sub-sea, if any, qualifies as a legal enclosed or semi-enclosed sea on the basis of Part IX of UNCLOS.[13] Amongst the geographical characteristics of the Mediterranean Sea it is important to emphasize again the restricted space and the presence of some major islands (Sicily, Balearic Islands and Crete), two island States (Malta and Cyprus) and a great number of smaller islands (e.g. Croatian islands, Spanish islands in front of the Moroccan coasts and Greek islands in the Aegean).[14] This, together with other factors, complicates the delimitation of maritime zones and, at least indirectly, also the process of extension of coastal State jurisdiction in the Mediterranean Sea.[15] The geographical difficulties are furthermore accentuated by some longstanding political problems as, for example, by the presence of the UK enclave of Gibraltar on the Iberian Peninsula and by the presence of the Spanish enclaves on the Moroccan coast coupled with the still difficult relationship of Israel with its Arab neighbours

12 Modelled on a figure found online, at <http://en.wikipedia.org/wiki/Mediterranean_Sea>.
13 See section 1.3.
14 See also Leanza, op. cit., pp. 7–11.
15 M. Grbec, 'Extension of Coastal State Jurisdiction in the Mediterranean: Quasi EEZs or real *sui generis* zones?', in N.A. Martínez Gutiérrez (ed.), *Serving the Rule of International Maritime Law: Essays in Honour of Professor David Joseph Attard*, London and New York: Routledge, 2010, p. 181.

(e.g. Lebanon).[16] The delimitation of maritime boundaries in the Eastern Mediterranean is furthermore complicated by the still divided status of Cyprus[17] and by the sometimes tense relations between Greece and Turkey in the Aegean. It is also imperative to note that not all Mediterranean States are parties to UNCLOS.[18]

From the standpoint of contemporary law of the sea there are at least three important implications of the size and configuration of the Mediterranean Sea. The first is that there are no points in the Mediterranean where the coasts of two States are more than 400 nmi apart.[19] In practical terms this means that Mediterranean coastal States are not in a position to extend their jurisdiction up to the maximum extent permitted by international law. Similarly, the limited maritime space available also means that almost every extension of jurisdiction creates new neighbours and triggers the need for delimitation of actual or potential zones of sovereign rights and/or jurisdiction with adjacent and opposite States. Second, due to the proximity between Mediterranean States, the extension of jurisdiction by one coastal State, in most cases, affects the interests of more than just another neighbouring State. An excellent example is the complicated geographical situation in the Central Mediterranean, where the extension of jurisdiction by one State up to the maximum extent permitted by international law would affect the interests of up to four neighbouring States, namely in the cases of Greece, Italy, Libya, Malta and Tunisia (see Figure 1.2).[20]

Lastly, since the continental shelf exists *ipso facto and ab initio*, it would seem that there is no space in the Mediterranean Sea for an outer continental shelf on the basis of Article 76 of UNCLOS, nor obviously for an 'International Area' in accordance with Part XI of UNCLOS. It is nonetheless noteworthy that while approximately 20 per cent of the Mediterranean Sea is represented by the natural continental shelf, the waters of the Adriatic, as one of its sub-seas, are almost completely situated over its natural continental shelf.[21]

1.2 The Adriatic Sea

As described by Vidas '[t]he Adriatic is a narrow, shallow and temperature warm semi-enclosed sea, forming a distinct sub-region within the Mediterranean Sea

---

16 See section 3.1.
17 See section 3.4.1.
18 Israel, Libya, Syria and Turkey are not parties to UNCLOS. See H. Slim and T. Scovazzi, 'Study of the current status of ratification, implementation and compliance with maritime agreements and conventions applicable to the Mediterranean Sea Basin: With a specific focus on the ENPI South Partner Countries', Part I, Tables of Participation to the Relevant Treaties, AGRECO Consortium, 2009, pp. 67–68.
19 D. Attard, 'The Delimitation of Maritime Zones: Some Mediterranean Experiences', Proceedings of the 5th International Conference on Traffic Science, Portorož, University of Ljubljana, Faculty of Maritime Studies and Transportation & Slovenian Society for Traffic Science, 27–30 October 2001, p. 1.
20 G. Francalanci and T. Scovazzi (eds), *The Mediterranean: Selected Maps*, Genova: Istituto Idrografico della Marina, 1992.
21 See Leanza, op. cit., p. 10.

10 *Extension of Coastal State Jurisdiction in Enclosed or Semi-enclosed Seas*

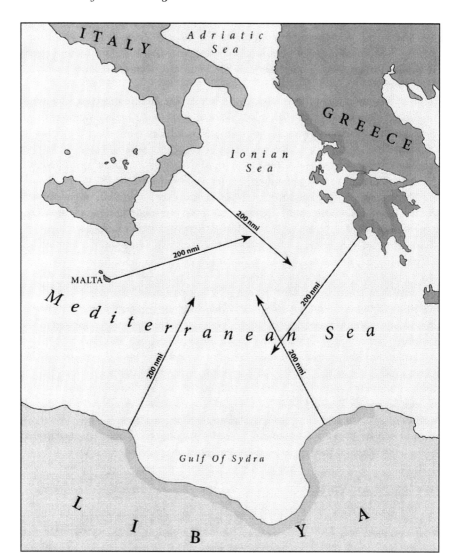

Figure 1.2 Overlapping claims in the Central Mediterranean[22]

Region [...]'.[23] The Adriatic Sea is nowadays surrounded by six States: Italy, Slovenia, Croatia, Bosnia and Herzegovina, Montenegro and Albania. Of interest is that the geographical co-ordinates of the Adriatic Sea slightly differ depending on the purpose of the specific measurement. From a practical point of view,

---

22 Modelled on a figure published in Francalanci and Scovazzi, op. cit. (cover).
23 See D. Vidas, 'Particularly Sensitive Sea Areas: The Need for Regional Cooperation in the Adriatic Sea', in K. Ott (ed.), *Croatian Accession to the European Union: Institutional Challenges*, Vol. 4, Zagreb: Institute of Public Finance, 2006, p. 347 at 359.

The Mediterranean and the Adriatic 11

of particular importance are co-ordinates contained in various IMO documents relating to safety of navigation in the Adriatic Sea. In the joint proposal submitted in 2003 by Albania, Croatia, Italy, Slovenia, Serbia and Montenegro on the establishment of new recommended Traffic Separation Schemes/Recommended Routes System and other new Routeing Measures in the Adriatic Sea, endorsed by the IMO, the Adriatic is described as follows:

> The Adriatic Sea is the part of the Mediterranean sea situated between Balkan and Appenine peninsulas, on the geographical longitude between 012°15' E and 019°45' E and the geographical latitude between 39°45' N and 45°45'N. The south border includes the whole area of the Strait of Otranto and leads on joint line of the Cape of Santa Maria di Leuca [Italy] – the north coast of the island of Krf [Corfu-Greece] – the mouth of the river Butrinit [Albania].[24]

Greece is at times also considered as an Adriatic State. This is mostly a result of the geographical position of the Greek island of Corfu located at the entrance, and due to some smaller Greek islands located within the Strait of Otranto.[25]

Due to its relatively long and narrow shape, the Adriatic is deeply indented into the European mainland and linked to the rest of the Mediterranean Sea (Ionian Sea) only through the Strait of Otranto. The surface of the Adriatic Sea amounts to 138,595 km², while the total length of the Adriatic coastline is around 7,912 km,[26] more than half of which is composed of the coastline of the numerous islands fringing particularly the Eastern Adriatic coasts. The length of the Adriatic Sea from Venice and the mouth of the River Butrinit in Albania amounts to almost 475 nmi.[27] It is noteworthy that the average width of the Adriatic is only 85 nmi.[28]

The Adriatic has also been an important route of international navigation. The main navigation route in the Adriatic Sea goes from the 'wider' Mediterranean Sea (Ionian) through the approximately 45 nmi wide Strait of Otranto and towards one of the Northern Adriatic ports: Trieste (Italy), Koper (Slovenia) and Rijeka (Croatia) (see Figure 1.3).[29]

---

24 IMO, 'Routeing of Ships, Ship Reporting and Related Matters: Establishment of new recommended Traffic Separation Schemes and other new Routing Measures in the Adriatic Sea. Submitted by Albania, Croatia, Italy, Slovenia and Serbia and Montenegro', NAV 49/3/7, 27 March 2003, p. 2. See also the discussion in section 5.4.1.1. The co-ordinates suggested by the International Hydrographic Organization are slightly different. See Introduction, fn 3.
25 See the discussion on the AII in section 5.4.1.
26 Cf fn 24.
27 Ibid.
28 M. Grbec, *Delimitation of the Maritime Boundary between the Republic of Slovenia and the Republic of Croatia*, LL.M. Thesis, Malta: IMO IMLI, 2001, pp. 1–2.
29 According to Vidas, an important characteristic of the 'Adriatic route' is the high and even increasing amount of oil (and other dangerous goods) transported particularly towards the Northern Adriatic ports of Trieste and Venice. The overall yearly amount of transported oil in 2005 on this route amounted to approximately 60 million tonnes, while in Adriatic as a whole the figure rose to approximately 70 million tonnes. Vidas is furthermore of the opinion that

12 *Extension of Coastal State Jurisdiction in Enclosed or Semi-enclosed Seas*

Figure 1.3 Adriatic Sea: Coastal States and main ports[30]

In 1991, the dissolution of the SFRY led to the emergence of four new littoral States (Croatia, Bosnia and Herzegovina, Montenegro and Slovenia) whose geographical positions within the Adriatic Sea differ substantially both with regard to the length and position of their coastlines. Croatia has by far the longest coastline fringed by more than 1,000 islands (almost 6,278 km, 4,398 km along islands) while Slovenia, on the other hand, has a coastline of around 47 km located within the Gulf of Trieste: a 'border bay' surrounded nowadays by Slovenia, Italy and Croatia. The position of the coastline of Bosnia and Herzegovina is remarkable from the standpoint of the law of the sea not only due to the specific position and

a significant increase in the transport of oil and other dangerous cargoes, including LNG may be expected during the second decade of the twenty-first century. See Vidas, op. cit., pp. 362–363.
30 Modelled on a figure published in Vidas, op. cit., p. 357.

shortness of its coastline (22 km), but also due to the fact that its maritime zones seem to be completely enclosed by the internal waters of the Republic of Croatia.[31] Montenegro has, on the other hand, 'inherited' the second longest coastline among the States successors of the former SFRY (294 km), while the length of the Albanian (Adriatic) coastline amounts to 362 km. The western side of the Adriatic shoreline is completely occupied by the fairly regular Italian coast extending to almost 1,300 km.[32] The political map of the sub-region still represents a division between EU Member States (Slovenia, Italy and Croatia) and other States, although it is important to note that all remaining States aspire to join the EU in the not too distant future. All Adriatic States are also parties to UNCLOS.[33]

The Adriatic marine environment is extremely sensitive and represents an almost unique ecosystem.[34] It has been alleged that its environmental conditions are mostly a result of the specific exchange of waters with the wider Mediterranean (Ionian Sea) through the Otranto Strait and the Palagruža threshold separating the shallower Northern Adriatic from the deeper Southern Adriatic, and furthermore by the inputs of freshwater from the mountains in the Eastern and the rivers in the Western part.[35] Its living resources can be generally qualified as 'highly diversified, with numerous species but low abundance',[36] which makes the Adriatic's ecosystem particularly vulnerable.

An important question for the purpose of this work is therefore whether the Adriatic, as a sub-sea of the Mediterranean Sea proper, forms also a separate juridical (legal) enclosed or semi-enclosed sea on the basis of the provision of Part IX of UNCLOS.

1.3 The Mediterranean and/or Adriatic: Enclosed or semi-enclosed seas?

The question whether UNCLOS should contain separate provisions on enclosed or semi-enclosed seas was highly controversial at UNCLOS III.[37] An even more intriguing issue was whether the Mediterranean should be classified as

---

31 See section 4.5.
32 Policy Research Corporation; 'The potential of Maritime Spatial Planning in the Mediterranean Sea. Case Study Report: The Adriatic Sea', Study carried out on behalf of the European Commission, Brussels, January 2011, pp. 3–4
33 Slim and Scovazzi, op. cit., pp. 67–68.
34 Joint Expert Group of the Adriatic States on the PSSA, 'Designation of the Adriatic Sea as a Particularly Sensitive Area', draft proposal, 2007, p. 2. Copy on file with the author. See also section 5.5.
35 Ibid.
36 The PSSA draft proposal, ibid, makes reference to the fact that more than 1,800 living species have been found only in the Slovenian part of the Gulf of Trieste, the northernmost and shallower part of the Adriatic. Furthermore, the biodiversity seems to be also high in front of the coast of Montenegro with almost 80 per cent of Mediterranean fish species found there. The draft proposal emphasizes, however, that high diversity is not supported by a high number of specimens. Ibid, p. 8.
37 See the discussion in section 2.2.

14 _Extension of Coastal State Jurisdiction in Enclosed or Semi-enclosed Seas_

a 'juridical' enclosed or semi-enclosed sea.[38] The opinions of States participating at UNCLOS III differed considerably.

It suffices here to mention that some delegations at UNCLOS III, particularly those representing maritime powers, were of the opinion that the situation of the Mediterranean Sea is so specific that it could not be granted a special regime as that envisaged for enclosed or semi-enclosed seas. A notable example is the former USSR which opposed the establishment of a special regime for semi-enclosed seas which, according to its interpretation, were 'large bodies of water' with several outlets through which passed international waterways'.[39] The USSR did not oppose, however, the possibility of inclusion of special rules for enclosed seas, which it regarded to be 'comparatively small seas that have no outlet to the ocean and do not serve as international shipping routes in the broadest sense'.[40]

The aforesaid Soviet interpretation is interesting, since it claimed that whilst the Mediterranean Sea would not qualify as 'juridical' enclosed or semi-enclosed sea, the various sub-seas forming part of it (e.g. the Adriatic Sea), would. Another line of thought was expressed by Alexander who considered that semi-enclosed seas only referred to primary seas, and not their sub-seas.[41] According to this view, the Mediterranean would be classified as a juridical enclosed or semi-enclosed sea, whilst the various sub-seas forming part of it would not (regardless of their characteristics and/or level of autonomy).[42]

In accordance with a modern view discussed in detail in Chapter 2, it is however clear that both the Mediterranean and the Adriatic are classified, on the basis of Part IX of UNCLOS (Article 122),[43] as legal enclosed or semi-enclosed seas.[44] Both seas are surrounded by more than one State, are linked to another sea or ocean through a narrow outlet (or outlets)[45] and, in case of proclamation of EEZs or other zones of jurisdiction, their surface would not just primarily, but most

---

38 Ibid. See particularly B. Vukas, 'Enclosed and Semi-Enclosed Seas', in B. Vukas, _The Law of the Sea: Selected Writings_, Publications on Ocean Development, Leiden and Boston, MA: Martinus Nijhoff Publishers, 2004, p. 263 at 273.

39 A/CONF.62/C.2/SR 38, 13 August 1974, para. 49.

40 Ibid. See also the discussion in Vukas, op. cit., p. 271.

41 L. M. Alexander, 'Regional Arrangements in the Oceans', AJIL, Vol. 71, No. 1, 1977, p. 84 at pp. 90–91. Quoted also in B. Vukas, 'The Mediterranean: An Enclosed or Semi-Enclosed Sea?', in B. Vukas; op. cit., p. 281 at 284.

42 Ibid, p. 284.

43 'For the purposes of this Convention [UNCLOS], "enclosed or semi-enclosed sea" means a gulf, basin or sea surrounded by two or more States and connected to another sea or the ocean by a narrow outlet or consisting entirely or primarily of the territorial seas and exclusive economic zones of two or more coastal States'. See the detailed discussion in section 2.2.

44 See Leanza, op. cit., p. 1. See also M. Škrk, 'Exclusive Economic Zones in Enclosed or Semi-Enclosed Sea', in B. Vukas (ed.), _The Legal Regime of Enclosed or Semi-Enclosed Seas: The Particular Case of the Mediterranean_, Prinosi za poredbeno proučavanje prava i međunarodno pravo, Vol. 19, No. 22, Zagreb, 1988, p. 159 at 164. See also B. Vukas, 'The Mediterranean: An Enclosed or Semi-Enclosed Sea?', op. cit., p. 284.

45 Even if one adopts the position that the approximately 40 nmi wide Strait of Otranto does not qualify as a 'narrow outlet', the Adriatic Sea still fulfils the second alternative requirement of Art. 122 of UNCLOS. See the discussion in section 2.2.2.3, and Škrk, op. cit., p. 164.

likely entirely be made up of EEZs and/or other jurisdictional zones of the surrounding States.[46]

It should be emphasized that the classification of the Mediterranean and/or the Adriatic Seas as juridical enclosed or semi-enclosed seas does not stem exclusively from the fulfillment of the prevalently geographical criteria embodied in Article 122 of UNCLOS. This fact may also be implied by the already established or envisaged co-operation amongst States bordering the Mediterranean and the Adriatic Seas which in certain cases even pre-dated the adoption of UNCLOS.[47] Furthermore, it seems reasonable to agree with Leanza that in the case of a sub-sea forming part of a wider 'juridical' enclosed or semi-enclosed sea, an important factor in its classification, in addition to the requirements embodied in Article 122 of UNCLOS, is also the level of autonomy which a certain sub-sea shows in relation to the principal sea.[48] It therefore follows that not all sub-seas which fulfill the relatively broad geographical criteria of Article 122 of UNCLOS, also qualify as separate juridical enclosed or semi-enclosed seas. Each sub-sea has its own characteristics and should be considered independently.

The classification of the Mediterranean and Adriatic as 'juridical' enclosed or semi-enclosed seas brings with it an enhanced requirement for its coastal States to co-operate in the implementation of their rights and duties under UNCLOS with particular emphasis on the areas of co-operation expressly referred to in Article 123.[49] The question which may be asked, and to which an answer is attempted in Chapter 2, is whether Article 123 of UNCLOS is mandatory or just hortatory in nature and whether it provides at least for an implied requirement for bordering States to endeavour to co-operate also when it comes to questions related to the extension of coastal State jurisdiction.

1.4 Concluding remarks

When it comes to the legal status of the waters of the Adriatic Sea the similarities with the Mediterranean Sea proper are unmistakable. Due to the narrowness of the Adriatic and the presence of six coastal States, there are obviously no points in the Adriatic Sea where the coasts of two States are more than 400 nmi apart. This points to the fact that none of the Adriatic States can extend its jurisdiction

---

46 Ibid.

47 See for example the adoption of the MAP in 1975 and the conclusion of the 1974 Belgrade Agreement between Italy and the SFRY. See the discussion in sections 5.1.1. and 5.4.

48 See Leanza, op. cit, p. 13. It is not completely clear what is the appropriate test to determine whether a certain sub-sea shows the necessary level of autonomy. It is suggested that a useful consideration, in addition to the already established level of co-operation among the bordering States, is whether a sub-sea is forming a separate management (functional) sub-region within the wider marine region. For an explanation of the possible meanings of the term 'region' (the formal, the functional and the political), see A. Boyle, 'Globalism and Regionalism in the Protection of the Marine Environment', in D. Vidas (ed.), *Protecting the Polar Marine Environment; Law and Policy for Pollution Prevention*, Cambridge: Cambridge University Press, 2000, p. 19 at p. 26. See also Vidas, op.cit, p. 359.

49 See the discussion in section 2.3.

up to the maximum extent permitted by international law. As a result, both the high seas of the Adriatic and of the Mediterranean are 'potential EEZs' awaiting delimitation.

It follows furthermore that the Adriatic qualifies as a (separate) 'juridical' enclosed or semi-enclosed sea, in addition to the Mediterranean Sea proper. It is accordingly suggested that States surrounding the Adriatic Sea are bound by the provisions of Part IX of UNCLOS.

2 The development of the concept of enclosed or semi-enclosed seas at UNCLOS III and its reflection in the contemporary law of the sea

The aim of this chapter is to provide a legal analysis of Part IX of UNCLOS in the light of the contemporary law of the sea. Particular attention is devoted to the question of whether the provisions of Article 123 of UNCLOS are mandatory or just hortatory in nature, and whether its scope of application is limited only to the three mentioned areas. Reference is also made to the potential relevance of Part IX of UNCLOS to the process of extension of coastal State jurisdiction and to the delimitation of maritime zones in the Mediterranean and Adriatic seas.

2.1 UNCLOS III

There is a consensus among scholars that UNCLOS III, which started in 1974 and led to the adoption of UNCLOS in 1982, was one of the most important international conferences in the history of mankind.[1] Never before or since has there been an attempt to regulate comprehensively, in a single document, all matters pertaining to the use of the oceans and seas.

The deliberations at UNCLOS III were extraordinary in many aspects. Unlike UNCLOS I, for which the ILC had prepared a single draft treaty which led to the adoption of the four Geneva Conventions,[2] the delegates who took part in the first session of UNCLOS III in Caracas commenced their deliberations without a single negotiating text. Bearing in mind that UNCLOS III's agenda encompassed almost 100 items, the Conference divided itself into three main committees.[3]

---

1 Almost 2000 delegates were present at its first meeting in Caracas and it took almost eight years from its inauguration in 1974 until the adoption of UNCLOS. See D. Attard, *The Mediterranean as an 'Enclosed Sea' in the New Law of the Sea*, Doctoral Thesis, Faculty of Laws, Malta: University of Malta, 1977, p. 8. For a detailed overview and commentary of UNCLOS, see M. H. Nordquist *et al.* (eds), *United Nations Convention on the Law of the Sea 1982: A Commentary*, Six Volumes, Dordrecht, Boston, MA and London: Martinus Nijhoff Publishers, 1985, 1989, 1991, 1993, 1995, 2002 (hereinafter the 'Virginia Commentary').

2 The four Conventions adopted at UNCLOS I were the Convention on the Territorial Sea and the Contiguous Zone (TSC), the Convention on the High Seas (CHS), the Convention on the Continental Shelf (CSC), and the Convention on Fishing and Conservation of the Living Resources of the High Seas.

3 Attard, op. cit., pp. 8–9, and T. Koh, 'The Art and Science of Chairing Major Inter-governmental Conferences', UN, Audiovisual Library of International Law. Available at <http://untreaty.un.org/cod/avl/ls/Koh_T_LS.html>.

18 *Extension of Coastal State Jurisdiction in Enclosed or Semi-enclosed Seas*

The First Committee addressed issues relating to the new regime of the international sea-bed area and the concept of the common heritage of mankind. The Second Committee was focused on questions related to the territorial sea and contiguous zone, straits used for international navigation, the EEZ, the continental shelf, the high seas, land-locked States, archipelagic States, the regime of islands, and settlement of disputes. The Third Committee, in turn, dealt with questions related to marine scientific research and environmental issues.[4]

The work of the Second Committee is of utmost importance for the purpose of this work since, within its deliberations, it dealt with the problems of enclosed or semi-enclosed seas. It should be noted that one of the principal outcomes of UNCLOS III was the codification of new zones of maritime jurisdiction, the most important being the EEZ. This resulted in a new law of the sea which, according to Leanza, gives priority to the exploitation of natural resources over the traditional freedoms of the seas, the most important being freedom of navigation.[5] Bearing this in mind, it should not come as a surprise that the problems of enclosed or semi-enclosed seas were debated at UNCLOS III by the Second Committee together with questions related to the territorial sea, the EEZ and the high seas.[6]

2.1.1 The pre-UNCLOS III period

One of the facts that led to the convening of UNCLOS III was that, particularly between the adoption of the 1958 Geneva Conventions and the convening of UNCLOS III in 1974, the oceans were being subjected to conflicting claims including sovereignty and jurisdictional disputes.[7] The latter were generated and fuelled by the fact that the 1958 Geneva Conventions did not address many pressing problems related to the world oceans, amongst which most notably was the breadth of the territorial sea, while other solutions (e.g. the breadth of the continental shelf linked to the concept of exploitability) led to uncertainty, unpredictability and conflicting claims.[8]

Another important topic not addressed by the 1958 Geneva Conventions was that relating to the specific problems of some 'regional seas' which, due to their size and particular hydrographical and ecological conditions, in many aspects differ from those of the world oceans. As pointed out by Attard, it is not possible:

> [...] to lose sight of their extremely diverse environmental conditions and of the wide differences they present from area to area under many

4 A/CONF.62/L.8/REV.1, 17 October 1974, Statement of activities of the Conference during its first and second sessions, Allocation of Work to Main Committees, para. 40. Ibid.
5 U. Leanza, *Il regime giuridico internazionale del mare Mediterraneo*, Studi e documenti di diritto internazionale e comunitario, No. 44, Napoli: Editioriale Scientifica, 2008, pp. 1–2.
6 Cf fn 4.
7 DOALOS, 'The United Nations Convention on the Law of the Sea: A historical perspective', available at <http://www.un.org/Depts/los/convention_agreements/convention_historical_perspective.htm>.
8 R. Churchill and V. Lowe, *The Law of the Sea*, 3rd edn, Manchester: Manchester University Press, 1999, p. 147.

standpoints (geographical, geological, biological, environmental, economic, physical, chemical and so on).[9]

It is noteworthy that the provisions of the 1958 Geneva Conventions were universal in nature, without containing any distinction based on geographical, historical or economic specificity of particular regions. This was mostly due to the fact that the biggest maritime powers of that time wanted to preserve, both substantially and geographically, the existing freedoms of the high seas, especially their freedom of navigation in such seas.[10] The question whether UNCLOS should contain special rules on enclosed or semi-enclosed seas was therefore one of the most controversial issues at UNCLOS III. Proof of this is the fact that until the very end of the Conference it was not clear whether UNCLOS would ultimately contain some specific rules in this regard.[11]

2.1.2 Position of states at UNCLOS III

It is noteworthy that almost half of the States participating at UNCLOS III were States surrounding enclosed or semi-enclosed seas and, if united, they could have represented an important negotiating block. However, not all States surrounding such seas favoured a separate (global) regime for enclosed or semi-enclosed seas. It seems that the positions of various States were particularly guided by their own strategic interests and/or by their geographic position in a particular enclosed or semi-enclosed sea.

The most notable example is the Aegean Sea, where Turkey was strongly in favour of a specific regime which would take into account the particular characteristics of a certain enclosed or semi-enclosed sea, and which would provide specific rules regarding the breadth of the territorial sea and the delimitation of maritime zones.[12] On the other hand, Greece found it legally difficult to accept an exceptional juridical regime for particular categories of enclosed or semi-enclosed seas and was particularly opposed to the introduction of specific rules regarding the breadth of the territorial sea, as well as the proclamation and delimitation of other zones in enclosed or semi-enclosed seas.[13]

A similar situation occurred in the Adriatic Sea, where the former SFRY supported the inclusion of specific rules on enclosed or semi-enclosed seas,[14] whilst Italy, at least during the early deliberations at UNCLOS III, seemed to oppose it. This was notwithstanding the fact that the that State was one of the promoters of the idea of enclosed or semi-enclosed seas within the

---

9 Attard, op. cit., p. 14. See also L. Alexander, 'Regionalism and the law of the sea: The case of semi-enclosed seas', ODIL, Vol. 2, Issue 2, 1974, pp. 151–186.
10 U. Leanza, *Il nuovo diritto del mare e la sua applicazione nel Mediterraneo*, Torino: G. Giappichelli Editore, 1993, p. 25, fn. 35.
11 See sections 2.3.1–2.3.3, and Virginia Commentary, Vol. III, op. cit., p. 360, para. 123.10.
12 See section 2.4.1.1.
13 A/CONF.62/C.2/SR.5, 13 August 1974, paras. 23–24.
14 See section 2.1.3.

20 *Extension of Coastal State Jurisdiction in Enclosed or Semi-enclosed Seas*

SBC.[15] The Italian position indicates that in some cases, the broader interest of the maritime powers bordering enclosed or semi-enclosed seas (e.g. freedom of navigation) prevailed over the benefits of the adoption of specific rules aimed at the protection and safeguard of such seas.

It is noteworthy that the few States which expressly opposed the inclusion of specific rules for enclosed or semi-enclosed seas at UNCLOS III were, already during the Conference's second session, outnumbered by States which emphasized the importance of according special treatment to such seas.[16] It seems that this was due to the fact that some States (e.g. France and Italy) lifted their opposition to the inclusion of particular rules for enclosed or semi-enclosed seas after it became clear that such rules would not deal with navigation and/or delimitation of maritime zones.[17]

2.1.3 Main reasons for the inclusion of specific rules on enclosed or semi-enclosed seas in UNCLOS

It is suggested that an analysis of the debates at UNCLOS III may shed some light on the main reasons why States believed that UNCLOS should contain specific rules on enclosed or semi-enclosed seas. In this respect, and amongst the many interventions at the Conference, it is important to highlight the intervention of the representative of Sweden, according to whom:

> […] the main reason for including item 17 [Enclosed and semi-enclosed seas] in the agenda was that there were basic differences between States situated along the oceans on the one hand and those bordering enclosed or semi-enclosed sea on the other. Those differences could be of a *political, economic, geological or ecological nature*. Each enclosed sea had its own particular problems and each case warranted its specific solution.[18]

---

15 In 1968, Italy submitted a Memorandum to the SBC advocating that 'enclosed seas' should receive special consideration in any future law of the sea treaty. Depuy called the Italian theory the 'Theory of the Mediterranean'. See Attard, op. cit., p. 18.

16 The Israeli representative made reference to 18 speakers, all from States surrounding enclosed or semi-enclosed seas, who had in the general debate declared themselves in favour of such an inclusion. See A/CONF.62/C.2/SR 38, 13 August 1974, para 10. See also B. Vukas, 'Enclosed or Semi-Enclosed Seas', in B. Vukas, *The Law of the Sea: Selected Writings*, Publications on Ocean Development, Leiden and Boston, MA: Martinus Nijhoff Publishers, 2004, p. 263 at pp. 266–267.

17 At the 127th Meeting of the Second Committee the French delegate pointed that '[…] the matters considered by the Second Committee reflected broad agreement on reasonable satisfactory compromise formulas concerning, *inter alia* […] enclosed and semi-enclosed seas […]'. See A/CONF.62/C.2/SR.127, 2 April 1980, para. 72.

18 Emphasis added. A/CONF.62/C.2/SR 38, 13 August 1974, para. 22. Quoted also in the Virginia Commentary, Vol. III, op. cit., p. 344, para. IX.3.

The representative of Iran also supported the inclusion of specific rules by stating that:

> The problems raised by the semi-enclosed seas with regard to the management of their resources, international navigation and the preservation of the marine environment justified granting them a particular status constituting an exception to the general rule [...][19]

He also emphasized that 'the fact that the total area of semi-enclosed seas lay above the continental shelf of the coastal States justified the working out of a special regime'.[20] It is also worth mentioning the intervention by the delegation of the former SFRY which drew attention to:

> [...] (a) the *complexity of navigation* in these seas and in outlets connecting them with the open seas due to their small surface and poor connection with other seas;
>
> (b) the *growing danger of all types of pollution*; because of their small size and poor interchange of their waters with adjacent seas; and
>
> (c) The *necessity of taking special precautionary measures in relation to the management, conservation and exploitation of the living resources* of such seas, as they are endangered by their natural characteristics and by pollution.[21]

In the light of the foregoing it is possible to conclude that the prevalent view of States participating at UNCLOS III was that there should be specific rules on enclosed or semi-enclosed seas providing 'exceptions' or at least 'additional duties' to the more general rules of UNCLOS, especially in areas where the characteristics of enclosed or semi-enclosed seas warranted particular solutions. The mentioned provisions should however be ideally implemented and upgraded in practice through bilateral and regional agreements. Such conclusions could perhaps be best explained by quoting the Swedish delegate, who stated that:

> [...] The Convention could not reasonably be expected to solve also the question of the various enclosed or semi-enclosed seas. In drawing up the Convention, however, the Conference should provide for exceptions to be made from its general provisions in all instances where the particular characteristics of enclosed or semi-enclosed seas warranted particular solutions.[22]

---

19 Ibid, para. 2.
20 Ibid, para. 3. See section 3.1.
21 Emphasis added. Quoted also in Vukas, 'Enclosed or Semi-Enclosed Seas', op. cit., p. 263 at p. 267.
22 A/CONF.62/C.2/SR.38, 13 August 1974, para. 24.

2.2 A legal definition of an enclosed or semi-enclosed sea

One of the main problems encountered within the Second Committee was the definition of enclosed and semi-enclosed seas. It should be recalled that some Mediterranean States, including France and Greece, at least during the early deliberations of the Second Committee, opposed the inclusion of specific rules on enclosed or semi-enclosed seas into UNCLOS on the basis that the concept was vague, undefined and purely geographical in nature.[23] For example, the Greek representative stated that '[...] to include a vague and undefined concept in the final instrument of the Conference would lead to insuperable problems'.[24]

It may also be noted that some States, including the USSR[25] and Iran,[26] tried to distinguish between enclosed and semi-enclosed seas, and even proposed different definitions for the two terms. Despite such differences there was consensus from the very early stages of UNCLOS III that the legal definition of enclosed or semi-enclosed seas should not include those 'geographically' enclosed and/or semi-enclosed seas bordered by only one State,[27] neither closed seas which do not have any connection to other seas or the oceans (e.g. the Aral Sea, the Dead Sea and the Caspian Sea).[28]

2.2.1 Evolution of Article 122 at UNCLOS III

There were many attempts during UNCLOS III to provide and/or clarify a legal definition of enclosed or semi-enclosed seas. The reason for this is not difficult to ascertain. If specific rules for enclosed or semi-enclosed seas were to be included in UNCLOS, it was crucial for the Convention to provide a legal definition which clearly set apart 'enclosed or semi-enclosed seas' from other seas and oceans.

This section deals with some of the proposals which influenced the final definition of 'enclosed or semi-enclosed seas' contained in Article 122 of UNCLOS and which can provide some help in the interpretation of its various ambiguous terms. It seems that the biggest influence on the legal definition of enclosed or semi-enclosed seas was exercised by the Iranian proposal[29] which, although providing separate definitions for 'enclosed' and 'semi-enclosed' seas, envisaged a common legal regime for both categories. While presenting the Iranian proposal at the 43rd Meeting of the Second Committee, the Iranian delegate explained his

---

23 See section 2.1.2.
24 Cf fn 13. See also Leanza, op. cit., 1993, p. 30, fn. 45.
25 A/CONF.62/C.2/SR 38, 13 August 1974, para. 49. See also section 1.3.
26 See section 2.3.1.
27 See Vukas, 'The Mediterranean: An Enclosed or Semi-Enclosed Sea?', in Vukas, op. cit., p. 281 at p. 283.
28 See Leanza, op. cit, 2008, p. 6.
29 A/CONF.62/C.2/L.72, 21st August 1974, Art. 1. See also Virginia Commentary, Vol. III, op. cit., p. 348, para. 122.2.

delegation's understanding of these terms and provided examples of seas which would fall under the two separate categories.[30] He stated that:

> [...] An enclosed sea was not a fully closed sea such as the Caspian Sea or the Aral Sea, which had no outlets to the oceans. It was, instead, a small body of inland water, such as the Persian Gulf and the Baltic Sea, which had at least one outlet to the open sea.[31]

On the other hand, he explained that the term 'semi-enclosed sea':

> [...] could be used in a broad sense to cover larger sea basins along the margins of the main ocean basins, more or less enclosed by a land mass – whether continental or insular – and with one or more narrow outlets to the oceans. [...][32]

The Iranian delegate referred to the Mediterranean as a 'semi-enclosed sea'. This is particularly important in the light of the divergent views existing at that time on this issue.[33] Although Vukas argued that the Iranian proposal was not satisfactory as it contained 'too many juridical and geographically vague notions (inland waters, open seas, narrow outlet, sea basins, main oceans basin)',[34] it follows that, particularly through its structure and underlying logic, it exercised a considerable influence on the final text embodied in Article 122 of UNCLOS.[35]

Another interesting proposal which also seems to have influenced the definition of 'enclosed or semi-enclosed seas' is the proposal submitted at the third session of UNCLOS III by the Informal group on enclosed or semi-enclosed seas. The Group defined a 'semi-enclosed sea' as:

> A sea surrounded by two or more States *which is of such extent and characteristics* as to prevent the full and entire application of one or more of the general provisions of this Convention with regards to maritime spaces and which is accessible from the other seas or oceans solely through straits or narrow passages *traditionally used for international navigation.*[36]

It is suggested that this proposal was the result of a realization by States surrounding enclosed or semi-enclosed seas that some general provisions of UNCLOS,

---

30 A/CONF. 62/C.2/SR.43, 23 August 1974, paras 31–32.
31 Ibid, para. 31.
32 Ibid, para. 32. See also M. Škrk, 'Exclusive Economic Zones in Enclosed or Semi-Enclosed Seas', in B. Vukas (ed.), *The Legal Regime of Enclosed or Semi-Enclosed Seas: The Particular Case of the Mediterranean*, Prinosi za poredbeno proučavanje prava i međunarodno pravo, Vol. 19, No. 22, Zagreb, 1988, p. 159 at p. 163. As examples of semi-enclosed seas the Iranian delegate mentioned the Caribbean Sea and the Andaman Sea.
33 See section 1.3.
34 Vukas, 'Enclosed or Semi-Enclosed Seas', op. cit., p. 272.
35 See section 2.2.1.1.
36 Emphasis added. Quoted in the Virginia Commentary, Vol. III, op. cit., p. 349, para. 122.3.

24　*Extension of Coastal State Jurisdiction in Enclosed or Semi-enclosed Seas*

particularly those regulating maritime spaces (e.g. the extension of the breadth of the territorial sea up to 12 nmi, of the EEZ up to 200 nmi, etc.), were not completely appropriate and could not be fully applied in enclosed or semi-enclosed seas.[37] The proposal therefore envisaged a new criteria for defining enclosed or semi-enclosed seas in addition to a 'two State requirement' and to a 'narrow outlet', namely 'the extent and characteristics of such seas which prevent the full and entire application of one or more general provisions of the Convention with regard to maritime spaces'. Unlike the Iranian proposal, the latter requirement and that of the 'narrow outlet' were not alternative, but cumulative.

Nevertheless, the Chairman of the Second Committee introduced into the ISNT a definition of an 'enclosed or semi-enclosed sea' modelled on the Iranian proposal, but which did not include 'the impossibility of the entire and full application of marine spaces as provided for in UNCLOS', as one of the criteria to determine enclosed or semi-enclosed seas.

2.2.1.1 *ISNT and RSNT*

Article 133 of ISNT provided that:

> *For the purposes of this part,* the term 'enclosed or semi-enclosed sea' means a gulf, basin, or sea surrounded by two or more States and connected to the open seas by a narrow outlet or consisting entirely or primarily of the territorial seas and exclusive economic zones of two or more coastal States.[38]

Like the Iranian proposal, the definition contained in the ISNT used both terms 'enclosed' and 'semi-enclosed seas'. However, there was a notable difference as in the ISNT the two concepts were joined in a single definition (enclosed or semi-enclosed seas). Such difference, though, is of limited practical value, since the same regime applies to both categories of seas.[39]

It is important to emphasize that although the definition contained in Article 133 of ISNT was applicable only to the part of the Convention dealing with enclosed or semi-enclosed seas, there were many States which were not satisfied with the broad nature of this definition and which sought to amend it during the following sessions of the Conference. Notwithstanding the various proposals in this respect, the Chairman of the Second Committee did not amend the definition, which was then incorporated into the RSNT[40] and later on, as explained below, with an important amendment which found its way into Article 122 of UNCLOS.

37　See section 1.1. See Leanza, op. cit., 2008, p. 2.
38　Emphasis added. ISNT/Part II. A/CONF.62/WP.8/Part II (ISNT, 1975), Art. 133 (Chairman, Second Committee), and Virginia Commentary, Vol. III, op. cit., p. 349, para. 122.3.
39　See Leanza, op. cit., 2008, p. 6.
40　See Virginia Commentary, Vol. III, op. cit., pp. 348–353, para. 122, and Vukas, 'Enclosed or Semi-Enclosed Seas', op. cit., pp. 272–274.

Following a Turkish proposal at the ninth session of the Conference, the definition was amended to read as follows:

> *For the purposes of this Convention*, 'enclosed or semi-enclosed sea' means a gulf, basin or sea surrounded by two or more States and connected to another sea or the ocean by a narrow outlet or consisting entirely or primarily of the territorial seas and exclusive economic zones of two or more coastal States.[41]

This was certainly a major amendment as it extended the scope of application of what later became Article 122 to other parts of UNCLOS.

2.2.2 Article 122 of UNCLOS

The definition of 'juridical' enclosed or semi-enclosed seas found in Article 122 of UNCLOS therefore applies 'for the purposes of UNCLOS' and it seems possible to assert that this extremely important change was triggered *inter alia* by the fact that references to the concept of 'enclosed or semi-enclosed' are found also in some other parts of UNCLOS.[42] As mentioned, the final text of Article 122 does not distinguish directly between 'enclosed' and 'semi-enclosed' seas, as both concepts are joined in a single definition. According to Leanza, the most notable defect of the definition contained in Article 122 of UNCLOS is that it confuses 'geographical' with 'juridical' criteria and that ultimately it is too broad.[43]

2.2.2.1 The two State requirements

The first requirement embodied in Article 122 is that a sea, gulf or basin must be *surrounded* by two or more States.[44] This is a legal and not a geographical criteria and it provides that a sea, gulf or basin which fulfils other criteria provided by Article 122 of UNCLOS, but which is not surrounded by at least two States, does not qualify as a 'juridical' enclosed or semi-enclosed sea. Article 122's definition therefore excludes from its scope of application geographical enclosed or semi-enclosed seas which are not surrounded by at least two States. As this requirement is legal or political in nature it obviously means that the legal status of a particular geographical enclosed or semi-enclosed sea may change, depending on political changes on its shores (e.g. secession of States).[45]

---

41 Emphasis added. A/CONF.62/WP.10/Rev.2 (ICNT/Rev.2, 1980), article 122 and Virginia Commentary, op. cit., p. 351, para. 122.8.

42 See the definition of a GDS contained in Article 70(2) of UNCLOS. For further reading see S.C. Vasciannie, *Land-Locked States and Geographically Disadvantaged States in the International Law of the Sea*, Oxford: Clarendon Press, 1990.

43 See Leanza, op. cit., p. 6.

44 See Vukas, 'Enclosed or Semi-Enclosed Seas', op. cit., p. 283. Note also the difference between the terms 'surrounded' in Article 122 and 'bordered' in Article 123 of UNCLOS. The term 'surrounded' seems to imply a substantial enclosure of a certain sea by the territories of at least two different States.

45 See the discussion on the potential implications of the secession of Québec in section 4.3.3.

26 *Extension of Coastal State Jurisdiction in Enclosed or Semi-enclosed Seas*

The fulfilment of the 'two State requirement' is however not enough. In addition, a certain gulf, basin or sea must fulfil at least one of the two alternative elements enumerated in the second element of Article 122: (a) it has to be connected to another sea or ocean by a narrow outlet; or (b) it has to consist entirely or primarily of the territorial seas or EEZs of two or more coastal States.[46] It is important to emphasize that the two requirements are not cumulative, which in turn implies a broad scope of application and consequently a considerable number of geographically enclosed or semi-enclosed seas falling under the definition contained in Article 122 of UNCLOS.[47]

2.2.2.2 Connection to another sea or the ocean by a narrow outlet

This requirement is a geographical one although it may potentially also have a legal dimension.[48] Independently of that, the interpretation of the first alternative requirement can only lead to the conclusion that every gulf, sea or basin bordered by two or more States connected to another sea or the oceans by a narrow outlet, qualifies as a legal enclosed or semi-enclosed sea. This holds true independently of the size of a certain sea and/or also independently of the second alternative requirement to which reference is made below.[49]

The rationale for such conclusion was explained by Vukas who was of the opinion that '[...] every sea connected to another sea or the ocean by a narrow outlet, even when of considerable size, is due to its poor connection to such other sea or ocean particularly vulnerable and deserves special protection'.[50] This is mostly a result of the slow exchange of waters through such narrow outlets which as a general rule renders such seas vulnerable to the risk of pollution from all sources. The mentioned provision is not however completely 'problem free' since the term 'narrow outlet' is not expressly defined by UNCLOS.[51]

Another interesting question relates to cases where a certain sea, gulf or basin is connected to another sea or oceans through more than one *narrow outlet* and/or one or more *artificial outlets*. A notable example is the Mediterranean which is connected to other seas and the oceans not only through the Strait of Gibraltar,

---

46 Cf fn 44.
47 See section 2.2.2.3.
48 Cf fn 51.
49 Cf fn 44.
50 Vukas, 'The Mediterranean: An Enclosed or Semi-Enclosed Sea?', op. cit., p. 283.
51 Some analogies may be traced between the term 'narrow outlet' and the legally more precise term 'channel'. The Arbitral Tribunal in the *Beagle Channel Case* referred to a definition of a 'channel' meaning '[...] A relatively narrow stretch of sea between two land masses connecting two more extensive areas of seas'. Even the latter definition is however vague and it was not used in the context of enclosed or semi-enclosed seas. See Beagle Channel Arbitration (Chile/Argentina), RIAA, Vol. XXI, 1977, para. 85. It is nonetheless suggested that a 'narrow outlet' is a *geographical* and not a *functional* category. See M.C. Stelekatos-Loverdos, 'The Contributions of Channels to the Definition of Straits Used for International Navigation', IJMCL, Vol. 13, No. 1, 1998, p. 71 at pp. 74–80.

but also through the Turkish straits of Bosporus and Dardanelles (with the Sea of Marmara and the Black Sea), and furthermore through the (artificial) Canal of Suez with the Red Sea and the Indian Ocean. As UNCLOS does not provide a clear answer it is necessary to resort to its *travaux préparatoires*.[52]

It should be noted that throughout the proceedings at UNCLOS III several proposals were put forward by States to change the term 'narrow outlet' into 'one or more outlets'. From the Virginia Commentary it derives that the majority of the informal proposals submitted at the sixth session of the Conference suggested a change from a 'narrow outlet' to 'one or more narrow straits or outlets'.[53] Despite substantial support, the Chairman of the Second Committee did not introduce that change into the RSNT, although it is clearly discernable from his statement at the introduction of the RSNT that this was due to the dissatisfaction of certain States with the provision requiring co-ordination of activities in enclosed or semi-enclosed seas, and not with the proposals advocating for the inclusion of the term 'one or more narrow outlets' in the definition of enclosed or semi-enclosed seas.[54]

From the *travaux préparatoires* it may be therefore clearly discerned that the majority of States participating at UNCLOS III supported the proposals according to which also 'gulfs, basins or seas' which are connected to another sea or ocean through more than one narrow or even by artificial outlets, should qualify as legal enclosed or semi-enclosed seas, and it may be implied that such interpretation was accepted also by the great majority of States at the moment of the signature of UNCLOS. It is indisputable that even a sea connected to another sea or ocean through more than one narrow outlet is still facing the same problems (environmental and others) as a sea connected to the oceans only through one narrow outlet. The exchange of water through outlets is generally still extremely slow and therefore such seas are not in a much better position than 'gulfs, basins or seas' which are connected to the open oceans through only one narrow outlet.[55]

Lastly, an interesting question is posed by the meaning of the expression 'another sea or ocean' to which the narrow outlet is connected and particularly by the expression 'another sea'. Does it refer to a sea which is not itself a 'juridical' enclosed or semi-enclosed sea? According to such interpretation, the Black Sea would not qualify as a juridical enclosed or semi-enclosed sea which would be a rather illogical conclusion. The correct interpretation seems to be that the expression 'another sea or ocean' does not distinguish between 'enclosed or semi-enclosed' and other seas and oceans and that it may refer also to another 'juridical' enclosed or semi-enclosed seas.[56]

---

52 See Article 32 of VCLT.
53 Virginia Commentary, Vol. III, op. cit., p. 350, para. 122.4.
54 See section 2.3.4.1.1.
55 Vukas, 'Enclosed or Semi-Enclosed Seas', op. cit., p. 273.
56 See section 1.3.

28 *Extension of Coastal State Jurisdiction in Enclosed or Semi-enclosed Seas*

2.2.2.3 Consisting entirely or primarily of the territorial seas and EEZs of two or more coastal States

The second alternative criteria is represented by the situation where a gulf, basin or sea consists entirely or primarily of the territorial seas and EEZs of two or more coastal States. That provision is again an interesting mixture of geographical and *prima facie* legal requirements. It seems to aim at protecting seas of limited dimensions and, accordingly, it no longer contains the 'narrow outlet' requirement.

The underlying logic of the second alternative was explained again by Vukas who stated that '[…] small seas are susceptible of being vulnerable to pollution and over-exploitation of their natural resources […]'.[57] Even that scholar, however, questioned whether the drafters of UNCLOS had not gone too far by drafting a provision according to which even such large seas as the Norwegian Sea, the Greenland Sea or the Tasman Sea may be considered as 'juridical' enclosed or semi-enclosed seas.[58] It seems however questionable whether, for example, the Tasman Sea may be deemed to be 'surrounded' by Australia and New Zealand as required by the definition of enclosed or semi-enclosed seas in Article 122 of UNCLOS, and similar considerations apply also to the Norwegian and the Greenland Sea.[59] Furthermore, as both Articles 122 and 123 of UNCLOS and the *chapeau* of Part IX of UNCLOS refer to 'enclosed or semi-enclosed seas', it would seem that this fact should also govern the application and interpretation of the whole of Article 122 of UNCLOS, thus limiting its geographical scope of application. This seems, at least to a certain extent, to rebut the argument that '[…] almost any sea could be called semi-enclosed'.[60]

Notwithstanding the above, one should be extremely cautious when using the term 'smaller sea' in relation to the criteria embodied in the second element of Article 122 of UNCLOS. If the maximum breadth of the EEZ (200 nmi from the baselines) is taken into account, it would follow that a sea which is entirely composed of the EEZs of its coastal States could be up to 400 nmi in width; and an obvious question is whether a sea of such dimensions is still a 'small' sea. Furthermore, the definition also covers seas, bays or basins which consist *primarily* of the territorial seas and EEZs. The term 'primarily' in this context is again not precise and can lead to different interpretations. Would it be possible to say that in order for a 'gulf, basin or sea' to qualify as an 'enclosed or semi-enclosed sea' more than half or eventually two-thirds of its surface shall be covered by territorial seas or EEZs of coastal States? Neither UNCLOS nor State practice provide a straightforward answer. However, if we interpret the provision in accordance with the ordinary meaning to be given to the terms of the Treaty,[61] it

---

57 Vukas, 'The Mediterranean: An Enclosed or Semi-Enclosed Sea?', op. cit., p. 283.
58 Ibid.
59 Cf fn 44.
60 Škrk, op. cit., pp. 163–164. In this regard Škrk quoted the statement of the Soviet delegate at UNCLOS III.
61 Article 31(1) of VCLT.

Enclosed or semi-enclosed seas   29

seems that the term 'primarily' implies a 'gulf, basin or sea' which is for the most part, that is mainly, composed of the territorial seas and EEZs of two or more coastal States. While a specific percentage cannot be given, it seems possible to argue that approximately two-thirds of the area of sea would have to be composed of territorial seas and EEZs in order to fulfil the requirement of *primarily* within the meaning of Article 122. It is suggested therefore that seas with prevailing areas of high seas within them would not qualify as a 'juridical' enclosed or semi-enclosed seas, notwithstanding the fact that they are *surrounded* by two or more 'States'.[62]

2.2.2.4 Should there be a proclaimed EEZ?

An interesting question also arises as to whether the wording of Article 122 of UNCLOS refers exclusively to a *proclaimed* EEZ or whether it also includes 'potential EEZs' or *sui generis* zones of jurisdiction.[63] This point again calls for an interpretation in the light of the 'object and purpose' of Part IX of UNCLOS in general and of Article 122 in particular.

The question at stake is therefore whether Article 122 of UNCLOS requires the formal proclamation of EEZs by two or more coastal States or whether it is sufficient that the breadth of a certain sea is such that it potentially allows for the extension of coastal State jurisdiction up to the extent referred to in the second element of Article 122.[64] This consideration is particularly relevant in the context of the Mediterranean and Adriatic Seas where just a few States have proclaimed full EEZs; some others have proclaimed *sui generis* zones based on the concept of the EEZ; while many States have so far refrained altogether from extending their maritime jurisdiction.[65] As mentioned above, the current situation in the Mediterranean may be described as one where the high seas still prevail.[66]

From a *prima facie* reading of Article 122, and after taking into account the ordinary meaning of the terms used, one may be tempted to conclude that the provision in question refers exclusively to proclaimed EEZs. But is this really the case? It should be recollected that the primary reason for the inclusion of the *second alternative requirement* within the definition of a juridical enclosed or semi-enclosed sea was the need for the protection of 'smaller seas' which are, due to their size, particularly vulnerable to all kinds of pollution.[67] Moreover, from the *travaux préparatoires* at UNCLOS III, it is possible to discern that what the majority of States had in mind were the *geographical* and *natural* characteristics of such seas

---

62 Scovazzi nonetheless opines that the Arctic Ocean falls under the definition of 'enclosed or semi-enclosed seas' provided by Article 122 of UNCLOS. See T. Scovazzi, 'Legal Issues Relating to Navigation through Arctic Waters', in A. Gudmundur *et al.* (eds), *The Yearbook of Polar Law*, Vol. 1, The Netherlands: Brill, 2009, p. 371 at p. 379.
63 See sections 1.4 and 3.2.
64 Cf fn 44.
65 See the discussion in Chapter 3.
66 See Leanza, op. cit., 2008, pp. 164–165.
67 See sections 2.1.2–2.1.3.

and not whether or not there is one or more proclaimed EEZ.[68] The relevant criteria, therefore, seems to be predominantly geographical in nature and not directly linked to the legal notion of the territorial sea and/or of the EEZ.[69] In other words, it is the ecological and geographical characteristics of such seas which require the application of enhanced co-operation among bordering States and not whether a certain State has extended up to the maximum extent the breadth of its territorial sea or has proclaimed an EEZ or similar zone of jurisdiction in an enclosed or semi-enclosed sea.

It seems therefore possible to agree with Škrk that the definition found in Article 122 suggests the 'presumed, not the established EEZ', as otherwise one would face the absurd situation where an endangered sea of limited dimensions becomes a 'juridical' enclosed or semi-enclosed sea only after the proclamation of EEZs by its coastal States.[70] Additionally, it follows that during the proceedings at UNCLOS III, not many States seriously envisaged a situation where certain States would refrain from proclaiming an EEZ and this may in turn explain why States participating at UNCLOS III did not feel the need to address the difference between the *actual* and *potential* EEZ in relation to what later became Article 122.[71]

It is possible to conclude that reference to the territorial sea and the EEZ in Article 122 refers to the *potential* or *presumed* EEZ (and territorial sea) and not to the actual (legal) extension of jurisdiction by coastal States. Therefore, for a certain 'gulf, basin or sea' to qualify as a legal enclosed or semi-enclosed sea, there is no need for an actual proclamation of EEZs, nor for the actual extension of the breadth of the territorial sea up to the maximum extent permitted by international law, as an 'inchoate' right to do this seems to be enough.

2.3 Rights and duties of states bordering an enclosed or semi-enclosed sea

Before embarking on a legal analysis of Article 123 of UNCLOS, it seems necessary to consider another question which was highly debated at UNCLOS III and which can assist in understanding the relation between the general rules of UNCLOS and the specific rules regulating the status of enclosed or semi-enclosed seas. Leanza identified two conflicting sets of proposals at UNCLOS III:

(i) The general rules of the Convention should be exercised in enclosed or semi-enclosed seas in a manner consistent with the general characteristics of such seas and the needs and interests of its coastal States;

---

68 Ibid.
69 It is suggested that the maximum breadth of the territorial sea (12 nmi) and of the EEZ (200 nmi) represent primarily a geographical aid in the determination of an 'enclosed or semi-enclosed sea' on the basis of Article 122 of UNCLOS.
70 Škrk, op. cit., p. 164.
71 Vukas, 'The Mediterranean: An Enclosed or Semi-Enclosed Sea?', op. cit., p. 284.

(ii) Specific rules on enclosed or semi-enclosed seas should be exercised in a manner consistent with the general rules of the Convention and shall not prejudice the rights and obligations of third States.[72]

The two main advocates of the first hypothesis were Iran and Turkey.[73] The Iranian proposal submitted at the Second Session of UNCLOS III was particularly important as it addressed the specific relation between the 'general rules' of the Convention and 'specific rules' on enclosed or semi-enclosed seas.[74] Furthermore, the Iranian proposal was the first to provide the formula of co-ordination of activities in enclosed or semi-enclosed seas[75] and also the first to refer to 'scientific research' as an area which should be regulated within the context of enclosed or semi-enclosed seas.[76] On the other hand, the various proposals by Turkey were more focused on the application of the general rules of the Convention regarding the extension of the breadth of the territorial sea and the application of the concept of the EEZ in enclosed or semi-enclosed seas.[77]

2.3.1 The Iranian proposal

Article 2 of the Iranian proposal provided that:

> The general rules set out in this Convention [UNCLOS] shall apply to an enclosed or semi-enclosed sea *in a manner consistent with the special characteristics of such seas and the needs and interest of their coastal States.*[78]

This proposal directly addressed the way in which the general rules of UNCLOS should be applied and exercised in enclosed or semi-enclosed seas. It is noteworthy that the proposal did not distinguish between 'States bordering such seas' and 'other users of such seas'. The proposal's main characteristic was ultimately that it provided for enhanced coastal State rights and greater duties by the relevant States in comparison with other seas or oceans. This can be clearly seen from Article 3 of the proposal which in the first part provides that '[t]he preservation and protection of the marine environment of an enclosed or semi-enclosed sea

---

72 Author's translation. See Leanza, op. cit., 2008, p. 4.
73 See section 2.4.1.1.
74 A/CONF.62/C.2/L.72; Iran: draft articles on enclosed or semi-enclosed seas, 21 August 1974.
75 Ibid, Art. 3. The proposal by Iraq contained reference to the two main areas in which cooperation between States bordering enclosed or semi-enclosed seas was deemed to be particularly necessary. The latter emphasized: (a) management, conservation and exploration of marine living resources beyond the territorial sea (Art. 2); and (b) preservation of the marine environment and the control of pollution (Art. 3). See A/CONF.62/C.2/L.71 and Add.1 and Add.2; Iraq: draft articles on enclosed or semi-enclosed seas, 21 August 1974.
76 Article 4 of the Iranian proposal provided: 'Scientific research in an enclosed or semi-enclosed sea shall be conducted only with the consent of the coastal State concerned'. Cf fn 74.
77 See section 2.4.1.1.
78 Emphasis added. Cf fn 74.

32 Extension of Coastal State Jurisdiction in Enclosed or Semi-enclosed Seas

and the management of its resources shall be the responsibility of the coastal States […]', while in the second part it provided that:

> To this end the coastal States may, *in addition to global norms*:
>
> (a) Adopt regional rules and standards aimed at the better protection of their environment against marine pollution;
> (b) Co-ordinate their activities in relation to the management and exploitation of the renewable resources of the enclosed or semi-enclosed seas under regional arrangements.[79]

Despite the term 'may', the second part of Article 3 of the proposal should be read in conjunction with the opening sentence of that Article, which provides that '[t]he preservation and protection of the marine environment of an enclosed or semi-enclosed sea and the management of its resources *shall* be the responsibility of the coastal States […]'.[80]

The importance attributed to co-operation in the two areas may also be seen in many other proposals by States participating at UNCLOS III. Besides the Iranian proposal, reference should be made to the Iraqi[81] and Turkish proposals[82] together with the paper submitted by the informal consultative group on enclosed or semi-enclosed seas.[83] It is noteworthy that the common denominator of all these proposals was their reference to the application of the general rules of the Convention in enclosed or semi-enclosed seas in a manner which would take into account *the specific characteristics of such seas*. In this respect it may be mentioned that, more than two decades later, the Memorial of Ireland in the Mox Plant Case[84] advocated that:

> The drafting history of Article 123 makes it clear that the States participating in UNCLOS III considered the duty to have regard for the 'special characteristics' of those areas to be a key element of the concept of enclosed and semi-enclosed seas […].[85]

---

79 Emphasis added.
80 Cf fn 74, Art. 3.
81 Cf fn 75.
82 A/CONF.62/C.2/L.56, Turkey: draft article on enclosed or semi-enclosed seas, 13 August 1974.
83 Cf fn 36.
84 On 25 October 2001, Ireland instituted arbitral proceedings against the UK pursuant to Art. 287, and Art. 1 of Annex VII of UNCLOS in the *Dispute Concerning the Mox Plant, International Movements of Radioactive Materials, and the Protection of the Marine Environment of the Irish Sea (Ireland v United Kingdom*, the Mox Plant Case). The case concerned discharges into the Irish Sea from a mixed oxide fuel (MOX) plant located at Sellafield nuclear facility in the UK, and related movements of radioactive materials through the Irish Sea. The case was eventually terminated without a judgment on the merits. See S. Boelaert Suominen, 'The European Community, the European Court of Justice and the Law of the Sea', IJMCL, Vol. 23, No. 4, 2008, p. 643 at pp. 673 679.
85 Mox Plant Case, Memorial of Ireland, 26 July 2002, p. 141, para. 8.12. It is noteworthy, however, that the UK in its Counter Memorial argued that that the text of the Iranian proposal was not reflected in the ISNT nor in the wording of the final text of Art. 123 of UNCLOS and that this was proof that States at UNCLOS III did not consider the duty to take account of the special

The Mox Plant Case (Arbitral Tribunal) has been one of the rare cases where the importance of Part IX of UNCLOS has been raised in the context of the interpretation and application of UNCLOS in enclosed or semi-enclosed seas. In the absence of direct relevant scholarly literature, reference will be made to the positions of both States (Ireland and the UK) as an aid to shed some light on the (potential) relevance of Part IX of UNCLOS in the contemporary law of the sea, including extension of coastal State jurisdiction and/or delimitation of maritime zones. In this context it is unfortunate that the Mox Plant Case did not end with a binding award by the arbitral tribunal.

2.3.2 ISNT

Neither the Iranian nor the Turkish proposals were included *verbatim* in the first drafts of the Convention. Nonetheless, the Iranian proposal substantially influenced the content of Article 134 of the ISNT both regarding the general 'duty of co-operation' for States bordering enclosed or semi-enclosed seas and regarding the way in which the general rules of UNCLOS should be exercised in enclosed and semi-enclosed seas.

It is submitted that the ISNT consolidated the ideas contained in the Iranian proposal, the Turkish proposal, and in the proposal by the Informal Consultative Group on enclosed or semi-enclosed seas[86] into a compromise text, which at that moment seemed an acceptable compromise to the majority of States participating at UNCLOS III. Many provisions of UNCLOS reflect the fact that, in many instances, the different opinions expressed at UNCLOS III were covered by drafting techniques and broad text which eluded clear meaning.[87] In fact, it may be argued that Article 134 of ISNT, and ultimately the adopted text of Article 123 of UNCLOS, are prime examples of such provisions. This in turn makes the task of its correct interpretation (by trying to establish to the maximum possible certainty what the common intention of the parties was) even more important.

It is also important to emphasize that the obligation to co-operate contained in Article 134 of the ISNT was limited to States bordering enclosed or semi-enclosed seas. That Article provided that:

> States bordering enclosed or semi-enclosed seas *shall co-operate* with each other in the exercise of their rights and duties under the present Convention. To

---

characteristics of semi-enclosed seas to be a key element of the concept of enclosed or semi-enclosed seas. See Mox Plant Case (Ireland v United Kingdom of Great Britain and Northern Ireland), Counter-Memorial of the United Kingdom, 9 January 2003, p. 141, para. 6.17.

86 The Paper was modeled on the Turkish and Iranian Proposals with an important addition providing that '[...] the riparian States may, as necessary, take account of the activities of the competent international organizations with a view to the adoption of regional rules and standards aimed at the better protection of their environment against marine pollution'. C.2/Blue Paper No. 13 (1975, mimeo.), Provisions 223 and 225 (WP.1). Quoted in the Virginia Commentary, op. cit., p. 359, para. 123.4.

87 See J. Harrison, 'Judicial Law-Making and the Developing Order for the Oceans', IJMCL, Vol. 22, No. 2, 2007, p. 283 at 287.

34 *Extension of Coastal State Jurisdiction in Enclosed or Semi-enclosed Seas*

this end *they shall*, directly or through an appropriate regional organization [...][88]

Although it is clear that the text of the Iranian proposal was not reflected in the ISNT, it is questionable whether this is really proof that States at UNCLOS III did not consider the duty to have regard for 'the special characteristics of such seas' to be a key element of the concept of enclosed or semi-enclosed seas, as for example advocated by the UK in the Mox Plant Case.[89] In fact, it follows that despite the fact that the text of Article 134 of the ISNT did not include *ad verbatim* the provision from the Iranian proposal, Article 134 of the ISNT embodied a 'method' on how States bordering enclosed or semi-enclosed seas shall exercise their rights and duties under the Convention.[90] In so doing, this Article, at least impliedly, regulated the relation between the general rules of UNCLOS and specific rules on enclosed or semi-enclosed seas.

By imposing on States bordering an enclosed or semi-enclosed seas a duty of co-operation in the exercise of their rights and duties under UNCLOS, it seems that the ISNT, at least impliedly, also imposed upon States bordering enclosed or semi-enclosed seas an obligation to take into account 'the specific characteristics of enclosed or semi-enclosed seas' in the exercise of their rights and duties under the Convention. Such a conclusion is supported by the underlying reason for the inclusion of specific rules on enclosed or semi-enclosed seas within UNCLOS, which may be subsumed as the protection of certain types of seas with specific characteristics, in which the 'unilateral exercise of rights and duties' by one coastal State may adversely affect the rights and interest of other coastal States.

2.3.3 RSNT

Notwithstanding many proposals to amend the text of Article 134 of the ISNT, the Chairman of the Second Committee decided to retain the original structure of the ISNT. There was, however, a change of utmost importance triggered by the proposals of Mexico and Tunisia at the Fourth Session of the Conference.[91] The amendment made the duties of co-operation and co-ordination in Article 134 of the ISNT less mandatory. As may be noted, the word 'shall' as used in the ISNT was replaced by the word 'should' in the RSNT.[92] Similarly, the requirements on States bordering enclosed or semi-enclosed seas to co-ordinate their activities with regard to living resources, preservat of the marine environment and scientific research policies were softened, by substituting 'shall' with 'shall endeavor'.

---

88 Emphasis added. A/CONF.62/WP.8/Part II (ISNT, 1975), Arts 134 and 135 (Chairman, Second Committee).
89 Cf fn 85.
90 See section 2.3.1.
91 See Vukas, 'The Mediterranean: An Enclosed or Semi-Enclosed Sea?', op. cit., p. 286. Vukas relied on his personal notes taken at the informal meeting of the Second Committee on 27 April 1976.
92 Škrk, op. cit., p. 172.

Enclosed or semi-enclosed seas 35

These changes have substantially lightened the burden of the general obligation of coastal States to co-operate in the exercise of their rights and duties under UNCLOS, and also on the duty of 'co-ordination of activities' in the three specific areas listed by Article 123 of UNCLOS. Such impact has been further accentuated by the clear statement made by the Chairman of the Second Committee at the introduction of the RSNT:

> On the issue of enclosed or semi-enclosed seas, I have responded to expressions of dissatisfaction with the provisions in the single negotiating text [ISNT] by making less mandatory the co-ordination of activities in such seas [...].[93]

As may be seen from the following sections, it is obvious that such a strong statement has had important repercussions on the 'construction' and 'interpretation' of Part IX of UNCLOS, as it leaves no doubt about the intention of the drafters.

2.3.4 Article 123 of UNCLOS

Article 123 of UNCLOS[94] is the only Article in the Convention to make direct reference to the rights and duties of States bordering enclosed or semi-enclosed seas. At least impliedly, it seems also to recognize the interdependence of States bordering enclosed or semi-enclosed seas and the fact that the unilateral action of one coastal State in such seas in most cases affects the interests of other coastal States and other users of the sea.[95] This seems to be the case particularly with regard to the three areas of co-operation expressly mentioned in the second element of Article 123 of UNCLOS. Therein, reference is made to co-operation with regard to the management, conservation, exploration and exploitation of the living resources of the sea, protection and preservation of the marine environment, and marine scientific research.

The first general observation is that the general law of the sea is, without exception, applicable also in 'juridical' enclosed or semi-enclosed seas.[96] This in turn means that States bordering enclosed or semi-enclosed seas do not have

---

93 A/CONF.62/WP.8/Rev.1/Part II (RSNT, 1976), Art. 130 (Chairman, Second Committee), Introductory Note, para. 21. Quoted also in the Virginia Commentary, Vol. III, op. cit., p. 362, para. 123.5.
94 For the full text of the Article, see Introduction, section II.
95 According to the Virginia Commentary, Art. 123 '[...] recognizes that the special geographical situation of enclosed and semi-enclosed seas requires cooperation among the States bordering them to coordinate their activities, in particular with regard to the matters listed in subparagraphs (a)–(d). In this respect, article 123 recognizes that activities undertaken by one State in an enclosed or semi-enclosed sea may have a direct impact on the rights, duties and interests of other States bordering that sea'. Virginia Commentary, Vol. III, op. cit., p. 365, para. 132. 12(a). See also M. Grbec, 'Problematika morskih pasov v (severnem) Jadranu', Podjetje in delo, No. 6/7, Year 23, Ljubljana, 2007, p. 1439 at p. 1442.
96 Virginia Commentary, Vol. III, op. cit., p. 365, para. 123.12(a).

36　*Extension of Coastal State Jurisdiction in Enclosed or Semi-enclosed Seas*

any additional rights in addition to those contemplated by UNCLOS[97] and, *argumentum ad contrario*, that other users of such seas do not have any additional duties beyond those expressly contemplated by UNCLOS. The latter therefore avails itself in enclosed or semi-enclosed seas, with the same rights and duties as in any other sea or ocean, depending of course on the specific maritime zone.[98] Furthermore, reference to the exercise of rights and performance of duties under UNCLOS by States bordering enclosed or semi-enclosed seas shall be understood as a reference to the general rules of, and deriving from, UNCLOS.

Article 123 therefore opted for a solution according to which the specific rules on enclosed or semi-enclosed seas should be exercised in a manner consistent with the general rules of UNCLOS and shall not prejudice the rights and obligations of third States. Such a general statement needs however some further clarification.

2.3.4.1 An obligation or just an exhortation to co-operate?

A crucial question which needs to be answered, and on which no consensus exists among scholars and practitioners alike, is whether the provisions of Article 123 of UNCLOS are mandatory in nature, or whether they represent just an 'exhortation' to co-operate. According to the Virginia commentary:

> […] The Article is couched in the language of exhortation, *declaring* that States bordering enclosed or semi-enclosed seas 'should co-operate' with each other and, in doing so, they 'shall endeavor' to co-ordinate the activities enumerated in the article […].[99]

On the other hand, Leanza, Scovazzi and Vukas seem to be of the opinion that the provisions of Article 123 are something more than a 'mere recommendation'.[100] Both groups of commentators share the opinion that there are differences between the legal value of the introductory statement of Article 123 and its second element.[101]

A common argument of the first group of commentators may be well represented by the opinion of Škrk, who in 1988 wrote that the 'RSNT changed the mandatory obligation to cooperate, imposed on the coastal States surrounding enclosed or semi-enclosed seas into a declaratory provision', which provision was later transposed into Article 123.[102] A similar view was echoed more than a decade later in the Counter-Memorial of the United Kingdom in the Mox Plant Case. The UK argued that the weak language introduced in the RSNT (i.e. 'should' and 'shall endeavor'), coupled with the statement by the Chairman of the Second

---

97　Ibid.

98　For a general discussion of the regimes of the maritime zones regulated by UNCLOS, see Churchill and Lowe, op. cit., Chapters 3, 4, 6–9. 11.

99　Emphasis added. Virginia Commentary, Vol. III, op. cit., p. 366, para. 123. 12(c).

100　See the discussion in sections 2.3.4.1–2.3.4.4.

101　See section 2.3.4.4.

102　Škrk, op. cit., p. 172.

Committee at the introduction of the RSNT and the fact that subsequent proposals by States to return to the language of obligations were not accepted, constitute proof that the provisions of Article 123 are hortatory only.[103]

2.3.4.1.1 RELEVANCE OF THE CHAIRMAN'S STATEMENT

It seems perfectly possible to agree that an important aid in the interpretation of the 'legal nature' of the provision of Article 123 of UNCLOS is represented by its *travaux préparatoires*, and particularly by the oft-quoted statement by the Chairman. There are also no doubts that the main importance of the statement lies in the fact that the Chairman made plainly clear that the changes in the wording of Article 134 of the ISNT were due to the dissatisfaction of States with the provision regulating the mandatory co-ordination of activities in enclosed or semi-enclosed seas, and that the aim of such changes was to make less mandatory the co-ordination of activities in such seas.

Two observations should be made in this regard. The first refers to the relation between the introductory statement and the second element of Article 123 of UNCLOS. In his statement, the Chairman of the Second Committee referred to the entire text of Article 134 of the ISNT and not just to the three areas of co-operation mentioned in the second element of what is nowadays Article 123 of UNCLOS. This can be clearly seen from the change of wording in the introductory statement where the word 'shall' was substituted with the legally less mandatory 'should'.[104] Second, the Chairman made reference to making 'less mandatory' the co-ordination of activities and not to make such provisions 'hortatory' or 'declaratory' in nature. The statement of the Chairman of the Second Committee could, therefore, be best interpreted in the sense that if according to the ISNT there was a 'strict' legal obligation for States bordering enclosed or semi-enclosed seas, first, to co-operate with each other in the exercise of their rights and duties under the Convention and, second, to co-ordinate their activities in the areas of management of living resources, protection and preservation of the marine environment and scientific research, the text of the RSNT lowered such obligation both with regard to the introductory statement and the second element of Article 123 of UNCLOS, although not necessarily to the same extent.[105]

The obvious question is what, in the context of Article 123 of UNCLOS, is a 'less mandatory obligation'? The answer seems to be suggested by the amended drafting language of the second element of Article 123. The latter provides that in order to achieve the goal stated in the introductory statement, therefore 'cooperation of States bordering enclosed or semi-enclosed seas in the exercise of their

---

103 Counter-Memorial of the United Kingdom (Mox Plant Case), op. cit., pp. 139–140, paras 6.11–6.13.

104 'States shall cooperate' was changed into 'State should cooperate'. The mentioned *dictum* was later incorporated into Article 123 of UNCLOS.

105 In the first part of the text the RSNT substituted 'shall' with 'should', while in the second part 'shall' was substituted with 'shall endeavor'.

38 *Extension of Coastal State Jurisdiction in Enclosed or Semi-enclosed Seas*

duties and in the performance of their rights under UNCLOS', States bordering enclosed or semi-enclosed seas *shall endeavour*, directly or through an appropriate regional organization, *to co-ordinate* their policies and/or activities in the three expressly mentioned areas in subparagraphs (a)–(c) and to invite, as appropriate, other interested States or international organizations to co-operate with them as provided by sub-paragraph (d).

It may be implied from the term 'shall endeavour' that it cannot, even with the most extensive interpretation, be defined as an obligation of result. Vukas has defined the latter as a *sui generis* obligation,[106] while Scovazzi has termed it a *bona fide* obligation.[107] It is, however, suggested that the obligation ultimately means an 'obligation of conduct', therefore an obligation for States bordering enclosed or semi-enclosed seas to endeavour to co-operate in *bona fide* in the exercise of their rights and in performance of their duties under the Convention. It is accordingly argued that although States are not bound to reach an agreement, they shall endeavour in good faith to achieve such goal. What Article 123 requires therefore is an effort by States, a certain conduct, not a guarantee of result.

It therefore follows that it is not enough for a coastal State to notify other States bordering enclosed or semi-enclosed seas about their intended activities. Instead, there should be a genuine good faith attempt to co-operate and co-ordinate its activities with other States, particularly potentially affected ones. Similarly, a refusal to undertake negotiations in good faith, or a rejection of all good faith proposals of other bordering States, would be contrary to Article 123 of UNCLOS.[108]

2.3.4.2 Areas of co-operation

A question also arises as to whether the list of areas of co-operation contained in the second element of Article 123 is exhaustive and, accordingly, whether the good faith duty of co-operation and co-ordination is limited to the areas mentioned. The answer to this question seems to be strictly tied to the legal nature of the introductory statement of Article 123 providing that:

> States bordering an enclosed or semi-enclosed sea should cooperate with each other in the exercise of their rights and in the performance of their duties under this Convention [UNCLOS].

---

106 Vukas, 'The Mediterranean: An Enclosed or Semi-Enclosed Sea?', op. cit., p. 286.
107 Ibid. T. Scovazzi, 'Implications of the new Law of the Sea for the Mediterranean', Marine Policy, Vol. 5, Issue 4, 1981, pp. 302–312.
108 See Vukas, 'The Mediterranean: An Enclosed or Semi-Enclosed Sea?', op. cit., p. 286. A similar position is advocated also by the Memorial of Ireland (The Mox Plant Case), although on a different basis. The Memorial provides that '[a]n outright, blanket refusal to co-operate or co-ordinate actions and plans would not be compatible with the implementation of the UNCLOS in good faith'. It is furthermore asserted that that would be the position even if the provisions of Art. 123 UNCLOS '[…] were regarded as no more than a declaration of policy'. See Memorial of Ireland, op. cit., pp. 144–145, paras. 8.30–8.31. See also Art. 300 of UNCLOS and the overall discussion in section 2.3.4.3.

The first observation is that the introductory statement of Article 123 is general in its scope of application, as it addresses the exercise of *all* rights and the performance of *all* duties on the basis of UNCLOS by States bordering enclosed and semi-enclosed seas. On the other hand, the second element is more specific and at least, *prima facie*, more stringent in its wording. This is a result of the fact that the latter specifically mentions the three areas in which States bordering enclosed or semi-enclosed seas 'shall endeavor to cooperate', and also due to the fact that it provides an indication of the way in which such co-operation should be undertaken (co-ordination of activities in the three areas).[109]

The differences between the introductory statement and the second element of Article 123 of UNCLOS were addressed also by Škrk, who stated that:

> [...] According to the present text the coastal States 'should' cooperate with each other but are, nevertheless, *legally obliged* 'to endeavor' to coordinate the foreseen activities, such as managing the living resources, protection of the environment, scientific research, and to invite third States and international organizations in furtherance of these activities.[110]

From this statement it may be seen that the author attributed different legal value to the second element of Article 123 from that of its introductory statement. Similarly, it may be noted that Vukas asserted that '[...] there is indeed a legal and not only a moral obligation to co-ordinate activities in the three mentioned fields', although he left some doubts about the legal nature of the introductory statement of Article 123. In this regard he pointed at the difference between the English text of Article 123 (States should co-operate) and the French version of the same text which *prima facie* seems to be less stringent.[111] He however admitted that it is doubtful whether the introductory statement provides only for a 'recommendation to cooperate'.[112]

2.3.4.3 The introductory statement of Article 123 and its influence on the application of the general rules of UNCLOS

One of the crucial questions for the purposes of this work relates to the legal value of the introductory statement of Article 123. *Prima facie* it would seem that that statement is too broad in its scope to represent a self-standing legal obligation. But is this really the case? It seems convenient to start this discussion by making reference to the Memorial of Ireland in the Mox Plant Case according to which '[a]rticle 123 contains a broader obligation in relation to cooperation and

---

109 Conservation and management of living resources, protection and preservation of the marine environment and marine scientific research. See also Vukas, 'Enclosed or Semi-Enclosed Seas', op. cit., p. 286.
110 Emphasis added. Škrk, op. cit., p. 172.
111 *'Les Etats [...] devraient coopèrer [...]'*. See Vukas, 'The Mediterranean: An Enclosed or Semi-Enclosed Sea?', op. cit., p. 286.
112 Ibid.

40 *Extension of Coastal State Jurisdiction in Enclosed or Semi-enclosed Seas*

coordination, *couched in the language of moral, rather than legal obligation* [...]'.[113] This passage is particularly interesting in the light of the fact that the drafters of the Irish Memorial made plainly clear that the latter does not mean that the introductory statement of Article 123 of UNCLOS is without legal effect.[114] The question is now how can a 'declaratory provision' or a 'moral obligation' have legal implications on the exercise of rights and performance of duties under UNCLOS.

An indication of this, which at the same time seems to provide also a preliminary answer on the relation between the general rules of UNCLOS and specific rules on enclosed or semi-enclosed seas in the contemporary law of the sea, may be found in the Memorial of Ireland (The Mox Plant Case), as further clarified during the oral pleadings by the Irish co-agent (V. Lowe). According to the latter the main importance of the introductory statement of Article 123 of UNCLOS is that it expressly provides for a *general policy of co-operation* for States bordering enclosed and semi-enclosed seas regarding the exercise of their rights and performance of their duties under UNCLOS, and that by doing this, it in turn influences the way in which States bordering enclosed or semi-enclosed seas should exercise their rights and perform their duties in enclosed or semi-enclosed seas. In other words, although the first element of Article 123 of UNCLOS does not represent a self-standing legal obligation, it influences, through its wording and structure, the way in which States bordering enclosed or semi-enclosed seas should perform their rights and exercise their duties on the basis of UNCLOS. As further explained by the Irish co-agent during the oral pleadings:

> [...] because it is influencing [Article 123] the interpretation of what are, plainly, themselves legally binding provisions in other UNCLOS Articles, it has the effect of modifying the application, the expectations in relation to the enforcement of those other Articles. [...] Article 123 makes plain that the substantive obligations and the way that they [*State bordering enclosed or semi-enclosed sea*] fulfil their legal obligation under other UNCLOS Articles has to be looked in the context of this broad duty of co-operation and consultation. This, in return, requires that regard be had to the nature of the activity giving rise to the obligation to co-operate, to the characteristic of the sea in question and to the impact of that activity on that sea.[115]

That explanation seems to represent a sound interpretation as it derives both from the structure and drafting language of Article 123 of UNCLOS and

---

113 Memorial of Ireland, op. cit., p. 143, para. 8.22.

114 Paragraph 8.23 of the Memorial of Ireland provides that '[...] the fact that this obligation is not couched in the language of immediately binding legal duties does not mean that it is without binding legal effect'. Ibid.

115 The Mox Plant Case; Proceedings, Day Five, Revised, 17 June 2003, pp. 24–25. Leanza similarly pointed out that '[...] anche l'applicazione di molti altri istituti disciplinati dalla Convenzione viene condizionata dal concetto di mare chiuso o semi-chiuso [...]'. See Leanza, op. cit., p. 7.

its *travaux préparatoires*[116] and as such it may be relied upon for the purposes of our discussion. It is indeed true that the requirement to take into account the characteristics of the sea in question and the impact of that activity in that sea are reflected only in the various proposals by States at UNCLOS III and (at least not directly) in any of the negotiating texts (ISNT, RSNT, etc.) and/or statements by the Chairman. This explanation seems however to be derived not only from the *travaux préparatoires* at UNCLOS III, but even more from the underlying logic for the inclusion of specific rules on enclosed or semi-enclosed seas into UNCLOS which according to the Virginia Commentary:

> [...] reflects recognition, that the special geographical situation of such seas requires co-operation between the States bordering them in managing activities in the marine environment.[117]

Such interpretation seems to be furthermore reinforced by the provision of Article 300 of UNCLOS (Good faith and abuse of rights) according to which:

> States Parties shall fulfill in good faith the obligations assumed under this Convention *and shall exercise the rights, jurisdiction and freedoms recognized in this Convention in a manner which would not constitute an abuse of right.*[118]

It seems possible to agree with Pavliha that Article 300 represents a 'key ethical rule' and even more importantly a 'binding promise' by States parties to UNCLOS implying that '[...] states should exercise their rights and jurisdictions recognized by UNCLOS in such a manner as not to unnecessarily or arbitrarily harm the rights of other countries or the interest of the international community as a whole [...]'.[119] This author reinforces further such argument by making reference to Article 26 of VCLT which provides that '[e]very treaty in force is binding upon the parties to it and *must be performed by them in good faith.*'[120]

It therefore follows that even accepting the opinion of some renown commentators[121] that Article 123 is just 'hortatory' and/or a non-binding 'declaration of policy', it would still be possible to claim also that in such a case there would be still an obligation on States bordering enclosed and semi-enclosed seas to take into account and/or fulfil such 'hortatory provision' on the basis of Article 300 of UNCLOS. As properly stated by the Irish co-agent in the Mox Plant Case, under

---

116 See section 2.1.3.
117 Virginia Commentary, Vol. III, op. cit., p. 343, para. IX.1.
118 Emphasis added.
119 M. Pavliha, 'Essay on Ethics in International Maritime Law', European Transport Law, Vol. XLVII, No. 5, 2012, p. 461 at p. 467. Pavliha, on the other hand, interprets the concept of 'abuse of rights' in the context of UNCLOS as '[...] the exercise by a state of a particular right in such a manner or in such circumstances as indicated that it was for that state an indirect means of avoiding an international obligation imposed upon that state, or was carried out with a wrong, illegitimate purpose *(in fraudem legis agere).* [...].'. Ibid.
120 Ibid. Emphasis added.
121 See section 2.3.4.1.

42   *Extension of Coastal State Jurisdiction in Enclosed or Semi-enclosed Seas*

no hypothesis could the situation be the same as it would have been if UNCLOS had provided that States bordering an enclosed or semi-enclosed sea were under no obligation[122] or if the Convention had stayed silent. Also in the light of the above, the assertion put forward by the UK in its Counter-Memorial stating that '[…] what is to be fulfilled in good faith under Article 300 are obligations assumed under this Convention […]', and that since Article 123 does not impose a legal obligation '[…] Article 300 adds nothing of present relevance […]', do not seem to be persuasive.[123]

It is therefore possible to assert that States bordering enclosed and semi-enclosed seas are under an obligation to exercise their rights and perform their duties under UNCLOS in the light of the general duty (policy) of co-operation embodied *inter alia* in the first element of Article 123. The latter may be qualified as synonymous with a good faith duty to endeavour to co-operate in the exercise of the rights and duties under UNCLOS.

2.3.4.4 Interrelation between the introductory and the second element of Article 123

Here follows a general overview of the differences in the legal value between the introductory (first) element and the second part of Article 123 of UNCLOS. Attention should be given to the fact that the introductory statement is comprehensive in its scope of application, as it addressees the exercise of *all* rights and the performance of *all* duties under UNCLOS by States bordering enclosed or semi-enclosed seas, and not only the three areas of co-operation expressly listed in the second element. It is therefore possible to agree with the position pleaded by Ireland in the Mox Plant Case, according to which the introductory element of Article 123:

> […] does not tie down the rights and duties to any particular right or duty under the Convention. Indeed, it applies to the whole range of provisions: […] not simply to Part XII of the Convention. […][124]

This assertion seems to be confirmed also by the *travaux préparatoires* of Article 123 at UNCLOS III and the Chairman's statement.[125] The introductory statement therefore affects the interpretation and application of the whole UNCLOS and this obviously includes *inter alia* the 'exercise of rights and performance of duties

---

122 Memorial of Ireland (Mox Plant Case), op. cit., pp. 145–146, paras. 8.34–8.38 and Proceedings Day 5 (Revised), op. cit., p. 24.
123 See Counter-Memorial of the UK (Mox Plant Case), op. cit., p. 143, para. 6.24.
124 Mox Plant Case, Proceedings, Day 5, op. cit., p. 26. As, however, stated by ITLOS in the 'provisional measure phase' of the Mox Plant Case: '[…] the duty to cooperate is a fundamental principle in the prevention of pollution of the marine environment under Part XII of the Convention [UNCLOS] and general international law […]'. See ITLOS, The Mox Plant Case (Ireland v United Kingdom), Request for provisional measures, Order, 3 December 2001, 41 ILM 405, 2002, para. 82.
125 See section 2.3.4.1.1.

by States bordering enclosed or semi-enclosed seas' related to the extension of coastal State jurisdiction and delimitation of various maritime zones.[126] Its functioning is triggered by the simple fact that a certain State is a riparian State of a 'juridical' enclosed and/or semi-enclosed sea.

It may accordingly be argued that the introductory statement of Article 123 of UNCLOS, although not in itself an enforceable obligation, affects the way in which other provisions of UNCLOS should be interpreted and applied by States bordering enclosed and/or semi-enclosed seas.[127]

The second part of Article 123 of UNCLOS on the other hand provides for a more stringent legal duty of co-operation as it additionally requires States bordering enclosed or semi-enclosed seas to endeavour to co-ordinate their activities and policies with regard to living resources, protection and preservation of the marine environment, and scientific research. Like the introductory element, the scope of application of the second element is broad, mostly due to the fact that it makes reference to the three areas of co-operation in general terms, which seems to imply that States bordering enclosed or semi-enclosed seas shall endeavour to co-ordinate all their rights and duties, directly or indirectly related particularly to the 'management, conservation, exploration and exploitation of the living resources of the sea'[128] and with respect to 'the protection and preservation of the marine environment'.[129]

This in turn implies a stringent duty of co-operation and *co-ordination of activities* in all those areas which are related, and may have a direct impact particularly on the conservation and exploitation of living marine resources and on the protection and preservation of the marine environment. Clear examples include the environmental aspect of navigation (safety at sea)[130] and following the same logic also the extension of coastal State jurisdiction by States bordering enclosed or semi-enclosed seas and co-operation regarding the delimitation and/or conclusion of provisional arrangement of a practical nature pending delimitation of such zones.[131] It is suggested that unco-ordinated activities in the two areas influences the 'management, conservation, exploration and exploitation of the living resources', the 'protection and preservation of the marine environment', and ultimately the overall governance of a particular enclosed or semi-enclosed sea.[132]

---

126 See section 2.4.
127 It is noteworthy that the co-agent of Ireland (Lowe) advocated the position that the duty of co-operation and co-ordination embodied in Art. 123 of UNCLOS is forming part of customary international law. See Mox Plant Case, Proceedings Day Five (Revised), op. cit., p. 23.
128 Article 123(a).
129 Article 123(b).
130 Possible examples may include cooperation regarding the establishment of routing measures and/or reporting systems in a particular enclosed or semi-enclosed sea. For the specific case of the Adriatic Sea, see the discussion in section 5.4.1.1.
131 See section 2.4.2.5.
132 For a particular case of the Mediterranean Sea, see T. Treves, 'Potential Exclusive Economic Zones in the Mediterranean', paper delivered at the 11th Mediterranean Research Meeting Florence and Montecatini Terme, 24–27 March 2010, p. 4. See also the discussion in Chapters 3 and 6.

44 *Extension of Coastal State Jurisdiction in Enclosed or Semi-enclosed Seas*

2.3.4.5 Institutional or non-institutional co-operation?

A related question is also whether co-operation and/or co-ordination of activities among States bordering enclosed or semi-enclosed seas should be undertaken directly (bilaterally or multilaterally) or through an established regional organization (institutional co-operation).

Generally speaking, States bordering enclosed or semi-enclosed seas are not always bound to co-operate and co-ordinate their activities bilaterally and/or directly. Article 123 of UNCLOS expressly provides, although directly referring only to the list of activities enumerated in its second element that States may co-operate also through an appropriate regional organization. In this respect, is particularly interesting the separate opinion of Judge Andersen (ITLOS) in the provisional measure phase of the Mox Plant Case. According to Andersen:

> [...] Article 123 does not require cooperation to be at the bilateral level so long as there is cooperation through an appropriate regional body [...] In other words, there does not have to be a bilateral 'Irish Sea Conference' along the lines of the North Sea Conferences in order to secure compliance with Article 123. [...][133]

Judge Andersen obviously took into account different existing forms of co-operation between the two States, both at the regional level and within the EU context, although ironically the Irish Sea does not form part of the North Sea and thus does not provide the best possible example.[134] Notwithstanding this fact, what Anderson seems to argue is that States have a choice as to whether they co-operate directly or through an existing organization (in this case, the OSPAR Commission and the EU), and that where they have already co-operated through the latter, they are not also obliged to co-operate directly.[135]

Nonetheless, this should not be understood in the sense that where a particular (larger) semi-enclosed sea, for example the Mediterranean Sea, is composed of smaller 'juridical' enclosed or semi-enclosed sub-seas (e.g. the Adriatic Sea), co-operation and co-ordination of activities through regional organizations on a broader (regional) Mediterranean level (e.g. through the Barcelona system) will eliminate the requirement for States bordering a 'sub-regional' enclosed or semi-enclosed sub-seas to additionally co-operate and co-ordinate their activities on 'sub-regional' level. This position, if accepted, would be contrary to the 'object and purpose' of the inclusion of specific rules on enclosed or semi-enclosed seas into UNCLOS which may be conveniently stated as the need to protect

---

133 Cf fn 124 (ITLOS). Separate Opinion of Judge Anderson, 3 December 2001, section 3. See also Mox Plant Case (Arbitral Tribunal), Counter-Memorial of the UK, op. cit., p. 142, para. 6.21.

134 See the definition of North Sea contained in Art. 4 of the 1882 North Seas Fisheries Convention and the delineation of the North Sea by the International Council for the Exploration of the Sea (sub-area IV). Available at <http://www.ices.dk/aboutus/icesareas.asp>.

135 Cf fn 133.

Enclosed or semi-enclosed seas 45

a specific category of enclosed or semi-enclosed seas without differentiating between 'main' and 'sub-seas'. The relation between the Mediterranean and the Adriatic Sea, which is further discussed in Chapter 5, is an excellent example of this.[136]

It is accordingly suggested that co-operation solely through regional organizations is not enough, and that it has to be, in many instances, complemented by direct co-operation between two or more affected States usually at an appropriate sub-regional level. The most appropriate way of co-operation and/or co-ordination of activities ('institutional' or 'direct') depends on the equities of a particular case, although due to the absence of sub-regional institutionalized organizations, direct co-operation (bilateral or multilateral) seems to prevail. Direct sub-regional co-operation is however possible also under the auspices and/or guidance of an established regional organization, the most notable example being the EU.[137]

2.3.4.6 Does Article 123 affect other users of enclosed or semi-enclosed seas?

The last question in this section relates to the implications of Part IX of UNCLOS on other users of such seas. Article 123(d) of UNCLOS provides that States bordering enclosed or semi-enclosed seas shall endeavour '[…] to invite, as appropriate, other interested States[138] or international organizations to cooperate with them in the furtherance of the provisions of this article'.

An analysis of the text of Article 123(d) seems to suggest that this is legally the least stringent part of Article 123 or according to some, even hortatory in nature. Its main aim seems to be just to encourage States bordering enclosed or semi-enclosed seas to invite other interested States and international organizations, particularly other users of such seas (e.g. fishing States, etc.) to co-operate with the bordering States in furtherance of the provisions of Article 123.[139] Moreover, it may be argued that this obligation is restricted to where it is 'appropriate', which leaves a great amount of discretion and a way out of this obligation for riparian States. It should be reiterated however that States bordering enclosed or semi-enclosed seas, and ultimately also third States, are also bound to undertake such 'obligation' in good faith (Article 300 of UNCLOS)[140] which in turn seems to imply that they should nonetheless endeavour to invite and/or consider proposals

---

136 See also the discussion Chapter 1.
137 See the discussions of the 'Integrated Maritime Policy for better governance of the Mediterranean' in section 3.5.2.2. and of the recent efforts of the EU aimed at the adoption of 'A Maritime Strategy for the Adriatic and Ionian Seas' in section 5.6. For an example of a direct (multilateral) sub-regional co-operation, see the discussion of the 'Sanctuary Agreement' concluded between Italy, France and Monaco (Ligurian Sea) in section 3.3.3.
138 For an explanation of the various dimension of the concept of 'Third State' (geographical, institutional, legal), see J. Juste Ruiz, 'Mediterranean Cooperation and Third States', paper delivered at the 11th Mediterranean Research Meeting, Florence and Montecatini Terme, 24–27 March 2010, p. 9.
139 Virginia Commentary, Vol. III, op. cit., p. 368, para. 123.12 (g).
140 See section 2.3.4.3.

46 *Extension of Coastal State Jurisdiction in Enclosed or Semi-enclosed Seas*

by other interested States or international organizations to co-operate with them in furtherance of the provisions of Article 123.

There is, however, no direct mandatory obligation for third (interested) non-riparian States and/or certain regional or global international organizations to co-operate with States bordering enclosed or semi-enclosed seas. This seems to be confirmed also by the Virginia Commentary which states that:

> [...] This language is not consistent with any mandatory obligation to join with the States bordering such seas in the activities specified in the article.[141]

It should also be recalled that other users of enclosed or semi-enclosed seas (third States) are under an obligation, particularly when approached by States bordering enclosed or semi-enclosed seas with a proposal for co-operation to act in good faith,[142] which in turn points to the fact that Article 123 is not without legal implications for other users of the sea.

2.4 Influence of Part IX of UNCLOS on the extension of coastal state jurisdiction in enclosed or semi-enclosed seas

When trying to assess the potential influence of Part IX of UNCLOS on the extension of coastal State jurisdiction in enclosed or semi-enclosed seas, it is first of all necessary to reiterate that all general rules of UNCLOS, including those regulating the regimes of various maritime zones and their delimitation are fully applicable in enclosed or semi-enclosed seas.[143] There is no doubt that States bordering 'juridical' enclosed or semi-enclosed seas have the same rights and the same duties in enclosed or semi-enclosed seas as their oceanic counterparts, and that this includes, *inter alia*, the right to extend their jurisdiction up to the limits permitted by international law. Account should, however, be taken of the fact that Article 123 of UNCLOS, in its introductory element, provides for a general (good faith) obligation on States bordering enclosed and/or semi-enclosed seas to co-operate in the exercise of *all* their rights and in the performance of *all* their duties under UNCLOS;[144] and that this obligation, although not enforceable *per se*, affects the way in which other articles of UNCLOS should be interpreted and applied by States bordering enclosed or semi-enclosed seas.[145]

The various proposals by States during the deliberations of the SBC and the early stages at UNCLOS III may be broadly divided in two groups: (a) proposals to include special rules with regard to the extension of the breadth and

---

141 Virginia Commentary, Vol. III, op. cit., p. 366, para. 123.12 (c).
142 Cf fn 140.
143 See section 2.3.4.
144 While referring to the scope of application of the first element of Art. 123, the Irish co-agent (Lowe) stated that '[...] Those rights and duties include the duties to protect and preserve the marine environment under Articles 192, 193, 194, 197 and so on, and also the exercises of rights, such as navigation. [...].'. The Mox Plant Case, Proceedings Day 5 (Revised), op. cit., p. 27.
145 See section 2.3.4.3.

Enclosed or semi-enclosed seas 47

the delimitation of the territorial sea in enclosed or semi-enclosed seas; and (b) proposals to include specific rules with regard to the application (or in certain cases, even non-application) of the concept of the EEZ in enclosed or semi-enclosed seas. Although the proposals were rejected and not directly reflected in the various negotiating texts, they point at the importance attributed by a considerable number of States to the two issues during the discussions (genesis) on the concept of enclosed or semi-enclosed seas at UNCLOS III.

2.4.1 Extension of the breadth of the territorial sea in enclosed or semi-enclosed seas

2.4.1.1 Proposals by states at UNCLOS III and within the SBC

As previously mentioned, during the deliberations of the SBC, the problems of enclosed or semi-enclosed seas were not treated separately. Instead, they were included in the more general discussion on the territorial sea and EEZ, particularly in the context of the delimitation and extension of the territorial sea in such areas.[146]

Of particular interest are the proposals submitted by Turkey, Uruguay and Iraq within the SBC and during the (early) sessions of UNCLOS III. These States insisted on the inclusion within UNCLOS of some specific provisions regarding the extension of the breadth of the territorial sea in enclosed and semi-enclosed seas. An example is the proposal by Turkey (SBC) where it advocated the inclusion into the Convention of the following provision:

> In *areas with special characteristics*, such as the semi-enclosed and enclosed seas, *where the exercise of this right by one State for the purpose of extending the breadth of its territorial sea may prejudice the rights and interest of other States* in the area, the determination of the breadth of the territorial sea [...] shall be affected by the agreement of the States in that area.[147]

Similar provisions were included in a proposal by Uruguay[148] submitted to the SBC in 1973.[149] The common denominator of the two proposals was therefore that, where the unilateral extension of the territorial sea, up to the maximum

---

146 Virginia Commentary, Vol. III, op. cit., p. 343, para. IX. 2 and Vol. I., op. cit., p. 32. For a discussion of the 1968 'Maltese move' and the genesis of the SBC, see *inter-alia* Attard, op. cit., pp. 4–8. See also the discussion in sections 2.1.1–2.1.2.

147 Emphasis added. A/AC.138/SC.II/L.16, para. 2, reproduced in III SBC Report 1973, p. 2. See Virginia Commentary, Vol. III, op. cit. p. 357, para. 123.2. See also A/CONF.62/C.2/L.8; Turkey: draft article on the breadth of the territorial sea; global or regional criteria, open seas and oceans, semi-enclosed seas or enclosed seas, 15 July 1974, para. 3.

148 'In regions, with special characteristics, such as semi-enclosed or inland seas, where it is impossible for coastal States to fix the maximum breadth of their territorial sea, the breadth of the said seas shall be determined by agreement between the coastal States of the same region'. A/AC.138/SC.II/L.24, Art. 2, para. 2, reproduced in III SBC Report 1973, pp. 23 and 25. See also Virginia Commentary, Vol. III, op. cit., p. 357, para. 123.2.

149 Ibid.

48 *Extension of Coastal State Jurisdiction in Enclosed or Semi-enclosed Seas*

extent permitted by international law in an enclosed or semi-enclosed sea, affects or may affect the interest of another coastal State, the breadth of the territorial sea shall be determined by agreement between the affected coastal States.[150] Turkey ultimately proposed the inclusion into the Convention of a provision which would be applicable both to the rules on the territorial sea and EEZ and which would provide that:

> The general rules set out in [the chapters relating to territorial sea and economic zone] of this Convention shall be applied, in enclosed and semi-enclosed seas, in a manner consistent with equity.[151]

However such and similar proposals referring to the inclusion of specific rules on the delimitation and/or extension of the breadth of the territorial sea in enclosed and semi-enclosed seas were opposed by the majority of States participating at UNCLOS III. It may be tentatively asserted that one of the main reasons why States participating at UNCLOS III did not provide more support for the efforts of Turkey and some other States, as happened for example with the various proposals relating to the application of the EEZ concept in enclosed or semi-enclosed seas,[152] is due to the fact that unlike the 200 nmi EEZ, the extension of the breadth of the territorial sea up to 12 nmi was not seen as a major problem by the majority of States bordering enclosed and semi-enclosed seas; or at least not outside the debate on straits used for international navigation.[153]

2.4.1.2 Extension of the territorial sea up to the maximum extent permitted by international law: A right or a duty?

UNCLOS does not contain specific rules regulating the extension of the breadth of the territorial sea in enclosed or semi-enclosed seas. The only general provision applicable to all seas and oceans is found in Article 3 which provides that:

> Every State has the right to establish the breadth of its territorial sea up to a limit not exceeding 12 nautical miles, measured from the baselines determined in accordance with this Convention.

---

150 See also A/CONF.62/C.2/L.71 and Add. 2; Iraq: draft articles on enclosed and semi-enclosed seas, 21 August 1974, Art. 6.
151 A/CONF.62/C.2/L.56; Turkey: draft article on enclosed and semi-enclosed seas, 13 August 1974.
152 See section 2.4.2.1.
153 According to the Virginia Commentary, the provisions of Art. 3 of UNCLOS (Breadth of the territorial sea) '[i]t is to be taken together with the consensus on the arrangements for navigation in the territorial sea and in straits used for international navigation.' See Virginia Commentary, Vol. II, op. cit., p. 77, para. 3.1.

This provision must be read in the light of Article 2(1) of UNCLOS according to which:

> The sovereignty of a coastal State extends, beyond its land territory and internal waters [...] to an adjacent belt of sea, described as the territorial sea.

The combination of these two provisions leads to the conclusion that there is *a duty* for a coastal State to exercise sovereignty over an adjacent belt of sea called a 'territorial sea', but on the other hand only *a right* to extend its breadth up to the maximum extent permitted by international law. States are therefore not under an obligation to extend their territorial sea up to the maximum extent permitted by international law. Thus it is possible to agree with the authors of the Virginia Commentary that a coastal State may establish different breadths of its territorial sea for different parts of its coasts.[154] Such is the case, for example, with Turkey which has a 6 nmi territorial sea in the Aegean while in the Black Sea area of territorial sea amounts to 12 nmi.[155]

It follows that in enclosed and or semi-enclosed seas coastal States should exercise their rights and perform their duties, and in general interpret the provisions of UNCLOS in the light of the 'general policy of co-operation' embodied in the introductory element of Article 123 of UNCLOS. That seems to suggest that the relevant States are under an obligation to (endeavour to) co-operate in good faith, without any obligation as to the result, and to do so also when they exercise their rights with regard to the extension of the breadth of the territorial sea in enclosed and/or semi-enclosed seas; and it would seem that such a good faith duty is greatly accentuated in cases where an extension of the territorial sea, up to the maximum extent permitted by international law, affects or is likely to affect the rights and/or interests of other States in the area, particularly neighbouring States.[156]

---

154 Virginia Commentary, Vol. II, op. cit., p. 81, para. 3.8.(a).

155 See H. Slim and T. Scovazzi, 'Study of the current status of ratification, implementation and compliance with maritime agreements and conventions applicable to the Mediterranean Sea Basin: With a specific focus on the ENPI South Partner Countries', Part II, Regional Report, AGRECO Consortium, 2009, p. 8.

156 An example could be a case when the extension of the breadth of the territorial sea of a State A up to 12 nmi (in an enclosed or semi-enclosed sea) would have the effect of 'cutting off' the territorial sea of State B from the high seas and/or zones of sovereign rights and jurisdiction. See N. Šebenik, '*Teritorialni dostop do odprtega morja v mednarodni sodni in arbitražni praksi*', Pravna Praksa, Vol. 28, No. 45–50, Ljubljana, 2009, Appendix, p. IV. Reference should be made to the fact that the 'cut-off effect' is nowadays not recognized by the international jurisprudence as an established 'relevant circumstance', particularly in cases involving the delimitation of the EEZ and/or continental shelf involving concave coastlines. See ITLOS, Dispute concerning delimitation of the maritime boundary between Bangladesh and Myanmar in the Bay of Bengal Bangladesh/Myanmar), Judgment, 14 March 2012, para. 292. See also the discussion of the second element of Art. 123 in section 2.3.4.4.

50   Extension of Coastal State Jurisdiction in Enclosed or Semi-enclosed Seas

2.4.1.3 Practice of states bordering enclosed or semi-enclosed seas

Cases where States bordering enclosed or semi-enclosed seas have refrained from extending the breadth of their territorial seas up to the maximum extent permitted by international law, particularly due to the specific (sometimes also political) characteristics of a certain enclosed or semi-enclosed sea are not rare, although one has to admit that it is extremely difficult to ascertain whether the latter have been directly or indirectly influenced by Part IX of UNCLOS or by the discussions on enclosed or semi-enclosed seas at UNCLOS III. The scope of this Section is accordingly limited. The fact that such cases are found almost exclusively in enclosed or semi-enclosed seas gives, however, some weight to this argument. The practice of States bordering the enclosed or semi-enclosed Baltic and Mediterranean Seas seems particularly relevant.

In the Mediterranean, the most notable examples include Greece and Turkey in the Aegean, whose territorial seas still stand at 6 nmi[157] and the two UK sovereign bases on the island of Cyprus (Akrotiri and Dhekelia) with a 3 nmi territorial sea,[158] while it would also be possible to include within the group the Spanish enclaves on the Moroccan coast (including Ceuta and Melila)[159] and Gibraltar (UK),[160] whose breadth and/or even the sole right to a territorial sea have been disputed. Furthermore, a most interesting case is found in the Baltic Sea (Gulf of Finland) where Finland and Estonia have undertaken not to extend their territorial seas up to the maximum extent possible by international law but instead have left at the centre of the gulf a 3 nmi wide corridor of EEZ/fishing zone. Though not expressly stated in their *Exchange of Notes*,[161] it seems that the main reason for such a decision was the need not to enclave the Russian territorial

---

157 Ibid.
158 See Slim and Scovazzi, op. cit, p. 8, and Ahnish, op. cit., pp. 256–258. Scovazzi opines that it is likely that the implicit objective of the sole granting of (territorial) waters to the two UK sovereign bases (Akrotiri and Dhekelia) agreed with the 1960 Treaty Concerning the Establishment of the Republic of Cyprus (signed by Cyprus, Greece, Turkey and the UK) was to '[...] preserve freedom of military navigation, in particular to avoid the application of the regime of innocent passage to British ships proceeding to or from SBAs.' See T. Scovazzi, 'Maritime Boundaries in the Eastern Mediterranean Sea', Policy Brief, Mediterranean Policy Program, Washington, DC: The German Marshal Fund of the United States, June 2012, pp. 6–7. See also the discussion in section 3.4.1.
159 See Ahnish, op. cit., pp. 278–284.
160 Ibid, pp. 288–295. According to Slim and Scovazzi, the territorial sea of Gibraltar amounts to 3 nmi. See Slim and Scovazzi, op. cit., p. 8.
161 See 'Exchange of Notes constituting an agreement on the procedure to be followed in the modification of the limits of the territorial waters in the Gulf of Finland' (Estonia-Finland), 6 April and 4 May 1994. According a note from Estonia:

> [...] If Finland were also to extend its own territorial waters by 12 nautical miles, *the international channel in the Gulf of Finland would be completely closed*. In order to maintain *free passage* through the Gulf of Finland, the Republic of Estonia is prepared to limit the width of its territorial waters in the Gulf of Finland *so that it extends no closer than 3 nautical miles from the centre line*. This is presuming that Finland, for its part, is prepared to limit the width of its own territorial waters correspondingly. [...]. (Emphasis added.)

> Finland accepted the proposal in a note dated 4 May 1994. This practice predated the entry into force of UNCLOS for Estonia (26 August 2005).

sea and to allow the exercise of the freedom of navigation for commercial and naval ships sailing to or from the Russian ports in the Gulf of Finland. This is, however, not the only case where the interest of other States, particularly in relation to freedom of navigation, has been taken into account by Baltic coastal States. It is suggested that Sweden and Denmark have also followed the policy of refraining from extending their territorial seas up to the maximum distance permitted by international law in cases where such an extension would close the navigable channel of high seas/EEZ between the territorial seas of the two States.[162] On the other side of the globe (in the Korea Strait), Japan and South Korea similarly refrained from extending their territorial seas beyond 3 nm with the aim of leaving at the centre of the strait a 'corridor' (of undivided EEZs) where all States could exercise their high seas' (communication) freedoms, particularly freedom of navigation.[163] Japan has, additionally, unilaterally refrained from extending its territorial waters in the Soya, Tsugaru and Osumi Straits, where the breadth of its territorial sea has remained fixed at 3 nmi.[164]

2.4.2 Proclamation of EEZs and similar zones in enclosed or semi-enclosed seas

2.4.2.1 Positions of States at UNCLOS III

Whilst Turkey and Uruguay did not manage to attract broader support and were relatively isolated in their efforts to include specific rules on the extension of the breadth and delimitation of the territorial sea at UNCLOS III, a considerable number of States, particularly States bordering enclosed or semi-enclosed seas, were expressing doubts and/or concerns about the application of the new concept of the EEZ in enclosed or semi-enclosed seas. The various proposals by States at UNCLOS III can be divided into different groups which, in turn, broadly reflect the main problems associated or felt at that time to be associated with the proclamations of EEZs in enclosed and semi-enclosed seas. The common denominator of all groups of proposals may be best expressed in the words of the representative of Algeria, who at the 28th Meeting of the Second Committee stated that:

> [...] in putting the idea of the 200-mile zone into practice certain accommodations would be required, particularly with regard to enclosed or semi-enclosed seas [...].[165]

---

162 Helsinki Commission, 'Guidelines on ensuring successful convictions of offenders of anti-pollution regulations at sea', Baltic Sea Environmental Proceedings, No. 78, 2000, see map at p. 41.

163 Also the mentioned practice of Japan and Korea goes back to 1977, therefore before the adoption of UNCLOS. Cf fn 164.

164 It has been alleged by former Japanese 'top officials' that Japan has avoided extending its territorial waters in the relevant straits in order to avoid political disputes arising from the passage of US warships carrying nuclear weapons within Japanese territorial waters. See *Japan Times Online*, 'Japan left key straits open for U.S. nukes', 22 June 2009.

165 A/CONF. 62/C.2/SR. 28, 6 August 1974, para. 70.

52 *Extension of Coastal State Jurisdiction in Enclosed or Semi-enclosed Seas*

2.4.2.1.1 A RIGHT TO PROCLAIM AN EEZ

It is noteworthy that certain States bordering enclosed or semi-enclosed seas went so far as to advocate that the concept of the EEZ should not be applied in such seas. Such concerns were particularly accentuated during the early sessions of the Conference and particularly at the 38th Meeting of the Second Committee which was almost entirely dedicated to the problems of enclosed or semi-enclosed seas. For example, the representative of the German Democratic Republic was of the opinion that:

> [...] the convention could include a general provision that for such coastal States [States bordering enclosed and semi-enclosed seas] the principle of the economic zone beyond the territorial sea or of the contiguous zone up to 12 miles should be applied only to the mineral resources of the sea-bed and its subsoil, and to their exploration and exploitation [...].[166]

The representative of Israel addressed the particular situation in the Mediterranean Sea and pointed out that '[...] a semi-enclosed sea poor in resources such as the Mediterranean did not lend itself to the kind of far reaching claims to oceans space sometimes associated with the concept of a an exclusive economic zone [...]'.[167] The representative of Iraq more generally stated that '[...] any area of the sea which was beyond the 12 nm zone and the internal waters of a State should be regarded as part of the high seas'.[168] From these proposals it can be seen that, at least during the early sessions of UNCLOS III, there was no consensus among participating States and/or States bordering enclosed or semi-enclosed seas on whether the new concept of the EEZ could be applied in (specific) enclosed or semi-enclosed seas at all.

2.4.2.1.2 DELIMITATION OF EEZs

One of the main concerns by States participating at UNCLOS III was the *delimitation of maritime zones*, particularly EEZs, in such (narrow) seas where in the great majority of cases States are not is a position to proclaim a full 200 nmi zone and where accordingly such situations are most likely to result in over-lapping claims involving in the majority of cases both adjacent and opposite States.[169] Such concerns were for example echoed in the interventions of the Soviet representative at the 38th Meeting of the Second Committee when he noted that:

> [...] The question of economic zones would cause no problems where the coastline faced the open sea, but a number of problems could arise in enclosed

---

166 A/CONF. 62/C.2/SR. 38, 13 August 1974, para. 41.
167 A/CONF. 62/C.2/SR. 22, 31 July 1974, para. 110.
168 A/CONF. 62/C.2/SR. 43, 23 August 1974, para. 29.
169 Cf fn 151.

or semi-enclosed seas [...] particularly in connexion with the delimitation of sea areas between States.[170]

The representative of Iran similarly pointed out that '[...] regional or bilateral arrangements seemed more appropriate [than global norms applicable to all oceans] in many areas, particularly in matters relating to the delimitation of areas under national jurisdiction'.[171] An interesting solution by then already had been proposed by the representative of the Republic of Korea, who noted that in many enclosed or semi-enclosed seas, including those surrounding the Korean peninsula, the claims of coastal States to maritime zones were bound to overlap. As in such cases the delimitation of the boundary would give rise to many problems, he proposed that if the parties concerned could not arrive at a mutually satisfactory agreement, or if one party had difficulty in accepting the claim of the other in the area where jurisdiction or claims overlaps, '[...] joint development schemes should be taken into consideration, as had been suggested by the International Court of Justice in its 1969 decision on the North Sea continental shelf case'.[172]

2.4.2.1.3 CONSERVATION OF LIVING RESOURCES AND PRESERVATION OF HISTORIC FISHING RIGHTS

Among the problems raised by States at UNCLOS III, of some significance was the particular concern by bordering States with regard to the preservation of historic fishing rights in enclosed or semi-enclosed seas. The representative of Denmark, for example, pointed out that:

> [...] Establishment of exclusive economic zones in such relatively narrow waters, without taking into account the interest of neighbouring coastal States and countries opposite to each other, would destroy the historic pattern of the fisheries which had long functioned satisfactory. [...][173]

More generally, States participating at UNCLOS III were afraid that the application of the EEZ concept in enclosed or semi-enclosed seas would provoke difficulties in the 'exploitation (distribution) and conservation of living resources' and accordingly many of them advocated the position that the application of the concept of the EEZ would be feasible in such seas only if supplemented by appropriate regional agreements. The representative of Bahrain stated that '[t]he application of the economic zone doctrine in [...] semi-enclosed seas would lead to difficulties of distribution which could probably be settled only by regional agreements based on equitable principles'.[174] SFRY's

---

170 A/CONF. 62/C.2/SR. 38, 13 August 1974, para. 50. See also the discussion in section 2.4.1.1.
171 A/CONF.62C.2/SR.6, 17 July 1974, para. 16.
172 A/CONF.62/C.2/SR.17, 26 July 1974, para. 29–30. See also section 2.4.2.5.
173 A/CONF.62/C.2/SR.38, 13 August 1974, para. 19.
174 A/CONF.62C.2/SR.22, 31 July 1974, para. 2.

54 Extension of Coastal State Jurisdiction in Enclosed or Semi-enclosed Seas

representative (Ibler) similarly pointed out, obviously alluding to enclosed or semi-enclosed seas, that:

> In cases where the creation of an economic zone of 200 nm was not possible, recourse to regional arrangements could solve the problems connected with the rights and duties of the coastal States. That arrangements should take into account the legitimate interest of all the countries concerned, particularly the land-locked and geographically disadvantaged countries.[175]

2.4.2.1.4 NAVIGATION

Navigation in enclosed and semi-enclosed seas, and particularly navigation through the EEZ of coastal States and/or outlets linking such seas with other seas and oceans, represented another 'hot' topic at UNCLOS III. In this respect noteworthy is the statement made by the Soviet representative at the 38th Meeting of the Second Committee where he pointed out that his country:

> [...] could not accept the establishment of a special regime benefiting any given country in waters that has traditionally been used by all countries for international shipping on a basis of equality. [...][176]

Some other States expressed concerns in the sense that the rights of the coastal State with regard to the exercise of jurisdiction over the establishment and use of artificial islands, installations and structures in its EEZ could have negative impacts on the freedom of navigation in enclosed or semi-enclosed seas. The proposal by Iraq at the fourth Session of the Conference for example reflected both (navigational) concerns. Iraq proposed at that time the introduction of an additional article in the text of ISNT (Article 134 *bis*) which would expressly confirm in paragraph 1 the '[...] right of the free transit passage through straits used for international navigation and connecting semi-enclosed seas with the open seas for all ships and aircraft [...]', while in paragraph 2, the proposal contained a provision stating that '[t]he existence of islands, artificial islands, installations and structures in the semi-enclosed seas shall not affect in any way the freedom of international navigation through the traditional sea lanes'.[177] A concern may be implied, particularly from the second part of that proposal, that the proclamations of EEZs in enclosed and semi-enclosed seas where the coastal State exercises jurisdiction also with regard to the establishment and use of artificial islands, installations and structures[178] may disrupt navigation in

---

175 Ibid, para. 39.
176 A/CONF.62C.2/SR.38, 13 August 1974, para. 49.
177 Emphasis added. See Iraq (1976, mimeo), Arts 134, 134 *bis* and 135. See also Virginia Commentary, Vol. III, op. cit., p. 361, para. 123.5.
178 Article 56(1)(b)(i).

Enclosed or semi-enclosed seas 55

traditional sea-lanes in such seas; a fact which would affect both other bordering States and the international community as a whole.[179]

Despite the many identified problems which may arise as a result of the proclamations and delimitations of EEZs in enclosed or semi-enclosed seas, neither the negotiating texts, nor the final text of UNCLOS contain specific rules on the application of the concept of the EEZ in enclosed or semi-enclosed seas. This does not mean, however, that there is a completely unqualified right to establish EEZs in such seas, as is explained below.

2.4.2.2 Proclamation of EEZs

At the outset of this discussion it should be reiterated again that the general rules of UNCLOS on the regime of maritime zones are, when geographically possible, fully applicable in enclosed or semi-enclosed seas. This is because, despite a variety of different proposals at UNCLOS III, the final text of UNCLOS does not contain specific rules relating to the concept or the delimitation of the EEZ in relation to enclosed or semi-enclosed seas. What should be taken into account – even if the language of Part V of UNCLOS may give a *prima facie* impression that the EEZ (like the continental shelf) exists *ipso facto* and *ab initio*,[180] is that there must be an express legal act usually in a form of an express (formal) proclamation in order for a coastal State to avail itself of the specific legal regime regulated by Part V of UNCLOS.[181] Part V of UNCLOS thus gives coastal States an inchoate *right*[182] – not an obligation – to proclaim an EEZ. It is asserted, however, that such right, similarly to other rights under UNCLOS by States bordering enclosed or semi-enclosed seas, should be interpreted and exercised in such seas in the light of the 'general policy of co-operation' embodied in the introductory part of Article 123.

Of particular interest are the arguments put forward by some scholars, particularly in the context of the Mediterranean Sea, in the sense that there may exist a specific regional custom preventing States from proclaiming EEZs in

---

179 Leanza, op. cit., pp. 173–177.
180 Article 55 of UNCLOS provides that '[t]he EEZ is an area beyond and adjacent to the territorial sea [...] in which according to Article 56 UNCLOS coastal state *has* [and not as Attard properly pointed out "may have"] specific rights'. See D. Attard, *Exclusive Economic Zone in International Law*, Oxford: Clarendon Press, 1987, p. 54.
181 According to Attard, such an interpretation is derived primarily from the *travaux préparatoires* at UNCLOS III and practice of the States (customary international law). Both Attard and Leanza agree that such interpretation derives also *argumentum ad contrario* from Art. 77(3) of UNCLOS which expressly provides that the rights over the continental shelf do not depend either on occupation or on any express proclamation. See Attard, *The Exclusive Economic Zone in International Law*, op. cit., pp. 54–61 and U. Leanza, '*La zona economica esclusiva nella evoluzione del diritto del mare*', in E. Turcho Bulgherini (ed.), *Studi in onore di Antonio Lefebvre D'Ovidio*, Tomo I, Milano: Giuffré Editore, 1995, p. 541 at pp. 553–554. See also section 3.1.
182 See however I. Vella, 'A new advent for renewable offshore resources', in N.A. Martínez Gutiérrez (ed.), *Serving the Rule of International Maritime Law: Essays in Honour of Professor David Joseph Attard*, p. 136 at pp. 149–151.

56   *Extension of Coastal State Jurisdiction in Enclosed or Semi-enclosed Seas*

particular enclosed or semi-enclosed seas.[183] However, as properly pointed out by Gestri, the sole definition of 'enclosed or semi-enclosed seas', embodied in Article 122 of UNCLOS admits the possibility of certain enclosed or semi-enclosed seas being completely covered by the EEZs of its coastal States.[184] Furthermore, as follows from our discussion in Chapter 3, the practice of States in relation to the extension of coastal State jurisdiction in the Mediterranean and Adriatic Seas has been a long way away from achieving the degree of uniformity which would be required for the creation of a 'regional' custom on this point.[185]

It is therefore suggested that all States bordering enclosed or semi-enclosed seas have the right to proclaim an EEZ, but that in enclosed or semi-enclosed seas such right, and particularly the implementation of the regime of the EEZ after its formal proclamation, should be undertaken in the light of Part IX of UNCLOS. This, however, does not mean, as properly pointed out by Scovazzi, that a State bordering enclosed or semi-enclosed seas cannot proceed to establish its EEZ without the agreement of its neighbouring States.[186]

2.4.2.3 Fixing external limits of EEZs

The breadth of the EEZ is regulated by Article 57 of UNCLOS which provides that:

> The exclusive economic zone shall not extend beyond 200 nautical miles measured from the baselines from which the breadth of the territorial sea is measured.[187]

It follows that a coastal State, while exercising its right with regard to the institution of an EEZ, may decide (and in certain cases indeed should decide) not to proclaim a full 200 nmi and it would seem that there are no restrictions whatsoever with regard to the minimum size of such zone.[188] It is also perfectly possible for a coastal State to proclaim an EEZ or EEZs only along a portion of its coasts,

---

183 See M. Gestri, '*I rapporti di vicinato marittimo tra l'Italia e gli Stati nati dalla dissoluzione della Iugoslavia*', in N. Ronzitti (ed.), *I raporti di vicinato dell'Italia con Croazia, Serbia-Montenegro e Slovenia*, Rome: Luiss University Press-Giuffrè, 2005, p. 177, at pp. 196–197.

184 Ibid. This view is shared by Škrk, who opines that the EEZ represents a 'Constitutive Element of Enclosed or Semi-Enclosed Seas'. See Škrk, op. cit., p.162.

185 See also Leanza, op. cit., 2008, pp. 164–181.

186 See T. Scovazzi, 'Recent Developments as regards Maritime Delimitation in the Adriatic Sea', in R. Lagoni and D. Vignes (eds), *Maritime Delimitation*, Leiden and Boston, MA: Martinus Nijhoff Publishers, 2006, p. 189 at p. 195.

187 If a State has a 12 nmi territorial sea, then the maximum breadth of its EEZ may be 188 nmi, with an adequate decrease if the breadth of the territorial sea is less. See Virginia Commentary, Vol. II, op. cit., p. 547, para. 57(1).

188 The difference between the territorial sea and the EEZ seems to be that, generally speaking, a coastal State shall extend its sovereignty over an adjacent belt of sea, described as the territorial sea, although not necessarily to the maximum extent permitted by international law and/or (geographic) circumstances, while in the case of the EEZ there are no obligations for a coastal State to proclaim an EEZ at all. See Attard, *The Exclusive Economic Zone in International Law*, op. cit., p. 54.

Enclosed or semi-enclosed seas 57

or to opt for different breadths of its EEZ along different parts of its coasts. Lastly, it seems that the right of a coastal State to proclaim a full 'EEZ' on the basis of Part V of UNCLOS also includes the right to proclaim only some elements of the latter (FPZ, ZEP, EFPZ), therefore different zones of (functional) jurisdiction.[189]

If we are to limit this discussion to those three subjects (proclamation of EEZs, their extension of up to 200 nmi, and impliedly also proclamation of only some elements of an EEZ), it seems possible to state that all the three cases deal with 'rights of a coastal State'. From this it follows that States bordering enclosed or semi-enclosed seas have a good faith obligation to co-operate[190] also when it comes to the proclamations of zones of sovereign rights and jurisdictions in such seas (EEZ, FPZ, ZEPs, etc.) and particularly, with regard to the implementation of the relevant regimes of such zones.[191] This argument is based, first, on the introductory statement of Article 123 of UNCLOS and, second, on the second element of Article 123 which advocates for a more stringent obligation for States bordering enclosed or semi-enclosed seas to endeavour to co-operate *and co-ordinate their activities* with regard to:

(a) the management, conservation, exploration and exploitation of the living resources of the sea;[192]
(b) the implementation of their rights and duties with respect to the protection and preservation of the marine environment;[193]
(c) their scientific research policies, and to undertake where appropriate joint programmes of scientific research in the area [...].[194]

The latter conclusion seems to be reinforced by the texts of Articles 56 and 123 of UNCLOS, from which it can be clearly seen that the three areas of co-operation and co-ordination of activities listed in Article 123 of UNCLOS match the areas in which coastal States have sovereign rights and jurisdiction in their EEZ on the basis of Article 56. The *travaux préparatoires* of Article 123 of UNCLOS indicate that such a 'match' was exactly the intention of the drafters.[195]

---

189 See the general discussion in Chapters 3 and 6.
190 See the discussion in section 2.3.4.3.
191 States bordering enclosed or semi-enclosed seas shall obviously take into account relevant (general) provisions of UNCLOS addressing co-operation within EEZs. See for example provisions on co-operation provided by Part V of UNCLOS in the field of management of living resources and relating to 'stocks occurring within the exclusive economic zones of two or more coastal States or both within the exclusive economic zone and in an area beyond and adjacent to it' (Art. 63), 'Highly Migratory Species' (Art. 64), 'Anadromous stocks' (Art. 66) and 'Catadromous species' (Art. 67). See also Škrk, op. cit., p. 173, and relevant provisions of the '1994 Fish Stocks Agreement'.
192 Article 123(a) of UNCLOS.
193 Article 123(b) of UNCLOS.
194 Article 123(c) of UNCLOS.
195 From the *travaux préparatoires* of Article 123 it follows that the drafting language of that article had been, upon the proposal by the Drafting Committee (ninth session, 1980) deliberately brought into line with the language of Articles 56(2) and 58(3) of EEZ. See Virginia Commentary, Vol. III, op. cit., p. 365, para. 123.10.

58 Extension of Coastal State Jurisdiction in Enclosed or Semi-enclosed Seas

It is suggested therefore that States bordering enclosed or semi-enclosed seas have a good faith obligation to co-operate also with regard to the proclamation of EEZs in particular enclosed or semi-enclosed seas. That good faith duty *prima facie* seems to include the duty to endeavour to: (a) co-operate and co-ordinate their activities with regard to the sole modalities of the proclamation of an EEZ and/or *sui generis* zone in a particular enclosed and or semi-enclosed sea; (b) co-operate and co-ordinate with regard to the definition of the breadth of such an EEZ; and (c) co-operate and co-ordinate their activities with regard to the practical application of the regime of the proclaimed zones.

It would appear that the 'obligation' under (a) may be, for example, executed through a co-ordinated extension of jurisdiction by the bordering States and/or establishment of (joint) common zones. The practice of States bordering enclosed or semi-enclosed seas on this point is, however, at least contradictory. As commented by Scovazzi:

> [...] Nor does it appear that the States which have established exclusive economic zones (or other *sui generis* zones) in enclosed or semi-enclosed seas, such as the Baltic, the Caribbean or the Black Seas and the Mediterranean as well, have acted only after having sought and obtained the permission of their neighbours.[196]

It is argued, however, that the matter is not about 'seeking and obtaining permission' but about informing potentially affected States, consulting with them and endeavouring to co-operate in this regard.

2.4.2.4 Delimitation of EEZs

After having completed the analysis of the good faith duty of co-operation and co-ordination of activities by States bordering enclosed or semi-enclosed seas, this section focuses on the relation between Part IX and Articles 74 and 83 of UNCLOS. As pointed out by Scovazzi:

> Art. 123 does not provide for a special obligation to co-operate as regards the delimitation of maritime boundaries. But such an obligation comes very clearly from Art. 74 and Art. 83 UNCLOS.[197]

As there already exist extensive literature on the 'law of maritime delimitation'[198] and taking into account that the general application of Articles 15, 74 and 83 of UNCLOS will be, at least in the context of the Adriatic Sea, touched upon in

---

196 See Scovazzi, 'Recent Developments as regards Maritime Delimitation in the Adriatic Sea', op. cit., p. 196.

197 Ibid, op. cit., p. 195, fn 18.

198 See for example P. Weil, *The Law of Maritime Delimitations–Reflections*, Cambridge: Grotius Publications Limited, 1989, and Y. Tanaka, *Predictability and Flexibility in the Law of Maritime Delimitation*, Oxford: Hart Publishing, 2006.

Enclosed or semi-enclosed seas 59

Chapter 4, it is proposed to focus in the next sections specifically on the application of the general duty embodied in Articles 74(3) and 83(3) of UNCLOS in the context of enclosed or semi-enclosed seas. Notwithstanding this, some general remarks should also be made with regard to the scope of application of Article 74(1) of UNCLOS, which states that:

> The delimitation of the exclusive economic zone between States with opposite or adjacent coasts shall be effected by agreement on the basis of international law, as referred to in Article 38 of the Statute of the International Court of Justice, in order to achieve an equitable solution.

Article 74(1) of UNCLOS, although being rather vague,[199] nonetheless provides for a general duty of co-operation in respect to the delimitation of the EEZ 'in order to achieve an equitable solution' without distinguishing between enclosed or semi-enclosed seas and other seas and oceans.[200] It is suggested, however, that when it comes to the delimitation of EEZs (and/or other zones of functional jurisdiction) in enclosed or semi-enclosed seas, such duty should again be interpreted and applied in the light of Part IX which seems to add a further duty to act in line with the provisions of Article 74 of UNCLOS, including its third paragraph.

This obviously does not mean that there are special rules which international courts or tribunals would have to follow when delimiting maritime boundaries in enclosed or semi-enclosed seas. On the other hand, there seems to be enough room for the 'specific characteristics of such seas' and/or eventually the 'legitimate interests of neighbouring States' to be treated as *special* or *relevant* circumstances in a particular case. The ICJ seems to have adopted (at least impliedly) this position in its 2009 Judgment in the Romania/Ukraine Case,[201] although it is

---

199 A crucial role in the interpretation of Arts 74(1) and 83(1) of UNCLOS is played by the jurisprudence of international courts and tribunals. For a legal interpretation of Arts 74(1) and 83(1) from the standpoint of the recent jurisprudence of international courts and tribunals, see the excellent analysis in the Award of the Arbitral Tribunal in the Matter of An Arbitration between Barbados and The Republic of Trinidad and Tobago (Barbados/Trinidad Tobago), The Hague, 11 April 2006, RIAA, Vol. XXVII, p. 147, paras 219–245.

200 According to Scovazzi '[...] UNCLOS provides for a general obligation of the states concerned to behave in good faith in order to reach an agreement on the delimitation of their exclusive economic zones or continental shelves [...]'. See Scovazzi, 'Maritime Boundaries in the Eastern Mediterranean Sea', op. cit., p. 10.

201 Romania argued that the '[...] enclosed nature of the Black Sea is also a relevant circumstance as part of the wider requirement to take account of the geographical context of the area to be delimited. In Romania's view, this geographical factor is to be considered together with any pre-existing delimitation agreements so that any new delimitation should not dramatically depart from the method previously used in the same sea between other riparian States in order not to produce an inequitable result'. Ukraine replied that '[...] there is no special régime governing delimitations taking place in an enclosed sea simply because of its nature' and, second, that '[...] in general terms, bilateral agreements cannot affect the rights of third parties and, as such, the existing maritime delimitation agreements in the Black Sea cannot influence the present dispute'. The ICJ just stated that it '[...] nevertheless considers that, in the light of the above-mentioned delimitation agreements and the enclosed nature of the Black Sea, no adjustment to the equidistance line as provisionally drawn is called for.' See Case Concerning Maritime Delimitation

60 *Extension of Coastal State Jurisdiction in Enclosed or Semi-enclosed Seas*

unfortunate that the ICJ did not dwell more comprehensively on this issue. Previously however, in the (1985) Libya/Malta Case, the ICJ made reference to the Mediterranean as a 'semi-enclosed sea' and to the position of the Maltese islands 'in the wider geographical context, particularly their position in a semi-enclosed seas'.[202] According to the ICJ:

> [...] relevant circumstances indicate that some northward shift of the boundary line is needed in order to produce an equitable result. These are first, *the general geographical context in which the islands of Malta appear as a relatively small feature in a semi-enclosed sea*; and secondly, the great disparity in the lengths of the relevant coasts of the two Parties [...].[203]

This, however, does not mean that the 'enclosed or semi-enclosed status' of a certain sea is *per se* a relevant circumstance.[204] In the Libya/Malta Case those were the characteristic of the relevant part of the semi-enclosed Mediterranean Sea which '[...] was thus a factor to be taken into account in order to achieve an equitable result, influencing the scope of the adjustment of the boundary northwards'.[205] As emphasized by ITLOS in a recent maritime delimitation case (Bangladesh/Myanmar):

> [...] The goal of achieving an equitable result must be the paramount consideration guiding the action of the Tribunal [...]. Therefore the method to be followed [in drawing the maritime delimitation line] should be one that, under the prevailing geographic realities and the particular circumstances of each case, can lead to an equitable result.[206]

---

    in the Black Sea (Romania/Ukraine), ICJ Reports 2009, p. 1, paras. 169, at pp. 172–173 and 178. See also the Memorial Submitted by Romania, 18 August 2005, pp. 62–72, at p. 128 and Counter-Memorial Submitted by Ukraine, 19 May 2006, pp. 43–47. See furthermore R. Churchill, 'Dispute Settlement under the UN Convention on the Law of the Sea: Survey for 2009', IJMCL, Vol. 25, No. 4, 2010, p. 458 at p. 475.

202 Continental Shelf (Libyan Arab Jamahiriya/Malta), Judgment, ICJ Reports, 1985, p. 13, para. 53.

203 Emphasis added. Ibid, para. 73. The ICJ furthermore observed that '[i]n a semi-enclosed sea like the Mediterranean, that reference to neighboring states is particularly apposite, for [...] it is the coastal relationship in the whole geographical context that are to be taken account of and respected'. Ibid, para. 47.

204 Case Concerning Maritime Delimitation in the Black Sea (Romania/Ukraine), Rejoinder Submitted by Ukraine, 6 July 2007, p. 102, para. 6.20.

205 Ibid, Reply Submitted by Romania, 22 December 2006, p. 204, para. 6.48.

206 ITLOS, Dispute concerning delimitation of the maritime boundary between Bangladesh and Myanmar in the Bay of Bengal (Bangladesh/Myanmar), op. cit., para. 235. In the latter case ITLOS took the position that the *concavity of the coast* of Bangladesh represents a relevant circumstance, as the (provisional) equidistance line produces a *cut-off effect* on that coast requiring an adjustment of that line. Emphasis added. Ibid, para. 297. The judgment, however, does not make specific reference to enclosed or semi-enclosed seas. It is also questionable whether the Bay of Bengal may be, due to its dimension (2.2 million km²), considered as a 'juridical' enclosed or semi-enclosed sea. See the discussion in section 2.2.2.

Enclosed or semi-enclosed seas 61

2.4.2.5 Conclusion of provisional arrangements of a practical nature pending delimitation (Article 74(3))

If good faith attempts by two or more States to co-operate in the final delimitation of their EEZ and/or other zones of functional jurisdiction are not (immediately) successful, and particularly if such a situation results in overlapping claims involving more than two States, it would seem necessary for the States involved to resort to the provisions of Article 74(3) of UNCLOS.[207] This Article provides for a general 'duty' applicable to all coastal States. However, in relation to coastal States bordering enclosed or semi-enclosed seas, it is argued that it should be interpreted and applied in the light of Part IX of UNCLOS. It is thus important to also mention that Article 74(3), as well as Article 83(3) on the continental shelf, provide as follows:

> Pending agreement as provided for in paragraph 1 [on the delimitation of the EEZ or continental shelf], the States concerned, in a spirit of understanding and cooperation, shall make every effort to enter into provisional arrangements of a practical nature and, during this transitional period, not to jeopardize or hamper the reaching of the final agreement. Such arrangements shall be without prejudice to the final delimitation.[208]

The proper and timely exercise of the mentioned duty seems to be particularly important in cases where the extension of jurisdiction by a certain State affects, or is likely to affect, the rights and/or interest of more than one State, a situation often found in enclosed or semi-enclosed seas.[209] It therefore follows that such obligation exists independently of the actual commencement of the negotiations on the relevant delimitation.[210] In other words, as soon as the proclamation of an EEZ or EEZs or even similar (derived) zones of jurisdiction result in overlapping claims, the States involved have a *duty* to make '*every effort to enter into provisional arrangements of a practical nature* and, during this transitional period, *not to jeopardize or hamper the reaching of the final agreement*'.[211]

An important contribution to the interpretation of the mentioned Articles has been provided by the 2007 Award of the Arbitral Tribunal in the Matter of an Arbitration between Guyana and Suriname.[212] On that occasion the Tribunal

---

207 See also Art. 83(3) of UNCLOS.
208 See T.A. Mensah, 'Joint Development Zones as an Alternative Dispute Settlement Approach in Maritime Boundary Delimitation', in Lagoni and Vignes (eds), op. cit., pp. 143–151. See also the overview of the practice on provisional arrangements in disputed areas provided in S.P. Kim, *Maritime Delimitation and Interim Arrangements in North East Asia*, Leiden and Boston, MA: Martinus Nijhoff Publishers, 2004, pp. 94–147.
209 See section 1.1 for the specific situation in the Central Mediterranean.
210 Virginia Commentary, Vol. II, op. cit., p. 815, para. 74.11(d).
211 '[…] The first element aims to promote the adoption of certain interim measures; the second seeks to limit the activities of the States concerned in the disputed area'. Ibid. See also Award of the Arbitral Tribunal in the Matter of an Arbitration between Guyana and Suriname, 17 September 2007, The Hague, pp. 152–153, para. 459.
212 Ibid.

62 *Extension of Coastal State Jurisdiction in Enclosed or Semi-enclosed Seas*

adopted the position not only that Articles 74(3) and 83(3) of UNCLOS impose upon States a 'duty to negotiate in good faith', but also that:

> [...] the inclusion of the phrase 'in a spirit of understanding and cooperation' indicates the drafters' intent to require of the parties a *conciliatory approach to negotiations,* pursuant to which they would be *prepared to make concessions in the pursuit of a provisional agreement.* Such an approach is particularly to be expected of the parties in view of the fact that any provisional arrangements arrived at are by definition temporary and will be without prejudice to the final delimitation [...][213]

The added value of the Award results also from the fact that in declaring that Guyana had violated its obligation to make every effort to enter into provisional arrangements of a practical nature *inter alia* on the basis of the fact that is had been preparing exploratory drilling for some time before the accident and should have, in a spirit of co-operation, informed Suriname directly of its plans, the Tribunal listed the various steps which Guyana could (and should) have taken in order to fulfil its obligation on the basis of Article 83(3) of UNCLOS. According to the Tribunal, the 'duty to make every effort to enter into provisional agreements' includes the *duty to notify, the duty to seek co-operation (to consult)* and the *duty to share the benefits (both scientific and financial).*[214] In this respect, it is possible to agree with Churchill that the Tribunal's pronouncement on the scope of the obligations under Articles 74(3) and 83(3) of UNCLOS are important and it is suggested that it may provide an extremely useful guidance to coastal States, including States bordering enclosed or semi-enclosed seas, as this is the first occasion when the mentioned provisions have been directly assessed by an international court or tribunal.[215] It should not come as a surprise therefore that Bangladesh, on 8 October 2009, while notifying Myanmar about the submission of the dispute regarding the delimitation of their maritime boundary to the arbitral procedure provided for in Annex VII of UNCLOS, made the following initial claim:

> Bangladesh also requests the Tribunal to declare that by authorizing its licensees to engage in drilling and other exploratory activities in maritime areas claimed by Bangladesh without prior notice and consent, Myanmar has violated its obligations to make every effort to reach a provisional arrangement pending delimitation of the maritime boundary as required by UNCLOS

---

213 See Guyana and Suriname Award, op. cit., p. 153, para. 461. Reference should, however, be made to para. 2 of Arts 74 and 83 of UNCLOS providing that '[i]f no agreement can be reached within a reasonable period of time, the States concerned shall resort to the procedures provided for in Part XV [Settlement of Disputes]'. See also S. Ramphal, *Triumph for UNCLOS; The Guyana-Suriname Maritime Arbitration,* London: Hansib Publications, 2008, pp. 283–293.

214 See Guyana and Suriname Award, op. cit., pp. 159–160, para. 477.

215 R. Churchill, 'Dispute Settlement under the UN Convention on the Law of the Sea: Survey for 2007', IJMCL, Vol. 23, No. 4, 2008, p. 601 at p. 639.

Articles 74(3) and 83(3), and further requests the Tribunal to order Myanmar to pay compensation to Bangladesh as appropriate.[216]

The specific duty of co-operation embodied in Articles 74(3) and 83(3) is therefore applicable to all coastal States although one can hardly miss the similarities with the various aspects of the general 'duty' of co-operation and co-ordination of activities embodied in Article 123 of UNCLOS. There is, however, an important legal difference between these provisions. Articles 74(3) and 83(3) of UNCLOS do not provide only for a good faith obligation to endeavour to co-operate but for a (legally) stricter duty according to which relevant States '*shall* make every effort to enter into provisional agreements of a practical nature pending delimitation and, during this transitional period, not to jeopardize or hamper the reaching of the final agreement'.

It should also be emphasized that the obligation for coastal States 'to make every effort to enter into provisional arrangements' on the basis of Article 74(3) does not only call for the conclusion of provisional arrangements of a practical nature regarding the 'exploitation of non-living resources of the sea-bed and subsoil' but obviously also for provisional arrangements relating to the 'exploitation and conservation of living resources' of the superjacent waters (e.g. joint fishing zones).[217] The latter two 'arrangements' have been in certain cases merged in order to form a 'joint development and fishing zone', while on (rare) occasions States have also formally agreed on 'joint EEZs'[218] as a provisional or even in certain cases as a permanent solution to their delimitation dispute.[219] In the absence of an *interim* agreement' on a 'joint EEZ', it is suggested that the interpretation and application of Article 74(3) (in the light of Part IX of UNCLOS) calls on States bordering enclosed or semi-enclosed seas to make every effort, in a spirit of understanding and co-operation, to enter also into

---

216 See Notifications under Art. 287 and Annex VII, Art. 1 of UNCLOS and the Statement of the Claim and Grounds on which it is based in the Dispute Concerning Delimitation of the Maritime Boundary between Bangladesh and Myanmar in the Bay of Bengal, Notification submitted by Bangladesh, 8 October 2009, para. 26. Both parties have later issued Declarations under Art. 287 of UNCLOS accepting the jurisdiction of ITLOS. See also Churchill, 'Dispute Settlement under the UN Convention on the Law of the Sea: Survey for 2009', op. cit., p. 465. The claim (compensation for violation of Arts 74(3) and 83(3) UNCLOS by Myanmar) was, however, not repeated in the Memorial of Bangladesh or in Bangladesh's Reply (Submissions). See ITLOS, Dispute concerning delimitation of the maritime boundary between Bangladesh and Myanmar in the Bay of Bengal (Bangladesh/Myanmar), Memorial of Bangladesh, 1 July 2010, and Reply of Bangladesh, 15 March 2011.
217 For an overview of the various possibilities regarding the establishment of joint fishing zones and an overview of State practice, see Kim, op. cit., pp. 108–132.
218 Ibid, pp. 132–141.
219 See the 'Joint Development and Fishing Zone' established with the 1993 'Maritime delimitation treaty between Jamaica and the Republic of Colombia' in the semi-enclosed Caribbean Sea which seems to be a *de facto* 'provisional' joint EEZ'. According to Art. 3(1) of the Agreement '"*[p]ending the determination of the jurisdictional limits of each party in the area designated below*", the Parties agree to establish therein a zone of joint management, control, exploration and exploitation of the living and non-living resources hereinafter called "The Joint Regime Area" [...]'. Emphasis added.

64 Extension of Coastal State Jurisdiction in Enclosed or Semi-enclosed Seas

'provisional arrangements of a practical nature relating to the protection and preservation of the marine environment of the disputed area' (e.g. joint ZEPs) and, if applicable, also into 'provisional arrangements with regard to the undertaking of marine scientific research programmes'.[220]

Furthermore, it is suggested that the interpretation of Article 15 of UNCLOS, in the light of Part IX of UNCLOS, seems to call on States bordering enclosed or semi-enclosed seas 'to make every effort to enter into provisional arrangements of a practical nature and, during this transitional period, not to jeopardize or hamper the reaching of the final agreement', also in cases where there is a pending delimitation of the territorial sea between two or more States, and particularly in cases where at least one involved State 'by reason of historic title or other special circumstances' does not agree with the median line as the 'provisional' delimitation.[221]

Besides agreements on joint development and/or joint zones (EEZs), an excellent example of a provisional arrangement of a practical nature pending delimitation of the maritime boundary is the Agreement on Provisional Arrangements for the Delimitation of the Maritime Boundaries between the Republic of Tunisia and the People's Democratic Republic of Algeria,[222] concluded on 11 February 2002. It is asserted that this Agreement could provide some guidance also to other Mediterranean States and other States bordering enclosed or semi-enclosed seas on how to provisionally solve their maritime delimitation issues, particularly in some geographically and/or politically complicated situations as it is indeed the case in some parts of the Adriatic Sea.[223]

2.4.2.5.1 2002 TUNISIA/ALGERIA AGREEMENT: APPLICATION OF ARTICLE 74(3) AND 83(3) OF UNCLOS IN THE LIGHT OF PART IX OF UNCLOS?

The Tunisia/Algeria *interim* Agreement represents not only one of the rare practical applications of Article 74(3) of UNCLOS in the context of the Mediterranean, but also in the broader context of enclosed or semi-enclosed seas.[224] In its Preamble, the Agreement makes express reference to Articles 74(3) and 83(3)

---

220 The 1978 Columbia/Dominican Republic Agreement provides for a joint zone that applies both to Fisheries and Marine Scientific Research (see Agreement on Delimitation of Marine and Submarine Areas and Maritime Cooperation between the Republic of Colombia and the Dominican Republic, 13 January 1978). For a discussion of the various arrangements of Japan and its neighboring States with regard to marine scientific research in areas where EEZ's claims of two States conflict, see A. Kanehara, 'A legal and practical arrangements of disputes concerning maritime boundaries pending their final solution and law enforcement: from a Japanese perspective', in N.A. Martínez Gutiérrez (ed.), op. cit., p. 95 at pp. 97–109.

221 See also the discussion in section 4.6. of the '2002 Protocol on the Interim Regime along the Southern Border between the Republic of Croatia and Serbia and Montenegro'. This agreement provisionally delimits the internal waters and territorial sea of the two States and provides for a *sui generis* regime of the disputed area.

222 LOS Bulletin, UN, No. 52, 2003, pp. 41–44.

223 Cf fn 221.

224 See nonetheless fn 219–221.

of UNCLOS, while in its main part it incorporates important provisions on co-operation and co-ordination of activities of the two States in different areas.[225]

Through this Agreement, the two States agreed on a provisional line of delimitation linking four points (P1–P4),[226] without however distinguishing between various zones of sovereignty, sovereign rights and jurisdiction. The direct result of such an approach is that the 'provisional line', which is actually a provisional single maritime boundary, is applicable both to the territorial sea, the continental shelf, the EEZ, fisheries protection zones and/or other functional zones of jurisdiction. This is clearly expressed in Article 3 of the Agreement which provides that:

> The Republic of Tunisia and the People's Democratic Republic of Algeria shall exercise their sovereignty, their sovereign rights and their jurisdiction east and west, respectively of this line.

Beyond the limits of the territorial sea, the agreed provisional line delimits the continental shelf and superjacent waters, and this both with regard to existing[227] and potential zones of jurisdiction. It is particularly interesting that there is a segment between points P3–P4 where Tunisia is entitled to exercise sovereign rights and jurisdiction in an area located in front of the Algerian coast – a solution which seems to have been influenced by the previously concluded 1971 Tunisia-Italy Shelf Delimitation Agreement.[228]

It should be emphasized, however, that the two States made it clear that such 'provisional arrangements' are without prejudice to the final delimitation of the maritime boundary between the two States and they also temporarily limited the duration of the provisional agreement to six years following the date of the exchange of the instruments of ratification.[229] At the end of this period, the parties undertook to conclude a final agreement on the delimitation of the maritime boundary, or alternatively to extend the period of validity of the Agreement or to revise it.[230]

The importance of this Agreement also lies in the fact that it seems to establish a link between Article 74(3) and the 'general policy of cooperation and coordination of activities' embodied in Part IX of UNCLOS. Although the 2002 Agreement does not make express reference to Part IX of UNCLOS (or its

---

225 Article 6.
226 See Figure 2.1.
227 Tunisian EEZ and the Fishing Zone of Algeria. See also section 3.3.4.
228 Point P4 coincides with point 1 of the 1971 (Italy-Tunisia) shelf agreement. See T. Scovazzi, 'Maritime Delimitations in the Mediterranean Sea', in J. Cordona Llorens (ed.), *Cursos Euromediterráneos Bancaja de Derecho Internacional*, Vol. VIII/IX, Castellón, 2004/2005, p. 357 at p. 419.
229 The instruments of ratifications were exchanged on 23 November 2003.
230 See the discussion in section 2.4.2.5.1. According to Slim and Scovazzi, Tunisia and Algeria reached in 2009 a final delimitation agreement based on the delimitation provided by the 2002 Agreement. See Slim and Scovazzi, op. cit. (Part 2), p. 11. The author was unable to consult the text of the agreement.

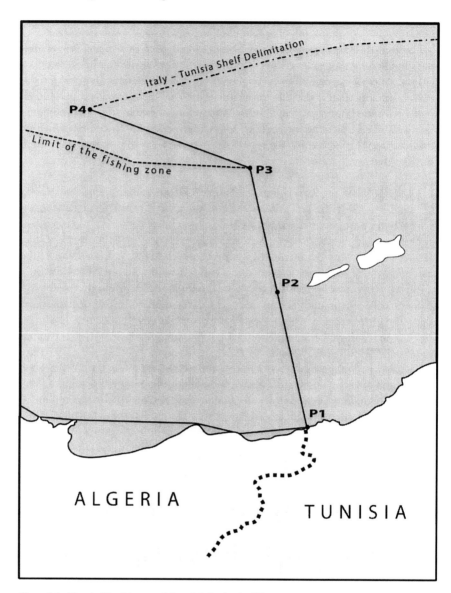

Figure 2.1 Algeria-Tunisia: provisional delimitation[231]

Article 123), the similarities with its drafting language and even more with its scope and objective are considerable. According to Article 6 of the Agreement the two Parties undertake *to co-operate and co-ordinate their activities* in the following areas: conservation of natural resources and in particular of living resources;

---

231 Modelled on a figure published in LOS Bulletin, UN, No. 52, 2003, p. 44.

search and rescue at sea; prevention and punishment of customs, sanitary and fiscal offences and of illegal immigration; prevention and punishment of illegal actions involving psychotropic substances, arms' trafficking and prevention of any act threatening the security of the two countries, and with regard to the application of conventional rules, particularly those concerning the safety of shipping and air traffic and protection of the marine environment.[232] In this respect, it is worth noting that the list of envisaged areas of co-operation provided by the 2002 Agreement is not limited to the three areas of co-operation expressly listed in the second element of Article 123 of UNCLOS.

The 2002 Agreement therefore represents an interesting example of a possible application of Articles 74(3) and 83(3) of UNCLOS in the light of Part IX of UNCLOS, and together with cases of joint development and/or joint zones of jurisdiction provides guidance to States bordering enclosed or semi-enclosed seas on how to provisionally solve their delimitation disputes pending the reaching of a final delimitation agreement. The discussion of the 2002 Agreement may accordingly serve also as a convenient introduction to our discussion in Chapter 3, which focusses on the recent process of extension of coastal State jurisdiction in the (enclosed or semi-enclosed) Adriatic and Mediterranean Seas.

2.5 Concluding remarks

It seems possible to conclude this chapter by arguing that States bordering enclosed and semi-enclosed seas are under a *bona fide* obligation to exercise their rights and perform their duties under UNCLOS in the light of the general duty (policy) of co-operation embodied in Part IX of UNCLOS. This assertion is *inter alia* based on the introductory element of Article 123 of UNCLOS which seems to provide a general good faith obligation for States bordering enclosed and/or semi-enclosed seas to endeavour to co-operate in the exercise of *all* their rights and in the performance of *all* their duties under UNCLOS, which also includes the exercise of their rights and performance of their duties regarding the delimitation and/or extension of coastal State jurisdiction in such seas. It is suggested that although such general obligation is not enforceable *per se*, it affects the way in which other articles of UNCLOS should be interpreted and applied by States bordering enclosed or semi-enclosed seas.

---

232 (Direct) There are no provisions, however, regarding co-operation in the field of marine scientific research.

3 Extension of coastal state jurisdiction in the Mediterranean: An Adriatic and EU perspective

This chapter provides an analysis of the recent trends in the field of extension of coastal State jurisdiction in the Mediterranean Sea where special attention is placed on the practice of Adriatic States regarding the proclamation of *sui generis* zones. This chapter seeks to determine whether those proclamations have created real *sui generis* zones or just 'mini EEZs', and studies the legal nature of the proclaimed zones and their relation with the EEZ. Particular attention is placed on the attitude of States regarding the proclamation and fixing of external limits (delimitation) of such zones, and on whether States have fulfilled their obligation to co-operate in this regard.

The chapter is divided into four sections: the first section offers a brief explanation of the *ipso facto* existence of the continental shelf and its influence on the legal regime and/or delimitation of superjacent waters; the second section deals with the recent practice of Adriatic and some Mediterranean States regarding the proclamation of *sui generis* zones of jurisdiction;[1] the third section deals with the recent practice of Mediterranean States regarding the proclamation of EEZs; and the fourth section focuses on the EU position on the matter throughout the last decade. The final aim of this chapter is to identify relevant trends at the Mediterranean and EU level which are likely to be reflected in the Adriatic Sea.

3.1 The continental shelf and the Mediterranean

The particular situation of the Mediterranean among the group of enclosed or semi-enclosed seas is particular not only because of its size and the status of an important international waterway, but also because of its hydrological and geological characteristics which in many aspects differ from other enclosed or semi-enclosed seas. Most areas of the Mediterranean Sea are quite deep, in most cases exceeding 1,000 m, and this still represents a considerable obstacle when it comes to the exploitation of the natural resources of its continental shelf.

---

1 An early version of the first two sections of Chapter 3 was published in M. Grbec, 'Extension of Coastal State Jurisdiction in the Mediterranean: Quasi EEZs or real *sui generis* zones?', in N.A. Martinez Gutiérrez (ed.), *Serving the Rule of International Maritime Law: Essays in Honour of Professor David Joseph Attard*, London and New York, NY: Routledge, 2010, pp. 181–202.

It is important to emphasize that the new regime of the EEZ as embodied in Part V of UNCLOS has not absorbed the continental shelf and that the two regimes coexist.[2] This was evidenced in the 1985 Libya/Malta Judgment where the ICJ held that the continental shelf and the EEZ coexist as two separate institutions as the latter has not absorbed the former,[3] and in the 2006 Arbitral Award in the dispute between Barbados and Trinidad and Tobago where the Arbitral Tribunal stated that '[...] the former does not displace the latter [...]'.[4] Among the many differences between the two regimes there is perhaps one which is crucial for a proper understanding of the legal relationship between the Mediterranean continental shelf and its superjacent waters. This difference, already mentioned in Chapter 2, arises from Article 77(3) of UNCLOS which provides that '[t]he rights of the coastal State over the continental shelf do not depend on occupation, effective or notional, or on any express proclamation'. Thus, unlike in the case of the EEZ which depends on an express proclamation, the rights over the continental shelf exist *ipso facto* and *ab initio*.[5] This means that each coastal State, if geographical circumstances so permit, has a continental shelf and the latter fact does not depend upon express proclamation, nor effective occupation.

In the geographical context of the Mediterranean Sea this means that the entire sea-bed and subsoil of the latter (including the seabed of the Adriatic Sea) is formed by the continental shelf of the coastal States and this independently of the legal status of the superjacent waters which may be that of high seas, EEZ, EFZ, or of one of the so-called *sui generis* zones.[6] As already emphasized, the prevalent position in the Mediterranean is still where the waters above the continental shelf have the status of 'high seas',[7] despite the fact that we have recently witnessed remarkable efforts by some Mediterranean States (including Adriatic coastal States) to extend their jurisdiction beyond the limits of the territorial sea.[8]

While stressing that the EEZ and the continental shelf remain independent regimes, it is necessary to also emphasize the close links between them. This coexistence between the two regimes is particularly felt in the case where a State proclaims its own EEZ in accordance with Article 56(3) of UNCLOS. In such a case the rights of the coastal State in the EEZ with respect to the sea-bed and

---

2 For an analysis on the relationship between the two zones, see D. Attard, *Exclusive Economic Zone in International Law*, Oxford: Clarendon Press, 1987, pp. 129–136.

3 Continental Shelf (Libyan Arab Jamahiriya/Malta), ICJ Reports 1985, p. 13, para. 33.

4 Award of the Arbitral Tribunal in the Matter of An Arbitration between Barbados and The Republic of Trinidad and Tobago (Barbados/Trinidad Tobago), The Hague, 11 April 2006, RIAA, Vol. XXVII, p. 147, para. 234.

5 See Attard, op. cit., p. 141. Sea also the North Sea Continental Shelf Cases, Judgment, ICJ Reports 1969, p. 3, para. 19.

6 See sections 3.2–3.3. As explained in Chapter 1, there is no space for an 'International Area' in the Mediterranean Sea, including the Adriatic. See section 1.1.

7 T. Treves, 'Potential Exclusive Economic Zones in the Mediterranean', paper delivered at the 11th Mediterranean Research Meeting Florence and Montecatini Terme, 24–27 March 2010, p. 4.

8 Cf fn 6.

70 Extension of Coastal State Jurisdiction in Enclosed or Semi-enclosed Seas

subsoil shall be exercised in accordance with Part VI of UNCLOS. There is, however, no legal need for the boundaries of the two zones to coincide, although this has recently been a widespread practice.[9]

As pointed out by Treves, in the absence of EEZs (and/or *sui generis* zones) the existence of the continental shelf of States surrounding the Mediterranean (and Adriatic) affects the exercise of the high seas' freedoms by other States. This is due to the fact that their exercise has to be reconciled with the exclusive sovereign rights of the coastal State(s) on their continental shelf.[10] Treves furthermore opines that the exercise of high seas' freedoms by other States may in certain cases interfere with the 'legitimate expectations of the coastal States regarding their EEZ rights'.[11] While there may be some perplexities regarding the latter statement,[12] it suffices here to reiterate regarding the former that the freedoms to lay submarine cables and pipelines and to construct artificial islands and other installations permitted under international law on the high seas are also subject to Part VI of UNCLOS.[13] It is therefore possible to support Treves' assertion that:

> [...] activities that belong to the freedom of the high seas when conducted in the high seas of the Mediterranean [...] are not as free as they would be if they were conducted on the high seas whose bottom lies beyond the limits of national jurisdiction [...]'.[14]

---

9 As the ICJ observed:

> [...] the concept of a single maritime boundary does not steam from multilateral treaty law but from State practice, and that finds its explanation in the wish of States to establish one uninterrupted boundary line delimiting the various partially coincident zones of maritime jurisdiction appertaining to them. (Maritime Delimitation and Territorial Questions between Qatar and Bahrain (*Qatar v Bahrain*), ICJ Reports, 2001, p. 40, para. 173).

10 Treves for example questioned whether '[...] research on the impact of sea-floor vents on water temperature and currents is shelf research or water column research [...]' and pointed at the problems of 'deep sea fisheries' whose main characteristic is that they are conducted with gear that is likely to come into contact with the sea floor. He concluded that: 'The exercise of the freedom of deep-sea fishing [including in the Adriatic] cannot be undertaken [*sic*] without taking into due consideration that there is an environmental interest (as well as a resource interest concerning sedentary species) of the coastal State'. See Treves, op. cit., pp. 7–8.

11 Treves proposed the following 'formula': 'Third States may consider potential EEZs as high seas as regards freedoms of the high seas set out in Article [*sic*] 58 UNCLOS. As regards activities that are free but may in the future fall under the coastal States' jurisdiction, they should behave in such a way as not to jeopardize the legitimate expectations of the coastal States'. See Treves, op. cit., p. 9. See also I. Vella, 'A new advent for renewable offshore resources', in N.A. Martínez Gutiérrez (ed.), op. cit., p. 136 at pp. 144–153.

12 Although it would be possible to agree with such a statement on a 'declaratory level' the problem seems to be the definition of 'the legitimate expectations of the coastal States' in any particular case. Would that mean that Italian fishermen are not to be allowed to fish for (potentially) endangered species on the Adriatic high seas just in order to safeguard the future 'legitimate expectations' of, for example, Croatian or Montenegrin fishermen? From the legal point of view the answer seems to be negative.

13 Article 87(c)–(d) of UNCLOS.

14 Treves, op. cit., p. 8. On this point see also J. Juste Ruiz, 'Mediterranean Cooperation and Third States', paper delivered at the 11th Mediterranean Research Meeting Florence and Montecatini Terme, 24–27 March 2010, p. 5.

3.1.1 Delimitation of the Mediterranean continental shelf

It is possible to claim that numerous problems encountered by the Mediterranean States while trying to delimit their continental shelf have played a part in the decision of the majority of Mediterranean States not to extend their jurisdiction beyond the limits of its territorial sea.[15] It has been calculated by Leanza that for a complete delimitation of the Mediterranean continental shelf 30 delimitation agreements would be necessary, while up to the present day only ten or so such agreements have been signed and entered into force (coupled with some provisional agreements).[16] In this respect it is noteworthy that almost half of the final shelf delimitation agreements were concluded by Italy with its maritime neighbours – former SFRY, Tunisia, Spain, Greece and Albania[17] – and that a great majority of them, with the exception of the 1992 Shelf Agreement with Albania, were concluded in the period between 1968 and 1977, at a time when the concept of the EEZ had not fully crystallized into a principle of customary international law. It is nonetheless important to emphasize that through the concluded agreements with the former SFRY and Albania, Italy has (almost) completely delimited the continental shelf of the Adriatic with the two opposite States.[18]

Additionally, France in 1984 delimited its territorial sea and continental shelf with Monaco[19] where it was also agreed that the boundary line for the shelf will be applicable also in case of an eventual proclamation of an EEZ or similar zone of jurisdiction.[20] The latter was the first delimitation agreement in the Mediterranean involving a single maritime boundary for all zones of jurisdiction, *actual and potential*, and the Principality of Monaco is the only State in the Mediterranean to have definitely resolved all its maritime delimitation issues with its neighbouring States. In the central Mediterranean, two partial delimitation

---

15 See the discussion in section 3.2.

16 U. Leanza, *Il regime giuridico internazionale del mare Mediterraneo, Studi e documenti di diritto internazionale e comunitario*, No. 44, Napoli: Editioriale Scientifica, 2008, p. 125.

17 For the text and an assessment of the agreements concluded by Italy, see G. Francalanci and P. Presciuttini, *A History of the Treaties and Negotiations for the Delimitation of the Continental Shelf and Territorial Waters between Italy and the Nations of the Mediterranean (1966–1992)*, Genova: Istituto Idrografico della Marina, 2000.

18 The only undelimited part of the Adriatic continental shelf affecting Italy is the 'tripoint' between Italy-Albania and nowadays Montenegro. For an assessment of the 1968 Italy-SFRY and of the 1992 Italy-Albania Shelf Agreements, see Francalanci and Presciuttini, ibid, pp. 15–39 and pp. 167–175. See also T. Scovazzi, 'The Delimitation of National Coastal Zones: The Agreements Concluded by Italy', paper delivered at the 11th Mediterranean Research Meeting Florence and Montecatini Terme, 24–27 March 2010, pp. 8–10 and pp. 22–23, and Leanza, op. cit., pp. 125–137. The 1968 Italy-SFRY Shelf Agreement represents the agreed shelf boundary between Italy and the States successors of the former SFRY. The lateral (shelf) boundaries between the States successors of the latter have not been delimited yet and the sole existence of the Slovenian right to its own continental shelf is disputed by Croatia. See the discussion in section 3.3.4–3.3.6, and Figure 3.4.

19 Convention on Maritime Delimitation between the Government of His Most Serene Highness the Prince of Monaco and the Government of the French Republic, 16 February 1984.

20 This is implied from Art. 2 which provides that '[t]he limits of the maritime areas situated beyond the territorial sea of Monaco *over which the Principality of Monaco exercises or shall exercise sovereign rights* in accordance with international law shall be the following: [...]'. Emphasis added. Ibid. See Figure 3.2.

72 Extension of Coastal State Jurisdiction in Enclosed or Semi-enclosed Seas

agreements have been concluded on the basis of the 1982 and 1985 ICJ Judgments between Tunisia and Libya[21] and Libya and Malta,[22] while in 2002, as discussed, a (provisional) delimitation agreement was agreed between Algeria and Tunisia, which provides for a single maritime boundary for both the shelf and superjacent waters (independently of their legal status).[23]

Lastly, three recent Delimitation Agreements have been concluded in the Eastern Mediterranean between Egypt and Cyprus in 2003,[24] Cyprus and Lebanon in 2007[25] and Cyprus and Israel in 2010[26] which, however, regulate the delimitation of their potential EEZs and not only of the continental shelf. Similarly, on 27 April 2009 Albania and Greece signed an Agreement between the Hellenic Republic and the Republic of Albania on the delimitation of their Respective Continental Shelf Areas and Other Maritime Zones to which they are entitled under International Law.[27] Also the latter agreement aims at delimiting the 'present' and 'future' maritime areas of the two States in the Ionian and to a shorter extent also in the Adriatic Sea (Strait of Otranto).

The aforesaid Agreements are interesting as they tried to delimit potential, rather than existing, EEZs. At the time of the conclusion of the Delimitation Agreement between Egypt and Cyprus in 2003, Cyprus did not have a proclaimed EEZ,[28] while the position of Egypt was not completely clear.[29] The same situation

---

21 Agreement between the Libyan Arab Socialist People's Jamahiriya and the Republic of Tunisia to Implement the Judgment of the International Court of Justice in the Tunisia/Libya Continental Shelf Case, 8 August 1988.

22 Agreement between the Great Socialist People's Libyan Arab Jamahiriya and the Republic of Malta implementing Article III of the Special Agreement and the Judgment of the International Court of Justice, 10 November 1986.

23 See section 2.4.2.5.1.

24 Agreement between the Republic of Cyprus and the Arab Republic of Egypt on the Delimitation of the Exclusive Economic Zone, 17 February 2003, LOS Bulletin, UN, No. 52, 2003, p. 45.

25 Not yet in force. Unofficial text of the Lebanon/Cyprus Agreement published in T. Scovazzi and I. Papanicolopulu, 'Cyprus Lebanon (Report Number 8–19)', in D.A. Colson and R.W. Smith (eds), *International Maritime Boundaries*, Vol. VI, ASIL, Leiden and Boston, MA: Martinus Nijhoff Publishers, 2011, p. 4445 at pp. 4452–4454. See also H. Slim and T. Scovazzi, 'Study of the current status of ratification, implementation and compliance with maritime agreements and conventions applicable to the Mediterranean Sea Basin: With a specific focus on the ENPI South Partner Countries', Part II, Regional Report, AGRECO Consortium, 2009, p. 11.

26 Agreement between the Government of the State of Israel and the Government of the Republic of Cyprus on the Delimitation of the Exclusive Economic Zone, 17 December 2010. Entry into force: 25 February 2011, LOS Bulletin, UN, No. 75, 2011, pp. 27–31.

27 Not yet in force. See unofficial text and general discussion of the signed agreement in T. Scovazzi and I. Papanicolopulu, 'Albania/Greece (Report Number 8–21)', in Colson and Smith (eds), op. cit., p. 4462. Scovazzi and Papanicolopulu made reference to the judgment of the Constitutional Court of Albania, dated 15 April 2010 which preceded the process of ratification by Albania. The Constitutional Court ruled out that the 2009 Agreement is subject to procedural and substantive violations of the Albanian Constitution and UNCLOS. Ibid, p. 4463. It is, accordingly, unlikely that Albania will ratify the 2009 Agreement in the near future.

28 Cyprus has on 2 April 2004, after the stipulation of the Delimitation Agreement with Egypt, adopted 'A Law to Provide for the Proclamation of the Exclusive Economic Zone by the Republic of Cyprus'. See LOS Bulletin, No. 55, UN, 2004, pp. 22–24. The 2003 Delimitation Agreement then entered into force on 7 April 2004. Cf fn 24. See also section 3.4.1.

29 Upon ratification of UNCLOS, Egypt declared that '[t]he Arab Republic of Egypt will exercise from this day the rights attributed to it by the provisions of Parts V and VI of the United Nations

Extension of jurisdiction in the Mediterranean Seas 73

occurred in 2007 with Lebanon,[30] in 2009 with Greece and Albania[31] and in 2010 with Israel.[32] For the later group of agreements it is characteristics that they attempt to delimit both the continental shelf and potential future zones (including the EEZ) of the States involved.[33]

Considering that Article 89 of UNCLOS provides that '[n]o State may validly purport to subject any part of the high seas to its sovereignty', it is argued that the provision should also be applicable to the exercise of sovereign rights and jurisdiction over that part of the sea beyond the limits of the territorial seas of a coastal State, but within the 200 nmi from the baselines, in the absence of an express proclamation of an EEZ or a similar (e.g. *sui generis*) zone.[34] The sole delimitation of 'potential' zones of jurisdiction does not in itself represent an automatic proclamation of such zone, nor the entry into force of the regime of the zone or zone(s) in question.

It is suggested that the importance of such *all purpose* delimitation agreements (including in the Mediterranean and Adriatic) may be at least twofold. On the one hand such agreements delimit the existing (actual) maritime zones of the States concerned (i.e. internal waters, territorial sea and the continental shelf), while on the other hand they provide for a (future) *single* maritime boundary for *actual* and

---

Convention on the Law of the Sea in the exclusive economic zone situated beyond and adjacent to its territorial sea in the Mediterranean Sea and in the Red Sea [...].' See LOS Bulletin, UN, No. 3, 1984, p. 14. It was, however, doubtful whether such declaration established an EEZ. See A. Del Vecchio Capotosti, 'In Maiore Stat Minus: A note on the EEZ and the Zones of Ecological Protection in the Mediterranean Sea', ODIL, Vol. 39, No. 3, 2008, p. 287 at p. 289.

30 It was only on 18 August 2011 that Lebanon formally proclaimed its EEZ through the adoption of a framework law. See Law No. 163 dated 18 August 2011 (Delineation and declaration of the maritime regions of the Republic of Lebanon), and T. Scovazzi, 'Maritime Boundaries in the Eastern Mediterranean Sea', Policy Brief, Mediterranean Policy Program, Washington, DC: The German Marshal Fund of the United States, June 2012, p. 6. See also Decree No. 6433 (Delineation of the boundaries of the exclusive economic zone of Lebanon), 16 November 2011. Previously, on 15 July 2010, Lebanon deposited with the Secretary-General, pursuant to Art. 75(2) of UNCLOS, charts and a list of geographical co-ordinates of points defining the Southern Limits of Lebanon's exclusive economic zone (Lebanon/Palestine) *based on the median line*. See LOS Bulletin, UN, No. 73, pp. 39–42. In addition, on 19 October 2010 Lebanon deposited charts and list of geographical co-ordinates of points defining the 'Southern part of the Western Median Line of Lebanon's exclusive economic zone'. See LOS Bulletin UN, No. 74, 2010, pp. 30–31.

31 On 4 April 2002 Albania adopted its law on the coast guard which seemed to represent a framework law for the proclamation of the Albanian EEZ. The latter should (provisionally) extend up to the median line with Italy. No national legislative action has followed since. Quoted in Del Vecchio Capotosti, op. cit., p. 289. Cf fn 27.

32 Cf fn 26.

33 The Preamble to the 2009 Albania/Greece Agreement is clear in this regard and provides as follows:

[...] AWARE of the need to delimit precisely the maritime spaces over which the two countries exercise *or shall exercise* sovereignty, sovereign rights and jurisdiction in accordance with international law [...].

Emphasis added. Cf fn 27.

The second Paragraph of the Preamble also made clear what was the main purpose of the agreement. It provides as follows: 'RECOGNIZING *in particular the importance of the delimitation of the continental shelf* for the purpose of development of both countries [...]'. Emphasis added.

34 See also Grbec, op. cit., p. 186.

74 *Extension of Coastal State Jurisdiction in Enclosed or Semi-enclosed Seas*

potential zones of sovereign rights and jurisdiction (e.g. EEZ, EFZ, ZEP). As such they may help improve legal certainty, prevent future conflicting claims and eventually facilitate the overall co-operation of coastal and third States in the governance of such seas.[35] The conclusion of such agreements may be furthermore seen as an expression of the 'legitimate expectations of the coastal States regarding their EEZ rights'[36] and/or the expression of their intention to proclaim an EEZ or *sui generis* zone in the (near) future, extending up to the agreed delimitation line. It is finally asserted that the sole signature of such delimitation agreement (also in the absence of its entry into force) may, and ultimately should, influence the future maritime claims of the signatory states on the basis of the relevant provision of VCLT.[37]

Thus, bearing in mind that the EEZ does not exist *ipso facto* and *ab initio*, Mediterranean and Adriatic States have, particularly during the last decade felt compelled to proclaim different maritime zones to safeguard their national interests. What follows is a discussion of the different proclamations and their compatibility with UNCLOS in general and with the 'general policy of co-operation and consultation' embodied in Part IX of UNCLOS in particular.

3.2 The Mediterranean *status quo* (jurisdictional landscape)

It is interesting to note that up to the late 1990s the majority of Mediterranean States (including all Adriatic States) had refrained from proclaiming an EEZ or even a fishery zone along their Mediterranean coast. It was most likely felt by the bordering States that an act of extension of jurisdiction in such a restricted space as the Mediterranean would provoke tensions and possible political problems with neighbouring States.[38] A factor which may have played a role in determining such an attitude of self-restraint was also the inclination of some Mediterranean States to give priority to interests such as free access to fisheries or mobility of commercial and military ships;[39] coupled with the fact that the

---

35 See Introduction, section III. Such agreements affect the rights (maritime claims) of third States. A notable example is represented by the recently concluded maritime delimitation agreements by Cyprus with its neighbouring States (Egypt, Lebanon and Israel) in the Eastern Mediterranean. See Scovazzi, op. cit., pp. 8–9, and the discussion in section 3.4.1.

36 Cf fn 11.

37 Article 18 of VCLT (*Obligation not to defeat the object and purpose of a treaty prior to its entry into force*) provides that '[a] State is *obliged to refrain from acts which would defeat the object and purpose of a treaty* when: (a) it has signed the treaty or has exchanged instruments constituting the treaty subject to ratification, acceptance or approval, *until it shall have made its intention clear not to become a party to the treaty*; or (b) it has expressed its consent to be bound by the treaty, pending the entry into force of the treaty and provided that such entry into force is not unduly delayed.' Emphasis added. Cf fn 25 and 27.

38 See section 1.1.

39 See T. Scovazzi, 'Maritime Delimitations in the Mediterranean Sea', in J. Cordona Llorens (ed.), *Cursos Euromediterráneos Bancaja de Derecho Internacional*, Vol. VIII/IX, Castellón, 2004/2005, p. 356 at p. 366.

Mediterranean fishing fleets have been, with the partial exception of the Spanish and Italian, prevalently 'artisanal' in nature.

The attitude of some Mediterranean States in the past, particularly of Spain and France, is quite interesting. In 1976 France adopted a law whereby it established an EEZ off the French coast bordering the North Sea, the English Channel, and the Atlantic from the French-Belgian border to the French-Spanish border, without however extending it to its Mediterranean coast.[40] Spain, similarly, when establishing its EEZ in 1977 did not apply it to its Mediterranean coasts[41] while a number of Adriatic States like Italy, SFRY and Albania did not proclaim an EEZ – or an EFZ – of their own.[42] Some other States like Morocco[43] and Egypt[44] formally proclaimed their EEZs without implementing them in the Mediterranean Sea. Other States like Tunisia,[45] Malta[46] and Algeria[47] limited their claims to relatively narrower EFZ, which with the exception of the Tunisian claim[48] have not affected the interests of neighbouring States. An interesting example is represented by Algeria, whose limits of its 'Reserved Fishing Zone' do not reach the median line.[49]

Overall, there seems to have been a sort of 'tacit agreement' between Mediterranean States, not to establish EEZs or other *sui generis* zones based on the concept of the EEZ in the Mediterranean, as long as other States would refrain from doing the same. What was also clear is that from the standpoint

---

40 *Loi no. 76-655 du 16 juillet 1976 relative à la zone économique au large des côtes du territoire de la République*, OGFR, No. 17, 18 July 1976. It was only on 12 October 2012 that France extended its (full) EEZ along its Mediterranean coasts. See section 3.3.2.

41 Cf fn 51.

42 See Grbec, op. cit., p. 187. Cf fn 27 and 31.

43 In 1981 Morocco proclaimed a 200 nmi EEZ which in principle applies to both Atlantic and the Mediterranean coast (Act No. 1-81 of 18 December 1980, Promulgated by Dahir No. 1-81-179 of 8 April 1981). Morocco, however, has not adopted any implementing legislation applicable to its Mediterranean EEZ, nor has it entered into any kind of delimitation negotiations with neighboring Mediterranean States. See also C. Chevalier, 'Governance of the Mediterranean Sea: Outlook for the Legal Regime', IUCN Malaga: Centre for Mediterranean Cooperation, 2005, p. 44.

44 Cf fn 29.

45 In 1951 Tunisia claimed an EFZ which is bordered for approximately half of its length by the 50 m isobath; a *unicum* in the practice of States on maritime delimitation. See Art. 3(b) of Decree of 26 July 1951 as modified by Law No. 63-49 of 30 December 1963. The result of the application of such method was that the external border of such zone was in certain points more than 70 nmi from the Tunisian coast and only 15 nmi from the Italian island of Lampedusa. See U. Leanza, *Il regime giuridico internazionale del mare Mediterraneo, Studi e documenti di diritto internazionale e comunitario*, No. 44, Napoli: Editoriale Scientifica, 2008, pp. 178–179.

46 In 1971 Malta proclaimed a 12 nmi fishing zone, extended in 1975 to 20 nmi and finally in 1978 to 25 nmi. See section 3 subsection (2) of Act XXXII of 10 December 1971 as amended. See also the discussion in section 3.4.5.

47 Legislative Decree No. 94-13 of 17 Dhu'lhijjah 1414, corresponding to 28 May 1994, establishing the general rules relating to fisheries. According to Art. 6 '[a] reserved fishing zone located beyond and adjacent to the national territorial waters is hereby established. The breadth of the zone measured from the baseline shall be *32 nautical miles* between the western maritime border and Ras Ténès and *52 nautical miles* between Ras Ténès and the eastern maritime border'. Emphasis added. See Figure 2.1, and the discussion in section 2.4.2.5.1.

48 Cf fn 45.

49 Cf fn 47.

76 *Extension of Coastal State Jurisdiction in Enclosed or Semi-enclosed Seas*

of international law there were no legal restriction for the proclamation of EEZs or similar zones[50] and it was also predictable that in the case of extension of jurisdiction by one State others would follow suit. It may be argued that the Mediterranean *status quo* was terminated on 1 August 1997 when the Council of Ministers of Spain approved Royal Decree No. 1315/1997,[51] through which a Spanish FPZ was established in the Mediterranean, extending from Cabo the Gata to the French border.[52] Such 'termination' was ultimately confirmed in 2003 with the adoption of the framework law and the subsequent proclamation of the French Mediterranean ZEP.[53] The restrain towards proclaiming full EEZs,[54] however, still persists in certain parts of the Mediterranean and seems to be particularly accentuated in the Adriatic Sea.

3.3 Extension of coastal state jurisdiction in the Mediterranean and Adriatic: *sui generis zones* or *quasi* EEZs?

It is suggested that the French and Spanish proclamations are important as they set a 'precedent' followed also by Adriatic States (Croatia, Slovenia, Italy) to proclaim zones of functional jurisdiction which are based on the EEZs, but are not EEZs proper (*sui generis* zones).[55] It should be noted that both Spain and France expressly based their proclamations on their right to proclaim a full EEZ.

3.3.1 Fisheries protection zone (Spain)

As early as in 1978, under Act No. 15 of 1978,[56] Spain had proclaimed an EEZ applicable to the Spanish coast facing the Atlantic Ocean and the Bay of Biscay. The law provided for its future application also to other areas of the Spanish coast, and the 1997 Decree is a manifestation of this power.[57] From the general

---

50 See, however, the discussion in section 2.4.2.2.
51 Royal Decree No. 1315/1997, OGKS No. 204, 26 August 1997. See LOS Bulletin, UN, No. 36, 1997, p. 47.
52 See section 3.3.1. During the same year, the joint declaration of Algeria, Egypt, Libya, Morocco and Syria at the 22nd Session of the GFCM called on Mediterranean States to '[…] urgently take steps to formulate a unified position towards this crucial question, by […] determining, speedily, practical measures, to raise again the question of establishing exclusive economic zones in the Mediterranean'. See GFCM, Report of the Twenty-Second Session, Rome, 1997, p. 49. See also Scovazzi, 'Maritime delimitations in the Mediterranean Sea', op. cit., p. 367.
53 See section 3.3.2, and fn 40.
54 Scovazzi termed such restraint the 'EEZ phobia'. See Scovazzi, 'Maritime delimitations in the Mediterranean Sea', op. cit., p. 365.
55 For a discussion on the legality of the establishment of *sui generis* zones from the standpoint of contemporary international law (law of the sea), see section 6.1.
56 OGKS, No. 46 of 23 February 1978.
57 According to para. 8 of the general provisions '[…] in exercise of the authority given by the first final provision of Act 15/1978, of 20th February, on the economic zone, it is deemed necessary to establish in the Mediterranean Sea a fisheries protection zone between Cabo the Gata and the French border […]'.

Extension of jurisdiction in the Mediterranean Seas 77

provisions of the Spanish Decree it is evident that the main reason for the proclamation of the Spanish zone in the Mediterranean was the fear of overexploitation of fisheries resources along its coast, particularly by distant water fleets (e.g. South Korea and Japan fishing for Atlantic tuna)[58] which necessitated the taking of appropriate resource conservation policy measures. Taking such measures would be more difficult or impossible to implement, if the measures were to be restricted to only the 12 miles of the territorial sea. The Decree furthermore makes reference to the fact that the EU conservation and control measures (EU rules and policies, e.g. CFP) are not generally applicable beyond 12 nmi measured from the baseline of the coastal States to vessels flying other flags[59] and to the need to maintain and preserve a labour-intensive, small-scale Spanish fleet in the Mediterranean. The latter are important considerations when it comes to the assessment of the recent attitude of Mediterranean EU Member States with regard to the extension of coastal State jurisdiction.[60]

The legal nature of the Spanish zone may be best seen from a comparison of the relevant elements of Article 56 of UNCLOS and Article 2 of the Decree. According to the latter:

> In the said zone, the Kingdom of Spain shall have sovereign rights for purposes of conservation of living marine resources, as well as for the management and control of fishery activity, without prejudice to the measures for protection and conservation of resources that have been or may be enacted by the European Union.

The scope of application of the Spanish Mediterranean zone is therefore narrower than an EEZ, as in the latter Spain does not exercise sovereign rights with regard to 'other activities for the economic exploitation and exploration of the zone, such as the production of energy from the water, currents and winds',[61] nor jurisdiction as provided for in the relevant provisions of UNCLOS with regard to '(i) the establishment and use of artificial islands, installations and structures; (ii) marine scientific research; (iii) the protection and preservation of the marine environment'.[62] The relevant provisions to be compared are, therefore, Article 2 of the 1997 Decree and Article 56(1)(a) of UNCLOS. Even in this case the Spanish Decree seems to be narrower than Article 56 of UNCLOS. While the first part of Article 56(1)(a) makes reference to 'sovereign

---

58 See Leanza, op. cit., p. 183.
59 Spain wanted to extend the EU standards in the matter, including conservation standards (the EU Common Fisheries Policy), to the newly established zone. See also the discussion in section 3.5.1.
60 See also the discussion in M. Reisman and M.H. Arsanjani, 'Some Reflections on the Effect of Artisanal Fishing on Maritime Boundary Delimitation', in M.T. Ndiaye and R. Wolfrum (eds), *Law of the Sea, Environmental Law and Settlement of Disputes: Liber Amicorum Judge Thomas A. Mensah*, Leiden and Boston, MA: Martinus Nijhoff Publishers, 2007, pp. 629–665.
61 See Art. 56(1)(a) of UNCLOS.
62 See Art. 56(1)(b)(i–iii) of UNCLOS.

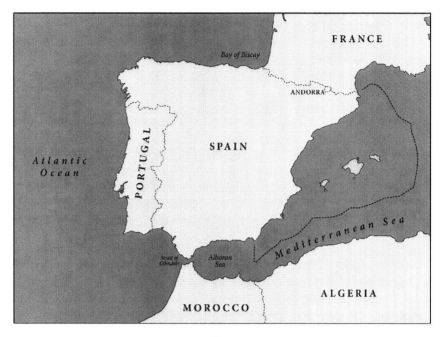

Figure 3.1 Outer limits of the Spanish FPZ[63]

rights for the purpose of exploring and exploiting, conserving and managing the (living) natural resources', Article 2 of the Spanish Decree makes reference to 'sovereign rights for purposes of conservation of living marine resources, as well as for the management and control of fishery activities'. It seems that the emphasis is slightly more on the 'management and control of fishery activities itself' than on the 'management of the living resources' and this also makes the Spanish zone similar or equivalent to an EFZ.[64] It should be noted, however, that Spain based the proclamation of its FPZ on the authority given by its Act 15/1978 on the EEZ, while the EFZ is regulated by customary international law.[65]

Two observations must be made with regard to the limits of the zone (see Figure 3.1). First, Spain showed self-restraint, as it did not extend the zone in that part of the sea overlooking the coasts of Morocco.[66] Second, with regard to France and Algeria, the method of equidistance was used. This triggered protests

63 Modelled on a figure published in LOS Bulletin, UN, No. 43, 2000, p. 104.
64 See also S. Kvinikhidze, 'Contemporary Exclusive Fishery Zones or Why Some States Still Claim an EFZ', IJMCL, No. 23, 2008, p. 271 at p. 273.
65 U. Leanza, '*L'Italia e la scelta di rafforzare la tutela del ambiente marino: L'istituzione di zone di protezione ecologica*', *Rivista di diritto internazionale*, Vol. LXXXIX, No. 2, Milano: Giuffrè, 2006, p. 309 at p. 314.
66 A proclamation of the Spanish FPZ in that part of the sea overlooking the coasts of Morocco (Alboran Sea) would have most likely triggered serious delimitation issues with Morocco, mostly due to the presence of the Spanish 'enclaves' on the Moroccan coasts and Spanish islands and islets in the close proximity. See F.A. Anish, *The International Law of Maritime Boundaries and the Practice of States in the Mediterranean Sea*, Oxford: Clarendon Press, 1993, pp. 278–285.

by France, a country which is known not to accept equidistance as a method for the delimitation of its EEZ and/or continental shelf along its coast in the Mediterranean.[67] According to the *Statement of position of the French Government with respect to the Spanish communication concerning the deposit of a list of geographical co-ordinates* of the FPZ:

> The French Government wishes to *protest against the part of this declaration that relates to the line delimiting the edge of the Spanish fisheries zone facing the French coasts.* It protests against this delimitation initiative conducted by Spain. In any event, it considers that the delimitation resulting from the line joining points specified in the Spanish communication cannot be invoked against it. The French Government recalls on this occasion that under international public law, the delimitation of the boundary must take place by agreement. *Moreover, in this specific case of a maritime boundary, such delimitation must result in an equitable solution, thus ruling out in this instance the use of the equidistant line employed by the Spanish side.*[68]

From the *Note Verbale* it is clear that, while France did not dispute the validity of the proclamation of the zone by Spain, as such, it was opposed to Spain's unilateral delimitation being based on the principle of equidistance. This might have been also due to the fact that the external limits of the Spanish FPZ appear *prima facie* not just provisional, pending delimitation agreements with neighbouring (affected) States, but (at least in the view of the Spanish) permanent.[69]

Italy, like France, shortly after the Spanish proclamation, protested against the unilateral delimitation by Spain, and it is suggested by Andreone that the formal protest of Italy was at the origin of the 'correction of the technical errors'[70] to the list of geographical co-ordinates provided and published by Spain in 1998.[71] According to Andreone, the new list of co-ordinates was first forwarded to Italy with a Spanish *Note Verbale* dated 19 May 1999[72] and only a couple of months later (13 April 2000) to the UN Secretary-General. For the purpose of this work it is

---

67 See 'List of geographical coordinates of points constituting the delimitation made by Spain of the Fisheries Protection Zone in the Mediterranean Sea, established by Royal Decree 1315/1997 of 1 August', LOS Bulletin, UN, No. 37, 1998, pp. 80–81. There is no mention to the fact that the list is provisional pending agreements with affected States.

68 Emphasis added. LOS Bulletin, UN, No. 38, 1998, p. 54.

69 Ibid.

70 See Spain; 'List of geographical coordinates defining the limits set by Spain for the Fisheries Protection Zone established by Decree No. 1313/1997 of 1 August 1997', LOS Bulletin, UN, No. 43, 2000, pp. 101–104. According to its second paragraph:

> Since a *number of technical errors* were discovered in the list, the Spanish authorities have corrected those errors *on the basis of the principle of equidistance,* hence the need to deposit the corrected list, which is transmitted with this note.

> Emphasis added. See also G. Andreone, '*La Zona Ecologica Italiana*', Il Diritto Marittimo, Anno CIX-Terza Serie, Vol. I, January–March, Genova, 2007, p. 1 at 7, fn 12.

71 Cf fn 67.

72 Note Verbale No. 177/18, Ministry of Foreign Affairs (Spain), 19 May 1999. See Andreone, op. cit., p. 7, fn 12.

80 *Extension of Coastal State Jurisdiction in Enclosed or Semi-enclosed Seas*

particularly relevant that Italy, with a *Note Verbale* sent from its Ministry of Foreign Affairs on 13 December 1999, accepted the 'provisional' modified limits of the Spanish zone under two conditions: (a) *there is an express understanding that the provisional limits of the Spanish FPZ do not coincide with the limits agreed with the 1974 continental shelf Agreement between the two States*; and (b) Italy reserves the right to ask for a different line of delimitation after the extension of its jurisdiction beyond 12 nmi.[73] It may thus be implied that at least regarding Italy, the list of co-ordinates represents a 'temporary line of delimitation'.

Algeria, on the other hand, has not protested formally and this may be also due to the fact that there is still a corridor of 'high seas' between the Algerian 'Reserved Fishing Zone'[74] and the Spanish FPZ. Overall, it seems possible to conclude that Spain did not endeavour to co-operate with other potentially affected States regarding (the modalities of) its extension of jurisdiction in the Mediterranean,[75] nor – at least before the formal proclamation of its FPZ – made every effort to enter into provisional arrangements of a practical nature pending agreement on a final delimitation.[76]

The proclamation of a Spanish zone triggered reactions from other Mediterranean States and together with two environmental disasters, *Erika* and *Prestige*, in front or adjacent to the French Atlantic coast – contributed to another cornerstone in the process of extension of coastal State jurisdiction in the Mediterranean Sea; the adoption of the Framework Law in 2003[77] and the actual institution by Decree[78] in 2004 of a ZEP along the French coast in the Mediterranean. The main aim of the French move was to extend the French jurisdiction regarding the preservation and protection of the marine environment to the area beyond the French territorial waters, which up until then were under the regime of the 'high seas'.

3.3.2 *Zone of ecological protection (France)*[79]

The first possible conclusion to be drawn from the text of the Framework Law and the 2004 Decree is that the French Mediterranean ZEP had been (from its entry into force in January 2004 till its upgrade into a fully fledged EEZ on 12 October 2012)[80] a functional zone of jurisdiction, which was however

---

73 See Andreone, op. cit., p. 7.
74 Cf fn 47.
75 There seems to have been no consultations with other Mediterranean or EU States previous to the proclamation of the Zone.
76 See Art. 74(3) of UNCLOS, and section 2.4.2.5.
77 *Loi No. 2003-346 du 15 avril 2003 relative à la création d'une zone de protection écologique au large des côtes du territoire de la République*, OGFR, No. 19, 16 April 2003.
78 *Décret no. 2004-33 du 8 janvier 2004 portant création d'une zone de protection écologique au large des côtes du territorie de la République en Méditerranèe*, OGFR, No. 8, 10 January 2004.
79 See *Décret No. 2012-1148 du 12 octobre 2012 portant création d'une zone économique exclusive au large des côtes du territoire de la République en Méditerranée*, OGRF (240), 14 October 2012.
80 Ibid. For a more detailed discussion on the new French Mediterranean EEZ, see section. 3.4.6.

broader than its name suggested. The latter gave to France not only jurisdiction with regard to the protection and preservation of the marine environment in the said zone, but also jurisdiction with regard to marine scientific research and the establishment and use of artificial islands, installations and structures.[81] This is interesting, as the latter two powers, particularly jurisdiction with regard to marine scientific research, do not seem to be directly related to the protection and preservation of the marine environment. When it comes to the legal nature of the French Mediterranean ZEP it can be seen from the two enactments that France did not see the zone as a *sui generis*, but instead as the exercise of certain EEZ rights, particularly those relating to protection and preservation of the marine environment.

The 2003 enactment is therefore just a framework law which gives France the possibility to proclaim ZEPs – therefore not just one zone – along its coasts, if international relations are not conducive to a full EEZ.[82] Not surprisingly, the first ZEP established by France was that along its Mediterranean coasts in 2004.[83] The French laws therefore make express reference to the regime of the EEZ, and the relevant provisions of the 2003 Law were amended to form part of a consolidated version of the 1976 French EEZ law[84] which was renamed the Law on the Exclusive Economic Zone and the Zone of Ecological Protection.[85] The latter also expressly provided that the provisions of the 1968 French Law on the continental shelf[86] are applicable to the said zone and this fact reinforced the ties between the EEZ which has been in force in relation to French oceanic coasts and the Mediterranean ZEP. There seems to be no doubt that the French Mediterranean ZEP was a zone derived from the EEZ in line with the maxim *in plus stat minus*. An additional proof of this is the fact that the latter does not give to the coastal State any additional right or different rights from those expressly contemplated by Article 56 of UNCLOS although it is, as mentioned, narrower in its scope of application.

Article 1 of the 2004 Decree establishes the outer limits of the ZEP in two parts: (a) the part overlooking Continental France; and (b) the part overlooking Corsica (see Figure 3.2). Towards Italy it follows broadly the median line,[87] which is not the case with regard to Spain, so the result is that the outer limits of the

---

81 See Art. 1(2) of the 2003 Law. Cf fn 77.
82 Article 1(2) of the 2003 Law amending Art. 4 of the 1976 French Law on the EEZ provides:

> *Lorsque, dans une zone délimitée ainsi qu'il est précisé à l'article 1er, les autorités françaises entendent,* pour des motifs tenant aux relations internationales, *n'exercer que les compétences mentionnées au premier alinéa, cette zone est dénommée zone de protection écologique.* [...]

Emphasis added.
83 Cf fn 78.
84 Cf fn 40.
85 *Loi relative à la zone économique et à la zone de protection écologique au large des côtes du territoire de la République.* See Art. 1 of the 2003 Law.
86 Article 2. See also French Act No. 68-1181 of 30 December 1968 relating to the exploration of the Continental Shelf and to the exploitation of its natural resources.
87 See the discussion of the Italian ZEP in section 3.3.5.

82 *Extension of Coastal State Jurisdiction in Enclosed or Semi-enclosed Seas*

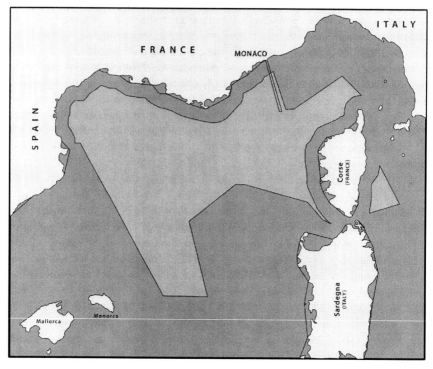

Figure 3.2 External limits of the French ZEP[88]

French Mediterranean zone overlaps with the Spanish FPZ.[89] However, the 2004 Decree (as also the previously mentioned 2012 EEZ law replacing the 2004 Decree) provides that the limits of the French zone may be modified as a result of future negotiations with neighbouring States.[90]

Like Spain, France did not enter into a process of consultations with other potentially affected States regarding the proclamation, nor regarding the external limits of its ZEP, or at least not before the formal proclamation of its ZEP in 2004.[91] Subsequent negotiations have not led to an agreement.[92]

Despite the fact that the 1997 Spanish and the 2004 French Declarations are extremely important, it is suggested that one of the first Mediterranean *sui generis* zones based on the maxima *in plus stat minus* was formally established in 1993. Reference is made here to the Joint Declaration for the Establishment of a

---

[88] The same external limits are nowadays applicable to the French (Mediterranean) EEZ. See section 3.4.6.
[89] See Leanza, '*L'Italia e la scelta di rafforzare la tutela del ambiente marino* …', op. cit., p. 321.
[90] The same outer limits and same rules regarding its future modifications are since 12 October 2012 applicable to the new French 'Mediterranean' EEZ. Cf Art. 1-2, and the discussion in section 3.4.6.
[91] See Leanza, '*Il regime giuridico internazionale del mare Mediterraneo*', op. cit., pp. 184–185.
[92] See also the discussion in section 3.3.5.

Sanctuary for the Protection of Marine Mammals in the Mediterranean, signed by the Ministers of the Environment of France and Italy, and the Minister of State of the Principality of Monaco on 22 March 1993.[93] This was implemented and superseded on 25 November 1999 through the adoption the Sanctuary Agreement between the three States, which entered into force on the 21 February 2002 and which *de facto* brought to life the regime of the 'Sanctuary'.[94]

The Sanctuary Agreement is particularly important also because it seems to provide a possible link between a joint *sui generis* zone and a transboundary SPAMI established on the basis of the Biodiversity Protocol to the Barcelona Convention.[95] As such it represents an interesting precedent which should be of interest for States bordering the Mediterranean and Adriatic Seas.

3.3.3 The Mediterranean (Pelagos) sanctuary: The first Mediterranean sui generis zone?

The 1993 Joint Declaration by France, Italy and Monaco represented an important landmark, as it seems to have formally proclaimed a joint management area of the three States which also included areas beyond their territorial seas (see Figure 3.3). Article 1 of the 1993 Declaration provided that:

> An international marine sanctuary is established in the marine area between Corsica (France), Liguria (Italy) and Provence (Monaco) with the objective of protecting all species of marine mammals.

It is argued that in the mentioned zone (particularly in the area beyond the limits of their territorial seas) the three States were entitled to exercise only some of the sovereign rights and/or jurisdiction *prima facie* limited to the area of protection of marine mammals.[96] Examples of such powers are stated by Article 5 of the 1993 Declaration which provides that the signatories should adopt provisions which are necessary to ensure a favourable level of conservation of marine mammals, in order to protect them and their habitats from negative impacts, both direct and indirect, and Article 6, prohibiting in the Sanctuary any deliberate catch or harassment of marine mammals, and furthermore completely banning the use and possession of driftnets.[97]

---

93 The 1993 Declaration is reproduced in Notarnartolo-Di-Schiara *et al.*, 'The Pelagos Sanctuary for the Mediterranean Marine Mammals', Aquatic Conservation: Marine and Freshwater Ecosystems, No. 18, Issue 4, Willey InterScience, 2008, p. 367 at pp. 385–387.
94 Agreement concerning the Creation of a Marine Mammal Sanctuary in the Mediterranean.
95 Protocol Concerning Specially Protected Areas and Biological Diversity in the Mediterranean. See the discussion in sections 5.1.2 and 5.1.3.1 and Chapter 6. See also T. Scovazzi (ed.), 'Note on the establishment of marine protected areas beyond national jurisdiction or in areas where the limits of national sovereignty or jurisdiction have not yet been defined in the Mediterranean Sea', UNEP, UNEP (DEPI)/MED WG.359/Inf.3 rev. 1, Tunis: RAC/SPA, 2011, pp. 32–37.
96 The intended 'joint management area' status of the Sanctuary can be furthermore implied from Art. 3 of the 1993 Declaration which envisages the establishment of a joint (international) authority entrusted with the competence of co-ordinating the management of the Sanctuary. See fn 93.
97 See also Art. 7 of the 1999 Agreement.

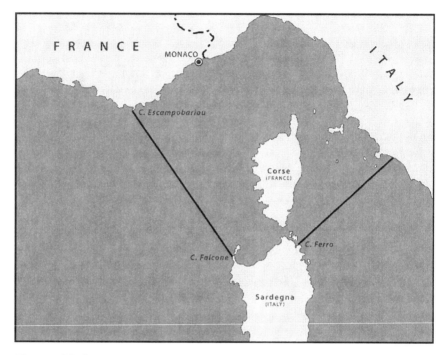

Figure 3.3 Mediterranean Sanctuary (1999 Sanctuary Agreement)[98]

Of particular interest is also Article 7 of the 1993 Declaration which provides that the signatories undertake to strengthen the monitoring in the Sanctuary and to increase the fight against any kind of pollution which may have a direct or indirect impact on the state of conservation. This provision is extremely broad, and also due to the fact that it makes reference to 'fight against any kind of pollution', it seems to suggest that the 1993 'joint area' located within the sanctuary, but beyond the territorial seas of the three states, may be eventually treated as the predecessor of the Mediterranean ZEP.[99] Mention should be made of the fact that the Declaration had the form of a 'declaration of principles' and therefore had to be implemented through the adoption of additional legislation and/or agreements by the three States.[100] It is suggested that the three main landmarks in this regard were the previously mentioned adoption of the 1999 Sanctuary Agreement, its entry into force in 2002, and the inclusion of the

---

98 Modelled on a map published in T. Scovazzi, 'The Mediterranean Marine Mammals Sanctuary: The Signature of an Agreement Establishing a Sanctuary for Marine Mammals', IJMCL, Vol. 16, No. 1, 2001, p. 132 at p. 135.
99 See also Art. 6 of the 1999 Agreement. In practical terms it would be extremely difficult to differentiate between pollution affecting the 'conservation of marine mammals' and pollution affecting the 'conservation of other living resources' and/or the ecosystem in general. See also the discussion in section 3.3.5.
100 See T. Scovazzi, 'The Declaration of a Sanctuary for the Protection of Marine Mammals in the Mediterranean', IJMCL, Vol. 8, No. 4, 1993, p. 510.

'Sanctuary' into the list of SPAMIs. The latter occurred at the conference of the States parties to the Barcelona Convention (Biodiversity Protocol) in 2001.[101]

Legally, the most challenging part of both the 1993 Declaration and the 1999 Sanctuary Agreement was that the competencies of the three signatory States were exercisable in an area which comprises parts of the internal waters and territorial seas of the three States, as well as parts of the high seas (nowadays prevalently forming part of the recently proclaimed French EEZ and Italian ZEP) between Corsica, Liguria and Provence.[102]

While there are no legal problems with the implementation of the rules of the Sanctuary in that part falling under the internal waters and territorial seas regime of the three States, some doubts have been cast about the legality of their application in the part of the 'Sanctuary' having the status of high seas. Although there are no relevant provisions in the 1993 Declaration explaining this, it is suggested that some help in our discussion may be provided by Article 14(2) of the 1999 Sanctuary Agreement. The latter provides as follows:

> In the other parts of the sanctuary [beyond the limits of the territorial sea], each of the State Parties is responsible for the application of the provisions of the present Agreement with respect to ships flying its flag as well as, *within the limits provided for by the rules of international law, with respect to ships flying the flag of third States.*

It seems clear that the rules of international law which could give the three coastal States specific rights (including enforcement rights) against third States in the field of the protection and preservation of marine mammals in that part of the sea located beyond their territorial seas, are the relevant provisions of UNCLOS on the EEZ, particularly Articles 56(1) and 65.[103] Article 65 in particular expressly

---

101 The SPAMI list may, on the basis of Art. 8(2) of the Biodiversity Protocol, include sites which are of either importance for conserving the components of biological diversity in the Mediterranean, contain ecosystems specific to the Mediterranean area or the habitats of endangered species or are of special interest at the scientific, aesthetic, cultural or educational level. The 'Sanctuary' has been on the basis of the provision of the mentioned Protocol to the Barcelona Convention included in the SPAMI List (2001) and has therefore become the first 'Mediterranean Transboundary Protected Area' and also the first High Seas Marine Protected Area (HSMPA) being established worldwide. See further the discussion in section 5.1.3.1.
102 See list of co-ordinates in Art. 3 of the 1999 Sanctuary Agreement. See also the discussion in sections 3.3.2 and 3.3.5.
103 Scovazzi, however, admits that Art. 14(2) of the Sanctuary Agreement is ambiguous and that another possible explanation could be that '[...] the State Parties cannot enforce the provisions of the Sanctuary Agreement with respect to foreign ships, as this action would be an encroachment upon the freedoms of the high seas'. See Scovazzi, 'The Mediterranean Marine Mammals Sanctuary ... ', op. cit., p. 138. Oral similarly stated that '[...] Whereas, if the Sanctuary has been established in the EEZ of the participating States much greater enforcement competence would have been available'. See N. Oral, 'Governance for the Protection of the Mediterranean Sea Marine Environment and the Role of Maritime Zones', paper delivered at the 11th Mediterranean Research Meeting Florence and Montecatini Terme, 24–27 March 2010, p. 7. Such interpretation seems however to contradict the 'object and purpose' of both the 1993 Declaration and that of the 1999 Sanctuary Agreement.

86   *Extension of Coastal State Jurisdiction in Enclosed or Semi-enclosed Seas*

grants the coastal State(s) the right to prohibit, limit or regulate the exploitation of marine mammals within its EEZs.[104]

A sound legal interpretation of the assessed provisions both of the 1993 and 1999 documents is that France, Italy and Monaco already with the 1993 Declaration formally proclaimed a zone *in plus stat minus* beyond the limits of their territorial seas, where only one element of the EEZ (protection of marine mammals) was directly applicable. As stated by Scovazzi '[...] the simple but sound argument that those who can do more can also do less seems sufficient in order to establish the lawfulness of the sanctuary'.[105]

The 'Mediterranean Sanctuary' seems therefore to be one of the earliest examples of the application of the principle *in plus stat minus* in the Mediterranean and one of the rare examples of a 'joint management zone' also involving superjacent waters in the mentioned Sea. Despite the fact that the recent proclamations of the French 'Mediterranean' EEZ (2012)[106] and of the Italian ZEP in the North-West Mediterranean, Ligurian and Tyrrhenian Sea (2011)[107] eliminated certain doubts about the applicability of the 'Sanctuary regime' and/ or about the legality of its enforcement against third States in the adjacent high seas, it is suggested that they have not altered the legal regime of the Sanctuary. The latter was from its very inception, at least in the area beyond the territorial seas of the States parties, based on the concept of the EEZ on the basis of the principle *in plus stat minus*.

It seems possible to conclude that the establishment of the Sanctuary may also be seen as a *prime* example of the general policy of co-operation in enclosed or semi-enclosed seas, advocated by Part IX of UNCLOS.[108]

Building particularly on the Spanish approach the EU, in a 2002 document laying down a Community Action Plan for the conservation and sustainable exploitation of fisheries resources in the Mediterranean,[109] advocated the proclamation of FPZs of up to 200 nmi as a means to improve fishery resources

---

104 Mention should also be made of the Agreement on the Conservation of Cetaceans of the Black Sea, Mediterranean Sea and Contiguous Atlantic (ACCOBAMS), adopted in 2002, which has a wide (Mediterranean) regional membership and which was concluded with the mandate of protecting cetaceans everywhere in the Mediterranean Sea, the Black Sea and contiguous Atlantic Ocean.

105 Ibid. See also Scovazzi, 'The Declaration of a Sanctuary for the Protection of Marine Mammals in the Mediterranean', op. cit., p. 514.

106 See sections 3.3.2. and 3.4.6.

107 See 'Decree of the President of the Republic (Italy), No. 209, 27 October 2011', and the discussion in section 3.3.5.

108 According to Art. 5 of the 1999 Sanctuary Agreement '[t]he parties *shall cooperate* with the intent of periodically assessing the marine mammal population status, the causes of mortality and the threats interfering on their habitat [...]'. 'The parties *exchange their views* in order to harmonise, as far as possible, the regulations' measures pursuant to the previous articles (Art. 10)'. 'The *parties invite other states*, exercising activities within the [Sanctuary], to take protection measures similar to those foreseen by the present Agreement (Art. 17)'.

109 Communication from the Commission to the Council and the European Parliament laying down a Community Action Plan for the conservation and sustainable exploitation of fisheries resources in the Mediterranean Sea under the Common Fishery Policy, COM(2002)535 final, Brussels, 9 October 2002.

management.[110] It was quite clear that such declaration would have a great impact on the (Mediterranean) EU Member States and even more on prospective – future – Member States. In fact, not long after the adoption of the French Framework Law on the ZEP, Croatia proclaimed its EFPZ in the Adriatic Sea, which in turn influenced similar moves from Slovenia and Italy and irrevocably opened a new era with regard to the extension of coastal State jurisdiction in the Adriatic Sea.

3.3.4 Ecological and fisheries protection zone (Croatia)

In 2003, the Croatian Parliament, with its Decision on the extension of the jurisdiction of the Republic of Croatia in the Adriatic Sea,[111] proclaimed its EFPZ notwithstanding strong protests by two of its maritime neighbours, Slovenia and Italy.[112] Croatia took advantage of the Spanish and French precedents and tried to join in a single document the most salient points of the two previous initiatives, creating *prima facie* a new *sui generis* zone. The relation between the latter and the EEZ is, however, unmistakable. Two observations should be made in this regard. The first is that the framework law for the adoption of the Croatian Decision was the 1994 Croatian Maritime Code which in Chapter IV defines the 'Economic zone' and the rights and jurisdiction which may be exercised in it. Article 1042 of the Code, however, provides that it is up to the Croatian Parliament to decide on the proclamation of the Croatian EEZ and states that the provisions of Articles 33 to 42 of the Code regulating the EEZ shall become applicable once the Croatian Parliament has decided to proclaim the EEZ.[113] The link between the two zones can be furthermore ascertained from Article 1 of the Croatian Decision, which provides that:

> The Croatian Parliament hereby proclaims the content of the exclusive economic zone related to the sovereign rights for the purpose of exploring and exploiting, conserving and managing the living resources beyond the outer limits of the territorial sea, as well as jurisdiction with regard to marine scientific research and the protection and preservation of the marine environment.

To make the interrelation between the Croatian zone and the EEZ even more evident, Article 2 of the Decision states that '[t]he Croatian Parliament reserves the right to proclaim, when it deems appropriate, the other elements of Chapter IV of the Maritime Code, in accordance with the United Nations Convention on the Law of the Sea'.[114]

---

110 See section 3.5.2.
111 OGRC, No. 157/2003. See also LOS Bulletin, UN, No. 53, 2004, pp. 68–69.
112 Cf fn 126 and 128.
113 The Maritime Code of Croatia, OGRC 17/1994.
114 See also Art. 1018 of the 2004 Maritime Code of Croatia, OGRC 181/2004.

88 *Extension of Coastal State Jurisdiction in Enclosed or Semi-enclosed Seas*

From an analysis of Article 1 of the Decision and the relevant provisions of the Croatian Maritime Code it can be inferred that the elements of the EEZ not expressly encompassed by the Croatian Decisions are: (a) sovereign rights with regard to other activities for the economic exploitation and exploration of the zone, such as the production of energy from water, currents and winds;[115] (b) jurisdiction with regard to the establishment and use of artificial islands, installations and structures;[116] and (c) other rights and duties provided by UNCLOS. The majority of the latter, however, may be exercised via other UNCLOS provisions, for example under Part VI on the continental shelf.[117] In fact, considering that, on the basis of Article 80 of UNCLOS, the provisions of Article 60 of UNCLOS regulating 'artificial islands, installations and structures in the exclusive economic zone' are applicable *mutatis mutandis* to artificial islands, installations and structures on the continental shelf, and bearing in mind that in the Decision the Republic of Croatia expressly reaffirmed its 'sovereign rights and jurisdiction which the Republic of Croatia, in conformity with international law is already exercising over its continental shelf',[118] it would seem that, with some minor exceptions, the Republic of Croatia is entitled to exercise in its zone a great majority of the powers which a coastal State is entitled to exercise in the EEZ on the basis of UNCLOS. It seems safe to conclude that the Croatian EFPZ is not a *sui generis* zone, but instead a derived zone, a *quasi EEZ* proclaimed by the Croatian Parliament in line with the maxim *in plus stat minus* (see Figure 3.4).[119]

The temporary limits of the Croatian zone are regulated by Article 6 of the Decision which provides that:

> Pending the conclusion of the delimitation agreements, the outer limits of the ecological and fisheries protection zone of the Republic of Croatia shall temporarily follow the delimitation line of the continental shelf established under the 1968 Agreement between the SFRY and the Italian Republic on Delimitation of the Continental Shelf, and, in adjacent delimitation, the line following the direction of and continuing the provisional delimitation line of the territorial seas, as defined in the 2002 Protocol on the Interim Regime along the Southern Border between the Republic of Croatia and Serbia and Montenegro.[120]

---

115 Article 56(1)(a) of UNCLOS.
116 Article 56(1)(b)(i).
117 As for example the right to establish safety zones around shelf installations. Ibid. See also Attard, op. cit., p. 49.
118 Cf fn 111, para. 10.
119 According to Vidas 'The belief has been swiftly created, especially in certain Croatian circles, that Croatia has in effect proclaimed an EEZ, though baptised under a different name'. See D. Vidas, 'Global Trends in Use of the Seas and the Legitimacy of Croatia's Extension of Jurisdiction in the Adriatic Sea', Zagreb: Croatian International Relations Review, Vol. 9, No. 32, 2003, p. 8.
120 See also Croatia; 'List of geographical coordinates defining the outer limit of the Ecological and Fisheries Protection Zone', LOS Bulletin, UN, No. 59, 2005, pp. 28–29.

Extension of jurisdiction in the Mediterranean Seas 89

Figure 3.4 Croatian EFPZ[121]

Article 6 of the Decision is interesting as it links the provisional borders of the Croatian zone to two agreements which were not meant to cover superjacent waters above the continental shelf – the 1968 Agreement[122] – and not even the continental shelf in the case of the 2002 Interim Delimitation Agreement between Croatia and Serbia and Montenegro.[123] Article 6 also departed from

---

121 Author's archive.
122 See Agreement between Italy and Yugoslavia Concerning the Delimitation of the Continental Shelf between the Two Countries, 8 January 1968. Article 4 of the 1968 Agreement expressly provided that '[t]he present agreement does not influence the juridical state of the waters or air space over the continental shelf'. The method of delimitation used was modified equidistance due to the reduced effect given to a certain number of (Yugoslav) islands located at the centre of the Adriatic Sea. It follows, however, that the interests of navigation were also indirectly taken into account. See Francalanci and Presciuttini, op. cit., p. 18 (and Figure 3.4).
123 See section 4.6.1. It is noteworthy that the third paragraph of Art. 42 of the 2004 Maritime Code of Croatia (previously Art. 43(3) of the 1994 Maritime Code) provides that:

> Until the agreement concerning the fixing boundaries of the continental shelf with Montenegro [...] is reached, the Republic of Croatia shall for the time being enjoy

90   Extension of Coastal State Jurisdiction in Enclosed or Semi-enclosed Seas

the 'unilaterally' established practice by Spain and France which linked the temporary borders of their Mediterranean zones prevalently to the median line.[124]

Slovenia protested vehemently against the unilateral proclamation and delimitation of the Croatian zone[125] stating *inter alia* that the said proclamation encroaches on the areas on which Slovenia exercised its sovereign rights and jurisdiction, that it prejudices the maritime border between the two States and purported to cut off the Slovenian territorial sea from the high seas.[126] As Article 6 of the Decision provides for the (temporary) delimitation of the Croatian Zone only with Italy and (Serbia) Montenegro, it impliedly also excludes the possibility that the waters falling under Slovenian jurisdiction could reach the high seas and consequently the possibility of Slovenia having its own continental shelf and an EEZ or *sui generis* zones of jurisdiction.[127]

Italy, on the other hand, protested against the way in which Croatia defined the provisional limits of its zone which coincide with the delimitation line contained in the 1968 Shelf Agreement concluded between Italy and the SFRY.[128] According to Italy such 'temporary' delimitation is against Italian interests in the Adriatic Sea and contrary to international law.[129] On this point it is worth reiterating that Article 4 of the 1968 Shelf Agreement expressly provides that the Agreement shall not be applicable to superjacent waters, nor to the airspace above the continental shelf.[130]

It is furthermore noteworthy that the ICJ in its judgment in the *Case Concerning the Arbitral Award of 31 July 1989 (Guinea Bissau v Senegal)* makes reference and

---

the sovereign rights in that zone *up to the median line* proceeding to the outer limit of the territorial sea in starting from the entrance of the Boka Kotorska Bay in the direction of the open sea.

Emphasis added. This points at two separate (provisional) lines of delimitation, one for the shelf and another for superjacent waters (EFPZ). The lateral continental shelf boundary with Slovenia is not even mentioned. Cf fn 125.

124 See sections 3.3.1–3.3.2.

125 LOS Bulletin, UN, No. 53, 2003, p. 70.

126 See Slovenia, 'Communication from the Government of Slovenia dated 30 August 2004, containing Statement of the position of the Slovenian Government with respect to the declaration by the Government of Croatia concerning the establishment of its own exclusive economic or ecological and fisheries protection zone', LOS Bulletin, No. 56, p. 139. See also sections 4.7–4.8.

127 See also the discussion in section 4.7.2.

128 Italy, 'Note by Italy concerning the declaration of an ecological and fisheries protection zone in the Adriatic Sea by the Republic of Croatia of 3 October 2003', 16 April 2004, LOS Bulletin, UN, No. 54, 2004, p. 129.

129 According to the Italian note:

… the automatic extension of the delimitation of the sea-bed, agreed in 1968, is not legally well founded because that limit was agreed on the basis of special circumstances that differ from the circumstances to be considered in the determination of superjacent waters. Furthermore, the 1968 delimitation was agreed in a moment in which the notion of the exclusive economic zone was not well defined in the international law of the sea.

130 Cf fn 122.

upholds the passage of the 1989 Arbitral Award according to which the 1960 Agreement concluded between Guinea Bissau and Senegal:

> ... had the force of law in relations between the parties 'with regard solely to the areas mentioned in that Agreement, namely the territorial sea, the contiguous zone and the continental shelf'. Consequently, 'the 1960 Agreement does not delimit those maritime spaces which did not exists at that date, whether they be termed exclusive economic zone, fishery zone or whatever ...'.[131]

It also seems differently as (at least impliedly) advocated by some renowned Croatian international lawyers[132] that the provision incorporated in Article 74(4) of UNCLOS stating that '[w]here there is an agreement in force between the States concerned, questions related to the delimitation of the exclusive economic zone shall be determined in accordance with the provisions of that agreement', addresses cases where there is already an agreement in force between the two States with regard to the delimitation of the EEZ, involving therefore also superjacent waters, and not only the continental shelf. Such view has been confirmed also in the 2009 Romania/Ukraine Judgment where the ICJ stated:

> ... The word 'agreement' in paragraph 4 (as elsewhere in the Article) refers to an agreement delimiting the exclusive economic zone (Article 74) or the continental shelf (Article 83) referred to in Paragraph 1. State practice indicates that the use of the boundary agreed for the delimitation of one maritime zone to delimit another zone is affected by a new agreement. This typically occurs when states agree to apply their continental shelf boundary to their exclusive economic zone ....[133]

For the purpose of this work, however, particularly interesting is the *Note Verbale* sent by Italy to the UN Secretary-General on 16 April 2004[134] which highlighted the breach of a duty of co-operation and co-ordination of activities among States bordering enclosed or semi-enclosed seas by Croatia. According to Italy:

> ... If the United Nations Convention on the Law of the Sea recognizes to coastal States the right to establish exclusive economic zones or other zones of functional State jurisdiction more limited in scope, in its Part IX

---

131 Arbitral Award of 31 July 1989, Judgment, ICJ Reports 1991, p. 53, paras 58–60.
132 See B. Vukas, 'The extension of the jursidiction of the coastal States in the Adriatic Sea', in N. Ronzitti (ed.), *I rapporti di vicinato dell' Italia con Croazia, Serbia-Montenegro e Slovenia*, Rome: Luiss University Press-Giuffrè, 2005, p. 251 at p. 267.
133 Case Concerning Maritime Delimitation in the Black Sea (*Romania v Ukraine*), ICJ Reports, 2009, p. 1, para. 69.
134 Cf fn128.

92 *Extension of Coastal State Jurisdiction in Enclosed or Semi-enclosed Seas*

it makes reference to various forms of co-operation, among coastal States in enclosed or semi-enclosed seas in situations in which the narrowness of marine spaces affect the claims of surrounding States to establish zones of functional jurisdiction beyond their territorial sea.

To this end, Article 123 of the 1982 Convention poses on contracting States that are bordering or not bordering enclosed or semi-enclosed seas the obligation to co-operate in the management, conservation, exploration or exploitation of living resources of the sea, in the protection and preservation of the marine environment and in scientific research, as a solution aimed at guaranteeing the respect of the various interests of the coastal States involved, thus in adherence to the spirit of the Convention.

This obligation to co-operate does not cease if a coastal State bordering an enclosed or semi-enclosed basin decides to establish reserved zones of functional jurisdiction. The above mentioned obligation should consist in the specific obligation to co-operate in determining the limits of the zone of functional jurisdiction, i.e., in agreeing on those limits with other interested States, also in compliance with Article 74 of the 1982 Convention.

The obligation to co-operate is even more evident in cases regarding enclosed or semi-enclosed basins that are particularly narrow, as is the case for the Adriatic Sea, where the proclamation of zones of functional jurisdiction beyond the territorial sea involves in a direct manner the interest of neighbouring states. *In those circumstances the co-ordination in determining the zone of functional jurisdiction is even indispensable ....*

Although the content of the Italian *Note Verbale* was criticized by Croatian[135] and even by some Italian experts,[136] it seems to represent a fair summary of the relevance of Part IX of UNCLOS to this particular case.[137] From the Italian *Note* it may in fact be seen that Italy did not challenge the sole right of Croatia to proclaim 'EEZs or zones of functional jurisdiction more limited in scope' in the semi-enclosed Adriatic Sea, but that instead it pointed at the failure of Croatia to '*coordinate in determining the zone of functional jurisdiction*' and to '*cooperate in determining the limits of such zones*'.[138] The latter obligation, also according to the

---

135 Vukas commented on the *Note Verbale* as follows: 'The main mistake in the Italian text is the erroneous link it tries to create between the establishment of the EFPZ and cooperation among the States bordering on an enclosed or semi-enclosed seas [...]'. See Vukas, 'The extension of the jurisdiction of the coastal States in the Adriatic Sea', op. cit., p. 265.

136 Scovazzi commented: 'If the note meant that a State bordering an enclosed or semi-enclosed seas cannot proceed to establish its exclusive economic zone (or other *sui generis* zones) without the agreement of its neighboring States, this would be wrong [...]'. See T. Scovazzi, 'Recent Developments as regards Maritime Delimitation in the Adriatic Sea', in R. Lagoni and D. Vignes (eds), *Maritime Delimitation*, Leiden and Boston, MA: Martinus Nijhoff Publishers, 2006, p. 189 at p. 195.

137 In the Preamble to the 2003 Decision, Croatia makes express reference to Part IX (Art. 122 of UNCLOS) and to the fact that '[...] the Adriatic Sea is an enclosed or semi-enclosed sea, which, because of its small size, is far more vulnerable to pollution than is the case with other seas [...]'. Cf fn 111, para. 7.

138 See the discussion in sections 2.4.2.2 2.4.2.5.

Extension of jurisdiction in the Mediterranean Seas 93

Italian *Note Verbale* derives from both Article 74 and Part IX (Article 123) of UNCLOS. In this regard it would seem that Croatia at least initially failed to fulfil its obligation to 'make every effort, in a spirit of understanding and cooperation, to enter into provisional arrangements of a practical nature', pending final agreement on delimitation.[139]

Due to strong opposition by its neighbours and particularly due to political pressures from the European Commission, the Croatian Parliament adopted on 3 June 2004 the Decision on Amending the Decision on the Extension of the Jurisdiction of the Republic of Croatia in the Adriatic Sea of 3 October 2003 which added a second paragraph to Article 3 of the 2003 Decision, providing that:

> With regard to the member States of the European Union, the implementation of the legal regime of the Ecological and Fisheries Protection Zone of the Republic of Croatia shall commence after the conclusion of the fisheries partnership agreement between the European Community and the Republic of Croatia.[140]

This created a rather curious situation which despite some legislative moves to suspend/revoke The Original Decision is still currently in force,[141] whereas the legal regime of the Croatian Zone is not applicable to ships flying the flags of the Members States of the EU – including for example Slovenia – but it is on the other hand applicable to ships flying the flag of a non-EU Member State, independently of the whether they are controlled by EU interests and whether or not they are sailing to an EU port.

In conclusion, it may be asserted that while there are indications that Croatia may have endeavoured to co-operate with other affected States regarding the establishment of its EFPZ (implementation of its regime),[142] it failed to co-operate

139 See Art. 74(3) of UNCLOS, and the discussion in 2.4.2.5.
140 LOS Bulletin, UN, No. 55, 2004, p. 31.
141 On 15 December 2006 the Croatian Parliament modified para. 3 (2) of the 2004 Decision with a new provision stating that '[f]or the Member States of the European Union the implementation of the legal regime of the [EFPZ] shall start not later than 1st January 2008, whereof, fisheries and ecological regulations of the Republic of Croatia shall be applied to fishing and other European Community vessels'. See 'Decision on Modifying and Amending the Decision on the Extension of the Jurisdiction of the Republic of Croatia in the Adriatic Sea', OGRC No.138/2006. On 13 March 2008, Art. 3(2) of the 2004 Decision was again modified by the Croatian Parliament and it currently provides that the EFPZ '[…] shall provisionally not apply to Member States of the European Union, as of March 15, 2008, *until a common agreement in the EU spirit is reached*'. Emphasis added. See 'Decision on Modifying the Decision on the Extension of the Jurisdiction of the Republic of Croatia in the Adriatic Sea', OGRC No. 31/2008. Translation and the discussion of the 2006 and 2008 decisions available in D. Vidas, 'The Adriatic Sea Governance and Maritime Delimitation Issue: The Case of Croatia's EEZ', paper delivered at the 11th Mediterranean Research Meeting Florence and Montecatini Terme, 24–27 March 2010, pp. 27–36.
142 Article 3 of the 2003 Decision for example provided that '[t]he implementation of the *legal regime* of the ecological and fisheries protection zone of the Republic of Croatia shall commence twelve months after its establishment. […] *The said period shall be used for preparing the implementation mechanism and for possible signing of agreements or making arrangements with interested States and the European Communities*'. Emphasis added. See fn 111.

94 *Extension of Coastal State Jurisdiction in Enclosed or Semi-enclosed Seas*

in the setting of its 'temporary limits'. It is argued, however, that the 'provisional non-application' of the legal regime of the EFPZ to the Member States of the EU, although somehow being 'enforced' on Croatia,[143] may still qualify as a 'provisional arrangement of a practical nature' in line with the provision of Article 74(3) of UNCLOS.

3.3.5 Zone(s) of ecological protection (Italy): An **in plus stat minus** *or a real* **sui generis** *zone?*

Despite strong protests against the proclamation of the Croatian EFPZ and obviously also as a result of it, and following precedents set by Spain and France in particular, Italy and Slovenia announced their intention in early 2005 to proclaim their ZEPs. The two States, although emphasizing that the primary reason for their intended moves was the need for the protection of the marine environment, made quite clear that they were influenced also by similar (unilateral) moves of other States. In the case of Italy that meant primarily the adoption of the French Framework Law (2003) and Decree in 2004 instituting the French Mediterranean ZEP,[144] while in the case of Slovenia the triggering precedents were the proclamation of the Croatian EFPZ and the publication of the Italian Draft Law on the establishment of an ZEP beyond the limits of the territorial sea.[145] The 'foreword' to the latter is straightforward in explaining the origins of the decision. In the first place it mentions the changing juridical character of the Mediterranean Sea due to recent initiatives to establish *sui generis* zones beyond the limits of the territorial sea, over which Mediterranean States exercise only some of the competences which the coastal State is entitled to exercise over its EEZ (*in plus stat minus*). Express reference is made also to the adoption of the French Framework Law No. 2003-346, at the origin of which, adoption was the necessity, felt also by Italy to better protect the marine environment, particularly from vessel source pollution.[146]

The urgency of the immediate institution of a similar zone, according to the Italian Draft Law, was the fact that France had not only proclaimed, but also provided the co-ordinates of its ZEP (with the 2004 Decree); and had Italy not taken action, this could have resulted in a situation wherein environmentally unsafe ships, particularly those flying the flags of convenience, would decide to sail on the Italian side, outwith the jurisdiction of the (French) coastal State, thereby taking advantage of the high seas regime. Such situation would, according to the Draft Law, result in a great danger to the environmental integrity of the Italian State.[147]

---

143 Cf Vidas, 'The Adriatic Sea Governance and Maritime Delimitation Issue', op. cit., pp. 27–36.
144 See section 3.3.2.
145 Camera dei Deputati, '*Disegno di legge: Istituzione di una zona di protezione ecologica oltre il limite esterno del mare territoriale*', Atti parlamentari, No. 5358, presented on 18 October 2004. Hereinafter 'Draft Law'.
146 See para. 4 of the introduction. Ibid.
147 See para. 5 of the introduction and the 'Analisi Technico-Normativa'. Ibid.

Another interesting consideration mentioned in the Draft Law was that in the absence of such proclamation, Italy would find itself in a disadvantaged situation in the event of bilateral negotiations with France for the delimitation of their (ecological) zones and also in a disadvantaged position with other States whose coasts are opposite or adjacent to Italy when they come in due course to proclaim their ecological and/or fisheries zones. This last consideration provides valuable insight into the motivation of Adriatic and other Mediterranean States which have recently extended or expressed their intention to extend their jurisdiction in the Mediterranean.

Following the Draft Law, Italy adopted on 8 February 2006 Law No. 61 on the establishment of an ecological protection zone beyond the outer limit of the territorial sea.[148] This Law also makes express reference to UNCLOS as according to Article 1(1) of the Law, '[i]n conformity with the provisions of the United Nations Convention on the law of the sea ... the establishment of an ecological protection zone is hereby authorized ...'.

It is important to point out that this enactment merely authorizes the institution of a zone or more zones along the Italian coast, and did not expressly proclaim a ZEP. From this it can be inferred that the Italian Law No. 61, like the French Law No. 2003-346[149] and Chapter IV of the 1994 Croatian Maritime Code[150] was just a framework law and did not represent the actual proclamation of the legal regime of such zone. Confirmation of this is found in Article 1(2) which provides that '[t]he establishment of the ecological protection zone will be provided for by the Decree of the President of the Republic ...'. An important consideration is that, unlike the 2005 Draft Law, Law No. 61 makes express reference to the establishment of 'ecological protection zones', therefore expressly envisaging the possibility of the institution of more than one ZEP along the Italian coast. That, in turn, means the possibility of establishing a ZEP or ZEPs only along certain parts of the Italian coasts and also with different breadths.[151] On 27 October 2011, the President of the Italian Republic issued a Decree establishing the first Italian ZEP in the North-West Mediterranean, Ligurian and Tyrrhenian Seas (see Figure 3.5).[152] The latter incorporates an area adjacent to the French zone, including parts of the Mediterranean (Pelagos) Sanctuary.

---

148 Legge 8 febbraio 2006, n. 61, '*Instituzione di zone di protezione ecologica oltre il limite esterno del mare territoriale*', OGRI, No. 52/2006. See also the translation published in the LOS Bulletin, UN, No. 61, p. 98. There is, however, a mistake in the English translation which in Art. 1 makes reference to 'the establishment of an ecological protection zone', while the original Italian text refers to the establishment of more zones of ecological protection (*zone di protezzione ecologica*).

149 See section 3.3.2.

150 See section 3.3.4.

151 See Andreone, op. cit., p. 23

152 Cf fn 107. Hereinafter the '2011 Decree'.

Figure 3.5 Italian ZEP in the North-West Mediterranean, Ligurian and Tyrrhenian Seas and its relation with the French zone[153]

When it comes to the rights and duties of Italy within such zone it would seem that there are some departures from the wording of Article 56 of UNCLOS. According to Article 2(1) of Law No. 61:

> In the framework of the ecological protection zone ... Italy exercises its jurisdiction in the area of protection and conservation of the marine environment, *including the archaeological and historical heritage*, in compliance with the provisions of the aforementioned United Nations Convention on the Law of the Sea Convention and the 2001 UNESCO Convention on the protection of the underwater cultural heritage, adopted in Paris on 2 November 2001 since the date of its entry into effect in Italy.[154]

It should be noted, however, that 'jurisdiction' with regard to the protection and preservation of the archaeological and historical heritage is not derived from the concept of the EEZ as embodied in Chapter V of UNCLOS, but rather has its basis on other provisions of UNCLOS and ultimately on (customary) international law. UNCLOS regulates the protection of 'underwater cultural objects' in Article 303, which obliges State Parties to co-operate with regard to such protection; but it does not elaborate further on the exact methods, nor it does provide a direct link to the regime or/and the extent of the EEZ.[155] In the second

---

153 Modelled on a map published by the 'Instituto Idrografico della Marina', Genova, February 2012.
154 Emphasis added. See also Art. 3(1) of the 2011 Decree.
155 According to Art. 303(1) of UNCLOS: 'States have the duty to protect objects of an archaeological and historical nature found at sea and shall cooperate for this purpose'.

paragraph of Article 303 express mention is made of the regime of the contiguous zone regulated by Article 33 of UNCLOS which in practice makes the contiguous zone to a certain extent also an 'archaeological zone'.[156] It has to be said, however, that the powers of the coastal State regarding the protection and preservation of underwater cultural heritage have been in the past many times linked to the sovereign rights the State exercises over its continental shelf, although such practice seems not to be in line with the UNCLOS.[157]

Nevertheless, Article 303(4) of UNCLOS provides that '[t]his article is without prejudice to other international agreements and rules of international law regarding the protection of objects of an archaeological and historical nature', and the latter article is also the basis for the adoption in 2001 of the UNESCO Convention, which entered into force on 2 January 2009 and to which reference is made in the Italian Law No. 61 of 2006. A detailed discussion of the UNESCO Convention is beyond the scope of this work[158] but as the 2006 Italian Law makes reference to it, it seems necessary to point out that the territorial scope of application of the UNESCO Convention is not, or at least not directly, linked to the concept of the EEZ. The UNESCO Convention in fact envisages specific regimes for co-operation between coastal, flag and if applicable other States, depending on the location (maritime zone) in which the underwater cultural heritage is found.[159] Regarding the EEZ and the continental shelf, the UNESCO Convention establishes an international co-operation regime which is based on notification and consultations (procedural mechanism), where the coastal State usually assumes a 'co-ordinating role'. As such it is in charge of the implementation of the agreed measures and may furthermore take all practical measures, if necessary even prior to consultation, to prevent any immediate danger to the underwater cultural heritage, whether arising from human activities or any other cause.[160] Such co-ordinating role, however, does not mean that the coastal State has jurisdiction in its EEZ in the field of the protection and preservation of underwater cultural heritage.

---

156 Article 303(2) provides that:

> In order to control traffic in such objects, the coastal State *may*, in applying Article 33, presume that their removal from the sea-bed in the zone referred to in that article without its approval would result in an infringement within its territory or territorial sea of the laws and regulations referred to in that article.

Emphasis added.

157 This is mostly a result of the fact that underwater cultural heritage is not a 'natural resource'. Examples of Mediterranean States which nonetheless extended their powers on the continental shelf also with regard to the protection and preservation of underwater cultural heritage include the former SFRY, France, Cyprus, Greece, Turkey and also Italy. See Leanza, *Il regime giuridico internazionale del mare Mediterraneo*, op. cit., p. 162.

158 For a general discussion, see R. Garabello and T. Scovazzi (eds), *The Protection of the Underwater Cultural Heritage Before and After the 2001 UNESCO Convention*, Leiden and Boston, MA: Martinus Nijhoff Publishers, 2003.

159 See T. Scovazzi, 'The entry into force of the 2001 UNESCO Convention on the Protection of the Underwater Cultural Heritage', *Aegean Rev Law Sea*, Vol. 1, No. 1, Berlin and Heildeberg: Springer, 2009, pp. 19–36.

160 See Art. 10.

98   Extension of Coastal State Jurisdiction in Enclosed or Semi-enclosed Seas

A potentially powerful provision for coastal States is also found in Article 10(2) of the UNESCO Convention which provides that:

> A State Party in whose exclusive economic zone or on whose continental shelf underwater cultural heritage is located has the right to prohibit or authorise any activity directed at such heritage to prevent interference with its sovereign rights and jurisdiction as provided for by the international law, including the United Nations Convention on the Law of the Sea.

This article is certainly potentially powerful both in relation to a full EEZ and ZEPs where the coastal State could for example claim interference with its jurisdiction with regard to the protection and preservation of the marine environment and interference with the sovereign rights that, at least as a general rule, exercises on the continental shelf below the superjacent waters of such a zone. The question which may arise is whether after the issuance of Presidential Decree proclaiming the Italian ZEP or ZEPs, and/or after the entry into force of the UNESCO Convention for Italy,[161] two different regimes shall be applicable with regard to underwater cultural heritage in the said zone: one within the 24 nmi in what could be the Italian contiguous (archaeological) zone,[162] and another in that part of the sea located between the limits of the 24 nmi zone and the external limits of the ZEP(s). From a legal standpoint the answer seems to be in the affirmative.[163] The latter position was ultimately confirmed by Article 4 of the Italian Law No. 157 on the ratification and implementation of the 2001 UNESCO Convention, dated 23 October 2009. This Article provides that the protection of the underwater cultural heritage within the Italian ZEPs *but beyond 24 nmi from the baseline of the Italian territorial sea*, should be undertaken in accordance with the relevant provisions of the 2001 UNESCO Convention. Special reference is made in this regard to Articles 9 and 10 and the Convention's Annexes.[164]

---

161 Italy deposited its instruments of ratifications on 8 January 2010. The 2001 UNESCO Convention is therefore in force for Italy.

162 Italy in 2004 proclaimed an 'Archaeological Zone' based on the provisions of Arts 33 and 303 of UNCLOS. According to Art. 94 of the Legislative Decree of 22 January 2004 (No. 41):

> *Gli oggetti archeologici e storici rinvenuti nei fondali della zona di mare estesa dodici miglia marine a partire dal limite esterno del mare territoriale sono tutelati ai sensi delle 'Regole relative agli interventi sul patrimonio culturale subaqueo' allegate alla Convenzione UNESCO sulla protezzione del patrimonio culturale subacqueo ….*

> See OGRI, supplement to No. 45 of 24 February 2004. Quoted in Scovazzi, 'Maritime delimitations in the Mediterranean Sea', op. cit., p. 360.

163 See also Art. 8 of the UNESCO Convention.

164 See 'Ratifica ed esecuzione della Convenzione sulla protezione del patrimonio culturale subacqueo, con Allegato, adottata a Parigi il 2 novembre 2001, e norme di adeguamento dell' ordinamento interno', OGRI No. 262, 10 November 2009. Article 4 regulates 'Underwater cultural heritage within ZEPs' and makes express reference to Law No. 61 of 8 February 2006. Cf fn 161.

Furthermore, Article 2(2) of Law No. 61 may be interpreted as establishing a zone which is something more than just a ZEP. Article 2(2) provides that:

> Inside the ecological protection zone the norms of Italian law, European Union Law, and international treaties in effect for Italy for the prevention and repression of all types of marine pollution, including pollution from ships and ballast waters, pollution from the sinking of trash, pollution from exploration activities and the exploitation of the sea-bed and pollution of atmospheric origin [*and in the fields of the protection of marine mammals and biodiversity and underwater cultural heritage*], will be applied also to ships flying foreign flags and persons of foreign nationality.[165]

The same text is then repeated in Article 3(1) of the 2011 Presidential Decree which legally sets in place the first Italian ZEP in the North-West Mediterranean, Ligurian and Tyrrhenian Seas.[166]

The Italian framework Law No. 61, therefore adopted a 'holistic' approach to the protection and preservation of the marine environment and the fact that EU and Italian laws on the protection of marine mammals and biodiversity are applicable within the Zone makes the latter, if one omits sovereign rights with regard to the exploitation of living resources, quite similar to an FPZ. It goes without saying that the application of the various laws and regulations on the conservation of marine mammals[167] and particularly those concerning the protection of biodiversity will influence the 'freedom of fishing' of third States in the zone. Account must be taken of the fact that the concept of 'biodiversity' is extremely broad (holistic) and accordingly the 'protection of biodiversity' within a ZEP cannot be undertaken only through the 'protection of the marine environment' and/or 'certain species of 'living resources'.[168] This view seems to be confirmed also by the definition of 'biodiversity' included in Article 2 of the CBD Convention to which Italy is a State Party. According to the latter:

> 'Biological diversity' means the variability among living organisms from all sources including, *inter alia*, terrestrial, marine and other aquatic ecosystems and the ecological complexes of which they are part; this includes diversity within species, between species and of ecosystems.

---

165 LOS Bulletin, UN, No. 61, 2006, p. 98. There is, however, a major omission in the English translation as the latter does not mention among the norms applicable in the ZEP those relating to the protection of marine mammals, biodiversity and underwater cultural heritage. Cf fn 147.

166 Cf fn 107.

167 In such right of the coastal State is included also the right of control and enforcement against vessels of third States exercising their freedom of fishing within the ZEP. In practical terms it would be extremely difficult to limit the conservation measures to marine mammals only without extending them also to complementary species. See Andreone, op. cit., p. 15.

168 Andreone, op. cit., p. 14.

100 *Extension of Coastal State Jurisdiction in Enclosed or Semi-enclosed Seas*

The protection of 'biodiversity' implies the conservation of 'living organisms from all sources' and ultimately of the 'entire ecosystem'. It seems possible to agree with Andreone[169] and Leanza,[170] who assert that the Italian ZEP is a zone halfway between an 'ecological' zone and a 'FPZ'; and it may be added that at least to a certain extent it is also a real *sui generis* zone.

Regarding the delimitation of the Italian zone, Article 1(3) states that '[t]he outer limits of the ecological protection zone are determined on the basis of agreements with the States involved ...' alluding obviously to neighbouring States. According to the second part of the Article '[u]ntil the date that said agreements enter into effect, the outer limits of the ecological protection zones follow the outline of the median line ...'. The practical result of this will most likely be that the provisional limits of the Italian ZEP(s) will not (fully) coincide with the already defined limits of the Italian continental shelf in respect of the majority of its maritime neighbours.[171]

It is, however, noteworthy that immediately after the adoption of Law No. 61 Italy started negotiations with France regarding the delimitation of their ZEPs. The negotiations have not led to an agreement. The negotiations stem from Article 2 of the 2011 Presidential Decree which provides for the provisional external limits of the proclaimed Italian ZEP in the North-West Mediterranean, Ligurian and Tyrrhenian Seas, *pending delimitation agreement with France and Spain*. Noteworthy is the fact that the provisional external limits of the first Italian ZEP generally do not go so far as to reach the French ZEP (EEZ). The two zones are generally divided by a small corridor of 'high seas'.[172]

It is possible to conclude that Italian Law No. 61 at least initially provided the Italian State with some competencies in such a zone, particularly with regard to the protection and preservation of underwater cultural heritage which have been so far characteristics of other zones and not the EEZ or are given to the coastal State by a self-standing international convention. From this perspective, at least the envisaged Italian ZEP may be deemed to be *sui generis*.

On the other hand, it should be acknowledged that the Italian approach of adopting first a framework law for its extension of jurisdiction in an enclosed or semi-enclosed sea (allowing for a proclamation of more than one zone along different parts of its coast), followed by a process of negotiations with its neighbouring States regarding the delimitation of such zone(s) before the actual implementation (proclamation) of its regime and before (ultimately) setting the provisional external limits of such zone or zones, seems to be in line with, and reflects the spirit of both Article 74 and Part IX of UNCLOS (Article 123).

In this context it also seems necessary to emphasize the provisions of Article 5 of the 2011 Decree which addresses the *de facto* implementation of the ZEP

---

169 Ibid, pp. 14–15.
170 See Leanza, '*L'Italia e la scelta di rafforzare la tutela del ambiente marino ...* ', op. cit., p. 334.
171 Leanza pointed out that with the inclusion of the 'median line' as a provisional delimitation, the Italian legislator emphasized the position of Italy of opposing the automatic extension of the continental shelf boundary to superjacent waters. Ibid, p. 332. See also sections 3.3.1 and 3.4.4.
172 See Figure 3.5.

regime within the first Italian ZEP in the Ligurian and Tyrrhenian Sea. This Article provides that the 'operative modalities' of the regime of the proclaimed ZEP will be provided on a case-by-case basis by a Decree issued by the Ministry of Environment. This fact highlights the extremely cautious approach adopted by Italy with regard to the *de facto* implementation (enforcement) of the ZEP regime and ultimately raises the question of whether the 2011 Decree represents something more than just (another) 'framework law', allowing for the potential future implementation of the ZEP regime within a specific geographical area.[173]

3.3.6 Zone of ecological protection (Slovenia)

The proclamation of the Croatian EFPZ, the adoption of the Italian Draft Law enabling Italy to proclaim its ZEP, combined with the news that Italy and Croatia were to renegotiate (without Slovenia) the 1968 Italy-SFRY Shelf Agreement[174] would appear to be the reasons behind the adoption by the Slovenian Parliament of the Ecological Protection Zone and Continental Shelf of the Republic of Slovenia Act on 22 October 2005.[175] With this, Slovenia established its ZEP in the Northern Adriatic and reaffirmed its rights to a continental shelf.[176]

The EPZCSA is not just a framework law, but legally represents a proper proclamation of the zone.[177] The reasoning behind the Slovenian proclamation can be best seen from wording of the proposal included in the draft law (legislative proposal)[178] prepared by the Slovenian Government, where it is difficult to miss similarities with the Italian 'Disegno di Legge'.[179] In the explanation of the proposal, emphasis is placed on the need to protect the marine environment, particularly due to heavy burdens on marine ecosystems and habitats which endanger marine biodiversity and lower the economic potential of the sea (fisheries, tourism, etc.). This is particularly important within the Adriatic which is, according to the draft law, due to its geographic position, shallowness, pollution from land-based sources and increasing traffic burdens is the most endangered sea within the Mediterranean basin.[180] Reference is also made to the changing juridical status of the Mediterranean Sea which has mostly occurred through

---

173 See also the discussion on the legal regime of the 'Mediterranean (Pelagos) Sanctuary in section 3.3.3. The latter is nowadays partially located within the (provisional) geographical limits of the Italian ZEP and of the newly proclaimed French (Mediterranean) EEZ. See also Figure 3.5, and the discussion in sections 3.3.2 and 3.4.6.
174 Cf fn 122.
175 Hereinafter the 'EPZCSA'. OGRS No. 93/2005. See also LOS Bulletin, No. 60, UN, 2006, pp. 56–57.
176 Article 2(1) of EPZCSA provides that '[t]he Republic of Slovenia has its own continental shelf'.
177 According to Art. 3: 'The Republic of Slovenia declares the ecological protection zone …'.
178 *Zakon o razglasitvi zaščitne ekološke cone Republike Slovenije in epikontinentalnem pasu* (draft). Copy on file with the author.
179 See section 3.3.5.
180 See section 1.2, and the overall discussion in Chapter 5.

102 *Extension of Coastal State Jurisdiction in Enclosed or Semi-enclosed Seas*

the proclamation of *sui generis* ZEPs whose primarily aim is the protection and preservation of the marine environment and/or conservation and management of marine resources.[181]

Lastly, it is stated that due to the ever-increasing maritime traffic in the Northern Adriatic and due to actual or announced extension of jurisdiction by other States in this regard (Croatia and Italy), it was deemed necessary that Slovenia also protects that part of the sea connected to but beyond the limits of its territorial sea.[182] Furthermore, in Section VI of the draft proposal which explains the reasons for the proposed urgent procedure for its adoption, the Slovenian Government expressly emphasized:

> ... that the Republic of Croatia has already proclaimed its EFPZ, that Italy is planning to proclaim its zone of ecological protection soon ... and that taking into account the fact that the maritime borders [with Croatia] have not been established yet, the Republic of Slovenia has to promptly protect its interest and provide for a proper environmental protection of that part of the continental shelf over which Slovenia is entitled to exercise sovereign rights in accordance with international law ....[183]

A comparison of the elements of the Slovenian EPZCSA with Article 56 of UNCLOS sheds light on the similarity of their content, although the drafting language differs to a certain extent. According to Article 3(1) of the EPZCSA, Slovenia in the zone:

> ... shall exercise its sovereign rights relating to research and sustainable use, preservation and management of marine wealth as well as its jurisdiction relating to scientific research and the preservation and protection of the marine environment in accordance with international law and obligations deriving from the European Union *acquis*.

This provision matches broadly the provisions of Article 56(1)(a) of UNCLOS, although leaving out the exploitation of living resources, other activities for the economic exploitation and exploration of the zone and jurisdiction with regard to artificial islands, installations and structures. When it comes to the exercise of jurisdiction the regime of the Slovenian zone lies somewhere between the Italian and the former French (ecological) zones, in the sense that is it is broader than that of the Italian ZEP(s) as it includes jurisdiction with regard to marine scientific research and narrower than that of the French zone as it does not include jurisdiction with regard to the establishment and use of artificial islands,

---

181 Paragraph I.1 of the Slovenian draft law.
182 Ibid.
183 Author's translation.

installsations and structures.[184] Article 6(1) of the EPZCSA furthermore states that:

> The legal order of the Republic of Slovenia and the European Union *acquis* in the areas of the protection and preservation of the marine environment, *including the archaeological heritage*, and the provisions of Part XII of the UN Convention on the Law of the Sea shall apply to the ecological protection zone.[185]

This provision, like the Italian framework law, establishes a link between the 'ZEP' and the 'archaeological zone' with similar consequences as already discussed with regard to the Italian ZEP(s).[186] Although the drafting language differs to a certain extent from the Italian Law No. 61, the 'substance' of the Slovenian zone is almost identical and therefore the same considerations apply.[187] As with the Italian, the Slovenian zone may be also qualified as a (partially) *sui generis* zone, halfway between a ZEP and an FPZ.

As to the temporary limits of the zone, Slovenia followed the Croatian precedent in the North by linking the provisional external border of the zone to:

> ... the delimitation line on the continental shelf as defined by the Agreement between the Government of the [SFRY] and the Government of the Italian Republic on the Delimitation of the Continental Shelf between the two states of 8th January 1968 ....[188]

As to the South, '[t]he provisional external border ... in the south shall run along the parallel 45 degrees and 10 minutes north latitude'.[189] The particularity

---

184 Article 3.
185 Emphasis added.
186 Slovenia deposited the instruments of ratifications of the 2001 UNESCO Convention on 18 September 2008.
187 The EPZCSA for example does not repeat *verbatim* the *dictum* 'protection of marine mammals and biodiversity' as it is the case with the Italian law, but instead 'protection and preservation of mammals and other animal and plant species aimed at the preservation of the integrity of the marine ecosystem'. See Art. 6. It is nonetheless peculiar that the 2006 Decree on the designation of the sea fishing area of the Republic of Slovenia defines the area of the Slovenian ZEP (and adjacent high seas) as 'fishing waters of the Republic of Slovenia'. See 'Decree on the Determination of Fisheries Areas of the Republic of Slovenia', OGRS, No. 2/2006 (Art. 4).
188 See Art. 4.1.
189 See Art. 4.2. This provision is particularly interesting as it seems that the temporary border in the South coincides with the limits of the 'joint fishing zone' instituted under the provisions of the 1997 Agreement on Cross-Border Traffic and Co-operation between Slovenia and Croatia (SOPS) which crosses the territorial sea of both States in the Northern Adriatic. See the discussion in section 4.7.3. Furthermore, Art. 5(3) of EPZCSA provides that '[t]he continental shelf of the Republic of Slovenia shall comprise sea-bed and subsoil in underwater areas, extending beyond the territorial sea of the Republic of Slovenia to the borders in compliance with international law.' This provision read in conjunction with Art. 4(2) of EPZSCA expressly admits the possibility of two separate (provisional) delimitation lines, one for the continental shelf and another for superjacent waters (ZEP). It is argued that this is also the current legal position on the basis of EPZCSA.

104　*Extension of Coastal State Jurisdiction in Enclosed or Semi-enclosed Seas*

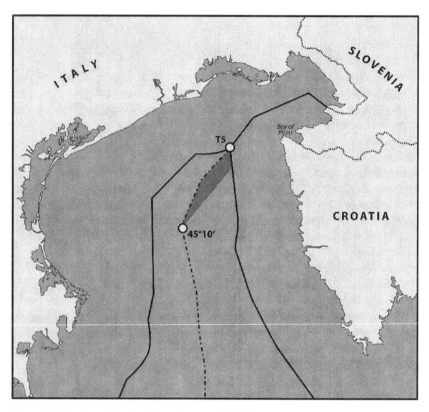

Figure 3.6 Provisional limits of the Slovenian ZEP[190]

of the Slovenian zone and of its temporary limits is obviously represented by the fact that the Slovenian zone is located along the Croatian coast. The latter fact, although not completely unique in the Mediterranean,[191] raises important questions from an international law standpoint (see Figure 3.6).[192]

Noteworthy is the fact that the Slovenian ZEP overlaps with the Croatian EFPZ and there is a risk that they will both partially overlap with the Italian zone(s) once

---

190　The line up to point T5 marks the territorial sea boundary in the Gulf of Trieste established with the 1975 (Italy-SFRY) Osimo Treaty. The two bold lines mark the external limits of the territorial sea of Italy and the former SFRY. The line in the middle is the 1968 shelf boundary agreed between Italy and SFRY.

191　Cyprus proclaimed its EEZ also along the two UK sovereign basis of Akrotiri and Dhekelia which have their own territorial sea (see section 3.4.1). Morocco formally proclaimed its EEZ along the Spanish 'enclaves' on its coast (see section 3.2.). Furthermore, Tunisia on the basis of the 2002 provisional delimitation agreement with Algeria exercises sovereign rights and jurisdiction also over an area of the sea located along the Algerian coast and located beyond the Algerian territorial sea and fishing zone (see sections 2.4.2.5.1 and 3.4.4). See also section 6.1.2 for reference to the specific regime of the waters in front of the Gaza Strip.

192　See also the discussion of the Croatian protest (*Note Verbale*) dated 31 May 2007 and issued (also) in relation to the proclamation of the Slovenian ZEP. See section 4.7.2.2.

Extension of jurisdiction in the Mediterranean Seas   105

the Italian regime is formally instituted in the (Northern) Adriatic.[193] It follows, therefore, that also Slovenia did not, or at least not entirely, fulfil its *bona fide* obligation to co-operate in the establishment of the zone nor seemingly did it make 'every effort to enter into provisional arrangements of a practical nature' pending its delimitation.[194]

3.4 Recently proclaimed EEZs in the Mediterranean: *de facto* or just virtual EEZs?

This section aims to analyze the 'recent' proclamations of EEZs in the Mediterranean Sea, starting from the proclamation by Cyprus in 2004 and ending with the proclamation of the French (Mediterranean) EEZ in October 2012. The aim is to assess whether these proclamations are just 'framework laws' or whether they actually establish EEZs. Of particular interest is the situation in the Eastern Mediterranean, whereby Cyprus has not just proclaimed an EEZ, but also concluded three (EEZ) delimitation agreements with its neighbours Egypt, Lebanon and Israel. This section also purports to identify recent trends at the Mediterranean level which are likely to influence the attitudes of Adriatic States regarding this question.

3.4.1 Cyprus

If the 1997 Spanish Proclamation confirmed a new era in the proclamation of *sui generis (in plus stat minus)* zones of jurisdiction in the Mediterranean, then the 2004 EEZ proclamation by Cyprus, effected through the adoption of its Law to Provide for the Proclamation of the Exclusive Economic Zone by the Republic of Cyprus[195] represented the next important milestone in the process of extension of coastal State jurisdiction in the (Eastern) Mediterranean. Its importance is represented also by the fact that up to that point in time practically all Mediterranean States had refrained from proclaiming or at least implementing full EEZs.[196] The Cypriot proclamation therefore represents an important precedent which was shortly followed by similar moves of some other Mediterranean States and seems to have had a particular influence on the Cypriot neighbouring States in the Eastern Mediterranean: Syria, Egypt, Lebanon, Israel and Turkey.[197] It is accordingly suggested that the Cypriot proclamation started a process of proclamations and delimitation of EEZs in the Eastern Mediterranean which,

---

193 As indicated, Italy does not recognize the continental shelf boundaries to be applicable also to superjacent waters. See sections 3.3.1 and 3.3.4. See, however, the discussion of the 2009 Arbitral Agreement between Slovenia and Croatia in section 4.8.

194 Slovenia proposed in 2004 to Croatia and Italy the establishment of a joint zone of jurisdiction of the three States in the Northern Adriatic. The proposal, although supported by Italy, was firmly rejected by Croatia. See Vidas, op. cit., pp. 27–28.

195 2 April 2004. See LOS Bulletin, UN, No. 55, 2004, pp. 22–24.

196 See section 3.2.

197 As for example Syria, section 3.4.2. See also the discussion in section 3.2.

106 *Extension of Coastal State Jurisdiction in Enclosed or Semi-enclosed Seas*

particularly during the last decade, differed substantially from other parts of the *Mare Nostrum*, including the Adriatic and/or Western Mediterranean.[198]

The Cypriot Proclamation is interesting from different points of view. The first consideration is that it occurred more than a year after the conclusion of the *Agreement between the Republic of Cyprus and the Arab Republic of Egypt on the Delimitation of the Exclusive Economic Zone, 17 February 2003*,[199] and the Cypriot Law provides for its retroactive application starting from 21 March 2003.[200] Second, the maritime areas in front of the two UK sovereign bases of Akrotiri and Dhekelia on the island of Cyprus which dispose of their own territorial sea[201] have not been expressly excluded from the proclamation which implies that they are deprived of their continental shelf and/or EEZ. This in turn means that the Cypriot EEZ is located in front of the coasts over which sovereignty is exercised by another State (UK) (see Figure 3.7).

Third, the Cypriot EEZ was proclaimed around the entire island of Cyprus without taking into account the (still) divided status of the island (Northern Cyprus).[202] Noteworthy is that, on 21 September 2011, the 'Turkish Republic of Northern Cyprus' signed an agreement on the delimitation of the continental shelf with Turkey, which includes areas formally included into the Cypriot EEZ.[203] This last consideration confirms the influence of political considerations on the proclamations and delimitation of maritime zones and emphasizes the need to

198 See the discussion in section 3.3.

199 Cf fn 24. See the discussion in section 3.1.1.

200 Cf fn 195, Art. 12.

201 For a general discussion, see F.A. Anish, *The International Law of Maritime Boundaries and the Practice of States in the Mediterranean Sea*, Oxford: Clarendon Press, 1993, pp. 256–258. The 1960 Treaty Concerning the Establishment of the Republic of Cyprus, signed by the UK, Cyprus, Turkey and Greece, provides in Art. 1 that the territory of the new State comprises the island of Cyprus with the exception of the two Sovereign Base Areas (SBAs) of Akrotiri and Dhekelia, which remained under the sovereignty of the UK. Section 3 of Annex 2 to the 1960 Treaty defines the waters pertaining to each SBA (see Figure 3.7), while the provisions of the Treaty obligates Cyprus not to claim the mentioned waters as part of its territorial sea. Scovazzi opinies that Cyprus is accordingly entitled to proclaim an EEZ in waters located beyond 12 nmi from the coast of the two SBAs. See Scovazzi, 'Maritime Boundaries in the Eastern Mediterranean Sea', op. cit., pp. 6–7. Reference should, however, be made to the fact that at the time of the conclusion of the 1960 Treaty the concept of the EEZ did not form part of (customary) international law and that the generally accepted breadth of the territorial sea at that time was still 3 nmi.

202 According to the 2006 *Note Verbale* sent by Cyprus to the UN Secretary-General in relation to the objections of Turkey to the 2003 Delimitation Agreement between Cyprus and Egypt: '[…] she [Turkey] continues to illegally occupy a sizeable part of the maritime zones of the Republic of Cyprus and prevents the latter from exercising effective control over a part of its sovereign territory […]'. See *Note Verbale* dated 19 October 2006 from the Permanent Mission Republic of Cyprus to the United Nations addressed to the Secretary-General of the United Nations concerning the communication dated 4 October 2005 from Turkey, LOS Bulletin, UN, No. 62, 2006, p. 164.

203 See Scovazzi, 'Maritime Boundaries in the Eastern Mediterranean Sea', op. cit., p. 9. On 27 April 2012, the Government of the Republic of Turkey granted hydrocarbon exploration licenses to the Turkish Petroleum Corporation (TPAO) in sea areas which fall, either partly or wholly, within the proclaimed EEZ and continental shelf of the Republic of Cyprus. See 'Letter dated 15 June 2012 from the Permanent Representative of Cyprus to the United Nations addressed to the Secretary-General', UN, General Assembly, Document A/66/851, Sixty-sixth session, Agenda item 76, Oceans and the law of the sea, 19 June 2012.

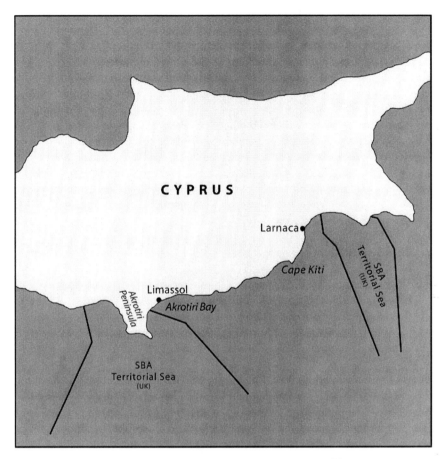

Figure 3.7 The territorial sea of the (UK) sovereign bases on Cyprus[204]

distinguish, particularly in the Mediterranean (and Adriatic) context between the formal proclamation of an EEZ (or *sui generis* zone) and the actual implementation of its regime.

The rights of Cyprus in its EEZ match completely the list of sovereign rights and jurisdictions enumerated in Article 56(1) of UNCLOS and the Cypriot law also expressly provides that Part VI of UNCLOS on the continental shelf is applicable in the Cypriot EEZ.[205] It may therefore be reasonable to argue that the Cypriot proclamation represents a proclamation of a full EEZ and not of a *sui generis* zone. The Cypriot Law is also quite detailed, as it regulates issues such as the determination of the total allowable catch,[206] offences and penalties,[207]

204 Modelled on a figure published in Anish, op. cit., p. 257.
205 Article 4(1) and (2).
206 Article 6.
207 Article 7(2).

108 *Extension of Coastal State Jurisdiction in Enclosed or Semi-enclosed Seas*

confiscation of vessels and their catch; from which it may be *prima facie* implied that the Cypriot legislator did not intend this law to be just 'framework law', requiring the adoption of additional implementing legislation.

The provisional limits of the 'Cypriot EEZ' are regulated by Article 3 of the Law. Article 3(1) includes a general provision stating that the outer limits of the Cypriot EEZ shall not extend beyond 200 nmi measured from the baseline. Article 3(1) then deals specifically with cases where part of the Cypriot EEZ overlaps with part of the EEZ of another State with an opposite facing coast, and for such cases the Cypriot proclamation provides that the delimitation shall be effected by agreement. However, in the absence of such agreement:

> ... the delimitation of this zone shall not extend beyond the *median line* or the *equidistance line* measured from the respective baselines from which the breadth of the territorial sea is measured.[208]

Article 3(3) furthermore provides that:

> The exact limits of the Exclusive Economic Zone at any given time, shall be made public by the Notification issued by the Minister of Foreign Affairs, to be published in the Official Gazette of the Republic, *as these limits will be shaped according to the specific areas and the possible delimitation agreements to be reached in accordance with the provisions of subsections (1) and (2).*[209]

From the latter provisions it may be clearly seen that Cyprus expressly envisaged a possibility of its EEZ having different breadths along 'specific areas' depending on 'possible delimitation agreements'. In the absence of agreement, however, the Cypriot law provides for the 'median line', as a temporary delimitation of the zone.[210] Such solution, although seemingly not in line with Article 74 of UNCLOS reflects the recent practice of (Mediterranean) States, particularly when it comes to the (provisional) delimitation of *sui generis* zones of jurisdiction in the Mediterranean.[211] Accordingly, such a position has been reflected also in

---

208 Emphasis added. Article 3(2).
209 Emphasis added. Article 3(3).
210 The median line as a method of delimitation in the region has been however strongly opposed by Turkey which in its 'Information note' sent to the UN Secretary-General on the 17 February 2003 stated:

> It is the considered opinion of the Republic of Turkey that the delimitation of the EEZ and the continental shelf beyond the western parts of the longitude 32°16'18" should be effected by agreement between the related states at the region based on the principle of equity.

> See Turkey, 'Information note concerning Turkey's objection to the Agreement between the Republic of Cyprus and the Arab Republic of Egypt on the Delimitation of the Exclusive Economic Zone', 17 February 2003, LOS Bulletin, UN, No. 54, 2004, p. 127.

211 See the discussion in sections 3.3.1, 3.3.2 and 3.3.5. According to the *Note Verbale* sent by Greece to the UN Secretary-General dated 24 February 2005:

> ... Greece, as one of the 'related States at the region', would like to reiterate its long-standing position that the delimitation of the continental shelf or the exclusive economic zone ... should take place in accordance with the pertinent rules of international law on the basis of

the two subsequent (EEZ) maritime delimitation agreements concluded by Cyprus after the formal proclamation of its EEZ in 2004. Both the 2007 delimitation agreement with Lebanon[212] and the 2010 delimitation agreement with Israel,[213] as the previously mentioned 2003 delimitation agreement with Egypt,[214] make express reference to the 'median line' as the method of delimitation (see Figure 3.8).

It is noteworthy that no Mediterranean State expressly opposed the right of Cyprus to proclaim a full EEZ in the Mediterranean Sea, although Turkey has not recognized the Delimitation Agreement between Cyprus and Egypt as opposable to it.[215] It is also important to note that Cyprus concluded the Delimitation Agreement with Egypt even before the formal proclamation of its EEZ and that shortly after its conclusion started negotiations with Lebanon and later Israel.[216] Cyprus therefore has taken a proactive approach and endeavoured to co-operate with some of its neighbouring States (Egypt and Lebanon)[217] with regard to the delimitation of its EEZs even before the formal proclamation of its EEZ.

Moreover, it appears from the three delimitation agreements concluded by Cyprus (Egypt, Lebanon and Israel) that interest of third (potentially) affected States have also been taken into account. All three delimitation agreements incorporate a 'standard clause' in Article 1(e) which expressly provides that on the basis of Article 74 of UNCLOS (or alternatively customary international law relating to the delimitation of EEZ between States),[218] the first and the last points of the agreed delimitation line(s):

> … could be reviewed and/or extended as necessary in the light of future delimitation of the exclusive economic zone *with other concerned neighbouring States* and in accordance with an agreement to be reached in this matter by the neighbouring States concerned.

> the principle equidistance/median line. This is confirmed by widespread, long-standing State practice ….

See Greece, 'Communication dated 24 February 2005 from the Government of Greece concerning Turkey's objection to the Agreement between the Republic of Cyprus and the Arab Republic of Egypt on the Delimitation of the Exclusive Economic Zone of 17 February 2003', LOS Bulletin, UN, No. 57, 2005, p. 129.

212 Cf fn 25, Art. 1(a).
213 Cf fn 26, Art. 1(a).
214 Cf fn 24, Art. 1(a).
215 Cf fn 210.
216 See the discussion in 3.1.1.
217 It is noteworthy that according to the *Note Verbale* by Cyprus to the UN Secretary-General, dated 19 October 2006 the Republic of Cyprus:

> … agrees with the following position by Turkey: 'Furthermore, according to one of the general principles of international law of the sea, States bordering an enclosed or semi-enclosed sea, such as the Mediterranean Sea, *are under an obligation to cooperate with each other in the exercise of their rights and in the performance of their duties*'.

Emphasis added. Cf fn 202.

218 See Art. 1(e) of the 2011 Israel-Cyprus delimitation agreement. See also the discussion in section 2.4.2.4.

110 *Extension of Coastal State Jurisdiction in Enclosed or Semi-enclosed Seas*

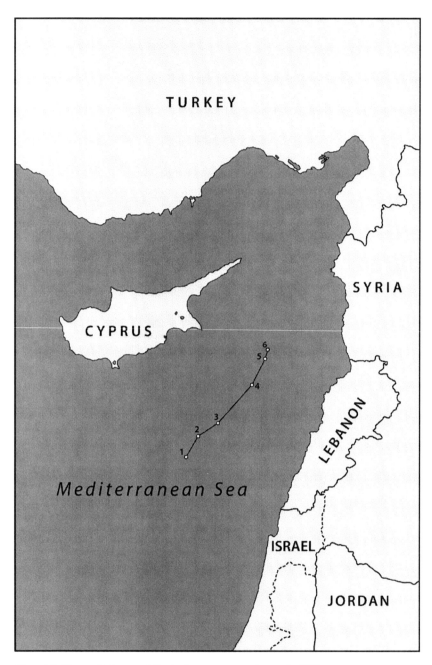

Figure 3.8 Cyprus-Lebanon delimitation agreement (unratified)[219]

219 Modelled on a figure published in T. Scovazzi and I. Papanicolopulu, 'Cyprus Lebanon (Report Number 8-19)', in Colson and Smith (eds), op. cit., p. 4454.

The first and the last points of the agreed delimitation line(s) could therefore be considered as provisional. The clause is furthermore supplemented by another standard provision incorporated in Article 3 of all three agreements. According to the latter:

> … [i]f either of the two Parties [to a delimitation agreement] is engaged in negotiations aimed at the delimitation of its exclusive economic zone with another State, that Party, before reaching a final agreement with the other State, shall notify and consult the other Party, if such delimitation is in connection with [the first and last] coordinates ….

Notwithstanding this, Lebanon protested vehemently against the application of the end point of the Cyprus-Lebanon delimitation line as a starting point for the Cyprus-Israeli delimitation line in 2011. Lebanon had pointed out that:

> … Point 1 does not therefore represent the southern end of the median line between the Lebanese Republic and the Republic of Cyprus that separates the exclusive economic zones of each country, and can only be viewed as a point that is shared by Lebanon and Cyprus. It is not a terminal point and therefore may not be taken as a starting point between Cyprus and any other country ….[220]

It seems that despite the clear text embodied in Article 3 of the 2007 Agreement, Cyprus did not 'notify and consult' Lebanon before the conclusion of the delimitation agreement with Israel in 2010.[221] Following the conclusion of this agreement, its entry into force in February 2011, and following the unilateral definition of the external limits of the territorial sea and EEZ of Israel in July

---

220 On 12 July 2011 Israel transmitted to the UN Secretary-General a 'List of Geographical Coordinates For the Delimitation of the Northern Limit of the Territorial Sea and Exclusive Economic Zone of the State of Israel' which (unilaterally) defines the maritime border with Lebanon. See LOS Bulletin, UN, No. 76, 2011, pp. 28–19. Lebanon promptly protested by *inter alia* stating:

> On the basis of the foregoing, it is clear that the geographical coordinates that were deposited with you by Israel violate the sovereign and economic rights of Lebanon over its territorial waters and exclusive economic zone, the coordinates of which are given in the attachment, and cut from those waters and that zone some 860 square kilometres. International peace and security could thus be imperilled, particularly if Israel, the occupying Power, should decide to pursue any economic activity in the aforementioned maritime area, which Lebanon considers to be an integral part of its territorial waters and exclusive economic zone.

Emphasis added. See 'A letter dated 3 September 2011 from the Minister for Foreign Affairs and Emigrants of Lebanon addressed to the Secretary-General of the United Nations concerning the geographical coordinates of the northern limit of the territorial sea and the exclusive economic zone transmitted by Israel'. See also fn 30, and Scovazzi, 'Maritime Boundaries in the Eastern Mediterranean', op. cit., p. 9.

221 It should be noted that the 2007 Cyprus-Lebanon delimitation agreement has not yet entered into force. Cf fn 25.

112 *Extension of Coastal State Jurisdiction in Enclosed or Semi-enclosed Seas*

2011,[222] in August 2011 Lebanon also formally proclaimed its EEZ.[223] The adoption of the 'EEZ framework law' was then followed by the adoption of the Decree in November 2011, which unilaterally provided for the (provisional) external limits of the newly proclaimed Lebanese EEZ.[224]

For the purpose of our discussion it is important that all three delimitation agreements incorporate in Article 2 a 'co-operation clause' which seems to reflect the 'general policy of co-operation' embodied in Part IX of UNCLOS (Article 123). The 'clause' provides that:

> … [i]n case there are *natural resources* [including hydrocarbon reservoirs][225] extending from the exclusive economic zone of one Party to the exclusive economic zone of the other, the two Parties *shall cooperate* in order to reach an agreement on the modalities of the exploitation of such resources.[226]

Such duty of co-operation relates, therefore, to both living and non-living (straddling) resources of the two EEZs, and not only to 'mineral deposits' as has been the case with many EEZ, and/or continental shelf delimitation agreements concluded in the past.

It seems possible to conclude that the EEZ delimitation agreements concluded by Cyprus may be interpreted also as an attempt of the application of Article 74 of UNCLOS in the light of the general policy of co-operation embodied in Part IX of UNCLOS.[227]

3.4.2 Syria

It would seem that the conclusion of the Delimitation Agreement between Egypt and Cyprus and the expected Cypriot proclamation of an EEZ[228] prompted its neighbouring State, Syria, to adopt on 8 November 2003 its own Law on maritime zones (Law No. 28).[229] Law No. 28 seems to represent also the formal

---

222 Cf fn 220.

223 Cf fn 30.

224 See Decree No. 6433 (Delineation of the boundaries of the exclusive economic zone of Lebanon), 16 November 2011. Cf fn 30. Article 3 of Decree No. 6433 provides, however, as follows:

> As needed, and in the light of negotiations with the relevant neighbouring States, the borders of the exclusive economic zone may be refined and improved and, consequently, the list of its coordinates amended, if more precise data becomes available.

225 Article 2 of the 2011 Israel-Cyprus Agreement makes express reference to 'hydrocarbon reservoirs', as part of the 'natural resources' of the two zones.

226 Emphasis added.

227 See the discussion in section 2.4.2.4.

228 See section 3.4.1.

229 Law No. 28 dated 19 November 2003 – 'Definition Act of Internal Waters and Territorial Sea Limits of the Syrian Arab Republic', OG of Syria, No. 51/2003. See LOS Bulletin, UN, No. 55, 2004, pp. 14–20.

Extension of jurisdiction in the Mediterranean Seas   113

proclamation of the Syrian EEZ in the Mediterranean[230] and in its Chapter V it regulates the regime of the Zone. According to Article 21 of the Law:

> The exclusive economic zone lies beyond the territorial sea and includes the entire contiguous zone, extending in the direction of the high seas for a distance of not more than 200 nautical miles measured from the baselines, subject to the provisions of international law.

The list of sovereign rights and jurisdiction which Syria is entitled to exercise in its EEZ is provided by Article 22 of the Law and exactly replicates the list embodied in Article 56 of UNCLOS. From the latter it may be *prima facie* seen that like the Cypriot zone, Law No. 28 has not established a *sui generis* (*in plus stat minus*) zone but a full EEZ based prevalently on the provisions of Chapter V of UNCLOS as reflected in customary international law.[231] It should be noted, however, that the freedom of navigation and overflight of other States in the Syrian EEZ is not expressly mentioned by the Syrian Law, while the laying of submarine cables and pipelines is subject to first acquiring a permit from the Syrian authorities.[232] The latter, however, does not seem to be in line with the relevant provisions of UNCLOS nor, as suggested, customary international law. Similarly, Article 23(b) of the Syrian Law provides that the '[t]he competent Syrian authorities shall have the right to *inspect, search, arrest and initiate legal actions against foreign ships* in case of violations of Syrian laws and regulations relating to the economic zone',[233] without differentiating between different scenarios based for example on the seriousness of the threat and/or damage as provided by Article 220 of UNCLOS regulating enforcement by coastal States in cases of ship source pollution in the EEZ.[234]

It is furthermore worth noting that Law No. 28 does not contain any provision on the delimitation of the EEZ, nor is there available data about whether Syria has started negotiations with neighbouring States in line with Article 74 of UNCLOS, including its third paragraph. This fact, together with the seeming absence of any implementing legislation and/or practical implementation of the regime of the Zone, seems to point to the fact that Chapter V of the Syrian Law No. 28, although legally representing a formal proclamation of an EEZ, is in

---

230 Ibid, Law No. 28 does not provide for any further requirement for the entry into force of the regime of the Syrian EEZ (e.g. proclamation by the President) from which it may be implied that Law No. 28 represents also a proclamation of the regime of the zone.
231 Syria is not a State Party to UNCLOS.
232 See Art. 24 of Act No. 28 and Arts 58 and 79 of UNCLOS.
233 Emphasis added.
234 As Syria is not a State Party to UNCLOS the relevant question is whether Art. 220 of UNCLOS reflects customary international law and the answer seems to be in the affirmative. As pointed out by Treves: 'On most issues the rules of UNCLOS reflect (or in the years after entry into force in 1994 have come to reflect) customary law ...'. Treves, op. cit., p. 1. Such conclusion seems to be confirmed also by the legislative history of Art. 220 of UNCLOS which shows that the latter was a carefully drafted compromise. See DOALOS, *The Law of the Sea: Enforcement by Coastal States, Legislative History of Article 220 of UNCLOS*, United Nations Publications, New York, NY: UN, 2005.

114 *Extension of Coastal State Jurisdiction in Enclosed or Semi-enclosed Seas*

practical terms a 'framework law' requiring the adoption of additional implementing legislation for the entry into force of the various elements of the EEZ regime for Syria.[235]

3.4.3 Libya: A transition from a sui generis zone to a full EEZ?

In the context of extension of coastal State jurisdiction in the Mediterranean, the specific case of Libya is particularly interesting. On 24 February 2005 Libya adopted its General People's Committee Decision No. 37 with which it proclaimed a FPZ in the Mediterranean Sea.[236] The proclamation includes two parts: the Decision itself and the annexed Declaration of a Libyan Fisheries Protection Zone in the Mediterranean Sea. The link between the two parts is provided by Article 1 of Decision No. 37 according to which '[a] Libyan fisheries protection zone in the Mediterranean Sea is hereby declared in accordance with the text of the annexed declaration'.

The two documents are therefore complementary and may be treated as a 'single' proclamation. While the Decision officially proclaims the zone and provides for a general prohibition against fishing,[237] the annexed declaration establishes the basis for the proclamation, the limits of the zone and impliedly also some international conventions, protocols and codes applicable in the Libyan zone.[238] At least *prima facie* it would seem that the Libyan proclamation and consequently the legal regime of the zone departs from the concept of the EEZ, and also from the majority of existing examples of EFZ or FPZ in the Mediterranean.

The first peculiarity of the zone is represented by the fact that fishing is as a general rule prohibited: both for foreigners and Libyan nationals alike, in the absence of a permit issued by the competent Libyan authority. Such prohibition is unequivocally stated in Article 2 of the Decision and reconfirmed by the second part of Article 1 of the Declaration. The latter provides that the Libyan zone is:

> [...] a fisheries zone subject to Libyan *sovereignty* and jurisdiction in which fishing, *be it domestic or national,* of any kind, for any purpose and by any means is prohibited, unless the competent Libyan authorities have issued a permit to the person or persons concerned to conduct fishing operations in such areas in accordance with the laws and regulations in force in the Great Jamahiriya.[239]

Another provision worth mentioning is found in Article 1 of the Libyan Declaration, which interestingly provides that the Libyan zone is a zone 'subject

---

235 See also Leanza, op. cit., p. 168, and Del Vecchio Capotosti, op. cit., p. 289.
236 General People's Committee Decision No. 37 Concerning the Declaration of a Libyan Fisheries Protection Zone in the Mediterranean Sea, LOS Bulletin, UN, No. 58, 2005, pp. 14–16.
237 Ibid.
238 See Preamble to the Declaration, ibid, p. 15.
239 Emphasis added.

Extension of jurisdiction in the Mediterranean Seas 115

to Libyan *sovereignty* and jurisdiction',[240] and not '*subject to sovereign* rights and jurisdiction', as provided by international law (UNCLOS and/or customary international law). Article 1 becomes even more interesting if one takes into account the Preamble to the Declaration as the latter makes express reference to the 1982 Protocol to the 1976 Barcelona Convention Concerning Mediterranean Specially Protected Areas, in addition, to two FAO documents; the Compliance Agreement[241] and the Code of Conduct for Responsible Fisheries.[242] It is, however, noteworthy that, unlike the (1995) Biodiversity Protocol,[243] the scope of application of the 1982 Protocol to the Barcelona Convention is limited only to the territorial waters.[244] An obvious question is therefore whether Libya equates its zone with a SPA and one has to admit that there are many similarities between the regime of the Libyan FPZ and a 'potential' regime of a SPA or SPAMI, particularly on the basis of the Biodiversity Protocol to the Barcelona Convention.[245]

An important aid in the interpretation of the nature of the Libyan proclamation and its zone may, however, be found in the last paragraph of the Preamble to the Declaration. From the latter it may be inferred that Libya proclaimed its zone also:

> With a view to promoting the Declaration of the Ministerial Conference for the Sustainable Development of Fisheries in the Mediterranean held in Venice on the 25 and 26 of November 2003, paragraph 10 of which states: 'we consider that the *creation of a fisheries protection zone* permits the improvements of conservation and control of fisheries and thus contributes to better resource management and to our common commitment to combat IUU [illegal, unreported and unregulated fishing'].[246]

A final question therefore seems to be, whether the Libyan zone is just an FPZ or whether it is, like other Mediterranean examples, a hybrid zone, halfway between an FPZ and a ZEP. This question is interesting *inter alia* in the light of the Preamble to the Declaration which makes reference also to international obligations (of Libya) in the area of protection of the marine environment of the Mediterranean Sea.

It is, however, doubtful whether Libya can extend the application of its environmental laws to its 'FPZ', located beyond the limits of its territorial sea

---

240 From the drafting language of the 'Decision' and the annexed 'Declaration' it would, however, appear that the rights of Libya in its zone are more akin to 'sovereign rights' than to 'sovereignty'.
241 Agreement adopted by FAO at its 28 Session, 24 November 1993, Resolution No. 15/93.
242 Agreement adopted by FAO at its 28 Session, 31 October 2005, Resolution 4/95.
243 See also the discussion in sections 5.1.3.1 and 3.3.3. Libya is not a State Party to the Biodiversity Protocol. See Slim and Scovazzi, op. cit. (Part 1), pp. 138–140.
244 See Art. 2.
245 An example seems to be the general prohibition of fishing, both for nationals and foreigners. See Art. 6 of the Biodiversity Protocol. Article 5(1) of the latter provides: 'Each Party may establish specially protected areas in the marine and coastal zones *subject to its sovereignty or jurisdiction*'. Emphasis added. For a possible link between a SPAMI and *sui generis* zones of jurisdiction, see the discussion in section 5.1.3.1 and Chapter 6.
246 Emphasis added. See also the discussion on the 'Venice Declaration' in section 3.5.2.1.

116 *Extension of Coastal State Jurisdiction in Enclosed or Semi-enclosed Seas*

by simply making reference to them in the Preamble to the Declaration. Such interpretation seems to be too extensive, at least in the absence of additional implementing legislation. It is nonetheless possible to agree with Del Vecchio Capotosti that:

> The Libyan Zone was established … with the intention of implementing: the Protocol Concerning Mediterranean Specially Protected Areas …, the FAO Agreement …, the FAO Code of Conduct … and the provisions laid down in the Declaration of the Ministerial Conference held in Venice in 2003 'to contribute in assuring a better management of these resources [fisheries] and combating against illegal, unorganized and undeclared marine fishing activities'.[247]

The Libyan zone is therefore an interesting mixture of an EFZ and an SPA, although ultimately its legal essence seems to be that of an FPZ.

3.4.3.1 The limits of the Libyan FPZ

The external limits of the Libyan zone are provided by Article 1 of the Declaration. The latter (geographically) describes the zone as:

> … the area of the Mediterranean Sea lying north of the boundaries of the Libyan territorial waters and extending seaward for a distance of 62 nautical miles, measured from the territorial sea line ….[248]

At first sight it would seem that Libya showed self-restraint and that due to the relatively limited breadth of the Libyan zone, which does not go so far as the median line, the latter will not give rise to overlapping claims and/or encroach (overlap) upon potential interest of other States. Nonetheless, the adoption by Libya of its General People's Committee Decision No. 104 of the year 1373 from the death of the Prophet (AD 2005) concerning straight baselines for measuring the breadth of the territorial sea and maritime zones of the Libyan Arab Jamahiriya,[249] and more specifically its General People's Committee Decision No. 105 of the year 1373 from the death of the Prophet (AD 2005) concerning the delimitation of the Libyan FPZ in the Mediterranean Sea,[250] has provoked protests by neighbouring States (e.g. Malta and Italy) and the EU.[251]

It is, however, interesting that the main reasons for the protests were not the sole proclamation of the Libyan zone, nor its (relatively) contained breadth; but the

---

247 See Del Vecchio Capotosti, op. cit., p. 293.
248 Libya therefore proclaimed a 50 nmi 'zone' in addition to the 12 nmi territorial sea.
249 See LOS Bulletin, UN, No. 59, 2005, pp. 15–18.
250 Ibid, p. 19.
251 See *Malta Today*, 'Libya's bridge to Europe', 29 April 2009.

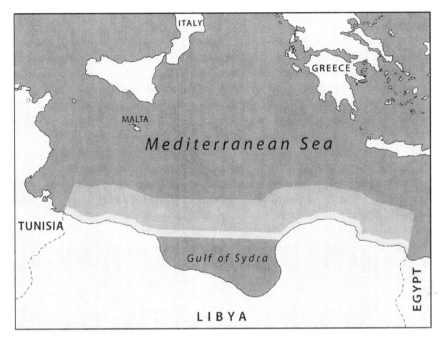

Figure 3.9 Baseline and external limits of the Libyan FPZ[252]

fact that Libya, in Decision No. 104 and 105 made plainly clear that the breadth of all its maritime zones, including its FPZ is measured *inter alia* from the straight baseline closing the Gulf of Sidra for which Libya claims, despite protest from many States, the status of a 'historic bay' (see Figure 3.9).[253]

There is no doubt that the closing of the Gulf of Sidra extends the limits of the Libyan territorial sea and FPZ substantially towards the centre of the Mediterranean Sea. However, even by using such a disputed baseline, the external limits of the Libyan zone, like that of the Algerian,[254] do not extend so far as to reach the median line with other States. Libya therefore, although seemingly not fulfilling its obligation of co-operation with its neighbouring States in fixing the external limits of the zone and/or with regard to the conclusion of provisional arrangements of a practical nature pending delimitation, has shown some restraint by defining the breadth of the zone which independently of the used baseline (low water mark or straight baselines) does not go so far as the median line with neighbouring States.

An interesting (related) question is, however, whether the provided limits of the Libyan zone are in the Libyan view 'final' or just 'provisional', pending

---

252 Author's archive.
253 For a thorough discussion of the legal status of the Gulf of Sidra, see Anish, op. cit., Part 7.
254 Cf fn 47.

118 *Extension of Coastal State Jurisdiction in Enclosed or Semi-enclosed Seas*

delimitation agreements with adjacent and opposite States. Article 1 of Decision No. 105 provides that:

> The Libyan fisheries zone in the Mediterranean Sea ... is delimited as follows, until such time as the Great Jamahiriya declares its own EEZ over which it exercises its right of sovereignty and jurisdiction which belong to it under its national legislation or international law [followed by a list of co-ordinates].

This provision is indeed noteworthy. It does not link the validity of the limits of the zone to the moment of the eventual conclusion of delimitation agreements with other potentially affected States, but instead to the proclamation of a full Libyan EEZ. The importance of the mentioned provision seems to be at least twofold: first, it clearly shows the Libyan intention to proclaim an EEZ at an appropriate moment; and, second, it made clear that the (limited) breadth of the Libyan EEZ will not be necessarily applicable also to the future Libyan EEZ. It may be furthermore implied that in the views of Libya, the *sui generis* FPZ represented just a transition from the high seas regime along its coasts to an EEZ regime, and that accordingly the ultimate goal was the proclamation of a full EEZ. This presumption was confirmed on 31 May 2009 when Libya adopted its General People's Committee Decision No. 260 of A.J. 1377 (A.D. 2009) concerning the declaration of the exclusive economic zone of the Great Socialist People's Libyan Arab Jamahiriya.[255]

3.4.3.2 The Libyan EEZ (2009)

With the 2009 Declaration, Libya formally proclaimed its EEZ beyond the limits of its territorial sea. However, the latest enactment consists only of three general articles and *prima facie* it seems that, although from the standpoint of international law representing a valid proclamation of the Libyan EEZ in the Mediterranean,[256] it is a *de facto* framework law requiring the adoption of additional implementing legislation for the entry into force of the various elements of the EEZ regime for Libya (in addition to the already established FPZ). At least *prima facie* it would therefore seem that the Libyan FPZ for the time being co-exists and is the only part of the EEZ regime[257] implemented by Libya.

---

255 The 'Decision' was based on the previous 'Declaration concerning the exclusive economic zone of the Great Socialist People's Libyan Arab Jamahiriya', adopted by the General People's Committee on 27 May 2009. The English translation of both documents is reproduced in the LOS Bulletin, UN, No. 72, 2010, pp. 78–79.

256 See Art. 1 of the 2009 Decision.

257 According to Art. 2 of the 2009 Decision, Libya:

> ... shall have sovereign rights in the exclusive economic zone for the purpose of exploring and exploiting, conserving and managing the natural resources, whether living or non-living of the waters superjacent to the sea-bed and its subsoil, and with regard to other activities for the economic exploitation and exploration of that zone, and shall have *jurisdictions over that zone in accordance with international law*.

Extension of jurisdiction in the Mediterranean Seas 119

Similar considerations apply in relation to the external limits of the Libyan EEZ. Article 1 of the Libyan Decision No. 260 provides that:

> An exclusive economic zone of the Great Socialist People's Libyan Arab Jamahiriya, adjacent to and extending as far beyond its territorial waters as permitted under international law, is hereby declared. *If necessary, the outer limits of this zone shall be established together with neighbouring States in accordance with instruments concluded on the basis of international law.*[258]

It seems, therefore, that the external limits of the Libyan FPZ are still in force. Libya, however, seems to have recognized that the latter are just 'provisional' and that they may be, if necessary, amended through (EEZ) delimitation agreements with neighbouring States. The 'Libyan' case therefore represents an interesting example of a gradual transition from a *sui generis* FPZ towards a full EEZ which influenced (and ultimately was influenced) also by the attitude of other Mediterranean States, particularly by two neighbours, Tunisia and Malta.

3.4.4 Tunisia

Following the proclamation by Cyprus and Syria (EEZs) and particularly of the Libyan FPZ in early 2005[259] Tunisia adopted in mid 2005 its Act No. 50/2005 dated 27 June 2005 concerning the EEZ off the Tunisian coast[260] with which it formally established its own EEZ in the Mediterranean Sea. This Act does not require any additional (formal) requirement for the entry into force of the regime of the zone (e.g. Proclamation by the President),[261] although reference should be made to Article 2(2) which provides that:

> These rights and jurisdictions [*EEZ regime*] shall be exercised [*in the Tunisian EEZ*] in accordance with the conditions and procedures set forth in this Act and *its implementing provisions.*[262]

The list of (sovereign) rights and jurisdictions which Tunisia is entitled to exercise in its zone follows closely the wording of Article 56 of UNCLOS and also the Act itself makes express reference to UNCLOS.[263] In this respect, it should be reiterated that Act No. 50/2005, at least from an international law standpoint

---

    Emphasis added. This provision matches broadly the list of competences embodied in the first part of Art. 56(1)(a) of UNCLOS and seem to make an implied reference also to its second part (Art. 56(1)(b)).

258 Emphasis added.
259 See section 3.4.3.
260 LOS Bulletin, UN, No. 58, 2005, p. 19.
261 'Pursuant to the present Act, an exclusive economic zone shall be established off the Tunisian coasts'. See Art. 1.
262 Emphasis added.
263 See Art. 2.

120 Extension of Coastal State Jurisdiction in Enclosed or Semi-enclosed Seas

represents a proper (legal) proclamation of the Tunisian EEZ.[264] This, however, does not automatically mean the entry into force of the regime of the zone itself. According to Article 4 of the Tunisian Act:

> Implementing orders shall govern the procedures for implementing the provisions of the present Act, including, where necessary, the establishment of *special fishing zones* or *protected fishing zones* or *environmental protection zones*.[265]

The latter provision is surprising, particularly if one takes into account that the regime of the EEZ *per se* includes the competences which a coastal State is normally entitled to exercise in 'special fishing zones, protected fishing zones or environmental protection zones'. From the latter provision it may be implied that the proclamation of a (full) Tunisian EEZ, although valid from the standpoint of international law, is in practical terms a 'framework law' and that in order for Tunisia to effectively exercise its sovereign rights and jurisdiction on the basis of the EEZ regime (in addition to the already existing Tunisian fishing zone)[266] additional implementing legislation (via implementing orders) is needed. Tunisia has therefore left the door open for a differentiated application of its sovereign rights and jurisdiction in its formally established EEZ, which may ultimately mean a selective application of the various EEZ powers along different segments of its coasts.

It seems therefore that, like the Libyan example, the existing Tunisian fishing zone[267] remains in force within its existing limits also after the proclamation of the Tunisian EEZ. The 2005 Tunisian Act is, although from an international law standpoint a proper proclamation of the EEZ, in practical terms more akin to a 'framework law' requiring the adoption of 'implementing orders' for the entry into force of the other elements of the EEZ regime.

The delimitation of the Tunisian EEZ is regulated by Article 3 which provides that:

> Without prejudice to the *relevant international conventions ratified by the Republic of Tunisia*, this zone may extend to the boundaries provided by international law. Where necessary, the outer boundaries of the exclusive economic zone shall be determined by agreement with the concerned neighbouring States.[268]

The reference to 'relevant international conventions ratified by the Republic of Tunisia' obviously refers to the already concluded (Shelf) Delimitation Agreements by Tunisia, namely the 1971 Agreement with Italy[269] and the 1988 Agreement with Libya.[270] The two (Shelf) Agreements, however, are not applicable

---

264 Cf fn 260.
265 Emphasis added. See also second paragraph of Art. 2.
266 Cf fn 45.
267 Ibid.
268 Emphasis added.
269 See section 2.4.2.5.1 (Figure 2.1).
270 Cf fn 21.

to superjacent waters and Italy, for example, has on many occasions firmly stated that it does recognize the continental shelf boundaries, particularly those which were concluded in the period before the advent of the EEZ, to be automatically applicable also to superjacent waters.[271] It therefore follows that even where there is a Shelf Delimitation Agreement in place, as with Libya and Italy, Tunisia will have to negotiate a (separate) Agreement covering superjacent waters which may or may not confirm the existing shelf line as applicable also to superjacent waters.[272] However, as discussed in Chapter 2, with Algeria, Tunisia concluded a 'provisional delimitation agreement' on the basis of Articles 74(3) and 83(3) of UNCLOS which temporarily delimits all maritime areas of the two States, including superjacent waters (potential EEZs). There are clear signs that the two States reached an agreement on the final settlement of a *single maritime boundary*, based on the provisions of the 2002 *interim* Agreement.[273]

The 2005 Act therefore allows for a flexible application of the various elements of the EEZ regime along different segments of the Tunisian coast; in a way which may allow Tunisia to take into account the specific geography of the (Central) Mediterranean[274] and the legitimate interests of its bordering States. It seems, nonetheless, possible to conclude that Tunisia has not fulfilled its obligation to endeavour to co-operate either with regard to the sole proclamation of the zone, or, apart from the discussed *interim* agreement with Algeria,[275] has made every effort to enter into provisional arrangement of a practical nature with the other two neighbouring States (Libya and Italy).

3.4.5 Malta

Following the proclamations of the Libyan FPZ and the Tunisian EEZ, Malta also adopted in 2005 the Fishing Waters (Designation) and Extended Maritime Jurisdiction Act[276] which is a framework law for the proclamation of the Maltese EEZ and/or other zones of jurisdiction. The latter gives to the Maltese Prime Minister the possibility by an order published in the 'Gazette', to claim all or some of the elements of the EEZ listed in Article 56 of UNCLOS[277] and this:

> ... over such areas of the marine waters beyond the limits laid down in Article 3(2) of the Territorial Waters and Contiguous Zone Act as may be

---

271 See the discussion in sections 3.3.1 and 3.3.4–3.3.5.
272 See the discussion in 3.4.4.
273 See section 2.4.2.5.1.
274 See Figure 1.2.
275 See section 2.4.2.5.1.
276 Chapter 479 of the Laws of Malta, 26 July 2005.
277 According to Arts 2 and 3 of the Act, '[t]he Prime Minister may by Order published in the Gazette claim sovereign rights for Malta, for the purpose of exploring and exploiting, conserving and managing the living and, or non-living natural resources therein ...' and '... provide for the exercise of jurisdiction beyond the territorial waters of Malta with regard to: (a) the establishment and use of artificial islands, installations and structures; (b) marine scientific research; and (c) the protection and preservation of the maritime environment'.

122 *Extension of Coastal State Jurisdiction in Enclosed or Semi-enclosed Seas*

designated in the order and thereupon the areas so designated shall form part of the fishing waters of Malta ....

The Act therefore gives the right to the Prime Minister of Malta to extend the existing Maltese EFZ[278] both in content and breadth; up to the point of transforming it into a full EEZ. It is also noteworthy that the Maltese Act, although completely based on the provisions of Article 56 of UNCLOS, does not make express reference to the concept of the EEZ. This still reinforces the impression that the intention of the drafters was to give to the Maltese Prime Minister the possibility to proclaim only some elements of the EEZ (*in plus stat minus*). The latter assertion seems to be confirmed also by the provisions of Article 2(1) of the Act which provides that the areas so designated may constitute part of the 'fishing waters of Malta' as provided in Article 3(c) of the (Maltese) Fisheries Conservation and Management Act.[279]

Regarding the limits of that zone, Article 2 provides that the zone may extend 'over such areas of the marine waters beyond the limits laid down in Article 3(2) of the Territorial Waters and Contiguous Zone Act[280] as may be designated in the Order ...'. The Act therefore impliedly also gives to the Maltese Prime Minister the power to define the external limits of the zone. The approach taken by the Maltese Act is extremely interesting, as it joins two different concepts, the 'EFZ' and the 'EEZ'. It would, therefore be perfectly possible for the Maltese 'EFZ' to be, in the future, supplemented with for example a ZEP and ultimately converted into a fully fledged EEZ.

3.4.6 French and Lebanese EEZs: The end of a 'sui generis zones era' in the Mediterranean?

The Mediterranean Sea has recently experienced two important EEZ proclamations for which it is suggested that they may potentially lead to the end of the *sui generis zones era* in the *Mare Nostrum*. Reference is hereby made to the EEZ proclamations by Lebanon in 2011,[281] and even more importantly to the EEZ proclamation by France in October 2012. The two proclamations, although far from being unexpected,[282] seem to confirm a new approach by Mediterranean coastal States when it comes to the extension of coastal State jurisdiction in this sea.

---

278 See fn 46.

279 Chapter 425 of the Laws of Malta, 4 June 2001.

280 Chapter 226 of the Laws of Malta, 10 December 1971. ACT XXXII of 1971, as amended by Acts XLVI of 1975, XXIV of 1978, XXVIII of 1981 and I of 2002.

281 For previous (EEZ) activities by Lebanon see fn 25 and 30.

282 On 25 August 2009 the French Minister of Environment, Jean-Louis Borloo expressed the intention of France to upgrade its Mediterranean ZEP to a full EEZ in the near future. It furthermore appealed to other State Parties of the Union for the Mediterranean (UFM) to follow suit. See Dnevnik, '*Francozi opozorili Hrvaško: Ne igrajte se z zaščiteno ekološko-ribolovno cono!*', Ljubljana, 28 September 2009.

Extension of jurisdiction in the Mediterranean Seas 123

While the Lebanese framework law(s) contains just a broad definition of the EEZ based on the relevant provisions of UNCLOS,[283] the 2012 French Decree with which France upgraded its (Mediterranean) ZEP into a fully fledged EEZ, provides some more insight into the main reasons for its adoption.[284]

The Preamble to the 2012 French Decree first of all makes clear that the Decree establishes an EEZ based on the relevant provisions of UNCLOS. The Preamble then makes reference to the main reasons and objectives of such a 'jurisdictional move'. Mention is made of the fact that the proclamation of a 'full' French EEZ in the Mediterranean will give to the French State sovereign rights for the purpose of exploring and exploiting, conserving and managing the natural resources, whether living or non-living, of the waters superjacent to the sea-bed and of the sea-bed and its subsoil within such (Mediterranean) zone. This was obviously not (fully) the case within the French Mediterranean ZEP. Second, reference is made to the fact that such EEZ proclamation shall further strengthen the ability of the French State to fight against all forms of pollution. Third, the Preamble makes reference to the fact that an EEZ, differently from the regime of the (former) French ZEP, will enable the French State to also carry out other activities for the economic exploitation and exploration of the (Mediterranean) zone, such as the production of energy from the water, currents and winds. Lastly, the entry into force of the 2012 Decree should allow France to 'establish and use' (therefore 'regulate') artificial islands, installations and structures, such as drilling platforms and wind turbines.[285] It should be acknowledged that, at least generally speaking, the French Republic was not entitled to exercise those sovereign rights and/or jurisdictions within its Mediterranean ZEP.[286]

Noteworthy is the fact that the initial intention of France was, at least in the immediate period following the proclamation of its (Mediterranean) ZEP, to establish an additional Mediterranean FPZ, which would be geographically located within the same boundaries and which would coexist with its ZEP.[287] France, however, ultimately opted for the upgrading of its (Mediterranean) ZEP into a full EEZ, allegedly as a result of a perception that the implementation of

---

283 Article 1 of the Lebanese Decree No. 6433 (Delineation of the boundaries of the exclusive economic zone of Lebanon) as of 16 November 2011 provides that:

> The exclusive economic zone [of Lebanon] is situated beyond the territorial sea and includes the whole of the contiguous zone, extending towards the high seas, measured from the baseline in accordance with the provisions of the United Nations Convention on the Law of the Sea.

Cf fn 30.

284 See '*Décret no 2012-1148 du 12 octobre 2012 portant création d'une zone économique exclusive au large des côtes du territoire de la République en Méditerranée*', and the overall discussion of the French (Mediterranean) ZEP in section 3.3.2. The Preamble of the Decree provides as its main aim (*objet*): '*création d'une zone économique exclusive en Méditerranée qui se substitue à la zone de protection écologique créée en 2003*'.

285 Author's translation. Jurisdiction rights with regard to marine scientific research were exercised by France already within its Mediterranean ZEP. See the discussion in section 3.3.2.

286 Ibid.

287 See the discussion in section 3.5.2. on the (recent) initiatives and positions of the EU regarding the extension of coastal State jurisdiction in the Mediterranean. See also the discussion on the Croatian EFPZ in section 3.3.4.

124 *Extension of Coastal State Jurisdiction in Enclosed or Semi-enclosed Seas*

the (full) EEZ regime '… would be more effective when acting on a sustainable approach towards (their part of) the Mediterranean than a combined Ecological and Fisheries Protection Zone (EFPZ)'.[288] This in turn seems to point at the growing realization by France (and potentially other Mediterranean States) that the 'holistic' sustainable governance of the Mediterranean Sea can be more effectively achieved through the proclamation of a full EEZ,[289] instead of making use of functional (sectoral) *sui generis* zones of jurisdiction.[290]

It is also important to point out that the external limits of the French (Mediterranean) EEZ coincide with the previous limits of the French ZEP.[291] Article 2 of the 2012 Decree provides that '… the provided limits [geographical points] will be modified, if necessary, subject to the conclusion of delimitation agreements with other neighbouring States, in accordance with Article 74 of UNCLOS.'[292] The 2012 EEZ Decree has therefore opted for the same approach with regard to external limits, as that envisaged by the 2004 ZEP Decree.[293]

3.5 Recent positions of the EU regarding the extension of coastal state jurisdiction in the Mediterranean

In the last part of this chapter it is proposed to assess the recent positions of the EU (in this particular case usually represented by the European Commission) regarding the extension of coastal State jurisdiction in the Mediterranean and Adriatic Seas. It is suggested that the role of the EU is already important and will be potentially crucial in the future governance of the Adriatic Sea. Italy and Slovenia are already Member States to the EU, Croatia and Montenegro[294] are candidate States (Croatia joined the EU on 1 July 2013),[295] while Bosnia Herzegovina[296] and Albania[297] are expected to acquire candidate status in the

---

288 See EU Commission; 'Exploring the potential of Maritime Spatial Planning in the Mediterranean' Country Report (France), EU Commission Study, Brussels, 2011, p. 2.
289 Cf fn 282. See also the discussion in section 3.4.2.2.
290 See the discussion in section in 3.5.2.2. of the (EU) Integrated Maritime Policy and particularly of its efforts 'Towards an Integrated Maritime Policy for better governance in the Mediterranean'.
291 See Art. 1 of the 2012 (EEZ) Decree.
292 Author's translation.
293 See the discussion in section 3.3.2. See also the discussion of the limits of the Italian ZEP in section 3.3.5 and Figure 3.5.
294 EU Council confirmed Montenegro as a candidate state on 17 December 2010. The accession negotiations started on 29 June 2012. For current information, see <http://ec.europa.eu/enlargement>.
295 On 9 December 2011 Croatia signed the Accession Treaty. Croatia joined the EU on 1 July 2013. Ibid.
296 Bosnia and Herzegovina was identified as a potential candidate for EU membership in 2003. In mid 2012 Bosnia and Herzegovina started preparatory work for submitting an application for EU membership. Ibid.
297 Albania submitted a formal application for EU membership in 2009. In October 2012, the EU Commission recommended that Albania should be granted EU candidate status, subject to completion of key measures in certain areas. Specific mention was made to judicial and public administration reform and to a need of revision of the parliamentary rules of procedures. Ibid.

Extension of jurisdiction in the Mediterranean Seas 125

years to come. It is submitted that the positions and/or policies of the EU have had and will affect the attitude of Adriatic States in this field and that the recent initiatives of the European Commission, together with Mediterranean practice, indicate possible future trends also in the Adriatic Sea.

3.5.1 Extension of coastal state jurisdiction and delimitation of maritime zones by EU Member States

If the division of competences between the EU[298] and its Member States is in some areas unclear, and subject to the discretion of the EU whether or not to exercise its regulatory powers,[299] there are no doubts that it is for each Member State to determine the extent and limits of its national territory. This in turn means that the decision whether to proclaim an EEZ and/or *sui generis* zones (and its modalities) lies within the competences of each Member State and not with the EU. However, as pointed out by Boelaert-Suominem:

> … any extension of the Member States' maritime jurisdiction automatically entails a concomitant extension of the EC's regulatory competence, insofar the Community [EU] is internally competent to regulate the subject matter concerned.[300]

That means that an EU Member State may in principle decide not to proclaim an EEZ or a *sui generis* zone, but if it does so then it automatically extends also the EU regulatory competences in a particular field.[301]

This, however, does not mean that the EU has not had any say whatsoever regarding the extension of coastal State jurisdiction by its Member States. An outstanding example is represented by the Resolution of the Council of the EC, dated 5 November 1976[302] with which the Council invited the Member States

---

298 On 1 December 2009, date of the entry into force of the Lisbon Treaty of 13 December 2007, the EU has succeeded to, and replaced the EC, and the consolidated version of the Treaty establishing the European Community has been renamed the Treaty on the Functioning of the European Union (TFEU). See also the consolidated version of the Treaty on European Union and the Treaty on the functioning of the European Union (TFEU), OJ C 115, 09.05.2008. The term 'EC' is used in this work for previously adopted documents.

299 See Part One, Title I. TFEU (Categories and areas of Union Competence), Art. 2-6 and Declaration concerning the competence of the European Community with regard to matters governed by the United Nations Convention on the Law of the Sea of 10 December 1982 and the Agreement of 28 July 1994 relating to the implementation of Part XI of the Convention, OJ L 179, 23.06.1998 (Annex). For a general discussion see S. Boelaert Suominem, 'The European Community, the European Court of Justice and the Law of the Sea', IJMCL, Vol. 23, 2008, pp. 643–713.

300 Ibid, p. 688.

301 The ECJ for example expressly confirmed the need for Member States to implement the Habitats Directive not only in relation to their territorial waters, but also with regard to the continental shelf and the EEZ. See Case C-6/04, *Commission v UK*, Judgment of 20 October 2005 [2005] ECR I-9017, paras. 115–117. See also the discussion in section 5.5 and Chapter 6.

302 Council Resolution of 3 November 1976 on certain external aspects of the creation of a 200-mile fishing zone in the Community with effect from 1 January 1977, OJ C 105, 7 May 1981.

126 *Extension of Coastal State Jurisdiction in Enclosed or Semi-enclosed Seas*

to extend by *a concerted action* (as from 1 January 1977) the limits of their fishing zones to 200 nmi. Although the resolution covered only the North Sea and North Atlantic coasts, it represents an important precedent and it also made clear that is without prejudice to similar action being taken for other fishing zones within the jurisdiction of Member States, such as in the Mediterranean.

3.5.2 The recent initiatives and positions of the EU (European Commission) regarding the extension of coastal state jurisdiction in the Mediterranean

The Mediterranean is currently the only EU Marine Region where EU Member States (with the exception of Cyprus and most recently France)[303] have not proclaimed (full) EEZs. Since 2002, however, the European Commission has on various instances impliedly expressed its support for the establishment of FPZ as a means to improve conservation and management of fishery resources in the Mediterranean. In the 2002 Communication laying down a Community Action Plan for the conservation and sustainable exploitation of fisheries resources in the Mediterranean Sea under the Common Fisheries Policy,[304] the EU Commission expressed the opinion that the Declaration of FPZ up to 200 nmi from baselines could be an important contribution to improving fisheries management, particularly in the light of the fact that 95 per cent of Community catches are taken within 50 nmi of the coast of the Mediterranean. According to the Communication the proclamation of FPZs in the Mediterranean would certainly facilitate control and contribute significantly to the fight against illegal, unreported and unregulated (IUU) fishing. The Commission advocated however the proclamation of FPZs and not of full EEZs and it made clear that '... FPZs, unlike EEZs, refer exclusively to the jurisdiction over fishery resources ....'[305]

The 2002 Communication identified both advantages and disadvantages of proclaiming FPZs in the Mediterranean. Among the advantages are listed: (a) the ability to apply fishery management over a much wider area; (b) a substantial improvement of control and enforcement; (c) the exclusion or, at least, the control of certain fleets (from the Far East) currently fishing in the Mediterranean's international waters; and (d) easier restriction of IUU fishing. Among the inconveniences the Commission noted: (a) the risk of loss of access to certain fishing grounds for EU vessels (if other non-EU States such as Tunisia were to

---

303 See sections 3.4.1. and 3.4.6.
304 Cf fn 109. For a thorough discussion of the EU Common Fisheries Policy, see R. Churchill and D. Owen, *The EU Common Fisheries Policy*, Oxford: Oxford University Press, 2010. See further European Commission, Communication from the Commission: Reform of the Common Fisheries Policy, COM(2011)417 final, Brussels, 13.7.2011. For the application of CFP in the Mediterranean (including the Adriatic Sea), see Council Regulation (EC) No. 1967/2006 of 21 December 2006 concerning management measures for the sustainable exploitation of fishery resources in the Mediterranean Sea, OJ L 409 of 30.12.2006; corrigendum: OJ L 36 of 8.2.2007.
305 Ibid (2002 Communication), section 3.1.

Extension of jurisdiction in the Mediterranean Seas 127

follow suit);[306] (b) significant political difficulties in certain areas; and (c) difficulties in establishing median lines (delimitation of such zones) in the narrower Mediterranean Sea. Although the benefits of proclaiming FPZs seem to have prevailed, the 2002 Communication emphasized that:

> […] such a declaration of FPZs would be much more effective *if carried out through concertation among all the countries involved*. A common approach to FPZs among Community Member States and, subsequently, among all the countries in the region would be therefore desirable.[307]

The 2002 Communication concluded that the initiative in this field should consist of inviting Member States (and candidate States) to debate at EU level the desirability of a common approach to this matter,[308] and if a clear (EU) position on the issue emerged, to convene a conference among coastal States of the Mediterranean in view of exploring a common Mediterranean wide approach in this matter. Such international conference was indeed convened the following year (2003) in Venice.

3.5.2.1 Venice Declaration (2003)

One of the main issues discussed at the Third Ministerial Conference on the Sustainable Development of Fisheries in the Mediterranean, held in Venice on 25–26 November 2003[309] and attended by the European Commission and governments of all States bordering the Mediterranean and some third States (Poland, Japan and Russia) was the possibility of proclaiming FPZs in the Mediterranean. In an opening speech the Member of the European Commission responsible for fisheries expressed the belief of the European Commission that it would be impossible to:

> … achieve a significant improvement of fisheries management in the Mediterranean without extending the jurisdiction of coastal states beyond their territorial waters and creating larger fisheries protection zones ….

However, he made clear that what it aimed to achieve is '… a co-ordinated extension of the jurisdiction as regards the exploitation of marine living resources and these only' and that there is a need '… to try and conserve as much as possible

---

306 See sections 3.3.4 and 3.4.4.
307 Emphasis added.
308 An open issue at that time was also whether and establishment of EFZ should include the limitation of access for third parties, or simply have as the main purpose an adequate control of fishing activities. See Section 3.1 of the 2002 Communication, p. 15.
309 The first Ministerial Conference was held in Crete on 10–12 December 1994, the second on 27–29 November 1996 in Venice. See Del Vecchio Capotosti, op. cit., p. 290.

128 *Extension of Coastal State Jurisdiction in Enclosed or Semi-enclosed Seas*

historical fishing patterns …'. He furthermore concluded that the proposed approach:

> … must be in line with the United Nations Conventions on the Law of the Sea, particularly *with regard to enclosed and semi-enclosed seas* and the *rights of states disadvantaged by geography.*[310]

It is important to note that at the 2003 Conference all Adriatic States in principle also supported the proclamation of FPZs. In the words of the Italian representative:

> … *L'obiettivo, infatti, é quello di aviare il percorso verso un* approccio concertato in materia di giurisdizione sulle acque, *in vista di una gestione responsabile delle risorse ittiche, senza perdere mai di vista l'importanza sociale ed economica della pesca e la specificitá di ciascun Paese. … Senza forzature unilaterali che possono diventare a tutti gli effeti, un ostacolo alto per lo sviluppo condiviso di un* bacino semichiuso qual é il Mar Mediterraneo.[311]

The representative of Slovenia also pointed at the status of the Mediterranean and Adriatic *as semi-enclosed seas* and that:

> It is absolutely necessary to approach the creation of fisheries protection zones *gradually*, with *concerted effort* based on equal dialogue among equal partners on both regional and sub-regional level … the execution of the sovereign rights of seaside states to declare that kind of zones should commence with an agreement on all related questions, including those of demarcation, exploitation of natural resources, the regime of the navigation control and similar issues, and only then carry out formal legal proclamations.[312]

The representative of (Serbia) Montenegro similarly saw:

> … the activities aimed to widen jurisdiction in the Adriatic by proclaiming ecological-fishery zone as legitimate ones, since each country has undisputable right to do so. However, I would like to emphasize that the issue of ecological [*sic*], fishery and every other kind of protection in the Adriatic is only possible to solve by multilateral and regional approach and agreement, with no disputes and unsolved bilateral issues.…[313]

---

310 Emphasis added. European Communities, 'Third Ministerial Conference on the Sustainable Development of Fisheries in the Mediterranean, Proceedings of the Conference', Venice, 25–26 November 2003, Luxemburg, 2004, p. 5.

311 Emphasis added. Ibid, p.1.

312 Emphasis added. Ibid, p. 54 at p. 55.

313 Ibid, p. 52.

Extension of jurisdiction in the Mediterranean Seas   129

On the other hand, the representative of Croatia, which only a month before proclaimed its EFPZ,[314] expressed his conviction that:

> ... the extension of national jurisdiction on the sea, combined with multilateral co-operation, is the only way to respond to the serious economic, social and environmental challenges today. The Exclusive Economic Zones, the Fishing and the Ecological and Fisheries Protection proclaimed so far, as well as those which will be proclaimed after this Conference, represent a cornerstone for the establishment of sustainable fisheries and the preservation of the Mediterranean bio-resources and ecosystem ....[315]

The common denominator of the great majorities of the interventions of Adriatic (and Mediterranean) States was therefore that there should be a concerted and regional approach towards the proclamation of FPZs. The latter position is also reflected in Section 10 of the final Declaration of the Conference (2003 Venice Declaration) which provides as follows:

> Against the background of a closer cooperation between all States benefiting from the biological wealth of the Mediterranean marine environment, *we consider that the creation of fisheries protection zones permits the improvement of conservation and control of fisheries and thus contributes to better resource management and to our common commitment to combat IUU fishing.*
>
> We consider that, without prejudice to the sovereign rights of States and in accordance with relevant international law, a more detailed examination should be made of the modalities for the creation of fisheries protection zones taking into account the precedents that exist, with a view to employing a *concerted and regional approach* suited to the needs of the fisheries concerned and based on *dialogue and coordination.* In order to progress in this direction, the Mediterranean states shall co-operate at the appropriate regional level.[316]

What is possible to discern both from the 1977 Council Resolutions, the 2002 Communication and the 2003 Venice Declaration is that, first, the approach advocated by the European Commission (on behalf of the EU) was *sectoral* (proclamation of FPZ) therefore limited to the extension of jurisdiction for fisheries purposes. Other elements of the EEZ, for example jurisdiction with regard to the protection and preservation of the marine environment and marine scientific research were not taken into account. What the EU seems to have advocated at that time was therefore the proclamation of derived zones *in plus stat minus* (FPZs) and not of full EEZs. Second, the longstanding position of the EU has been that a *concerted* approach, first among EU Member States and

---

314 See section 3.3.4.
315 See Proceedings, op. cit., p. 37 at p. 39.
316 Emphasis added. Declaration of the Ministerial Conference for the Sustainable Development of Fisheries in the Mediterranean, 25–26 November 2003, Proceedings, op. cit., p. 89 at p. 92.

130 *Extension of Coastal State Jurisdiction in Enclosed or Semi-enclosed Seas*

subsequently among all the countries of the region (or sub-region), should be preferred to unilateral action. In the case of the (unilateral) proclamation of the Croatian EFPZ the mentioned position has been extended also to candidate States.[317]

3.5.2.2 Towards an integrated maritime policy for better governance of the Mediterranean?

Despite the fact that the 2003 Venice Declaration called for a *concerted and regional approach*, the latter was followed both in the Mediterranean and Adriatic Seas by a series of unco-ordinated (unilateral) extensions of jurisdictions both with regard to the content of the zones (EEZs, ZEPs, EFPZs) and their external limits.[318] Somewhat ironically, the only FPZ which was proclaimed in the Mediterranean Sea in the aftermath of the 2003 Venice Declaration and which expressly made reference to the latter was that of Libya in 2005.[319]

In 2007 the European Commission, after a one-year process of consultation, presented its 'vision document', a *Blue Book on an Integrated Maritime Policy for the EU* (the Blue Book),[320] based on an inter-sectoral (holistic) approach to maritime activities. The Blue Book had as its central goal the creation of optimal conditions for the growth of maritime sectors and coastal regions, while ensuring that the objectives of EU environmental legislation, including those of the Marine Strategy Directive are met.[321] Particularly, the adoption of the Blue Book seems to have influenced also the discussed (sectoral) approach of the EU towards the proclamations of maritime zones (FPZs) in the Mediterranean. An important landmark occurred on 10 June 2008, when the European Commission, the Slovenian Presidency of the EU and the Euro-Mediterranean University (EMUNI) organised in Piran (Slovenia) the first ever international high level conference on maritime policy and governance in the Mediterranean which aimed to discuss the need of developing a holistic approach to the management of maritime sectors and activities in the Mediterranean basin. The *Conference*

---

317 See 'Communication from the Commission: Opinion on Croatia's Application for Membership of the European Union', COM (2004)257 final, Brussels, 20 April 2004. Quoted also in D. Vidas, 'The UN Convention on the Law of the Sea, the European Union and the Rule of Law: What is going on in the Adriatic', IJMCL, Vol. 24, 2009, pp. 1–66, at 18.

318 See the discussion in sections 3.2–3.3.

319 See section 3.4.3.

320 See 'Communication from the Commission: Integrated Maritime Policy for the EU', COM(2007)575 final, 10.10.2007. See also 'Progress Report on the EU's integrated maritime policy', COM(2009)540 final of 15.10.2009, and 'Developing the international dimensions of the Integrated Maritime Policy for the European Union', COM(2009)536 final of 15.10.2009. For a recent assessment, see 'Report from the Commission: Progress of the EU's Integrated Maritime Policy', COM(2012)491 final, 11.9.2012. See also M. Pavliha, 'New European maritime policy for cleaner ocean and seas', in Martínez Gutiérrez (ed.), op. cit., p. 22 at pp. 26–28.

321 Article 11 FEU (previously Article 6 TEC) provides that '[e]nvironmental protection require-ments must be integrated into the definition and implementation of the Union policies and activities, in particular with the view of promoting sustainable development'. See also the discussion in section 5.6.

Communique in addition to addressing problems in individual sectors such as transport, fisheries, the environment, etc. expressly mentioned that future discussions should focus also on two cross-cutting issues, one of them being '[t]he absence of Exclusive Economic Zones and the ways to find acceptable solutions to solve the difficulties this situation is generating'.[322]

Shortly after, on 14–15 January 2009, the European Commission convened a meeting of experts on the Mediterranean for the purpose of gathering independent expert advice on issues relating to the governance of the Mediterranean Sea. As a result, the experts produced a *Report on the role of maritime zones in promoting effective governance for protection of the Mediterranean marine environment.*[323] The Report assessed the advantages and disadvantages of establishing EEZs.[324] One of its recommendations was to '[c]onduct further studies for establishing maritime zones and *alternative joint zones* in overlapping areas of potential EEZs'.[325] The Report makes reference to potential EEZs and not EFZs while with regard to possible delimitations problems it emphasizes that:

> ... The *development of common zones* is a possible way forward that has been used in other seas where there are similar problems of delimitation of maritime zones due to overlapping zones and other factors making delimitation by mutual agreement problematic.[326]

Based on this process of consultation, and within the framework of the EU Integrated Maritime Policy, the European Commission adopted on 11 November 2009 a Communication Towards an Integrated Maritime Policy for better governance in the Mediterranean[327] which proposed a set of actions aimed at driving coastal States towards a more co-ordinated and holistic approach to the management of activities impacting on the sea and oceans. According to the 2009 Communication one of the main governance weakness in the Mediterranean is that: '[...] the large proportion of marine space made up of high seas makes it difficult for coastal States to plan, organise and regulate activities that directly affect their territorial sea and coasts'.[328]

---

322 The other cross-cutting issue was surveillance and the way to create joint ownership of cross-sectoral surveillance in the region, among EU and non-EU countries. See 'Conference on Maritime Policy in the Mediterranean Sea', 10 June 2008, Piran-Portorož (Slovenia), Conference Communiqué.

323 N. Oral *et al.*, 'The Role of Maritime Zones in Promoting Effective Governance for the Protection of the Mediterranean', Report of the Expert Group on Governance of the Mediterranean Sea, Prepared for the European Commission, Directorate General for Maritime Affairs and Fisheries: Mediterranean and Black Sea, 2009.

324 Ibid, p. 40.

325 Ibid, Recommendations, No. 20, p. 50.

326 Emphasis added. Ibid, pp. 43–44.

327 European Commission, 'Towards an Integrated Maritime Policy for better governance of the Mediterranean', Communication from the Commission to the Council and the European Parliament, COM (2009) 466, Brussels, 11.11.2009.

328 Ibid, section 3.

132 *Extension of Coastal State Jurisdiction in Enclosed or Semi-enclosed Seas*

Although the outcome of the process is still difficult to predict, there are strong indicators that the EU is leaning away from *sectoral* FPZ (and other functional zones of jurisdiction, e.g. ZEP) towards *holistic* EEZs. The latter process has also been influenced by the fact that a number of States in the wider Mediterranean Sea have, particularly in the period following the 2003 Venice Conference, proclaimed (*Cyprus, Syria, Tunisia, Libya and recently Lebanon and France*) and in certain cases even delimited *actual* or *potential* EEZs (*Egypt-Cyprus, Cyprus-Lebanon, Cyprus-Israel*).[329] It is particularly noteworthy that on 25 August 2009 France expressed its determination to upgrade its Mediterranean ZEP into a full EEZ, which ultimately was realized in October 2012.[330] It seems that at least in the Eastern but potentially also in the Central and Western Mediterranean the formal proclamation of EEZs will represent a 'lowest common denominator' and that the discussion of a 'concerted approach' will be most likely focused on the actual implementation of the regime of the EEZ.

The situation in the Adriatic is, however, rather different, as Croatia is the only State to have so far proclaimed an EFPZ, Slovenia has proclaimed a ZEP, while Italy has adopted a framework law for the adoption of a ZEP or more ZEPs along its coast, without formally proclaiming its regime in the Adriatic Sea.[331] As mentioned, there has been no move by Albania[332] or Montenegro to extend their jurisdiction in the Adriatic Sea. This seems to point to the need to discuss problems related to the extension of coastal State jurisdiction not only at the regional (Mediterranean level), but also at an appropriate sub-regional Adriatic level.[333] As pointed out in the Conclusions of the (2004) IUCN workshop:

> The lack of coordination of national initiatives of extension of jurisdiction *ratione materiae* (fishery, marine pollution …) is [also] a major obstacle to the development of coordinated legal framework for integrated resource management. Extension should be promoted on a voluntary and regional basis in a concerted manner.[334]

---

329 See section 3.1.1.
330 See section 3.4.6.
331 See the discussion in section 3.3.5.
332 Cf fn 27.
333 See the discussion in Chapters 5 and 6.
334 IUCN, 'Towards an Improved Governance in the Mediterranean Beyond the Territorial Sea', Workshop's Conclusions, 15–16 March 2004. Available at <http://cmsdata.iucn.org/downloads/conclusions_en.pdf>. The workshop's conclusions make reference also to '[t]he idea of an informal structure to be used as a forum for the management and prevention of litigation and for developing compromising solutions …' in the field of extension of coastal State jurisdiction and (presumably) also delimitation of maritime zone in the Mediterranean Sea. On this point, see also I. Papanicolopulu, 'Tools for the Governance of Regional Seas: A Comparative Study of the Mediterranean and the Caribbean', paper delivered at the 11th Mediterranean Research Meeting Florence and Montecatini Terme, 24–27 March 2010, pp. 17–21.

3.6 Concluding remarks

Most of the recent extension of jurisdictions in the Mediterranean Sea (proclamation of new zones) represents an interesting case of an actual or potential transition from a 'high seas' regime to an 'EEZ regime' passing through the proclamation of EFZ and/or ZEP and having as a final step the adoption of a framework law formally establishing an EEZ, although not necessarily also its *de facto* regime. Such an approach has been followed by a considerable number of Mediterranean States including Libya, Tunisia, Malta and most recently France, and seems to be on the horizon also for (some) Adriatic States.[335]

From this chapter's discussion it may be inferred that Adriatic and Mediterranean States have, generally speaking, not shown enough spirit of co-operation neither with regard the recent process of extension of coastal State jurisdiction nor with regard to the 'provisional' or 'final' delimitation of the newly arisen zones of sovereign rights and/or jurisdiction. It is suggested, therefore, that more efforts should be directed first of all to the co-ordination of national initiatives in the field of extension of coastal State jurisdiction and particularly in the quest for solutions which would reflect the spirit of Part IX of UNCLOS and override the various problems related to the delimitation of such zones (e.g. common zones).

Independently of that, the assessed proclamations in the Adriatic Sea are important as they reinforce the practice of some Mediterranean States to proclaim zones of functional jurisdiction *in plus stat minus* which are based on the EEZ, but are not EEZs proper. Such practice seems generally speaking completely in line with (customary) international law. As pointed out by Scovazzi:

> ... nothing in the UNCLOS or in customary international law prevents the establishment of special (or sui generis) zones beyond the 12–mile limit of the territorial sea, such as fishing zones or ecological zones, where the coastal States choose to exercise only some of the competences to which they are entitled under a full EEZ.[336]

There are, however, strong indicators that also the preference of the EU (European Commission) has been shifting from *sectoral* FPZs (and other functional zones of jurisdiction, e.g. ZEPs) towards the proclamation of *holistic* EEZs in the Mediterranean Sea.

---

335 See discussion in Chapter 6.
336 See Scovazzi, 'Recent Developments as regards Maritime Delimitation in the Adriatic Sea', op. cit., p. 202.

4 Delimitation of maritime boundaries in the (Eastern) Adriatic Sea: Border bays, *uti possidetis* and an enclosed or semi-enclosed sea

After assessing the recent process of extension of coastal State jurisdiction in the Adriatic Sea both from the Mediterranean and EU perspectives, this chapter discusses the three main maritime delimitation disputes which arose as a result of the dissolution of the former SFRY (Slovenia-Croatia, Croatia-Bosnia and Herzegovina, Croatia-Montenegro). Particular attention is paid to two questions which are common to all three cases and seem to require a clarification from the standpoint of international law: the application of the principle of *uti possidetis* (*effectivités*) to maritime delimitations and the status of border bays in international law. The discussion then focuses on the characteristics of each case, particularly on the attempts to solve the disputes and to enhance levels of co-operation among Adriatic States. Special attention is given to the case of Bosnia and Herzegovina (least discussed in contemporary literature) and to the salient points of the 2009 Arbitral Agreement concluded between Slovenia and Croatia.

4.1 *Uti possidetis*

If Articles 11 and 12 of the 1978 Vienna Convention[1] represent the 'external' dimension of the rules on State succession of boundaries and/or territorial regimes, then it would seem possible to assert that its 'internal dimension' is represented by the principle of *uti possidetis (juris).*[2] This principle provides, as pointed out by Ratner, that States emerging from decolonization shall inherit the colonial administrative boundaries they held at the time of independence.[3] As provided by the ICJ in the case of *Burkina Faso v Mali*, '… the principle of *uti possidetis* freezes the territorial title; *it stops the clock*, but does not put back the hands …'.[4] As later reiterated by the Chamber of the ICJ in the Case concerning the

---

1 The provisions of Arts 11 and 12 of the 1978 Vienna Convention are deemed to form part of customary international law. For their application in the Adriatic Sea, see M. Seršič, 'The Crisis in the Eastern Adriatic and the Law of the Sea', ODIL, Vol. 24, No. 3, 1993, p. 291 at pp. 291–295.
2 For a general overview, see M. Shaw, 'The Heritage of States: The Principle of *Uti Possidetis Juris* Today', BYIL, Vol. 67, 1996, p. 75.
3 See also S. Ratner, 'Drawing a better line: *Uti possidetis* and the border of new States', AJIL, Vol. 90, No. 4, 1996, p. 590.
4 Emphasis added. Frontier Dispute, Judgment, ICJ Reports 1986, p. 554, para. 30.

Maritime boundaries in the (Eastern) Adriatic 135

Land, Island and Maritime Frontier (*El Salvador v Honduras: Nicaragua intervening*), '... The essence of the principle lies in its primary aim of securing respect for the territorial boundaries at the moment when independence is achieved ...'.[5] Although the 'automatic' application of the principle of *uti possidetis* outside the framework of decolonization has been criticized by some writers,[6] it seems possible to agree with Shaw that the principle of *uti possidetis* is relevant to the process of creation of new States as a general rule and is not limited to the specific situation of decolonization'.[7]

4.2 *Uti possidetis* and the dissolution of the former SFRY

The crucial importance of the principle of *uti possidetis* in the context of the dissolution of the former SFRY was confirmed by the (Badinter) Arbitration Committee on the Conference on Yugoslavia[8] with its Opinion No. 3, although reference to it was also made in its Opinion No. 2.[9] With the latter, the Badinter Commission recollected that '... whatever the circumstances, *the right to self-determination must not involve changes to existing frontiers at the time of independence* (uti possidetis juris) *except where the States concerned agreed otherwise*'.[10] The Opinion therefore distinguished between two important principles of international law, namely the 'territorial integrity of a State' and the principle of 'self-determination of people', where the principle of *uti possidetis*, a reflection of the principle of the 'territorial integrity of States', prevailed.[11] While commenting on this principle Pellet noted that:

> ... this great principle of peace, indispensable to international stability ... has today acquired the character of a universal, and peremptory norm.

---

5 Land, Island and Maritime Frontier Dispute (*El Salvador v Honduras: Nicaragua intervening*), Judgment, ICJ Reports, 1992, p. 351, para. 42.
6 Ratner, op. cit., pp. 591–593, and M. Craven, 'The EC Arbitration Commission on Yugoslavia', BYIL, Vol. 66, 1995, p. 388. See also P. Radan, 'Post-Secession International Borders: A Critical Analysis of the Opinions of the Badinter Arbitration Commission', Melbourne University Law Review, Vol. 24, No. 3, Melbourne, 2000, pp. 50–76.
7 M. Shaw, 'People, Territorialism and Boundaries', EJIL, No. 8, 1997, p. 497. Cf fn 12.
8 The (Badinter) Arbitration Committee was created by the EC and its Members States at the time of the convening of the Peace Conference on Yugoslavia (27 August 1991). It was chaired by Mr Robert Badinter and had as members the presidents of the German and Italian Constitutional Courts and the presidents of the Belgian Court of Arbitration and the Spanish Constitutional Tribunal. Hereinafter the "Badinter Commission". See A. Pellet, 'The Opinions of the Badinter Arbitration Committee: A Second Breath for the Self-Determination of Peoples', EJIL, No. 3, 1992, p. 178, and the discussion in sections 4.2–4.3.
9 Badinter Commission: Opinions on Questions Arising from the Dissolution of Yugoslavia, January 11 and July 4 1992, 31 ILM 1488, 1992. See Opinion No. 2.
10 Emphasis added. See Para. 1 of Opinion No. 2.
11 See, however, 'Accordance with International Law of the Unilateral Declaration of Independence in Respect of Kosovo', Advisory Opinion, ICJ Reports 2010, p. 453, paras 80–81. See also M. Shaw, *International Law*, 6th edn, Cambridge: Cambridge University Press, 2008, p. 523.

136 *Extension of Coastal State Jurisdiction in Enclosed or Semi-enclosed Seas*

The people of former colonial countries were wise to apply it; Europeans must not commit the folly of dispensing with it.[12]

The relevance of the principle of *uti possidetis* in the context of the dissolution of the former SFRY, however, can be best seen from Opinion No. 3 of the Badinter Commission.[13] Its third paragraph provides that:

> Except where otherwise agreed, the former boundaries [between former SFRY's Republics] become frontiers protected by international law. This conclusion follows from the principle of respect for the territorial status quo and, in particular, from the principle of *uti possidetis*. *Uti possidetis*, though initially applied in settling decolonization issues in America and Africa, is today recognized as a general principle as stated by the International Court of Justice in the case between Burkina Faso and Mali ... Nevertheless, the principle is not a special rule which pertains to one specific system of international law. It is a general principle, which is logically connected with the phenomenon of the obtaining of independence, wherever it occurs. Its obvious purpose is to prevent the independence and stability by new states being endangered by fratricidal struggles ....

The first observation is that Opinion No. 3 raised the application of the principle of *uti possidetis* from the context of decolonization to a general principle of international law 'which is logically connected to the phenomenon of the obtainment of independence, whenever it occurs'.[14] As emphasized by Türk, this was the first time that the *uti possidetis* principle was directly applied in Europe.[15]

One may obviously question the legal validity of the opinions, as the latter were, strictly speaking, delivered to the EC Conference on Yugoslavia in a consultative capacity, and therefore not directly binding. The fact remains, however, that States successors of the former SFRY accepted the latter as binding and that compliance and respect for the opinions was furthermore one of the conditions for the recognition of *inter alia* Slovenia and Croatia by Member States of the EC.[16]

It is also noteworthy that Opinion No. 3 does not expressly differentiate between the 'boundaries on land' and the 'boundaries at sea', as it makes reference only to 'boundaries', 'frontiers' and 'territories' of the former Republics. Obviously, a

---

12 Pellet, op. cit., p. 180.
13 Cf fn 9. Opinion No. 3.
14 Opinion No. 3, para. 3. See, however, Shaw, *International Law*, op. cit., p. 528, and fn 6.
15 D. Türk, 'Recognition of States: A Comment', EJIL, Vol. 4, 1993, p. 66 at p. 70. According to Pazartis and Blay, the 'break up' of the former SFRY was 'the first test of post-colonial type secessionist conflict in Europe'. Quoted in P. Pazartis, 'Secession and International Law: the European dimension', in M.G. Kohen (ed.), *Secession: International Law Perspectives*, Cambridge and New York, NY: Cambridge University Press, 2006, p. 355 at p. 364.
16 See EC Council, 'Declaration on the Guidelines on the Recognition of New States in Eastern Europe and in the Soviet Union' (16 December 1991), and EC Council, 'Declaration on Yugoslavia' (Extraordinary EPC Ministerial Meeting, Brussels, 16 December 1991), reproduced in D. Türk, op. cit., p. 66, Annexes 1 and 2.

Maritime boundaries in the (Eastern) Adriatic   137

reference to the application of the principle of *uti possidetis* to 'boundaries' and 'territory' at least *prima facie* seems to imply its application at least to the delimitation of 'internal waters and/or territorial sea',[17] as a constituent part of the territory of a State.[18] This is even more so in the light of the fact that the Badinter Commission, in its Opinion No. 3, makes an express link between the application of the principles of *uti possidetis* and the 'territory' of the SFRY Republics during the time of the former SFRY. According to its second paragraph:

> The principle [*uti possidetis*] applies all the more readily to the Republics since the second and fourth paragraphs of Article 5 of the Constitution of the SFRY stipulated that the Republics' territories and boundaries could not be altered without their consent.

Noteworthy is the fact, as also reiterated by Türk, that '... the federal units – the [SFRY] Republics – were constitutionally defined as "states" with both defined borders and a considerable amount of constitutional power, which included authority in the field of international relations'.[19]

Opinion No. 3 therefore makes an express reference to Article 5 of the (1974) Constitution of the former SFRY[20] which in its first Paragraph provided that '[t]he territory of the SFRY is unified and is composed of the territories of the Socialist Republics', while according to its Preamble '[t]he working people and citizens exercise their sovereign rights in the Socialist Republics and Socialists Autonomous Provinces and – when determined by the Constitution to be of common interest – in the SFRY'. From the said statements it may be possible to imply, as emphasized by Kunič, that during the times of the former SFRY all parts of the territory of the former SFRY (including its internal waters and territorial sea) "belonged" to a particular coastal republic and that therefore *constitutionally* there was nothing such as "federal territorial sea" over which only the SFRY would exercise its sovereignty.[21] This seems to be the case despite the undisputed absence of formal administrative maritime boundaries between the (former) SFRY's federal Republics.[22]

---

17 It is suggested that the term 'maritime boundary' should nowadays be interpreted as also including line(s) delimiting zones of sovereign rights and jurisdictions (e.g. EEZs). This seems to derive from State practice regarding the succession of (maritime) delimitation treaties on the basis of Art. 11 of the 1978 Vienna Convention (e.g. former SFRY, USSR) and from the (almost) unification of principles regulating the delimitation of the territorial sea and/or the continental shelf/EEZ (equidistance/special circumstances, equitable principles/relevant circumstances). See Maritime Delimitation and Territorial Questions between Qatar and Bahrain (*Qatar v Bahrain*), ICJ Reports, 2001, p. 40, para. 231.

18 See I. Brownlie, *Principles of Public International Law*, 7th edn, Oxford: Oxford University Press, 2008, pp. 70–72.

19 See Türk, op. cit., p. 71.

20 OG SFRY, No. 9/1974.

21 See in this regard J. Kunič, 'The Slovenian-Croatian Border Question', IFIMES, Ljubljana, 2007. Available at <http://www.ifimes.org/default.cfm?Jezik=En&Kat=10&ID=313>.

22 See M. Kohen, Uti Possidetis and Maritime Delimitations, ppt presentation, Geneva: The Graduate Institute, 2009. Available at <http://untreaty.un.org/cod/avl/ls/Kohen_BD.html>.

138 *Extension of Coastal State Jurisdiction in Enclosed or Semi-enclosed Seas*

Provisions such as those contained in Article 1 of the (SFRY) Act concerning the Coastal Sea and the Continental Shelf of 23 July 1987[23] declaring that '[t]he sovereignty of the Socialist Federal Republic of Yugoslavia ... shall extend to the coastal sea [internal and territorial waters] to the airspace above it and to the sea-bed and subsoil of that sea', should be understood in its 'external dimension (against the international community)' while with regard to the relations between the coastal Republics, it seems that it could be better read in the light of Article 5 of the 1974 SFRY Constitution, in the sense that being a "territory of the SFRY" (which included the internal waters and territorial sea), each point at sea belonged to one of the former (coastal) SFRY Republics.[24]

The factual exercise of "jurisdiction" over the territorial sea and internal waters was, on the other hand, shared between the Federation (areas of common interest: e.g. defence, customs, protection of the marine environment, etc.) and the coastal Republics (economic exploitation of the sea, police supervision, certain tasks with regard to the protection and preservation of the marine environment, protection of underwater cultural heritage, etc.) in line with the provisions of the 1974 Constitution.[25] Also outside the context of the dissolution of the former SFRY, the Opinions of the Badinter Commission have had great impact and have been said to be 'non-binding but authoritative statements of the relevant law'.[26]

Unlike the (administrative) borders on land, the administrative borders at sea, as already pointed out, were not expressly defined, although at the moment of independence it was somewhat unclear which federal entity exercised *de facto* jurisdiction over which part of the 'common SFRY sea'. Generally speaking, the exercise of jurisdiction by the various republics was regulated by the principle 'land dominates the sea' whereby each (coastal) republic exercised jurisdiction over the waters in front of its coasts. At least in two instances (in the cases of the former 'juridical' bays of Piran and Boka Kotorska) claims have been made that the *de facto* jurisdiction over the entire Bay was, at the moment of independence, exercised by only one Republic: by Slovenia in the case of the Bay of Piran[27] and supposedly Montenegro in the case of the Bay of Boka Kotorska.[28]

While it is arguable that the land borders of the States' successors of the former SFRY are governed by the principle of *uti possidetis (juris)*,[29] some basic questions

---

23 OG SFRY, No. 49/1987 and 57/1989. Hereinafter the "1987 SFRY Law".
24 Article 3 of the 1974 SFRY Constitution defined the former SFRY Republics as "States" and provided that the Republic's territories and boundaries cannot be altered without their consent. See Türk, op. cit., pp. 70–71, and cf fn 19.
25 See also Kunič, op. cit.
26 See Craven, op. cit., pp. 333–334.
27 See section 4.7.2.
28 See section 4.6.
29 See also the Constitutional documents of Slovenia and Croatia adopted at the time of independence. According to Art. 2 of the Basic Constitutional Charter on the Independence and Sovereignty of the Republic of Slovenia of 25 June 1991: 'The ... frontier [of Slovenia] with the Republic of Croatia is the frontier within the hitherto SFRY'. According to Art. V of the Constitutional Decision on the Sovereignty and Independence of the Republic of Croatia of 25 June 1991: 'The State boundaries of the Republic of Croatia are ... the boundaries between the Republic of Slovenia and the Republic of Croatia ... within the framework of the present-day

Maritime boundaries in the (Eastern) Adriatic   139

should be answered regarding the possible application of the principle of *uti possidetis* at sea. The *first* is whether the principle of *uti possidetis* is applicable at all to maritime delimitations; the *second* is whether in the absence of an internal administrative (maritime) boundary at the time of independence (*uti possidetis (juris)*) the States may rely on the doctrine of 'effective control' (*effectivités*); while the *third* question relates to the application of the principle of *uti possidetis* in cases where it conflicts with another generally recognized rule or principle of (customary) international law (e.g. land dominates the sea).[30]

It should be emphasized nonetheless that the principle of *uti possidetis* does not represent *jus cogens* and that therefore its application may be excluded through an 'agreement freely arrived at'.[31] This may in turn occur through the conclusion of a 'boundary agreement' based for example on other criteria (including political aspects). Its application may however also be expressly or impliedly[32] excluded with a 'Special Agreement' by which two States agree to submit their (maritime) delimitation dispute to a binding third party adjudication.

4.3 *Uti possidetis* and maritime delimitations

The first question is, therefore, whether the principle of *uti possidetis* is applicable to cases of maritime delimitation at all, and one may say that the answer to this seems more straightforward after the 2007 ICJ judgment in the *Nicaragua v Honduras* case than it was before. In that judgment, the ICJ expressly confirmed that the '*uti possidetis juris* may in principle apply to offshore possession and maritime spaces' which seems to have represented a breakthrough in the matter.[33] Even before this decision, however, the jurisprudence of international courts (ICJ) and arbitral tribunals showed a gradual acceptance of the application of the principle of *uti possidetis* to maritime delimitations which in turn emphasizes the fact that the 2007 judgment did not come "out of the blue". The ICJ in fact based its decision on earlier judgments, amongst which featured the 1992 Land, Island and Maritime Frontier Case (*El Salvador v Honduras: Nicaragua intervening*).[34]

SFRY'. Both documents reproduced in J.I. Charney and L.M. Alexander (eds), *International Maritime Boundaries*, ASIL, Vol. III, The Hague, Boston, MA and London: Martinus Nijhoff Publishers, 2004, pp. 2439–2442.

30 See section 4.3.3.

31 '*Except as otherwise agreed*, the former boundaries become frontiers protected by international law. …'. Emphasis added. Cf fn 14 (Opinion No. 3).

32 An example could be the setting of a 'critical date' different from that of independence or even a decision *ex aqueo at bono*, where it is asserted that the court or arbitral tribunal would have the discretion to depart from the principle of *uti possidetis*. See also section 4.8.4.

33 Case Concerning Territorial and Maritime Dispute between Nicaragua and Honduras in the Carribean Sea (*Nicaragua v Honduras*), Judgment, ICJ Reports, 2007, p. 659, para. 156. Tanaka, nonetheless, opines that with regard to maritime delimitations '… as in the Nicaragua/Honduras case, it appears that the role of this principle [*uti possidetis*] remains modest in this field …. Y. Tanaka, 'Reflections on Maritime Delimitation in the *Nicaragua/Honduras* Case', *Zeitschrift für ausländisches öffentliches Recht und Völkerrecht*, Vol. 68. No. 4, 2009, Max Planck Institute, p. 903 at 907.

34 Cf fn 5.

140 *Extension of Coastal State Jurisdiction in Enclosed or Semi-enclosed Seas*

4.3.1 Pre-2007 jurisprudence on **uti possidetis**

It seems possible to start this general analysis by mentioning that the principle of *uti possidetis* had already been impliedly used in the 1917 Gulf of Fonseca judgment[35] where one of the keys to the *sui generis* solution was the legal status of the waters at the moment of Spanish decolonization in 1821.[36] In the 1992 Land, Island and Maritime Frontier Case, which 'reconfirmed' the 1917 judgment, the ICJ Chamber however based its judgment expressly on the functioning of the principle of *uti possidetis*. The ICJ stated on that occasion that 'the principle of *uti possidetis juris* should apply to the waters of the Gulf as well as to the land' and declared that '… a joint succession of the three States to the maritime area seems in these circumstances to be the logical outcome of the principle of *uti possidetis juris* itself'.[37] In the 1982 Tunisia-Libya Case, the Court made reference to the principle of *uti possidetis* indirectly, by referring to the 1964 OAU Cairo Resolution[38] and to the rule of continuity *ipso jure* of boundary and territorial treaties embodied in the 1978 Vienna Convention.[39]

A couple of years later in 1989, the Arbitral Tribunal in the Guinea Bissau/Senegal Case[40] was asked to rule upon the legal validity of an exchange of letters between France and Portugal from 1960 which allegedly fixed the maritime boundaries between Portuguese Guinea and French Senegal. One of the main arguments of Guinea Bissau was that State succession and by implication *uti possidetis juris* was not applicable to maritime delimitation *inter alia* due to the absence of relevant State practice and case law. According to the tribunal:

> … While it is true that there are not many cases of State succession to maritime boundaries, it is equally true that Guinea Bissau, for its part, has not been able to invoke any precedent in which the *tabula rasa* rule was applied to a maritime boundary applied in the colonial era.[41]

The principle of *uti possidetis* has been also relied upon by the ICJ in the 2002 Cameroon/Nigeria Case,[42] although it has not been applied to the maritime border *inter alia* due to the existence of a delimitation agreement concluded by the two States after independence.[43] In the context of delimitation on navigable rivers

---

35 Central American Court of Justice, Case concerning El Salvador vs Nicaragua, Opinion and Decision of the Court, San José, 9 March 1917. Published in AJIL, Vol. 11, No. 3, 1917, p. 674.

36 See also Kohen, '*Uti possidetis* and Maritime Delimitation', op. cit.

37 Cf fn 5, paras 386 and 405.

38 With the 1964 OAU Declaration the States parties pledged themselves 'to respect the borders existing on their achievement of independence'. See I. Brownlie, *African Boundaries, Legal and Diplomatic Encyclopedia*, Royal Institute of International Law, Guildford, London and Worchester: Billing & Sons Limited, 1979, p. 11.

39 Continental Shelf (Tunisia/Libyan Arab Jamahiriya), ICJ Reports, 1982, para. 84.

40 Guinea Bissau/Senegal Case, Award of the Arbitral Tribunal, 94 RGDIP, 1990, p. 204.

41 Ibid, para. 37. Cf fn 36 (Kohen).

42 Land and Maritime Boundary between Cameroon and Nigeria (*Cameroon v. Nigeria: Equatorial Guinea Intervening*), ICJ Reports, 2002, p. 303.

43 Ibid, paras 262–268.

the 2005 ICJ judgment in the Case Concerning the Frontier Dispute (Benin-Niger) is also extremely important.[44] There seems to be enough evidence that at least the judicial opinion has been in favour of the application of the principle of *uti possidetis* to maritime delimitations.

4.3.2 The applicability of the doctrine of 'effective control' (effectivités) to cases of maritime delimitation

While there seems to be a considerable body of international jurisprudence supporting the application of the principle of *uti possidetis* in cases where the 'administrative' maritime boundary was formalized at the time of independence (therefore in cases of a pre-existing title 'juris'), a far more complex question is whether the principle of *uti possidetis* may be applied to maritime delimitations in cases where, at the moment of independence, there was just a factual exercise of jurisdiction (effective control) by one of the administrative (e.g. federal) units over a certain sea area. Reference is made here to the *doctrine of effectivités*.[45]

The jurisprudence and/or available bibliography regarding the application of the doctrine of *effectivités* is relatively scarce and in a great part relates to boundaries on land. A landmark case in this regard is the 1986 Frontier Case (Burkina Faso/Mali)[46] where the ICJ clearly sets the relation between 'legal title' (*uti possidetis juris*) and 'effective possession' (*effectivités*) and where absolute pre-eminence was given to 'legal title'. The ICJ explained that '… the first aspect, emphasized by the Latin genitive *juris*, is found in the pre-eminence accorded to legal title over effective possession, as a basis of sovereignty'.[47] The ICJ also unequivocally explained the relation between legal title (*uti possidetis juris*) and effective possession stating that:

> Where the act does not correspond to the law, where the territory which is the subject of the dispute is effectively administered by a State other than the one possessing the legal title, preference should be given to the holder of the title. In the case that *effectivité* does not co-exist with any legal title, it must invariably be taken into consideration. Finally, there are cases where the legal title is not capable of showing exactly the territorial expanse to which it relates. The *effectivités* can then play an essential role in showing how the title is interpreted in practice.[48]

Regarding the application of the doctrine of *effectivités* to cases of maritime delimitation, there seems to be a tendency in the recent jurisprudence of

---

44 Frontier Dispute (Benin/Niger), ICJ Reports, 2005, p. 90. See also S. Allen, 'Case Concerning the Frontier Dispute (Benin/Niger)', ICLQ, Vol. 55, 2006, pp. 729–768.
45 See section 4.3.2.
46 Cf fn 4. See also Shaw, *International Law*, op. cit., pp. 529–530.
47 Ibid, para. 23.
48 Ibid, para. 63.

142 *Extension of Coastal State Jurisdiction in Enclosed or Semi-enclosed Seas*

international courts and tribunals towards the presumption that "internal maritime lines" between various administrative (federal) entities may become international boundaries. This may be derived from the El Salvador-Honduras (Nicaragua intervening) Case where the ICJ took the position that not only "lines", but also the absence of lines and/or a specific legal situation (e.g. condominium), could be inherited on the basis of the principle of *uti possidetis*. According to the Chamber 'there seems to be no reason in principle why a succession should not create a joint sovereignty where a single and undivided maritime area passes to two or more new States'.[49]

A decade before, in the 1982 Tunisia/Libya Case, the ICJ was called to adjudicate upon the legal value of various lines for different purposes which existed between the parties. A line unilaterally established by Italy with regard to sponge banking was, due to the absence of protest from the French side, deemed to represent a *modus vivendi,* which was taken into account by the Court as a 'historical justification for the choice of the method for the delimitation of the continental shelf between the two States, to the extent that the historic rights claimed by Tunisia could not be opposable to Libya east of the *modus vivendi* line'.[50] A similar treatment was given by the ICJ to the *de facto* line resulting from a longstanding practice of granting adjoining (offshore) oil and gas concessions. According to the ICJ:

> … This line of adjoining concessions, which was tacitly respected for a number of years … which had in the past been observed as a *de facto* maritime limit does appear to the Court to constitute a circumstance of great relevance for the delimitation.…[51]

The *modus vivendi* line, although not being recognized as a 'maritime boundary' was treated by ICJ as a 'relevant circumstance' which the Court should take into account while delimiting the continental shelf.[52] This in turn points to another possible application (relevance) of the principle of *uti possidetis,* particularly in relation to the doctrine of *effectivités.*[53]

There are at least another two cases from which it is possible to get some guidance about the application of the doctrine of *effectivités* to maritime

---

49 Cf fn 5, para. 399. See, however, the dissenting opinion of Judge Oda.
50 Cf fn 39, para. 95, and fn 36 (Kohen).
51 Ibid, para. 96.
52 In the words of the ICJ: '… This line of adjoining concessions, which was tacitly respected for a number of years, and which approximately corresponds furthermore to the line perpendicular to the coast at the frontier point which had in the past been observed as a *de facto* maritime limit, does appear to the Court to constitute a circumstance of great relevance for the delimitation.…'. Cf fn 39, para. 96.
53 See the discussion in 4.3.2.

Maritime boundaries in the (Eastern) Adriatic 143

delimitation.[54] The first is the Benin-Niger Case,[55] where the dispute *inter alia* concerned the question of sovereignty over 25 islands and delimitation of the boundary in the watercourse of the River Niger. Although the latter did not deal with 'maritime delimitation', it can nonetheless provide some guidance due to the fact that it shows, as pointed out by Allen, the complex interrelationship between 'law' and 'fact' within the framework of a single principle of international law (*uti possidetis*).[56] In the Special Agreement, the parties made express reference to the '*principle of state succession to the boundaries inherited from colonization, that is to say to the intangibility of frontiers*',[57] which the Court interpreted as reference to the principle of *uti possidetis juris*. Also in this case the Court decided to follow the approach adopted in the 1986 Burkina Faso/Mali Case in the sense that 'preeminence is accorded to legal title over effective possession as a basis for sovereignty'.[58]

The latter *dictum* therefore sets up the order of priorities for a Court and/or an arbitral tribunal which has primarily to consider the (internal) regulative and administrative instruments (title) and only later on, if necessary, the various *effectivités* advanced by the parties.[59] As the ICJ was not able to define the exact boundary solely on the basis of regulative and administrative colonial instruments, it resorted in the second phase to 'State *effectivités*', where an utmost important role was attributed to an existing *modus vivendi* and to the question of which party exercised jurisdiction over the disputed islands at the time of independence. As further emphasized by Allen, this fact demonstrates that in ambiguous situations and also where the title exists but it is not clear, 'facts rather than "law" may determine the application of *uti possidetis juris*'.[60]

The application of the principle of *uti possidetis* (*doctrine of effectivités*) has been further assessed in the 2007 Nicaragua/Honduras Case where the ICJ not only expressly declared the applicability of the principle to maritime delimitation, but it furthermore provided a list of 'colonial *effectivités*' to which the Court resorted after having concluded that the question of sovereignty over the disputed islands cannot be resolved on the basis of administrative and/or legislative texts. The 'test of colonial *effectivités*' has been defined by the Court as 'the conduct of the administrative authorities as proof of the effective exercise of territorial jurisdiction in the region during the colonial period …'.[61]

---

54 Three other ICJ cases assessing the relation between 'legal title' and *effectivités* include: Case Concerning the Land and Maritime Boundary (*Cameroon v Nigeria: Equatorial Guinea intervening*), Judgment, ICJ Reports, 2002, p. 303; Case concerning Sovereignty over Pulau Ligitan and Pulau Sipadan (Indonesia/Malaysia), Judgment, ICJ Reports, 2002, p. 625 and most recently: Territorial and Maritime Dispute (*Nicaragua v Colombia*), ICJ, Judgment, 19 November 2012. See also Award of the Arbitral Tribunal in the First Stage – Territorial Sovereignty and Scope of the Dispute (Eritrea/Yemen), Award, 9 October 1998.

55 Cf fn 44.

56 See Allen, op. cit., pp. 729–730.

57 Special Agreement (French). Available at <http://www.icj-cij.org/docket/files/125/7068.pdf>.

58 Cf fn 4, para. 23.

59 Allen, op. cit., p. 733.

60 Ibid, p. 738.

61 Cf fn 33, para. 165.

144 *Extension of Coastal State Jurisdiction in Enclosed or Semi-enclosed Seas*

It is suggested that this 'list' may by analogy represent an important guideline also when it comes to the application of the doctrine of *effectivités* to cases of maritime delimitation. In the 2007 case the ICJ, however, found that information about such conduct by administrative colonial authorities is lacking and that it could 'neither found nor confirm on this basis a title to territory over the islands in question'.[62] In such an absence, the Court had to resort to various categories of *post-colonial effectivités*[63] presented by the parties, including Legislative and Administrative Control,[64] Application and Enforcement of Criminal and Civil law,[65] Regulation of Immigration,[66] Regulation of Fisheries Activities,[67] Naval Patrols,[68] Oil Concessions[69] and Public Works.[70] This in turn confirms what was already stated by the ICJ in the Benin-Niger Frontier Case and which seems to be relevant also in the context of the Adriatic Sea[71] that 'sources subsequent to the critical date may be relevant to the determination of the *uti possidetis juris* at the time of independence'.[72] The added value of these provisions is obviously that they provide an illustrative and 'open-ended' list which may be taken into account also with the aim of 'clarifying' or even 'asserting' title over certain maritime areas.

There seems therefore to be enough evidence also for the assertion that not only is the principle of *uti possidetis* applicable to maritime delimitation, but also that in cases where the title over a certain (marine) area at the day of independence was for example not clear, '*effectivités* can play an essential role in showing how title is interpreted in practice'.

4.3.3 The application of the principle of uti possidetis (and/or doctrine of effectivitiés) in cases where it conflicts with generally recognized rules and principles of international law (law of the sea)

This work has so far showed not only that there is substantial agreement about the application of the principle of *uti possidetis* (inc. *effectivités*) to maritime

---

62 Ibid, para. 166.
63 Emphasis added. See also *Legal Status of the Eastern Grenland*, P.C.I.J. Series A/B, No. 53, (1933), pp. 45–46.
64 Cf fn 33, paras 177–181.
65 Ibid, paras 182–185.
66 Ibid, paras 186–189.
67 Ibid, paras 190–198.
68 Ibid, paras 199–201.
69 Ibid, paras 202–204.
70 Ibid, paras 205–207.
71 See also the discussion in section 4.8.4.
72 Cf fn 44, para. 26, and Allen, op. cit., pp. 736–737. See also Case concerning Sovereignty over Pulau Ligitan and Pulau Sipadan (Indonesia/Malaysia), op. cit., para. 135. According to the ICJ: 'The Court further observes that it cannot take into consideration acts having taken place after the date on which the dispute between the Parties crystallized *unless such acts are a normal continuation of prior acts and are not undertaken for the purpose of improving the legal position of the Party which relies on them* (see Arbitral Award in the Palena case, 38 International Law Reports (ILR), pp. 79–80) …'. Emphasis added. Ibid, para. 135.

Maritime boundaries in the (Eastern) Adriatic 145

delimitations, but also that the principle may be *inter alia* applied in cases where the (legal) title over maritime areas at the day of independence was not completely clear or, according to some, even non-existent (e.g. the dissolution of the former SFRY).[73] An interesting question is, however, posed by the application of the principle of *uti possidetis* in cases where the latter conflicts with another established rule and/or principle of international law (law of the sea), as for example the sole right of a coastal State to its own territorial sea and other zones (land dominates the sea) and/or for example the rule regulating the maximum allowable breadth of the territorial sea (12 nmi). Both situations are relevant in the (former) juridical bays of Piran (bordered nowadays by Slovenia and Croatia)[74] and seemingly also in the Bay of Boka Kotorska (bordered by Croatia and Montenegro)[75] where claims have been made that on the day of independence (of Croatia) only one of the two bordering republics exercised *effective control* over the two bays. The (automatic) application of the principle of *uti possidetis* in that case would, however, lead to a situation where the sovereignty of one of the States successors of the former SFRY (Croatia) would end up at the shores of the relevant bays. It is furthermore asserted by Slovenia that at the moment of independence it exercised 'effective control' up to the point where the former 'SFRY' territorial sea met the high seas in the Adriatic (Point T5),[76] and therefore to a point which is nowadays located exactly 12 nmi from the Croatian coast (baseline) and more than 15 nmi from the Slovenian coast (and/or baseline).[77]

There seems to be no international jurisprudence dealing with similar cases and not surprisingly the opinions of particularly Slovenian and Croatian experts on whether for example Slovenia is entitled to exercise sovereignty over the entire Bay of Piran and/or whether it has territorial access to the high seas (Point T5) differs diametrically.[78] It would, however, seem possible to draw an analogy to another similar scenario in the context of (potential) 'secession' and/or 'dissolution' of States which although it has not materialized, it has been nonetheless discussed hypothetically by some leading international law experts. Reference is

---

73 See section 4.2. Degan disagrees with the opinion that the doctrine of *effectivités* cannot be applied to sea areas, but in the absence of title, only to land territory, particularly smaller uninhabited islands. The Croatian expert is furthermore of the opinion that title to sea areas always derive from the principle 'land dominates the sea' and that *effectivités* should not play a role in maritime delimitations. See V.D. Degan, '*Pravni naslov i efektivnost kao osnove suverenosti*', PPP, Vol. 47, No. 162, Zagreb, 2008, p. 1 at p. 37.

74 See section 4.7.2.1. Cf fn 73.

75 See section 4.6.

76 Point T5 is the last point (5) of the borderline with which the former SFRY and Italy delimited the territorial sea in the Gulf of Trieste (1975 Osimo Treaty) and the starting point (1) of the 1968 Italy-SFRY Shelf Agreement. Nowadays it represents the 'unilaterally' set starting points of the Croatian EFPZ and of the Slovenian ZEP. See the discussion in 3.3.4 and 3.3.6. See also Figures 3.4 and 3.6.

77 See section 4.7.2.2. See also Z. Gržetić *et al.*, '*O granicama u sjevernom Jadranu (1948–2009) s posebnim osvrtom na kronološki kartografski prikaz*', PPP, Vol. 49, No. 164, Zagreb, 2010, p. 19 at 63.

78 Ibid.

146 *Extension of Coastal State Jurisdiction in Enclosed or Semi-enclosed Seas*

made here to the (potential) secession of Québec whose geographical relation with other provinces and/or Canada is to a certain extent similar to that existing among the States successors of the former SFRY (e.g. Slovenia/Croatia). The case is interesting as it would seem from the various documents forming the Constitution of Canada (including the 1867 Constitutional Act)[79] that the waters contiguous to the coastline of Québec are in fact either Canadian 'historic' and/or 'internal' waters over which sovereignty and jurisdiction is exercised by Canada and not by the various provinces.[80] Facing the perspective of the secession, the Québec National Assembly asked Charney in 1992 to provide a legal opinion on the Maritime Boundaries of Québec if it were to become a sovereign State (independent of Canada), and ten years later (in 2001) it was asked to amend those conclusions, as necessary. One of the questions which that scholar was expressly asked to raise in his Report[81] was whether 'there would be any change in the legal status of these waters should Québec attain sovereignty, given that the territorial sea off the Québec shore comes actually under the jurisdiction of the federal government of Canada', and in this regard Charney clearly answered that Quèbec would be entitled to all maritime areas provided by international law. A related question was also what would happen at the moment of secession with the current "Canadian historic waters" within the historic gulfs bordered also by Québec (e.g. Hudson Bay, Gulf of St Lawrence). Charney interestingly allowed for two possibilities:

> … either the historic water status would be extinguished causing the waters to revert to the normal zones of the territorial sea, exclusive economic zone or exclusive fisheries zones, and continental shelf; *or Québec would be entitled to share the internal [historic] waters it helped to create by a division through the delimitation of maritime boundaries, or the establishment of joint or condominium rights in the entire area.*[82]

The latter view was also reflected in a contemporary Report[83] on the same subject, prepared by Pellet, Higgins, Franck, Shaw and Tomuscat. According to the latter:

> … it is not at all certain that, even if the waters immediately contiguous to the Québec coastline were, at present, considered to be Canadian inland

---

79 See section 6 of the 1867 Canada Constitution Act. See also comparison with Art. 5 of the 1974 SFRY's Constitution. See section 4.2.

80 Quebéc borders Hudson Bay and Hudson Strait, and the Gulf of St Lawrence. Those areas are currently 'closed' as Canadian historic bays.

81 J.I. Charney, 'The Maritime Boundaries of Québec', Report, March 9, 1992 as amended by the '2001 Update of the Maritime Boundaries of Québec (updated and complementary texts of 2001), November 14, 2001.

82 Emphasis added. Ibid, 2001, Update, pp. 5–6.

83 A. Pellet *et al.* 'The Territorial Integrity of Québec in the Event of the Attainment of Sovereignty', Report prepared for the Québec's Ministére des relations internationals (Translation by William Boulet), 1992. The Report was not directly focused on the issue of maritime boundaries and made express reference to the previous Report prepared by Charney. Cf fn 81.

waters, *the principles applicable to State succession would defeat the universally recognized rules governing the allocation of maritime territory.* On the contrary, it seems to us that Québec, like any other State, could, in the event of sovereignty, demand the application of these rules and assert its 'inherent right' to territorial sovereignty or sovereign rights over the sea adjacent to its coastlines, it being understood:

> – that if *Hudson Bay and Hudson Strait, or even the Gulf of St Lawrence,* were deemed to be historical bays, classified as inland waters, the question would arise whether they should be apportioned between the coastal States or whether it would be appropriate to consider them as historical bays falling under the joint jurisdiction of such States, in the manner of the legal regime that probably governs the Gulf of Fonseca ....[84]

In the Adriatic context[85] it is particularly relevant that in its 2001 Update of the 1992 Report, Charney also addressed the question of access of Québec (navigation) to the 'open sea' (high seas), particularly in the light of the 1992 Judgment in the 1992 Land, Island and Maritime Frontier Dispute Case (*El Salvador/Honduras: Nicaragua intervening*)[86] and of the 1992 Award of the Arbitral Tribunal in the St Pierre et Miquelon Case (France/Canada).[87] While admitting that the best navigation for an independent Québec to and from the 'open sea' would be through Cabot straits, he realized that with the application of the method of (modified) equidistance Québec would not have maritime zones of its own, extending from its land territory to that point. He however stated that '... if, however, Québec established condominium rights in the Gulf then the Gulf of Fonseca Judgment would support Québec's right to a share of the closing line at Cabot Strait and rights seaward ...'.[88] Charney therefore saw the 'condominium' over the nowadays Canadian 'historic-internal' waters of the Gulf of St Lawrence as the only possibility which would allow Québec's 'territorial contact' with the high seas through and beyond Cabot Strait.

In the light of the foregoing it seems reasonable to agree with Shaw that the application of the principle of *uti possidetis* to cases of maritime delimitation is, although a presumption, 'a rebuttable presumption', as it should not be contrary at least to the fundamental provisions of UNCLOS and/or customary international law governing the allocation of maritime territory.[89] Whether they

---

84 Emphasis added. Ibid, sections 2.35–2.36.

85 See the discussion of the Slovenian claim regarding its 'direct territorial access to the high seas'. See section 4.7.2.2.

86 Cf fn 5.

87 St Pierre and Miquelon Case (France/Canada), 31 ILM 1145–1219 (1992). See also L. De La Fayette, 'The Award in the Canada-France Maritime Boundary Arbitration', IJMCL, Vol. 8, No. 1, 1993, pp. 77–103, and G.P. Politakis, 'The French-Canadian Arbitration around St Pierre and Miquelon: Unmasked Opportunism and the Triumph of the Unexpected', IJMCL, Vol. 8, No. 1, 1993, pp. 105–134.

88 See Charney, op. cit., p. 10. See also J.J. Smith, 'An independent Québec's Maritime Claims in the Gulf of St Lawrence and Beyond', Can.Y.B. Int'l L., 1997, pp. 113–127.

89 Unpublished report.

148 *Extension of Coastal State Jurisdiction in Enclosed or Semi-enclosed Seas*

are such 'fundamental' rules of UNCLOS, and whether 'fundamental' is a synonymous also for 'peremptory' (*ius cogens*) is subject to discussion.[90]

4.4 Border bays in international law

The next important question for the resolution of all three cases of maritime delimitation disputes between the States' successors of the former SFRY and particularly in relations between Slovenia-Croatia (Bay of Piran) and Croatia-Montenegro (Bay of Boka Kotorska)[91] is what is the status of 'border bays' in the contemporary law of the sea? A related question which is also relevant in the context of the Croatia-Bosnia and Herzegovina dispute is whether the 'juridical' status of the waters within such bays and/or waters (which were during 'federal times' bordered by only one State) automatically switched from 'internal waters' to 'territorial sea'. It is suggested that some clarity over these matters may help Adriatic States in the formulation of their future positions and hopefully in their pursuit of 'innovative' solutions reflecting the spirit of Part IX of UNCLOS.[92]

4.4.1 State practice regarding bays bordered by more than one state (border bays)

The definition of a (juridical) bay is contained in Article 7 of the 1958 TSC and this definition was incorporated almost entirely into Article 10 of UNCLOS where it defines a "bay" as:

> … a well-marked indentation whose penetration is in such proportion to the width of its mouth as to contain land-locked waters and constitute more than a mere curvature of the coast. An indentation shall not, however, be regarded as a bay unless its area is as large or larger than, that of the semi-circle whose diameter is a line drawn across the mouth of that indentation.[93]

This provision however does not apply where straight baselines were used to close historic bays[94] and, at least as a general rule, not to 'border bays'. Churchill and

---

90 It may be tentatively asserted that the rule of UNCLOS and customary international law regulating the maximum breadth of the territorial sea (12 nmi) in principle prevails over the 'strict' application of the principle of *uti possidetis*. It is nonetheless suggested that the situation may be different if two or more States exercise joint sovereignty (condominium rights) over a certain part of the territorial sea. That area, however, should not be located more than 12 nmi from the coast of at least one State. See M. Grbec, *Delimitation of the Maritime Boundary between the Republic of Slovenia and the Republic of Croatia*, LL.M. Thesis, IMO IMLI, 2001, p. 75, and M. Pavliha, '*To morje je vse, kar imam*', Pravna praksa, No. 5, Ljubljana, 2001, p. 33.

91 See the discussion in sections 4.6. and 4.7.

92 See for example section 4.7.3.

93 See G.S. Westerman, *The Juridical Bay*, Oxford: Clarendon Press, 1987.

94 According to a 'Study of the juridical regime of the historic waters, including historic bays', prepared by the UN Secretariat in 1962, '[t]he state may validly claim title to a bay on historic grounds if it can show that it has for a considerable period of time claimed the bay as internal waters and has effectively, openly and continuously exercised its authority therein, and that during

Maritime boundaries in the (Eastern) Adriatic 149

Lowe indicate that '… the normal rule of customary international law in relation to such bays [border bays] would appear to be that … they cannot be closed by a line drawn across their mouth'.[95] They, however, admit that '[e]xceptionally it may be possible for the riparian States to show that the position is different by reason of historic title'.[96]

However, there seems to be no valid reason why two (or more) States could not retain the 'internal waters' status within a border bay, particularly if the rights of third States are not affected. According to Symmons:

> … an emerging view seems to be that States may *at least by agreement* close off the mouth of a shared border bay, and so use the resulting straight baseline *as the generating point of any respective exterior maritime zones* derived from the enclosed internal waters ….[97]

This seems to be a feasible option, particularly with border bays which have arisen as a result of succession and/or secessions of States and which had been during 'federal' times closed as 'historic' or just 'juridical' bays. Examples include the two border bays arising out of the dissolution of the former SFRY (the Bay of Piran and the Bay of Boka Kotorska) while an interesting case is also that of Lough Foyle and Carlingford Lough, bordered by Ireland and the UK (Northern Ireland). The latter case is interesting as it seems that it was only following the entry into force of the Belfast Agreement in 1999[98] and the consequent change to the Constitution of Ireland[99] that there is now a notional maritime boundary running down the mentioned 'Loughs'.[100] It is noteworthy that before 1999 all waters of the Bay(s) and even all territorial waters around Northern Ireland were claimed by Ireland as its internal and/or territorial sea.[101]

Following the Belfast Agreement and the amendments to Article 2 of the Constitution of Ireland, it seems that Ireland recognizes to Northern Ireland (UK) the right to generate its own maritime areas, although it is not clear whether the juridical status of the waters within such bays is currently that of internal

---

this time the claim has received acquiescence by other States'. UN Doc. A/CN.4/143, 9 March 1962. For a thorough discussion on historic bays and waters, see C.R. Symmons, *Historic Waters in the Law of the Sea: A Modern Re-appraisal*, Publications on Ocean Development, Leiden and Boston, MA: Martinus Nijhoff Publishers, 2008.

95 R. Churchill and V. Lowe, *The Law of the Sea*, 3rd edn, Manchester: Manchester University Press, 1999, p. 45.

96 Ibid, p. 46.

97 Emphasis added. C.R. Symmons, 'The Maritime Border Areas of Ireland, North and South', IJMC, Vol. 24, No. 3, 2009, p. 457 at pp. 466–467. Symmons reinforces such assertion also with the lack of protest against such practice.

98 Northern Ireland Peace Agreement: The Belfast Agreement (UK/Ireland), 10 April 1998, in force since 10 December 1999.

99 See the Nineteenth Amendment of the Constitution Act 1998 which amended Arts 2 and 3 of the Constitution of Ireland. Prior to 1999, Arts 2 and 3 claimed that the whole island of Ireland formed one single 'national territory'.

100 Cf fn 97, p. 463.

101 See also the discussion in section 4.7.2.1.

150 *Extension of Coastal State Jurisdiction in Enclosed or Semi-enclosed Seas*

waters and/or territorial sea.[102] Overall there seems to be no valid reason why Ireland and the UK could not jointly 'confirm' that the waters within the two bays have the status of internal (or even historic) waters and retain the two bays closed within a straight baseline.

4.4.1.1 The Sea of Azov and the Strait of Kerch

Another interesting example is that of the Sea of Azov and the Strait of Kerch, bordered nowadays by Russia and Ukraine but which during the time of the former USSR had the status of a 'closed sea', and were therefore internal (historic) or in the words of some Soviet commentators even 'inland' waters. With the Joint Statement of the President of Ukraine and the President of the Russian Federation on the Sea of Azov and Strait of Kerch, 24 December 2003[103] the two States 'confirmed their common understanding',[104] that:

> ... *historically* the Sea of Azov and the Strait of Kerch are *inland waters* of Ukraine and Russia, and settlement of matters related to the said area of water is realized by agreement between the Ukraine and Russia in accordance with international law ....[105]

The importance of the 2003 Joint Statement derives also from the fact that with the latter, the two States impliedly confirmed that there was not an automatic conversion of the 'internal-historical waters' within the Sea of Azov and the Strait of Kerch into 'territorial seas', at the time of the dissolution of the former USSR. This may be implied particularly from paragraph 1 of the Joint Statement providing that '... the Azov-Kerch area of water is *preserved* as an integral economic and natural complex used in the interests of both States'.[106] The latter wording seems to imply a condominium (joint sovereignty) of the two States over the 'Azov Kerch area'. The joint statement furthermore regulates in broader terms co-operation between the two States which could also be termed as a sort of *de facto* 'joint management' of the shared waters. The latter includes:

> ... their common activity in the sphere of navigation, including its regulation and navigation and hydrographical provisions, fishing, protection of the marine environment, environmental safety ....[107]

The *sui generis* status of the Sea of Azov and the Strait of Kerch seem to be *inter alia* perfectly in line with the often cited decision of the ICJ and previously of the

---

102 Cf fn 97, p. 461.
103 LOS Bulletin, No. 54, 2004, p. 131.
104 Ibid, Preamble.
105 Ibid, Paragraph 2.
106 Emphasis added.
107 Preamble, para. 5.

Maritime boundaries in the (Eastern) Adriatic 151

Central American Court of Arbitration regarding the legal status of the Gulf of Fonseca.[108] It should nonetheless be noted that according to the 2003 Joint Statement 'military ships under the flags of other States can enter the Sea of Azov and go through the Strait of Kerch only by invitation of Ukraine and Russia, *agreed with the other State*'.[109] This in turn seems to deny a type of a 'right of innocent passage' which exists in the Gulf of Fonseca.[110] Independently of that, it seems difficult to agree with Degan that '... with one commonly recognized exception [the Gulf of Fonseca], the coast of all historic bays belongs to a single State'.[111]

4.4.1.2 Delimitation of historic waters (India-Sri Lanka and the Mozambique-Tanzania Agreement)

There are at least two other interesting cases which illustrate the practice of States applicable to border bays. The first is the 1974 Agreement on the Boundary in Historic Waters and Related Matters (Sri Lanka and India)[112] with which the two countries delimited the 'historic waters' between Palk Bay and Palk Strait in the Bay of Bengal. It is noteworthy that the latter acquired its 'historic' status during the times of the British dominion in the region, therefore prior to the independence of both States. That case, coupled with the 2003 Joint Statement by Russia and Ukraine, casts some serious doubt over the position of Croatia[113] that historic rights can arise only after a certain State acquires its independence. Degan for example stated that:

> ... these rights can only appear after such an event [achievement of independence] and after many years of peaceful exercise of exclusive jurisdiction by the respective State, without protests from other States ...[114]

The fact that *strictly speaking* there are no legal impediments for the riparian States of a certain border bay to delimit the 'historic' and eventually also 'internal

---

108 It was held by the ICJ in the 'Land, Island and Maritime Frontier Dispute Case, (El Salvador/Honduras: Nicaragua Intervening)' that the status of the waters of the Gulf of Fonseca is *sui generis* (co-ownership), although essentially that of internal waters through which however there exist the right of innocent passage. Cf fn 5, para. 412. See also C.M. Gutiérez Fons, *The Legal Status of the Gulf of Fonseca: Is a condominium of the enclosed waters possible?*, LL.M. Thesis, Malta: IMO IMLI, 2004.

109 Cf fn 103, para. 4.

110 Cf fn 108.

111 See Đ.V. Degan, 'Consolidation of Legal Principles on Maritime Delimitation: Implications for the Dispute between Slovenia and Croatia in the North Adriatic', CJIL, Vol. 6, No. 3, 2007, p. 601 at p. 626.

112 See also J. Charney and L. Alexander (eds), *International Maritime Boundaries*, Vol. II, ASIL, Dordrecht, Boston, MA and London: Martinus Nijhoff Publishers, 1989, pp. 1409–1419.

113 See section 4.7.2.1.

114 Degan, op. cit., pp. 625–626, para. 134.

152 Extension of Coastal State Jurisdiction in Enclosed or Semi-enclosed Seas

waters' among themselves[115] seems also to follow from the ICJ's judgment in the Land, Island and Maritime Frontier Dispute. According to the Court:

> ... the waters at the central portion of the closing line of the Gulf [of Fonseca] ... are subject to the joint entitlement of all three States of the Gulf *unless and until a delimitation of the relevant maritime areas be effected.*[116]

A second and somehow more controversial precedent seems to be, however, that of the 1988 Tanzania-Mozambique Agreement[117] which provides for a closing line across the border bay of Ravuma. The latter links specified co-ordinates on the shorelines of both States, while Article 2 of the Treaty expressly provides that all waters 'on the landward side of this line' constitute the internal waters of the two States. Article 3 then delimits the enclosed 'internal waters' between the two States. It is noteworthy that the mentioned agreement does not make, as the 1974 India–Sri Lanka Agreement or the 2003 Joint Statement by Ukraine and Russia (Sea of Azov) any reference to a 'historic title' or 'historic bay' doctrine. This in turn makes the 1988 Agreement, at least according to some commentators, questionable from the standpoint of the contemporary law of the sea.[118]

Reference should be finally made to the fact that the closure of border bays with a straight baseline shall not affect the interest of third States, particularly regarding the exercise of their communication freedoms (e.g. navigation). In the case of border bays arising out of the dissolution or succession of States (e.g. the Bay of Piran and/or the Bay of Boka Kotorska in the Adriatic) this is far less likely to happen due to an already existing (historical) situation in place. Overall it seems possible to agree with Symmons, that:

> [...] in the light of the flexibility that the law of the sea gives to *agreed* delimitation solutions, a closing or straight baseline which is in fact *formally* agreed between two or more littoral states in a border bay of border river situation would gain international approval and recognition.[119]

Lastly, it is suggested that there are no obstacles for an international court or Tribunal to adopt a 'Gulf of Fonseca' type of solution in disputed border bays,[120] both within and outside the bay (territorial sea, zones of sovereign rights and jurisdiction), and that this is not a completely impossible scenario in

---

115 This seems to be the case particularly with border bays arising out of dissolution of States (e.g. Bay of Piran, Bay of Boka Kotorska, Strait of Kerch, etc.), as such an Agreement just preserves an already existing situation.

116 Emphasis added. Cf fn 5, para. 432.

117 Agreement between the Government of the United Republic of Tanzania and the Government of the People's Republic of Mozambique regarding the Tanzania/Mozambique Boundary, 28 December 1988.

118 See Churchill and Lowe, op. cit., p. 46, and Symmons, 'The Maritime Border Areas of Ireland ...', op. cit., p. 469.

119 Ibid, Symmons, 'The Maritime Border Areas of Ireland ...', op. cit., p. 467.

120 See sections 4.3.2–4.3.3.

the two disputed Adriatic border bays.[121] It is furthermore suggested that it is perfectly possible for an international court or tribunal to retain the 'internal waters' status within a shared border bay. This is also the case in the absence of consensus on the juridical status of the bay's waters between the two contending riparian States.[122]

4.5 Croatia/Bosnia and Herzegovina: Is a solution in line with Part IX of UNCLOS possible?

The particular position of the coastline of Bosnia and Herzegovina and its waters is interesting not only in the context of the Adriatic and Mediterranean Seas, but worldwide. The reason lies in the (geographical) fact that Bosnia and Herzegovina exercises sovereignty over a narrow strip of territory called the 'Klek-Neum Corridor' enclosed between two parts of the Croatian coastline[123] and in the (legal) fact that the maritime areas of Bosnia and Herzegovina were both (on the basis of the 1994 and 2004 Croatian Maritime Code)[124] enclosed within the Croatian system of straight baselines.[125] It should also be noted that, although the length of the coastline of Bosnia and Herzegovina amounts officially to 21 km, its coastal front, as it takes the form of the letter 'Z', amounts to less than 10 km.[126] Furthermore, the width of the waters of Bosnia and Herzegovina between the peninsula of Klek and the much bigger Croatian peninsula of Pelješac (median line) is less than 2 nmi. To render the situation even more complicated, the waters of Bosnia and Herzegovina lie not only behind the Croatian peninsula of Pelješac but also behind a chain of several other Croatian islands (see Figure 4.1). The relevant legal question for Bosnia and Herzegovina is therefore not 'extension of coastal State jurisdiction' but instead its (navigational) access to the high seas and/or zones of sovereign rights and jurisdiction in the Adriatic Sea.

Taking into account the 'extreme' geographical characteristics of the coastline of Bosnia and Herzegovina and the surrounding Croatian islands, it seems reasonable to assert that, due to the particular position of its coastline and its maritime zone(s), Bosnia and Herzegovina does not have its own continental shelf nor the possibility of proclaiming an EEZ or other zones of functional jurisdiction in the Adriatic. It may thus be concluded that Bosnia and Herzegovina fulfils the requirements to qualify as a geographically disadvantaged State on the basis of Article 70 of UNCLOS.[127]

---

121 See the discussions in sections 4.6.1 and 4.7.2.1. Slovenia has throughout the years strongly opposed any kind of condominium solution for the Bay of Piran.
122 See also the discussion in 4.8.2 (Bay of Piran).
123 For a historical overview, see D. Topalović and G. H. Blake, 'The Maritime Boundaries of the Adriatic Sea', Maritime Briefing, Vol. 1, No. 8, University of Durham, 1996, pp. 36–41, and V. Ibler, *Medunarodno pravo mora i Hrvatska*, Zagreb: Barbat, 2001, pp. 188–191.
124 See OGRC, No. 17/1994 and 181/2004.
125 See Art. 19 of the 1994, and Art. 18 of the 2004 Maritime Code of Croatia. Ibid.
126 Blake and Topalović, op. cit., p. 34.
127 'For the purposes of this Part "geographically disadvantaged States" means coastal States, including States bordering enclosed or semi-enclosed seas ... which can claim no exclusive

Figure 4.1 Relationship between the coastlines of Croatia and Bosnia and Herzegovina[128]

In addition to the sole delimitation (e.g. the signed 1999 Border Treaty), there are at least two other aspects of this dispute which are interesting from the standpoint of the contemporary law of the sea and relevant for the purpose of this work. The first is the legality of the Croatian enclosure of the maritime zones of Bosnia and Herzegovina into its system of straight baselines, while the second is the right of navigation of Bosnia and Herzegovina through Croatian (internal) waters to the high seas (potential EEZs) in the Adriatic Sea.

economic zone of their own'. See Art. 70(2) of UNCLOS. For a thorough discussion, see S.C. Vasciannie, *Land-Locked and Geographically Disadvantaged States in the International Law of the Sea*, Oxford: Clarendon Press, 1990.
128 Modelled on a figure published in Blake and Topalović, op. cit., p. 9.

4.5.1 The legality of the enclosure of the maritime zone(s) of Bosnia and Herzegovina within the Croatian system of straight baselines

It is noteworthy that on the basis of the 1987 SFRY Law[129] the current maritime zones of Bosnia and Herzegovina were closed within a SFRY system of straight baselines (see Figure 4.2).[130] After attaining independence, Bosnia and Herzegovina has not expressed any official position on the legal status of its waters, nor can there be any clue derived from the (non-ratified) 1999 Border Treaty with Croatia.[131]

While the drawing of straight baselines and the enclosure of the Croatian peninsula of Pelješac and of the coastline of the then 'federal' Republic of Bosnia and Herzegovina within the 'SFRY' system of straight baselines was fully in line with the relevant provisions of the TSC and customary international law,[132] it seems questionable whether Croatia acted in line with the relevant provisions of UNCLOS (as reflected also in customary law) when in 1994 and 2004 it incorporated *ad verbatim* the previous SFRY system of straight baselines in its Maritime Code, without leaving any 'openings' or 'interruptions' and/or 'corridor' within which Bosnia and Herzegovina would exercise its right of navigation through Croatian waters.[133] It is also suggested that such a decision was not in accordance with the general policy of co-operation advocated by Part IX of UNCLOS.

From a legal standpoint, the adoption by Croatia of its 1994 Maritime Code[134] represented a *de novo* drawing of baselines (and not just the automatic 'succession' of the former SFRY system).[135] Therefore, it seems that Croatia should have taken into account a fundamental change of circumstances on the previous SFRY shores, namely the existence of the newly-independent coastal State of Bosnia and Herzegovina.[136] More specifically, while drawing straight baselines along its

---

129 Cf fn 23. The 1987 SFRY Law is still in force for Bosnia and Herzegovina.

130 Ibid. Article 16.

131 See section 4.5.2. It is argued that the current 'juridical' status of the waters of Bosnia and Herzegovina is that of a territorial sea (see Art. 2(1) in conjunction with Art. 5 of UNCLOS). See, however, B. Vukas, 'Sea Boundary Delimitation and Internal Waters', in T.M. Ndiaye and R. Wolfrum (eds), *Law of the Sea, Environmental Law and Settlement of Disputes: Liber Amicorum Judge Thomas A. Mensah*, Leiden and Boston, MA: Martinus Nijhoff Publishers, 2007, p. 553 at p. 561.

132 Churchill and Lowe expressed the opinion that the provisions of the TSC and the corresponding provisions of UNCLOS relating to straight baselines have, to the extent that they differ from the customary rules before 1958, passed into customary international law. See Churchill and Lowe, op. cit., p. 54.

133 See Art. 19 of 1994, and Art. 18 of the Maritime Code of Croatia. Cf fn 124.

134 Ibid.

135 V. Prescott and C. Schofield, *The Maritime Political Boundaries of the World*, 2nd edn, Leiden and Boston, MA: Martinus Nijhoff Publishers, 2005, p. 161.

136 It is noteworthy that Charney, when asked about what would happen with the Canadian system of straight baselines in case Québec attains sovereignty (secession from Canada) stated as follows: 'If Québec became an independent state the Canadian system of straight baselines would become invalid *if it were to close waters between the land territory of Québec and the high seas ...*'. Emphasis added. See Charney, op. cit. (2001 Update), p. 4. See the discussion in 4.3.3.

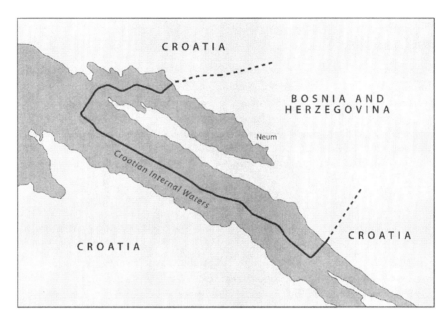

Figure 4.2 'Bosnian' maritime zones (1999 Border Treaty)[137]

coasts *de novo*, Croatia should have taken into account Article 7(6) of UNCLOS[138] which provides that '... the system of straight baselines may not be applied by a State in such a manner *as to cut off the territorial sea of another State from the high seas or an exclusive economic zone*'.[139]

It is noteworthy that some authors recognize that the latter provision was incorporated into the TSC and later transferred into UNCLOS in order to regulate similar cases to that of Bosnia and Herzegovina. In this respect, Churchill and Lowe are of the opinion that:

> This provision deals with highly exceptional situations, where a smaller territory is embedded within a larger territory (e.g. Monaco in France) or where small islands belonging to one State lie close to the coast of another State (e.g., Greek islands lying close to the coast of Turkey).[140]

Bosnia and Herzegovina fulfils both conditions. Its coastline is embedded within the much larger territory of Croatia, while the Croatian peninsula of Pelješac is located in front of its coast. As stated by Prescott and Schofield:

> The final Paragraph of Article 7 [UNCLOS] it contains no ambiguities. It prohibits states from drawing straight baselines that would cut off the

---

137 Modelled on a figure published in Vukas, op. cit., p. 564.
138 Article 4(5) of the TSC.
139 Emphasis added.
140 Churchill and Lowe, op. cit., p. 37.

Maritime boundaries in the (Eastern) Adriatic 157

territorial waters of a neighboring state from the high sea or the exclusive economic zone.[111]

It is particularly relevant that Prescott and Schofield make reference to two (unresolved) situations in the Mediterranean where the coastal States seem to have breached the obligations deriving from Article 7(6) of UNCLOS (Article 4(5) of the 1958 TSC). The first mentioned case is that of Morocco which in 1975 drew straight baselines along its Mediterranean coast in a manner that encloses the Spanish coast of Ceuta and Melila and the associated Spanish islands within its system of straight baselines.[142] The second case is that of Cyprus which in 1993 enclosed within its system of straight baselines the two UK sovereign bases of Akrotiri and Dhekelia.[143] On the other hand, the same authors also made reference to the case of France, which in 1967 drew baselines on its Mediterranean coast in a manner that allows Monaco unrestricted access to the high seas.[144]

It seems possible to claim that if a State is not entitled to draw straight baselines in a manner to cut off the territorial sea of another State from the high seas or an EEZ, then obviously it is even less entitled to draw straight baselines in such a way as to enclose the territorial waters of another State into its system of straight baselines. It would therefore follow that a proper application of Article 7 of UNCLOS (Articles 4 and 5 of the TSC) would have required the interruption of the Croatian system of straight baselines in a way which would allow the territorial contact of the 'Bosnian' territorial sea with the Croatian territorial sea, and which would not leave any doubt about the right of navigation (innocent passage) of Bosnia and Herzegovina through Croatian waters.[145]

Following by analogy the often quoted passage of the ICJ in the Fisheries Case,[146] it would seem that the 'straight baseline' closing the waters of Bosnia and Herzegovina within the Croatian system of straight baselines is, legally speaking, Bosnia and Herzegovina nor to any other State which would object to it. It is however noteworthy that, for the time being, neither Bosnia and Herzegovina nor any other State has protested against such enclosure.[147] This may be at least partially attributed to the current absence of (international) commercial ports on the Bosnian coast.

---

141 Prescott and Schofield, op. cit., pp. 160–161.
142 See E.A. Anish, *The International Law of Maritime Boundaries and the Practice of States in the Mediterranean Sea*, Oxford: Clarendon Press, 1993, p. 190.
143 See Prescott and Schofield, op. cit., p. 161 and section 3.4.1.
144 Ibid. See also section 3.1.1.
145 See section 4.5.4.
146 'The delimitation of sea areas has always an international aspect; it cannot be dependent merely upon the will of the coastal state as expressed in municipal law …'. Fisheries Case (*United Kingdom v Norway*), ICJ Reports 1951, p. 116 atp. 132.
147 'where a baseline is clearly contrary to international law, it will not be valid, certainly in respect of States which have objected it, although a State which has accepted the baseline (for example in a boundary treaty) might be estopped from latter denying its validity …'. See Churchill and Lowe, op. cit., p. 57.

158 *Extension of Coastal State Jurisdiction in Enclosed or Semi-enclosed Seas*

4.5.2 Treaty on the state border between the Republic of Croatia and the Republic of Bosnia and Herzegovina[148]

It is important to note that the 1999 Treaty regulates both the boundary on land and the maritime boundary between the two States. There can however be no doubts about the priorities of the two States at the time of its conclusion. Out of 24 articles only one (Article 4) deals with both the maritime[149] and the border on navigable rivers.[150] The latter, particularly taking into account the extremely difficult geographical position of the coastline of Bosnia and Herzegovina and the already at that time existing enclosure of its maritime areas within the Croatian system of straight baselines, is rather unusual.[151]

The Preamble shows that the two guiding references for the conclusion of the Agreement are the provisions of the Dayton Agreement[152] signed on 14 December 1995 and the Opinion No. 3 of the Badinter Commission, which as previously discussed, makes express reference to the application of the principle *of uti possidetis*.[153] It is worth noting that the two States did not distinguish between delimitation on land and at sea which in turn clearly points to the fact that they applied the principle of *uti possidetis* (*effectivités*) also to maritime delimitation. Although the latter principle is not expressly mentioned by its 'technical' name, reference to it is clearly visible from the direct reference to Opinion No. 3 of the Badinter Commission (Preamble) and furthermore from the first paragraph of Article 2(1) of the 1999 Treaty. According to the latter:

> The state border between the Republic of Croatia and Bosnia and Herzegovina is determined on the basis of the state of the borders at the time of the end of the Socialist Federal Republic of Yugoslavia in 1991 and the mutual recognition of the Republic of Croatia and Bosnia and Herzegovina in 1992 ... on the basis of the dividing line which divided the authorities of the Socialist Republic of Croatia and the Socialist Republic of Bosnia and Herzegovina.

---

148 Concluded on 30 July 1999. Not yet in force. Text reproduced in T. Scovazzi and G. Francalanci, 'Bosnia and Herzegovina-Croatia (Report Number 8-14)', in J.I. Charney and R.W. Smith (eds), *International Maritime Boundaries*, Vol. IV, op. cit., 2002, p. 2887 at p. 2891.

149 Article 4, para. 3.

150 Article 4, para. 2.

151 In 1998 the two States concluded an 'Agreement on Free Transit through the Territory of Croatia to and from the Port of Ploče and through the Territory of Bosnia and Herzegovina at Neum'. Bosnia-Herzegovina would be on the basis of the Treaty, entitled to 'custom free' passage through the territory of Croatia and to the participation in the management of the nearby Port of Ploče (Croatia). One of the aims of the 1998 Agreement was therefore to solve the 'access' of Bosnia and Herzegovina to the Adriatic Sea and it is suggested that the 1998 Agreement influenced the 'structure' of the 1999 Border Treaty. The Agreement, however, has not been ratified by Croatia and has not entered into force. See Ž. Rogošić, 'Bosnia forbids passage of Dubrovnik motorway through its territory', Nacional, No. 651, 5 May 2008. See also Blake and Topalović, op. cit., pp. 39–40.

152 See General Framework Peace Accord for Bosnia and Herzegovina, initialed in Dayton, 21 November 1995. Signed in Paris on 14 December 1995.

153 See section 4.3.2.

It is noteworthy that the 1999 Treaty does not even use the expression 'delimitation of the (maritime) boundary', but instead 'identification, marking, maintenance and ensuring the visibility of the common State border'.[154]

The maritime border between the two States is regulated by Article 4(3) of the 1999 Treaty, according to which:

> The State border on the sea stretches along the *median line* of the sea between the territories of the Republic of Croatia and Bosnia and Herzegovina in accordance with the 1982 Convention on Sea Rights [UNCLOS].[155]

Although the latter provision may be defined as 'short and sweet' as it happens to reflect both the application of the principle of *uti possidetis* (*effectivités*) to the particular case, as well as the general rule embodied in Article 15 of UNCLOS regarding the delimitation of the territorial sea (median line), it nonetheless seems that the 1999 Treaty and/or a separate agreement should have dealt with some important questions relating also to the (territorial) regime of the area in question, particularly regarding the regime of navigation from the maritime areas of Bosnia and Herzegovina through Croatian 'internal' waters, through which strictly speaking no right of innocent passage exists.[156] Quite interestingly, 'navigation' was a decisive criteria for the establishment of the boundary on the 'international navigable rivers with a regulated navigation course' for which the Treaty expressly provides that the boundary in such cases 'stretches along the *kinet* [*thalweg*]' of the navigation course'.[157]

Before embarking on a discussion of navigational issues related to the 'access' of Bosnia and Herzegovina to the high seas (and/or zones of sovereign rights and jurisdiction)[158] it seems necessary to dwell on another provision of the 1999 Treaty which is also remarkable, particularly in the light of the principle of 'intangibility' and 'stability of frontiers'.[159] Article 22(1) provides that the Treaty shall only be temporarily in force since the date of its signature. The fact that the 1999 Treaty has at the time of writing not been ratified by the Republic of Croatia, means that the Treaty has since 30 July 1999 represented just a 'provisional regime'. Article 22(3) furthermore provides that:

> Each Party can cancel this Treaty at any time with prior written notice to the other party sent through diplomatic channels. In that case, the Treaty shall become void six months after the date of receipt of the notice on the cancellation of the Treaty by the other Party.

---

154 Preamble, para. 4.
155 Emphasis added. See Figure 4.2.
156 See section 4.5.3.
157 See Article 4(2).
158 See section 4.5.3.
159 See section 4.1.

160   *Extension of Coastal State Jurisdiction in Enclosed or Semi-enclosed Seas*

Although the drafting language is ambiguous, it seems that the proper interpretation of this provision is that such 'cancellation' is possible only up to the moment when the Treaty enters into force.[160] Taking into account that there is no great prospect of its ratification by the Croatian Parliament and therefore for its entry into force,[161] it would seem that the 'provisional regime', coupled with the possibility of its cancellation, brings instability into an allegedly already unstable region (Western Balkans). Nonetheless, it seems possible to agree with Klemenčič that:

> The [1999] treaty was the first post-Yugoslav boundary agreement and all other similar agreements which will sooner or later inevitably follow will have to take into account the contents and principles applied ....[162]

4.5.3 Access of Bosnia and Herzegovina to the Adriatic's high seas / EEZs

An 'omission' from the 1999 Treaty is obviously that it does not regulate the regime of navigation for Bosnia and Herzegovina through Croatian (internal) waters (nor is it regulated in any previous or subsequent agreement). It seems therefore useful to determine which provisions of UNCLOS and/or customary international law Bosnia and Herzegovina could rely on in order to assert its right of (innocent) passage through Croatian internal waters. Reference should be made again to the fact that according to (customary) international law, as reflected in both the 1958 TSC and UNCLOS, there is no right of innocent passage through the internal waters of another State, although as with the majority of 'general rules' there are exceptions to the latter. The most important seems to be provided by Article 8(2) of UNCLOS, which provides that:

> Where the establishment of a straight baseline in accordance with the method set forth in Article 7 has the effect of enclosing as internal waters areas which has not previously been considered as such, a right of innocent passage as provided by this Convention shall exist in those waters.[163]

It would seem possible to argue, as advocated by Charney in the theoretical case of an independent Québec, that at the moment of the dissolution of the SFRY its

---

160 This could be implied from the fact that the provision is found in Art. 22 which regulates the 'temporary implementation' of the 1999 Treaty.

161 The current Croatian government led by Prime Minister Milanovic seems, however, favourable to the ratification of the 1999 Treaty by Croatia. According to the current Croatian Prime Minister, the 1999 Treaty may be ratified by the Croatian Parliament (Sabor) in 2013. See D. Vodovnik, '*Hrvaška in njene sosede: Država z začasnimi mejami*', Delo, Ljubljana, 11 August 2012, pp. 16–17.

162 See M. Klemenčič, 'The Border Agreement between Croatia and Bosnia and Herzegovina: The first, but not the last', IBRU Boundary and Security Bulletin, Winter 1999–2000, p. 96 at p. 100.

163 Churchill and Lowe are of the opinion that while this is the position under the two Conventions (TSC, UNCLOS), the position under customary law is less certain, as the Anglo-Norwegian Fisheries Case made no reference to the preservation of rights of innocent passage in those circumstances. See Churchill and Lowe, op. cit., p. 61 and cf fn 147.

Maritime boundaries in the (Eastern) Adriatic 161

system of straight baselines became invalid, at least in that part where it closed the access of Bosnia and Herzegovina to the high seas, and that therefore the waters in that part reverted to a status which was not dependent upon those baselines.[164] Following the same line of thought one may then argue that with the adoption of its 1994 Maritime Code, Croatia enclosed, as internal waters, areas which have not previously been considered as such and that according to both Article 5 of the TSC and Article 8 of UNCLOS, 'a right of innocent passage shall exist in those waters'.

From the standpoint of contemporary law of the sea, the interpretation according to which the segment of the Croatian system of straight baselines in that part which 'closes' the coastline of Bosnia and Herzegovina is not opposable to the latter State, nor to third States which would oppose it, seems however much more sound.[165] There also seem to be grounds for arguing that part of the Croatian waters situated among the coastline of Bosnia and Herzegovina and further along the Pelješac peninsula up to the 'high seas' (currently the Croatian EFPZ) could be considered as a 'strait used for international navigation'.[166] However, as that would link part of the high seas or an EEZ and the territorial sea of a foreign State, the regime of navigation through the latter should be regulated by Article 45 of UNCLOS, which provides that:

> The regime of innocent passage, in accordance with Part II, section 3, shall apply in straits used for international navigation … (b) between a part of the high seas or an exclusive economic zone and the territorial sea of a foreign State…. There shall be no suspension of innocent passage through such straits.

According to the latter interpretation Bosnia and Herzegovina has or it may have a 'non-suspendable right of innocent passage' through such a strait. The mentioned navigable route between two parts of the Croatian territory represent the closest and the most convenient route between the territory of Bosnia and Herzegovina and the high seas and/or EEZ in the Adriatic, and it suggested that the past or current absence of strong international shipping should not be decisive.[167] It seems therefore safe to conclude that Bosnia and Herzegovina should be entitled to exercise through Croatian (internal) waters at least the rights of non-suspendable innocent passage[168] and that such right should be expressly recognized by Croatia.

---

164 Cf fn 81.
165 Cf fn 147.
166 See Figure 4.2.
167 See M.C. Stelekatos-Loverdos, 'The Contribution of Channels to the Definition of Straits Used for International Navigation', IJMCL, Vol. 13, No. 1, 1998, p. 71 at pp. 76–80.
168 It is noteworthy that Art. 16(4) of the 1958 TSC, a 'predecessor' of Art. 45 of UNCLOS was primarily included within the 1958 TSC with the aim to secure the access of Israel to its port of Eliat through the Strait of Tiran and the Gulf of Aqaba. See Churchill and Lowe, op. cit., pp. 110–111.

162 *Extension of Coastal State Jurisdiction in Enclosed or Semi-enclosed Seas*

It is accordingly suggested that the two States should start negotiations, in good faith, on how the right of (unsuspended) innocent passage for Bosnia and Herzegovina will be fully preserved.[169]

4.6 Delimitation of the maritime (and land) boundary between Croatia and Montenegro

The dispute between Croatia and Montenegro relates to the Prevlaka peninsula area from where it is possible to control the entrance to the strategically important Bay of Boka Kotorska, home of the main naval base of the former SFRY[170] and up to the independence of Montenegro in 2006 of that of the federal State of Serbia and Montenegro.[171] If the claim over the Prevlaka peninsula were to be upheld then the entire coastline of the Bay of Boka Kotorska were to fall under the sovereignty of Montenegro. During the times of the former SFRY the Prevlaka peninsula was a 'closed area' by the SFRY army,[172] although *de jure* forming part of the territory of the 'federal' Republic of Croatia.[173]

The issue of the (maritime) and land border between the Croatia and (Serbia) Montenegro has been particularly acute in the early 1990s due to the ranging war in the Balkans, which had one of its epicentres in the bombardment of the ancient town of Dubrovnik in December 1991. It was only in 1992 that the Serbian and Montenegrin forces withdrew from Prevlaka on the basis of an agreement between at that time Croatian and Yugoslav presidents which provided that 'the security of Prevlaka would be resolved by demilitarization and the deployment of UN monitors'. Following the agreement, the Prevlaka peninsula was actually demilitarized and put under the control of UNPROFOR,[174] a situation which lasted until 2002.

A major breakthrough in the relations between the two States occurred on 10 December 2002 when the Ministers of Foreign Affairs of the two States signed a Protocol on the interim regime along the southern border between the Republic of Croatia and Serbia and Montenegro.[175] The latter is complex and temporarily regulates both the regime in the disputed area on land, including demilitarization, landmine removal and customs affairs, while at sea it provides for an extremely interesting 'delimitation line' and *interim* regime of co-operation

---

169 The need for such co-operation is further accentuated by the plans of Croatia to build a 'suspension bridge' close to the Bosnian coast and which will be most likely located over the only 'navigable access (strait)' to the maritime areas of Bosnia and Herzegovina. Cf fn 151 (Rogošić) and 161 (Vodovnik).
170 See Blake and Topalović, op. cit., pp. 42–45.
171 Montenegro is on the basis of Arts 11 and 12 of the 1978 Vienna Convention a State successors to the delimitation agreements concluded by the former SFRY (e.g. the 1968 Shelf Agreement), and by those concluded by the FRY and Serbia and Montenegro in the period 1991–2006 relating to boundaries and/or territorial regimes. See section 4.6.1.
172 For a historical overview, see Blake and Topalović, op.cit, pp. 46–52.
173 Cf fn 177.
174 UN, Security Council Resolution 1066, 15 July 1996.
175 Hereinafter the '2002 Protocol'. Copy on file with the author.

which includes, for example, provisions dealing with the protection and preservation of the marine environment and *inter alia* fisheries.[176] However, this discussion will be prevalently focused on the *sui generis* regime and on the provisional line of delimitation established by the two States within the 'border bay' of Boka Kotorska.[177]

4.6.1 The 2002 Protocol: Provisional arrangements of a practical nature applicable to internal waters and territorial sea?

The 2002 Protocol established a 'temporary regime', applicable both on land and at sea pending the conclusion of a final delimitation agreement between the two States. Regarding the 'exercise of jurisdiction' on land, Article 4 provides that Croatia shall *temporarily* exercise jurisdiction southwest of Cape Konfin, while the (Serbia) Montenegro should exercise jurisdiction north of that point. The temporary delimitation on land seems to follow the administrative border between the two republics which existed during the times of the former SFRY (*uti possidetis*). It may be argued, however, that with the conclusion of the 2002 Protocol the two States impliedly recognized that sovereignty over the entire coastline previously controlled by UNPROFOR is in dispute (see Figure 4.3).

When it comes to the setting of a provisional delimitation line and the temporary regime within the Bay of Boka Kotorska it seems, and this despite the fact that the 2002 Protocol does not make any reference to UNCLOS that the latter could be by analogy compared to an agreement on 'provisional arrangement of a practical nature' as regulated by Articles 74(3) and 83(3) of UNCLOS. The 2002 Protocol is however applicable only to an area of internal waters and/or territorial sea, including a border bay[178] and not to the EEZ or the continental shelf, although as already discussed, Croatia in 2003 (unilaterally) linked the temporary border of its EFPZ to '... the direction of and continuing the provisional delimitation line of the territorial seas, as defined in the 2002 Protocol ...'.[179] The latter seems to give weight to the assertion that the (final) delimitation of 'present' and/or 'potential' zones of sovereign rights and jurisdictions between Croatia and Montenegro will be influenced by the achieved solutions within and outside the Bay of Boka Kotorska. The 2002 Protocol, however, provides that the regime is 'just provisional pending the conclusion of a final delimitation agreement' and

---

176 According to the Preamble, the main goal of the 2002 Protocol is to improve the living standard of the inhabitants of both States in the border region, to promote the development of tourism *and to facilitate the establishment of a final boundary line between the two States.* Emphasis added. Author's translation.

177 When explaining the reasons for the departing from the 'median line' and for the *sui generis* regime (December 2002), the head of the Croatian delegation, Josip Paro, explained that Croatia *had never exercised jurisdiction over the waters of Boka Kotorska during the times of the former SFRY* and that the (Serbia) Montenegro *bases its claim on historic title.* Emphasis added. See R. Kajzer, *'Potek meje bosta urejali pred ICJ*, Delo, Ljubljana, 14 January 2009.

178 See section 2.4.2.5.

179 See section 3.3.4.

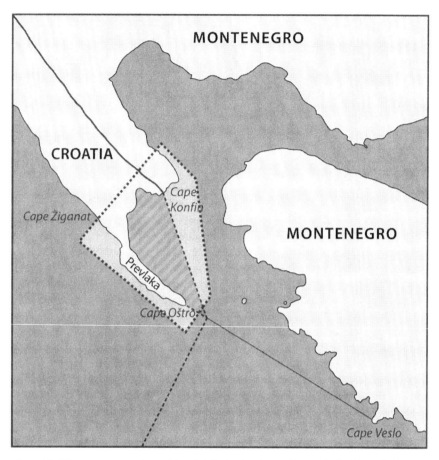

Figure 4.3 Disputed area and provisional delimitation in the Bay of Boka Kotorska[180]

that the provisions of the Protocol 'shall be without prejudice to the final delimitation'.[181] Furthermore, Article 1 contains an 'obligation' for the two States to continue negotiations in *good faith* with the aim to reach a final delimitation agreement'.[182]

The solutions adopted by the two States in the Bay of Boka Kotorska are indeed remarkable. The first interesting feature is that the entrance to the Bay of Boka Kotorska is, as during the times of the former SFRY, closed with a straight baseline linking Cape Oštro on the southernmost part of the Prevlaka peninsula (Croatia) with Cape Veslo in Montenegro. This in turn means that the waters on the landward side of the closing line (within the bay) have retained the status

---

180 Modelled on a figure published in the newspaper *Delo*, Ljubljana.
181 Article 1. See similarities with Arts 74(3) and 83(3) of UNCLOS.
182 See section 2.4.2.5.

Maritime boundaries in the (Eastern) Adriatic 165

of internal waters, subject to an extremely interesting *sui generis* regime.[183] Although the legal status of the waters on the landward side of the closing line is not expressly mentioned, the fact that the breadth of the territorial sea is measured from the straight baseline closing the Bay,[184] does not allow for any other conclusion apart from that the waters within the Bay have retained the status of internal waters. It seems therefore difficult to agree with Vukas that on the basis of the 2002 Protocol '... the legal status of the waters at the entrance of the Hercegnovski Gulf ... remains unclear ...'.[185] The only potential dilemma could in fact be whether the legal status of the waters on the landward side of the 'closing line' is that of 'internal waters' or of its equivalent 'historic waters'.[186]

The two States therefore delimited their 'internal waters' by a straight line joining Cape Konfin with a point located 3 cables (approximately 185 m) from Cape Oštro on a closing line of the Bay, thus creating a 'triangle' (formally) under Croatian jurisdictions and referred to by the 2002 Protocol as the 'Zone'.[187] It is noteworthy, however, that while the Protocol does not impose any major restrictions on the Montenegrin side of the Bay,[188] the regime within the 'Zone' is highly regulated and seems to be under a sort of 'joint jurisdiction' of both States. The elements of a 'condominium' are indeed not difficult to spott.

First of all, there is a provision which prohibits the entrance into the 'Zone' to the police and naval forces of both States (not just to the (Serbia) Montenegro)[189] while the patrolling of the Zone is in charge of a mixed police boat with a Croatian-Montenegrin crew bound to sail without a national flag.[190] The latter should also be in charge of any salvage and/or co-ordination of salvage operations. Furthermore, while commercial fishing, including artisanal fishing and aquaculture, is expressly prohibited in the Zone, 'recreational fishing' is

---

183 Regarding the Bay of Piran, Croatia has permanently advocated the position that a 'border bay' cannot be closed with a straight baseline. See section 4.7.2.
184 Article 6 of the Protocol provides that '[t]he provisional delimitation of the territorial sea starts at a point located 3 cables [approximately 185 m] from Cape Oštro on a line linking Cape Oštro and Cape Veslo and it continues with a straight line 12 nmi long, having the azimuth of 206 towards the high seas' (author's translation).
185 Vukas, op. cit., p. 561.
186 It is questionable whether the Bay of Boka Kotorska (at least in its disputed part) could be qualified as a 'historic bay'. In the past it used to be shared by *inter alia* the Republic of Dubrovnik, the Ottoman Empire, Venice and/or the Austro-Hungarian Empire. See Blake and Topalović, op. cit., pp. 46–48.
187 See Figure 4.3.
188 The only obligation for (Serbia) Montenegro is not to hold naval exercises between the line Cape Kobila-Cape Durov Kam and the straight baseline closing the Bay while its submarines are bound to sail within the area on the surface and flying its flag. The entrance of Croatian naval forces in that part of the Bay is altogether prohibited. See Art. 15 of the Protocol, and Figure 4.3.
189 Article 5.
190 Article 7. This provision is interesting as such vessel could be on the high seas associated with a 'ship without nationality' which is subject to boarding and/or seizure. See Arts 92 and 110 of UNCLOS.

166 *Extension of Coastal State Jurisdiction in Enclosed or Semi-enclosed Seas*

allowed on a basis of a specific license issued by the relevant authorities of one of the two States.[191] Both States are furthermore charged with the protection and preservation of the marine environment and must jointly undertake the necessary monitoring.[192] The 2002 Protocol therefore created a situation whereby the (internal) waters of a former juridical bay have been divided by the two States in such a way as to create on one side of the former juridical bay a 'Zone' where both States exercise jurisdiction while the other part of the Bay has remained under the exclusive sovereignty of only one State (Montenegro). It is also important to emphasize that the regime of 'joint jurisdiction' is applicable only within the 'Zone' (within a 'border bay'), and not in the territorial sea on the seaward side of the 'closing line'. Despite these issues, reference should be made to the fact that the 2002 Protocol has worked remarkably well during the last decade and has substantially contributed to the normalisation of relations between the two Adriatic States.[193]

The provisions of the 2002 Protocol seem therefore to add some weight to the assertion that States may close and/or retain a straight baseline in a border bay arising for example from a dissolution of a federal State.[194] The Protocol seems also to be an example of the application of Article 15 of UNCLOS in the light of Part IX of UNCLOS[195] and seems to reinforce this work's assertions on the importance of the agreement on the 'regime of a certain area' in addition to sole delimitation.[196] Lastly, it is also important to point out that Montenegro has not formally protested against the 'unilateral' delimitation of the Croatian EFPZ in 2003[197] and that Croatia and Montenegro started negotiations in 2009 to submit their maritime and land boundary dispute for a final adjudication to an international court or tribunal.[198]

4.7 Slovenia-Croatia maritime delimitation dispute: Looking for solutions in the spirit of Part IX of UNCLOS?

After assessing the main issues involved in the Croatia-Montenegro and Croatia-Bosnia and Herzegovina (maritime) delimitation disputes, it seems necessary to consider the third and last case of maritime delimitation disputed between the States' successors of the former SFRY; and the one which has been so far most widely debated at the national and for the first time also at the EU level.[199] The dispute involves those questions regarding the application of the

---

191 Article 8.
192 Article 24.
193 Cf fn 161 (Vodovnik).
194 See section 4.4.
195 See section 2.4.2.5.
196 See section 4.7.4.
197 See section 3.3.4.
198 Cf fn 161 and 177 (Kajzer).
199 See D. Vidas, 'The UN Convention on the Law of the Sea, the European Union and the Rule of Law: What is going on in the Adriatic', IJMCL, Vol. 24. No. 1, 2009, pp. 1–66.

Maritime boundaries in the (Eastern) Adriatic   167

principle of *uti possidetis* and border bays seen above coupled with the specific Slovenian claim regarding its 'territorial contact with the high seas' and questions regarding the legality of the Slovenian claim to a continental shelf and/or zones of sovereign rights and jurisdiction.[200]

The case seems therefore to highlight the many problems associated with the delimitation of maritime boundaries and/or extension of coastal State jurisdiction in enclosed or semi-enclosed seas, and seems to call for an (innovative) solution in line with Part IX of UNCLOS.[201]

4.7.1 Geographical characteristics and general historical background

The Slovenian coastline, which is approximately 46 km long, is one of the ten shortest coastlines in the world.[202] The 'concave' Slovenian coastline is totally located in the north-east corner of the border bay of Trieste, whose coastline nowadays belongs to Italy, Croatia and Slovenia and which is itself located in the north-east corner of the 'juridical' semi-enclosed Adriatic Sea. The region bordering the Gulf of Trieste was, until the First World War, mostly under the sovereignty of Venice[203] followed by Austria, while before the two Wars the region was under the unique sovereignty of the Kingdom of Italy.[204] Following the Second World War, the region was for a short period (1947–1954) part of the Free Territory of Trieste[205] followed by the SFRY.[206] After the dissolution of the Free Territory of Trieste in 1954 the shores of the Bay of Piran were within a single State (SFRY) administratively divided between two federal entities (Slovenia and Croatia).[207] However, there seems to be substantial evidence that the waters of the Bay of Piran had been, until the time of the dissolution of the former SFRY administered by Slovenia (Municipality of Piran).[208]

---

200 See section 3.3.6.
201 See sections 2.3–2.5.
202 Slovenia belongs to the group of approximately ten coastal States with coastlines shorter than 100 km. See M. Škrk, '*Pomorski zakonik Republike Slovenije v luči mednarodnega prava*', X. *Dnevi javnega prava*, Proceedings, Portorož, 2004, p. 493 at p. 497.
203 See D. Mihelič, *Ribič, kje zdaj tvoja barka plava? Piransko ribolovno območje skozi čas*, Koper: Založba Annales, 2007, pp. 23–40.
204 Ibid, pp. 47–80.
205 Ibid, pp. 101–111.
206 See B. Bohte and M. Škrk, 'Predgovor', *Pariška mirovna pogodba*, Ljubljana: Ministry of Foreign Affairs, 1997, p. v–xii, and Degan, op. cit., p. 625.
207 The administrative boundary on land followed the borders of the 'border municipalities'. See for example '*Zakon o postopku za ustanovitev, združitev oziroma spremembo območja občine ter o območjih občin*', OG(S)RS, No. 28/80 as amended.
208 See for example the documents reproduced in the 'White Paper on the Border between the Republic of Slovenia and the Republic of Croatia', Ministry of Foreign Affairs of Slovenia, Delo, Ljubljana, 2006. Cf fn 73 (Degan).

168 Extension of Coastal State Jurisdiction in Enclosed or Semi-enclosed Seas

4.7.2 Delimitation of the (maritime) boundary between the Republic of Croatia and the Republic of Slovenia

There are two main problems relating to the delimitation of the maritime boundary between Slovenia and Croatia, which are nonetheless closely interrelated. The first is the delimitation and/or the status of the waters within the 'border bay' of Piran, while the second is the question of the 'territorial access of Slovenia to the high seas in the Northern Adriatic'. The latter may be also understood as a reflection of the claim of Slovenia to its right to extend its jurisdiction over the (current) high seas and/or 'potential EEZs' in the Adriatic.[209] Slovenia obviously wants to avoid a situation wherein its territorial sea would remain completely 'enclaved' between the territorial seas of Italy and Croatia.[210]

As the general aspects of the Slovenia-Croatia maritime boundary have been already amply discussed in the contemporary literature,[211] it is proposed to focus within the next sections on the possible application and/or relevance of the principle of *uti possidetis* within (and outside) the border bay of Piran and on the various possibilities (and past attempts) to satisfy the Slovenian claim of a 'territorial access to the high seas'.[212] A general overview of the dispute will then be provided through an analysis of the 2009 Arbitration Agreement between the Government of the Republic of Slovenia and the Government of the Republic of Croatia, concluded after almost 18 years of negotiations on 4 November 2009.[213]

---

209 See section 4.7.2.2.
210 Ibid.
211 See the cited work by Degan, Ibler, Grbec, Pavliha, Škrk, Vidas, Vukas (op. cit.). See in addition M. Grbec, '*Razmejitev morskih pasov v mednarodnem pravu*', Pravnik, Vol. 57, No. 4–5, Ljubljana, 2002, p. 255; K. Turkalj, *Piranski zaljev: Razgraničenje teritorijalnog mora između Hrvatske i Slovenije*, Pravo 29, Zagreb: Organizator, 2001; D. Vidas, *Hrvatsko-slovensko razgraničenje*, Zagreb: Školska knjiga, 2009; D. Arnaut, 'Stormy Waters on the Way to the High Seas. The Case of the Territorial Sea Delimitation Between Croatia and Slovenia', *Ocean and Coastal Law Journal*, Vol. 8, No. 1, Portland, OR: University of Maine, 2002; M. Avbelj and J. Letnar Černič, 'The Conundrum of the Piran Bay. Slovenia v. Croatia – The Case of Maritime Delimitation', *Journal of International Law and Policy, The University of Pennsylvania Journal of International Law & Policy*, Vol. 5, No. 2, 2007.
212 See section 4.7.3. See also M. Pavliha, '*Tunel do odprtega morja*', Delo, Sobotna priloga, Ljubljana, 23 August 2003, pp. 29–30.
213 The Arbitration Agreement was signed on 4 November 2009 in Stockholm and was ratified in the Parliaments of both States and entered into force on 29 November 2010, following the exchange of relevant diplomatic notes by the two States expressing their consent to be bound by the Agreement. Croatia ratified the Agreement in 29 October 2009, while Slovenia had to wait for the opinion of its Constitutional Court regarding the consistency of the Agreement with the Constitution of the Republic of Slovenia. In its Opinion (Rm 1/09-30, OG RS 25/2010), the Constitutional Court confirmed that the Arbitral Agreement is not inconsistent with Art. 4 of the Constitution of the Republic of Slovenia in conjunction with Section II of the Basic Constitutional Chapter on the Sovereignty and Independence of the Republic of Slovenia. The Agreement was then ratified by the Slovenian Parliament on 19 April, and confirmed, although with a small majority (51.54%) at a legislative referendum on 6 June 2010. Finally, the Agreement was again reconfirmed by the Slovenian Constitutional Court on 7 October 2010. See V. Sancin, 'Slovenia-Croatia Border Dispute: From "Drnovšek-Račan" to "Pahor-Kosor" Agreement, European Perspectives', *Journal of European Perspectives of the Western Balkans*, Vol. 2, No. 2, 2010, p. 93 at p. 100, and general discussion on the Arbitration Agreement in section 4.8.

4.7.2.1 Border Bay of Piran

The Bay of Piran forms part of the wider Gulf of Trieste. The mouth of the bay is 3.2 nmi long while at its widest it is 3.5 nmi. There are no islands in the Bay and the coast is quite regular. The southern part of the Bay is not inhabited (or at least that was the case at the time of the dissolution of the former SFRY) although there are some tourist complexes, while on the Northern (Slovenian) side lies the town of Piran with the holiday resort towns of Bernardin and Portorož.[214] In the former SFRY the Bay of Piran qualified as a juridical bay, and was closed with a straight baseline linking Cape Madona and Cape Savudrija.[215] Following the dissolution of the former SFRY in 1991, the Bay of Piran for the first time in its history acquired the status of 'border bay' (see Figure 4.4).[216]

The first interesting question is whether the status of its waters switched at the moment of independence from 'internal waters' to 'territorial sea', and whether the straight baseline closing the (juridical) Bay of Piran during the times of the former SFRY has survived its dissolution.[217] The answer to this question seems important, as it will point to the relevant baselines from which the breadth of the territorial sea and other maritime zones will be measured outside the Bay of Piran.

It should be mentioned, however, that the positions of the two States regarding the legal status of the waters of the Bay of Piran and/or the delimitation within the Bay of Piran has differed diametrically. In the 1993 Memorandum on the Bay of Piran[218] Slovenia claimed sovereignty and jurisdiction over the entire Bay on the basis of historic title and other special circumstances. Slovenia therefore rejected equidistance as a method for a delimitation of the territorial sea between the two States. It based its claim on the fact that it had effective control and jurisdiction over the entire Bay during the times of the former SFRY and that this was the situation at the time of the achievement of independence of both States. Taking into account that (formal) administrative maritime boundaries did not exist between the former SFRY republics (*legal title*), this statement points to the fact that Slovenia is basing its argument on the doctrine of *effectivités*, or in the words of the Slovenian Constitutional Court in its 2010 Opinion, on *uti possidetis de facto*.[219]

---

214 See Grbec, op. cit., pp. 20–21. See also Gržetić *et al.*, op. cit., pp. 38–40
215 Bay closing lines, differently from straight baselines did not have to be shown on official SFRY charts. See Art. 16 of the 1987 SFRY Law. Cf fn 23.
216 The reference to the Bay of Piran as a 'border-bay' refers exclusively to the fact that it is bordered by the shores of two States, and does not prejudice the juridical status of its waters. Cf fn 221.
217 See the discussion in section 4.4.
218 Adopted by the Slovenian Parliament on 26 May 1993.
219 Cf fn 236.

170 *Extension of Coastal State Jurisdiction in Enclosed or Semi-enclosed Seas*

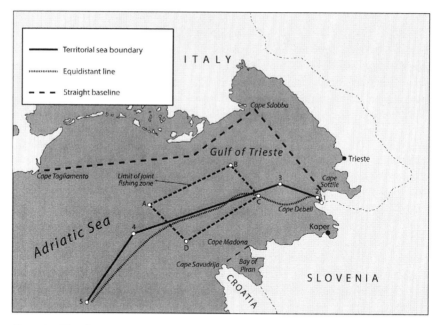

Figure 4.4 The Bay of Piran and the territorial sea boundary within the Gulf of Trieste[220]

According to Croatia's document, *Standpoints of the Republic of Croatia in Regard to the Delimitation within the Bay of Piran*,[221] Croatia firmly rejected the Slovenian position that the entire Bay should be under the sovereignty of Slovenia. It asserted that the 'equidistant line' has been used in almost all cases of lateral delimitation, especially if the coast is regular as is the case in the Bay of Piran. It furthermore argued that there are no special circumstances which would entitle Slovenia to a modified median line. Additionally, it was added that both Croatia and Slovenia are newly independent States and therefore none of them can claim historic title.[222] The position of Croatia is that the boundary on the sea between the two States has not yet been established and consequently the principle of *uti possidetis* cannot be used. Croatia therefore rejected altogether

---

220 Modelled on a figure published in Blake and Topalović, op. cit., p. 17. The territorial sea in the Gulf of Trieste was delimited by Italy and the former SFRY with the 1975 Treaty of Osimo. The boundary was, however, adjusted (modified equidistance) in a way to guarantee '… that routes of navigation to and from the main port of each country (Trieste and Koper) would only pass through the territorial sea of the state to which the port belongs'. See T. Scovazzi and G. Francalanci, 'Italy-Yugoslavia (Territorial Sea)', in J.I. Charney and L.M. Alexander (eds), *International Maritime Boundaries*, Vol. II, op. cit., p. 1639. Slovenia expressly notified Italy of its succession to the 1975 Osimo Treaty in 1992.
221 Adopted by the Croatian Parliament (Sabor) on 18 November 1999. See Ibler, op. cit., p. 555, and Grbec, op. cit., p. 22.
222 See sections 4.4.1–4.4.2.

Maritime boundaries in the (Eastern) Adriatic 171

the application of the principle of *uti possidetis* and even the possibility of the existence of a historic title over the disputed waters.[223]

Taking into account the earlier discussion on the application of the principle of *uti possidetis* (*effectivités*) to maritime delimitations and on the status of border bays in international law (including the practice of the States), the following general observations can be made regarding the potential status of the Bay of Piran. It is first of all argued that there are no obstacles from the standpoint of contemporary law of the sea for the Bay of Piran to retain its 'internal water status', and therefore to remain closed within a straight baseline. The internal waters status could be for example confirmed by a joint statement of the two States, similar to that of Ukraine and Russia in relation with the Sea of Azov,[224] or more likely in the particular case by the Award of the Arbitral Tribunal to which Slovenia and Croatia submitted their land and maritime dispute.[225] It is worth mentioning that the Republic of Slovenia has already, through its national legislation, confirmed the internal water status of the Bay of Piran under its 'sole' sovereignty[226] on the basis of the fact that it exercised effective control over the entire bay, on the critical day of independence, and that furthermore such position has been impliedly confirmed also by the Slovenian Constitutional Court in its 2010 Decision.[227] As the Municipality of Piran (Slovenia) has exercised *effective control* over the entire Bay of Piran since time immemorial, and this independently of the State entity to which it was forming part (Venice, Austria, Italy, Free Territory of Trieste, SFRY), there seems to be grounds for claiming that the Bay of Piran has acquired the status of a 'historic bay'.[228]

Also from the earlier discussion on *uti possidetis* it seems that it is unlikely, although not completely impossible, that the application of the principle of *uti possidetis* (*effectivités*), for example by the Arbitral Tribunal, may result in a situation wherein the sovereignty of Croatia will end at its shore. A more probable scenario is that the exclusive or at least prevalent exercise of jurisdiction over the entire Bay of Piran at the time of independence of both States will be treated as a 'special circumstance' in favour of Slovenia.[229] Croatia would in such case, similarly to some previously attempted solutions, retain sovereignty over a (narrow) strip of sea adjacent to its coasts. If the waters within the Bay of Piran retain their internal or historic waters status, then the latter may be divided between Slovenia and Croatia as for example occurred between India and Sri Lanka in 1974.[230] As already stated, it is not impossible to envisage a solution whereby part of

---

223 See Degan, op. cit., pp. 622–627.
224 Such statement should be ideally reinforced through some kind of reference to 'historic title' which may have its origin even before the SFRY-era, therefore prior to 1954. Cf fn 229.
225 See section 4.8.
226 Decree on the Determination of Fisheries Areas of the Republic of Slovenia, OGRS, No. 2/2006 (Art. 2).
227 Cf fn 236.
228 See section 4.4.1, and cf fn 94. For a discussion of the Bay of Piran as a potential 'historic bay', see Grbec, op. cit., pp. 26–35.
229 See sections 4.3.1–4.3.2.
230 See section 4.4.1.2.

172 *Extension of Coastal State Jurisdiction in Enclosed or Semi-enclosed Seas*

the Bay of Piran, not necessarily its central part,[231] would be under a sort of a 'condominium' of both States, which may continue also outside the closing line (territorial sea) and generate further zones of sovereign rights and jurisdiction. The chance of such solution becoming a reality seems however rather slim due to the longstanding opposition of Slovenia to a condominium solution within the Bay of Piran area.[232]

4.7.2.2 Territorial contact of Slovenia with the high seas: A reflection of the Slovenian claim to its own continental shelf and EEZ?

As a result of the narrowness of the Gulf of Trieste (geographic consideration) and due to the already established boundary with the Republic of Italy[233] (legal consideration), the Republic of Slovenia is facing the danger of becoming 'enclaved' between the territorial seas of Croatia and Italy, and thus cut off from the high seas and/or areas of sovereign rights and jurisdictions. Slovenia has, however, since independence (1991) advocated the position that 'the preservation of the direct territorial exit to the high seas is its vital interest'. Only such solution would in fact allow Slovenia to fully and uninterruptedly exercise its communication freedoms (from its territory to the high seas/EEZ), which apart from the freedom of navigation additionally includes at least freedom of overflight and freedom to lay submarine cables and pipelines.[234] Although statements and declarations of Slovenia on the legal basis of such claim have been at times *prima facie* conflicting,[235] it would show that Slovenia has throughout the years relied on the *territorial status quo* which existed at the time of independence (25 June 1991), in other words on the principle of *uti possidetis*.

The position of Slovenia seems to have been clarified in 2010 by the Slovenian Constitutional Court with its Opinion No. Rm-1/09-26.[236] This Opinion provides that according to the Basic Constitutional Charter on the Sovereignty and Independence of the Republic of Slovenia[237] the constitutionally protected border at sea between Slovenia and Croatia is the line up to which Slovenia exercised

---

231 See section 4.6.1. For an analysis of possible solutions in the Bay of Piran, see Grbec, op. cit., pp. 52–55.

232 See also the discussion on the relevant provision of the 2009 Arbitral Agreement in section 4.8.3. Article 3(1)(a) of the 2009 Arbitral Agreement is furthermore quite clear in providing that the task of the Arbitral Tribunal is *inter alia* to determine (shall determine) 'the *course of the maritime and land boundary* between the Republic of Slovenia and the Republic of Croatia'. Emphasis added.

233 See Figure 4.4. See also Gržetić *et al.*, op. cit., p. 31.

234 See Arts 58 and 87 of UNCLOS. 'Territorial access to the high sea/EEZ' is therefore not an issue relevant only for the purposes of navigation. See, however, Vidas, op. cit., pp. 33–35.

235 See 'Declaration by Slovenia upon Succession to the United Nations Convention on the Law of the Sea (16 June 1995)', LOS Bulletin, UN, No. 28, 1995, p. 5.

236 Opinion Rm-1/09-26 dated 18.03.2010, points II and III of the Award. See discussion in 5.8. It is, however, suggested that the Arbitral Tribunal will not be bound by the positions adopted by national (inc. Constitutional) Courts and/or Parliaments of both States, but only by the provisions of the Arbitration Agreement. Article 3(4) of the Arbitral Agreement is furthermore straightforward in providing that (only) '[t]he Arbitral Tribunal has the power to interpret the present [Arbitration] Agreement'.

237 Ibid.

effective control before independence up to the high seas; a statement which obviously makes reference to the application of the doctrine of *effectivités* or in the words of the Constitutional Court to *uti possidetis de facto*. Although not expressly stressed by the Constitutional Court, Slovenia has in many instances expressed its position (later confirmed also with its national legislation) that on the day of its independence it exercised effective control up to Point T5 in the Adriatic Sea.[238]

The current position of Croatia may be gleaned from its *Note Verbale*, dated 31 May 2007, issued in relation to the proclamation of the Slovenian ZEP, according to which:

> ... The lateral sea border between the Republic of Croatia and the Republic of Slovenia has not yet been formally established but it lies in the Bay of Savudria/Piran where the coasts of the two States are opposite to each other ... Due to the aforementioned facts the territorial sea of the Republic of Slovenia is not adjacent to the high seas; *consequently the Republic of Slovenia does not have its own continental shelf and it is not entitled to declare an ecological protection zone* ... the Zone of the Republic of Slovenia, apart from being proclaimed along the Croatian coast in violation of the principle of Article 2 of the 1982 Convention and the principle that the sea dominates and, lies as much as 15 nautical miles off the Slovenian coast, which is 3 nautical more than the 1982 Convention (Article 3) allows a coastal state to extend the breadth of its territorial sea, provided that the geographical position tolerates such a maximum extension.[239]

From the above we can see *inter alia* that issues of Slovenian access to the high seas and its consequent entitlement to a continental shelf and an **EEZ** (or other zones of functional jurisdiction) also arise, and raise important questions from the standpoint of international law as well as confronting several valid principles of the law of the sea. The two most important dilemmas seem to involve the confrontation of the principle of *uti possidetis* and Article 2 of UNCLOS (land dominates the sea), coupled with the non cut off principle and the provision of Article 3 of UNCLOS regulating the maximum breadth of the territorial sea.[240] The Croatian *Note Verbale* is, however, based on the presumption that the (juridical) status of the waters of the Bay of Piran is that of territorial sea and that Slovenia and/or Croatia shall 'inherit' the same (maximum) breadth of the territorial sea in the disputed area as that of the former SFRY. It would seem to follow that this is not automatically the case and it is furthermore suggested that the two States should endeavour to exercise their rights and perform their duties under UNCLOS and/ or to look for solutions also in the spirit of Part IX of UNCLOS.[241]

---

238 See Figure 4.4, and fn 226 (Art. 3). See also Ministry of Foreign Affairs (Slovenia), op. cit. '(White Paper)', pp. 10–13.
239 Emphasis added. See LOS Bulletin, UN, No. 64, 2007, pp. 40–41.
240 See section 4.3.3.
241 See section 2.4.1.2. For a discussion of the Slovenian claim regarding its right to a 'territorial access to the high seas' and potential solutions, see Grbec, op. cit., pp. 56–79. See also N. Šebenik,

174 *Extension of Coastal State Jurisdiction in Enclosed or Semi-enclosed Seas*

The most serious attempt to solve the dispute in the period 1991–2001 was the 'initialling' of the Treaty between the Republic of Slovenia and the Republic of Croatia on the Common State Border,[242] usually referred to as the Drnovšek-Račan Treaty. The latter was endorsed in Slovenia by the Committee on Foreign Policy of the National Assembly of the Republic of Slovenia and publicly supported by the Croatian Prime Minister (Račan), although it is necessary to point out that Croatia later withdrew from the solutions reached.[243] It is nonetheless asserted that the proposed solutions may be, at least indirectly, relevant also in the current arbitration proceedings between Slovenia and Croatia.[244] The Treaty in fact seems to have accommodated in an innovative way (and in a spirit of co-operation) the legitimate vital interests of both States. Furthermore, the solutions envisaged were at least at a certain point in time perceived by both States to be 'equitable compromises'. We therefore assess the most salient points of the Treaty.

4.7.3 Drnovšek-Račan Treaty (2001)

At the outset it must be mentioned that the 'draft treaty' attempted to finally settle both the disputed segments of the land boundary (including the three disputed villages on the shores of the Bay of Piran) and the maritime border between the two States including the 'territorial access' of Slovenia to the high seas. As such it was viewed by many as a 'package deal' giving allegedly some 'advantages' to Croatia on land and some 'gains' to Slovenia at sea.[245] In its maritime part it tried to reconcile the legitimate interests of both States and the aforesaid competing principles of international law in an innovative *sui generis* way, which seems to be wholly in line with international law. As reiterated by the (UN) *Handbook on the Delimitation of Maritime Boundaries*:

> The most important consequence of the fundamental rule that maritime boundary delimitation should be effected by agreement is that the parties are free to adopt whatever delimitation line they wish, whether the line is based on *political, economical, geographic or any other kind of considerations....*[246]

'*Teritorialni dostop do odprtega morja v mednarodni sodni in arbitražni praksi*', Pravna praksa, No. 49–50, Ljubljana, 2009, Appendix; and D. Rudolf ml. and I. Kardum, '*Sporazum o arbitraži između Hrvatske i Slovenije*', PPP, Vol. 49, No. 164, Zagreb, 2010, p. 3 at pp. 13–14.

242 Initialed on 20 July 2001. See also Sancin, op. cit., pp. 96–97.

243 See also Rudolf ml. and Kardum, op. cit., p. 13. Until 2005, Slovenia presented the latter as 'Agreement or record of an agreement reached', while Croatia as a 'draft agreement'. See Vidas, op. cit., p. 29.

244 See section 4.8.

245 Sovereignty over three disputed border villages close to the shores of the Bay of Piran (Mlini, Bužini, Škrile) would have been on the basis of the draft treaty exercised by Croatia. See Section III (State Border on Land) in relation to Annex II. of the Draft Treaty (verbal description and co-ordinates of State border on land). See also Blake and Topalović, op. cit., pp. 24–28.

246 Emphasis added. DOALOS, New York, NY: UN, 2000, p. 2.

On the other hand, it is important to keep in mind that '[d]elimitation by judicial settlement is a legal operation which can only be based on the application of the relevant legal provisions'.[247]

Regarding the 'juridical status' of the Bay of Piran the two States reached a compromise wherein the waters within it would have the status of a territorial sea, and where approximately 80 per cent of it would fall under the sovereignty of Slovenia.[248] Such a line seems to have been influenced by the indirect application of the principle of *uti possidetis* (*effectivités*) by seemingly taking into account an informal line of police control in the Bay agreed between the 'police authority' of the two federal republics a couple of months before their independence.[249] By giving a narrow strip of territorial waters to Croatia (circa 300 m from the shore) the two States skilfully avoided a conflict between the application of the principle of *uti possidetis* and Article 2 of UNCLOS as reflected in one of the central principles of the law of maritime delimitation, 'land dominates the sea'.[250]

The Slovenian claim regarding a 'territorial contact to the high seas' or in other words to the 'non-enclavement' of its maritime areas between the territorial sea of Croatia and Italy has been accommodated by an innovative *sui generis* solution for which it may be suggested that it reflects the spirit of Part IX of UNCLOS. The agreed solution in fact takes into account the specific (geographical) characteristics of the area (Northern Adriatic), the legitimate-vital interests of both States, and does not affect the rights of third States (see Figure 4.5).[251]

Taking into account the extremely difficult geographical position of the concave Slovenian coastline within the Gulf of Trieste and the position of Point T5 (located more than 12 nmi from the Slovenian coast), the parties decided to convert part of the previous 'SFRY's territorial sea located in the disputed area' into 'a corridor of high seas'[252] linking the Slovenian territorial sea[253] and 'Point T5' in the Northern Adriatic. Such a solution is completely in line with Article 3 of UNCLOS which defines 12 nmi as the maximum breadth of the territorial sea. The envisaged solution seems also to represent one of the potential applications of Article 3 of UNCLOS to the specific case in the light of Part IX of UNCLOS.[254]

---

247 Ibid, pp. 17–18.
248 The latter solution should, however, be seen as a part of an 'overall package deal' and not as a waiver of the longstanding Slovenian position regarding the 'internal water status' of the Bay of Piran. See section 4.7.2.1.
249 February 1991. Personal interview with Slovenian negotiators of the draft treaty (2008).
250 See section 4.3.3.
251 Article 4 of the draft treaty is entitled '*Junction* of the Territorial Sea of the Republic of Slovenia with the High Seas'. See also the discussion of the 2009 Arbitral Agreement (Slovenia's *junction* to the high seas) in section 4.8.4. Emphasis added. The agreement would have regulated only the area on the former SFRY side of the 'Osimo' border, therefore, without affecting the rights of Italy.
252 'The Contracting Parties agree that the sea surface limited with points … shall be high seas'. Article 4(1). The breadth of the 'corridor' was equivalent to 75 per cent of the 'former' straight baseline closing the Bay of Piran. See Art. 4(2).
253 Article 3(1).
254 See section 2.4.1.2.

176 *Extension of Coastal State Jurisdiction in Enclosed or Semi-enclosed Seas*

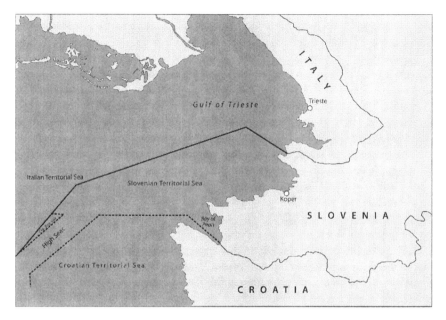

Figure 4.5 Drnovšek-Račan Treaty (envisaged solutions)[255]

One of the most innovative, but at the same time also criticized solutions embodied in the Drnovšek-Račan draft treaty was the enclave of Croatian territorial waters located near the 1975 Osimo border line (therefore on the border with the territorial sea of Italy) and separated from the remaining Croatian territorial sea by the 'high seas corridor'.[256] The latter was a result of a compromise between the positions of the two States, as Croatia throughout the negotiations insisted on 'preserving' its (territorial) maritime border with Italy in the Gulf of Trieste. Such solution wherein the territorial sea of one State is cut in two by a corridor of high seas is theoretically at least not in accordance with international law.[257]

It should be recalled, however, that States are free to adopt by agreement whatever solution they wish and that such a solution, although *sui generis*, would not affect the rights of third States. To the contrary, the 'international community' would be provided with some additional rights in the 'corridor' where all States would have the rights to exercise not just the right of innocent passage, but it seems full high seas freedoms in accordance with Article 87 of UNCLOS.[258]

255 Modelled on a figure published in LOS Bulletin, UN, No. 56, 2005, p. 142.
256 Article 5. It should be noted that the title of Art. 5 is '*Junction* between the Territorial Sea of the Republic of Croatia and the Italian Republic'. Emphasis added.
257 See B. Mekina, 'Interview with Vladimir Ibler', Mladina, No. 34, Ljubljana, 2007, pp. 39–42.
258 Article 4(5) provided: '*No sovereign rights* may be acquired in relation to the water column under the sea surface [of the corridor] hereof. The contracting parties shall, *in their mutual relations, refrain from exercising sovereign rights in the sea-bed and the relevant subsoil* under the sea surface referred to in Paragraph 1 hereof'. Emphasis added.

Maritime boundaries in the (Eastern) Adriatic 177

A final question is whether Slovenia would be entitled to extend its jurisdiction, proclaiming its zone of jurisdiction (EEZ) beyond the 'high seas corridor', therefore beyond point T5. In this respect, Škrk was of the opinion that, by refraining from the exercise of sovereign rights (although not necessary jurisdiction) in the corridor, Slovenia impliedly waived its rights to a continental shelf and the EEZ outside the high seas corridor.[259] The fact is, however, that the draft agreement was silent on the matter and one cannot see a valid reason why Slovenia, particularly taking into account the (joint and/or undivided) status of the continental shelf within the corridor, would not have been able to extend alone (or jointly with Croatia) its jurisdiction beyond Point T5.

4.7.4 Joint fishing zone (SOPS): Preservation of historic fishing rights in the Northern Adriatic?

When discussing the Drnovšek-Račan Treaty, it is necessary to mention that it was intended to be complemented by another treaty already concluded between the two States back in 1997, but ratified by the Republic of Slovenia only in the weeks following the initialling of the Drnovšek-Račan draft treaty in 2001. Reference is made here to the Agreement between the Republic of Slovenia and the Republic of Croatia on Border Traffic and Co-operation (SOPS)[260] with which the two States *inter alia* established a *de facto* 'joint fishing zone' straddling the territorial seas of both States in the Northern Adriatic. The logic of the Agreement followed the structure and rationale of a similar zone established by the 1983 Exchange of Letters between Italy and the former SFRY in the Gulf of Trieste.[261] It is asserted that the aim of both agreements was the preservation of traditional (historic) fishing rights of local inhabitants in the area (see Figure 4.6).[262]

Article 1 of SOPS defines *the joint fishing zone* as an area encompassing the entire *territorial sea of Slovenia* and the *territorial sea of Croatia, up to the longitude of 45°10'* along the western part of Istria.[263] The total area of the 'joint fishing zone' amounted to no less than 1183,3 km^2.[264] Fishing in the area of the other contracting party would, however, be permitted only by fishermen and/or fishing companies having their permanent residence within the expressly mentioned 'border municipalities' within the two States and was to be limited to only a certain number of fishing boats (25 daily, for each State), having specific characteristics and fishing equipment, based on the principle of reciprocity.[265]

---

259 Ibid. See Škrk, op. cit., p. 498, and Vidas, op. cit., pp. 29–30.
260 Act on ratification published in the OGRS (International Treaties) No. 20/2001. Agreement signed on 28 April 1997 and entered into force on 5 September 2001.
261 See Figure 4.4, and Scovazzi and Francalanci, op. cit. (Italy-Yugoslavia), p. 1641.
262 Ibid. See also Art. 47 of SOPS.
263 See Figure 4.6. Note that Slovenia used the same co-ordinates for the provisional limits of its ZEP in the area adjacent to the 'joint fishing zone'. See section 3.3.6. (Figure 3.6)
264 See Figure 4.6, and Gržetić *et al.*, op. cit., p. 40. According to Croatian sources, the area of the Croatian territorial sea in which Slovenian fisherman would be entitled to exercise their 'traditional' fishing rights was measured for the hypothetical median line in the Gulf of Piran, six times that of the relevant area of the Slovenian territorial sea.
265 Article 49.

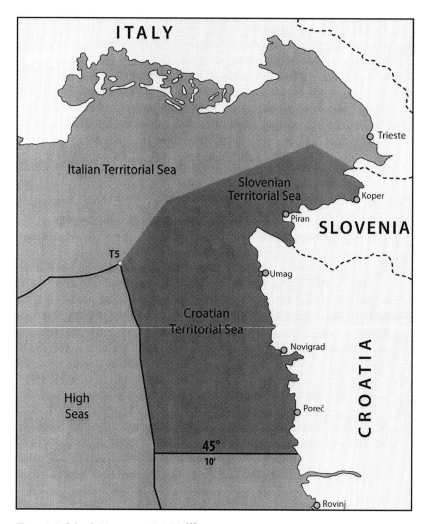

Figure 4.6 'Joint fishing zone' (SOPS)[266]

Allowable fishing gear should be according to the agreement defined by a permanent mixed Croatian-Slovenian commission, while each party would apply its legislation (in a non-discriminatory manner) in its own territorial sea.[267] The problem before the 'initialling' of the Drnovšek-Račan Treaty was obviously that the border line between the territorial sea of both States was not agreed which could (and most likely would) create 'grey areas', within which both States would attempt to exercise their fisheries jurisdiction. Another fear on the Slovenian side

---

266 Modelled on a Figure published in Gržetič *et al.*, op. cit., p. 40.
267 Article 48.

Maritime boundaries in the (Eastern) Adriatic 179

was that the provisions of the Agreement may prejudice the final settlement of the land and particularly the maritime boundary between the two States, and this despite the express 'disclaimer provision' embodied in Article 59 of the Treaty.[268] With the 'initialling' of the Drnovšek-Račan Treaty such concerns seemed *prima facie* overturned.[269]

Quite unfortunately, Croatia had made public its intention not to sign the Drnovšek-Račan Treaty as soon as 2002.[270] The SOPS had entered into force in 2001, although its provisions, particularly those regarding fisheries had not been implemented in practice, mostly due to the opposition of Croatia (and/or its fishermen). Upon its accession to the EU on 1 May 2004 Slovenia also formally 'suspended' the fisheries provisions of SOPS.[271]

It may nonetheless be asserted that the various solutions embodied in the SOPS (e.g. joint fishing zone) further emphasize the need for States bordering the Adriatic and/or the Mediterranean Seas to agree not only on delimitation, but also on a regime for the disputed (maritime) areas. Of particular importance seems to be the preservation of historic fishing rights of local inhabitants and issues related to the regime of navigation.[272] Both issues (safety of navigation and/or historic fishing rights) had already been addressed by Slovenia and Croatia on a multilateral level (IMO and/or EU).[273]

Despite the fact that the regime of the 'joint fishing zone' (SOPS) had not been implemented in practice, and independently of the fact that Slovenia also formally suspended its application upon its accession to the EU (1 May 2004), it would follow that the historic fishing rights of the local inhabitants of both States have been (at least impliedly) recognized in the 2011 Treaty between the EU Member States and the Republic of Croatia concerning the accession of the Republic of Croatia to the European Union, signed on 9 December 2011.[274] Annex III of the 2011 Accession Treaty provides in this regard that Annex I of Council Regulation (EC) No 2371/2002 of 20 December 2002 on the conservation and sustainable exploitation of fisheries resources under the Common

---

268 Article 59 of SOPS provides that the provisions of the Agreement shall not in any way prejudice the course of the maritime and land boundary between the two States. See also Opinion of the Constitutional Court of Slovenia No. Rm-1/00-29, dated 19 April 2001.

269 It is suggested that an eventual entry into force of the Drnovšek-Račan Treaty would have required an amendment to Art. 1 of SOPS. The latter defined (also) the waters in the envisaged 'high seas corridor' as the territorial seas of the two States.

270 See section 4.7.3.

271 The Agreement was concluded for a period of three years with a tacit renewal for another year in the absence of an express cancellation by one of the two States at least six months before its expiry. See Art. 60(3). On its accession to the EU (2004), Slovenia, however, temporarily suspended only the provisions of SOPS relating to the 'joint fishing zone', while other provisions of the Agreement remained in force.

272 See section 4.8.

273 See also the discussion on the 'Memorandum of Understanding between Slovenia, Croatia and Italy (endorsed by IMO in 2003) on the Establishment of a Common Routeing System and Traffic Separation Scheme in the Northern Part of the Northern Adriatic', in section 5.4.1.1.

274 Hereinafter '2011 Accession Treaty'. See OJ EU L112, 24 April 2012, p. 14. It is expected that all EU Member States will ratify it. Croatia joined the EU on 1 July 2013. See also the discussion in section 3.6.

180 *Extension of Coastal State Jurisdiction in Enclosed or Semi-enclosed Seas*

Fisheries Policy[275] which regulates access to coastal (territorial) waters of Member States by 'fishing vessels that traditionally fish in those waters from adjacent states'[276] should be amended with certain provisions (for which there cannot be any doubt) that are modelled on the relevant 'fisheries' provisions of the SOPS Agreement.

The '2011 Accession Treaty' provides in this regard that Annex I of the 2002 Regulation shall be amended and that it should provide for the right of (local) Slovenian fisherman to fish in the territorial sea of Croatia north of the *45 degrees and 10 minutes parallel*, along the West Istrian coast, therefore within the geographical area of the SOPS 'joint fishing zone'.[277] Such a right is, however, limited to 100 tonnes yearly for a maximum number of 25 fishing vessels, including five fishing vessels equipped with trawl nets.[278] An equivalent right is then provided also for 25 Croatian fishing vessels to fish within '12 miles limited to the sea area under the sovereignty of Slovenia situated to the north of the 45 degrees and 10 minutes parallel north latitude along the west Istrian coast'.[279]

Some general conclusions may be reached in this regard. First, there can be no doubt that the inclusion of the 'right of access' of Slovenian and Croatian fisherman within the 2011 Croatia's Accession Treaty (and indirectly within the 2002 Regulation), represent an implied recognition by the two States and the EU of the existence of historic fishing rights of both Slovenian and Croatian fisherman within the territorial waters of both States. Such 'historic rights' may now also be geographically limited, at least with regard to the territorial seas of both States, to the geographical area of the SOPS 'joint fishing zone'. The second important consideration is that the *de facto* transposition into the European *acquis* of the most important (fisheries) provisions of SOPS, means that the effective exercise of 'historic fishing rights' by Slovenian and Croatian fisherman within the territorial seas of both States, it is no longer dependent on the legal validity of SOPS. This is of crucial importance, as the bilateral

---

275 OJ EU L 358, 31 December 2002, p. 59. Hereinafter 'the 2002 Regulation'.
276 Article 17(2) of the 2002 Regulation establishes a derogation for the 12 nmi zone of Member States (territorial sea) from the general equal access rule for EU fishing vessels to EU waters and resources. It provides as follows:

> In waters up to 12 nautical miles from baselines under their sovereignty or jurisdiction, Member States shall be authorised from 1 January 2003 to 31 December 2012 to restrict fishing to fishing vessels *that traditionally fish in those waters from ports on the adjacent coast* [...] fixing for each Member State the geographical zones within the coastal bands of other Member States where fishing activities are pursued and the species concerned.

> Emphasis added. The duration of the mentioned provision has been extended to 31.12.2014 and is expected to be prolonged until 31.12.2022. See Regulation of the European Parliament and of the Council Amending Council Regulation (EC) No. 2371/2002 on the Conservation and Sustainable Exploitation of Fisheries Resources under the Common Fisheries Policy, COM(2012) 277 final, Brussels, 7.6.2012, Art. 1. See also Art. 6(2) of the Proposal for a regulation of the European Parliament and of the Council on the Common Fisheries Policy, COM(2011) 425 final, Brussels, 13.7.2011.

277 See Figure 4.6.
278 Cf fn 276, Annex 3, Section 5 (Fisheries), p. 50.
279 Ibid.

Maritime boundaries in the (Eastern) Adriatic 181

agreement can be unilaterally terminated by one of the two State Parties on notice if given within six months' minimum.[280]

However, it is striking that despite the forthcoming accession of the Republic of Croatia to the EU,[281] the discussed 'access regime' will enter into force only from the date of the 'full implementation of the arbitration award resulting from the Arbitration Agreement between the Government of the Republic of Slovenia and the Government of the Republic of Croatia, signed in Stockholm on 4 November 2009.[282] The two States were obviously afraid of the various (already experienced) problems which could have arisen as a result of the undefined maritime border between the two States, particularly with regard to the exercise of fisheries jurisdiction in the disputed area. The fact that Slovenian fishermen have been entitled to different forms of compensation from EU (fisheries) funds due to the temporary impossibility of their fishing within Croatian territorial waters pending the award of the Arbitral Tribunal seems, however, to be more proof of the implied recognition of the 'historic fishing rights' of the Slovenian fisherman within the area.[283]

Lastly, reference should be made to the fact that the agreed 'right of access' for the fisherman of both States to the territorial waters of the other State seems to represent an agreed 'regime of the area', which will most likely be taken into account by the Arbitral Tribunal in the current arbitral proceedings between Slovenia and Croatia. The Arbitral Tribunal, as discussed in the next section, has been entrusted not only with the task to determine 'the course of the maritime and land boundary' and 'Slovenia's junction to the high seas' but also with the task of determining the 'regime for the use of the relevant maritime areas'.[284] It seems unlikely that the Arbitral Tribunal will adopt a different solution than that already agreed and forming part of the European *acquis*.[285]

4.8 2009 Arbitral Agreement between Slovenia and Croatia: Reflecting the spirit of Part IX of UNCLOS?

The (maritime) delimitation dispute between Slovenia and Croatia has been ongoing for more than 20 years and during this period the two States have taken various diplomatic stances during the different rounds of negotiation. In addition to negotiations at various levels, two 'Slovenian-Croatian' border commissions and the 'good offices' of the former US Defense-Secretary William Perry were established.[286] The most important breakthrough in the relations between

280 Cf fn 274.
281 Cf fn 276.
282 Cf fn 213.
283 STA, '*Židan: Slovenskim ribičem priznane zgodovinske pravice*', Ljubljana, 6 June 2011.
284 Ibid. See Art. 3(1) and the discussion in section 4.8.
285 As mentioned, in the area beyond the 'joint fishing zone', Slovenia proclaimed its ZEP in 2005, while in 2006 it included the mentioned area within its 'fishing waters'. Croatia included the same area within its EFPZ in 2003. See the discussion in sections 3.3.4 and 3.3.6, and Gržetić, op. cit., pp. 64–66.
286 See Sancin, op. cit., pp. 96–98.

182 *Extension of Coastal State Jurisdiction in Enclosed or Semi-enclosed Seas*

the two States was the 'initialling' of the Drnovšek-Račan Treaty in 2001.[287] It was only in 2005 that Slovenia at least impliedly agreed to the continuation of negotiations.[288] On 27 August 2007 the prime ministers of the two States, Janez Janša and Ivo Sanader, reached an informal agreement to submit the dispute to a binding settlement procedure, with particular emphasis being placed on the ICJ.[289]

The two States then set in place a joint diplomatic commission of international law experts[290] entrusted with the task of agreeing on the text of a 'special agreement' and submitting the latter for approval to their governments.[291] While the experts could in principle agree that the jurisdiction of court/tribunal should include both the delimitation of the sea and land, and that the critical date would be 25 June 1991 (date of independence of both States), they were unable to reach an agreement of the forum (whether that would be the ICJ or an *ad hoc* arbitration) and most importantly on the applicable law. Slovenia advocated the position that taking into account the specific characteristics of its coastline and the Northern Adriatic and other relevant factors (including 'historic'), coupled with the already established boundary with Italy in the Gulf of Trieste, the dispute should be resolved on the basis of paragraph 2 of Article 38 of the ICJ Statute, i.e. *ex aqueo et bono*.[292]

Towards the end of 2008 Slovenia warned Croatia that some of its EU pre-accession materials (maps, laws, decrees, etc.) prejudiced the final settlement of the border issue, and following the refusal of Croatia to withdraw them it provided, at the December 2008 pre-accession conference, reservations to the opening of eight and to the closure of two negotiating chapters of Croatia. That in turn triggered the 'facilitation' of the EU through the Commissioner for Enlargement (Olli Rehn).[293] It is noteworthy that up to that time the European Commission treated the Slovenia-Croatia boundary dispute as a purely bilateral issue, outside its competence. After different attempts to agree on a compromise text (and following the change of the Croatian Prime Minister), the two States signed on 4 November 2009 in Stockholm the Arbitral Agreement between the Government

---

287 See section 4.7.3.

288 See Brioni Declaration, '*Skupna izjava o izogibanju incidentov*', Government of the Republic of Slovenia and the Government of the Republic of Croatia, Brioni, 10 June 2005.

289 Minutes of the meeting. Available at <http://www.vlada.si/fileadmin/dokumenti/si/projekti/2010/Arbitrazni_sporazum/5._Magnetogram_Jan%C5%A1a-Sanader_Bled.pdf>.

290 The author was in the period 2007–2009 a member of the Joint Commission (nominated by Slovenia).

291 Slovenian negotiators were bound by 'guidelines' (Basis for Negotiations), set by the Slovenian government and parliament. Emphasis was placed on an adjudication based (at least) on 'equitable principles' coupled with a determination of both the land and maritime boundary, while the critical date was to be set as 25 June 1991.

292 See 'Draft Special Agreement', submitted by Slovenian negotiators to the Croatian side in May 2008. English translation available at <http://www.vlada.si/fileadmin/dokumenti/si/projekti/2010/Arbitrazni_sporazum/7.a_Slovenski_predlog_Posebnega_sporazuma.pdf>. See also fn 315.

293 See Sancin, op. cit., pp. 98–99.

of the Republic of Slovenia and the Government of the Republic of Croatia.[294] The latter is specific as it linked the resolution of the (maritime) boundary issue with the unblocking of the pre-accession negotiations of Croatia with the EU, and seems to entrust the tribunal to take into account the specific (geographical) position of the Slovenian coastline within the 'border bay' of Trieste, all relevant factors and vital interests of both States.

4.8.1 The EU element

The involvement of the EU within the process may *prima facie* be visible from the Preamble which expressly welcomes the 'facilitation by the European Commission' and from the fact that the Agreement has been counter-signed by the Presidency of the EU Council (as witnesses). It is particularly noteworthy that the European Commission played a role of utmost importance in the appointment of the arbitrators. Article 2(1) of the Agreement provides that:

> Both Parties shall appoint by common agreement the President of the Arbitral Tribunal, and two members *recognized for their competence in international law* within fifteen days *drawn from the list of candidates established by the President and the member responsible for the enlargement of the European Commission*. In case that they cannot agree within this time-period, the President and the two members of the Arbitral Tribunal *shall be appointed by the President of the International Court of Justice from the list.*[295]

This provision represents a 'skilful' compromise between the positions of the two States. While Slovenia advocated a 'mediation' or 'arbitration' with the involvement of the EU, Croatia was strongly in favour of the submission of the dispute to the ICJ. However, the powers given to the EU in the present case seem to outweigh those given to the ICJ President, as it is the European Commission which had to draw a list of potential arbitrators from which the two parties together (or alternatively the ICJ President) would have to designate three arbitrators. Surprisingly however, Slovenia and Croatia, somehow, through the facilitation of the European Commission, managed to find a 'common agreement on the President of the Arbitral Tribunal, and two members' without the intervention of the ICJ President. On 17 January 2012 the two States jointly appointed Judge Gilbert Guillaume (former ICJ President) as President, and Professor Vaughan Lowe QC and Judge Bruno Simma as members of the Arbitral Tribunal.[296] There is no doubt that the appointed experts are 'recognized

---

294 Text of the 'Arbitration Agreement' available at <http://www.vlada.si/fileadmin/dokumenti/ si/projekti/2010/Arbitrazni_sporazum/10.a_Arbitra%C5%BEni_sporazum_-_podpisan_ EN.pdf>.
295 Emphasis added.
296 A. Brstovšek, '*Arbitražno sodišče je dobilo tri imena*', Dnevnik, Ljubljana, 18 January 2012.

184 Extension of Coastal State Jurisdiction in Enclosed or Semi-enclosed Seas

for their competence in international law' as requested by Article 2(1) of the Arbitration Agreement.

Regarding the remaining two arbitrators Article 2(1) provides that:

> Each Party shall appoint a further member of the Arbitral Tribunal within fifteen days after the appointments referred to in paragraph 1 have been finalised. In case that no appointment has been made within this delay, the respective member shall be appointed by the President of the Arbitral Tribunal.

In this context, a 'third party intervention' by the President of the Arbitral Tribunal was not necessary. Following the joint appointments of the President and two members, Slovenia and Croatia appointed, within the provided time limits, two more members of the Arbitral Tribunal. Slovenia appointed Dr Jernej Sekolec as arbitrator, while Croatia appointed Professor Budislav Vukas.[297]

Articles 8 and 9 of the Arbitration Agreement, on the other hand, expressly address the issue of the 'EU accession negotiation documents' which should not prejudice the work of the Arbitral Tribunal.[298] Article 9 even provided a 'roadmap' for Croatian EU accession negotiations according to the negotiating framework. The latter article is 'unique' as it links the 'lifting' of the reservations of Slovenia regarding the opening and closing of negotiating chapters where the obstacle is related to the dispute to the signature of the arbitral agreement.

Not surprisingly, Article 6(7) provides that the place of arbitration should be Brussels and the European Commission was also invited to provide Secretarial support to the Arbitral Tribunal.[299] The ultimate proof of the relation between the Croatian pre-accession negotiations and the 'Special agreement' is provided in Article 11(3) which provides that '... all procedural timelines expressed in this Agreement shall start to apply from the *date of the signature of Croatia's EU Accession Treaty*'.[300] The sole signature is enough, which means that procedural timelines started running before the entry into force of the Accession Treaty, in other words before ratifications by the 27 EU Member States. Croatia's Accession Treaty was signed and procedural timelines started to run on 9 December 2011.[301]

---

297 See PCA (Cases), 'Arbitration Between The Republic of Croatia and The Republic of Slovenia'. Available at <http://www.pca-cpa.org/showpage.asp?pag_id=1443>.

298 Article 8(1).

299 The two States and the European Commission later, however, agreed that the secretarial support (Registry) should be provided by the PCA in The Hague. Cf fn 297.

300 Emphasis added. This includes the 12 month time-limit for the submissions of the Memorials. See Art. 6(1).

301 Nonetheless, at the first procedural meeting held on 13 April 2012, the Arbitral Tribunal accepted the proposal of both parties according to which 'the Parties' first memorials would be simultaneously submitted on 11 February 2013, that the Parties' counter-memorials would be simultaneously submitted on 11 November 2013, and that a hearing would be held in the spring of 2014'. See PCA, 'Arbitration Between the Republic of Croatia and the Republic of Slovenia: Arbitral Tribunal Holds First Procedural Meeting with the Parties', Press Release, The Hague, 13 April 2012. Cf fn 297.

4.8.2 The Bay of Piran

According to the draft special agreement (2008) prepared by the Slovenian part of the joint commission of international law experts, the two States would authorize the ICJ/PCA/Ad Hoc Arbitration at sea: (a) to establish the baseline used for measuring the breadth of the maritime zones; (b) to decide on the legal status within the Bay of Piran; (c) to determine the lateral boundary of the respective territorial seas of either party; (d) to determine the lateral boundary of the respective continental shelf of either party and; (e) to determine the lateral boundaries of the maritime areas of sovereign rights.[302] The Republic of Croatia on the other hand proposed a wording according to which the *ICJ* should decide '[…] what is the course of the maritime boundary that divides the maritime area of the Republic of Croatia and the maritime space of the Republic of Slovenia'.[303] Also in this regard the 2009 Arbitral Agreement represents a compromise, although it is noteworthy that it does not mention directly the question of the 'juridical status of the Bay of Piran'.[304] Independently of that, one of the first tasks of the Arbitral Tribunal was to be the determination of the baselines from which the breadth of the maritime areas will be measured which will unavoidably require a decision on the 'juridical' status of the waters within the Bay of Piran. Furthermore, another of the tasks of the Arbitral Tribunal was to be to determine 'the regime for the use of the relevant maritime areas',[305] which in the case of the Bay of Piran might depend also on the status of its waters (internal and/or territorial).[306] One should also note Article 3(2) according to which:

> The parties shall specify the details of the subject matter of the dispute within one month. If they fail to do so, the Arbitral Tribunal shall use the submissions of the parties for the determination of the exact scope of the maritime and territorial dispute and claims between the Parties.

As the parties did not specify the subject matter of the dispute within one month from the signature of Croatia's Accession Treaty (9 December 2011), the Arbitral Tribunal will have to use the submissions of the parties for the determination of the exact scope of the maritime and territorial dispute and for the determination of the exact claims of both States. It seems quite possible that Slovenia will insist within its Memorial upon the 'internal waters' status of the (entire) Bay of Piran, while Croatia will almost certainly oppose it.[307] It seems safe to conclude that the Arbitral Tribunal will be, despite the absence of an express mention, compelled to determine the 'juridical' status of the waters within the Bay of Piran.

---

302 Article 3(2). Cf fn 292.
303 Article 2(1)(b). Text available at <http://www.vlada.si/fileadmin/dokumenti/si/projekti/2010/Arbitrazni_sporazum/8._Protipredlog_HR_september2008.pdf>.
304 Reference is made (only) to 'the determination of "the maritime" and "land" boundary', Art. 3(1)(a).
305 Article 3(1)(c).
306 See the discussion in section 4.7.4. on the 'access regime' by local fisherman within the *territorial sea of both States* regulated by the 2011 Accession Treaty of Croatia.
307 See the discussion in section 4.7.2.1.

4.8.3 Applicable law and the principle of uti possidetis

Article 3(1)(a) of the Agreement provides as one of the central tasks of the Tribunal the determination of 'the course of the maritime and land boundary'. This should be done by applying 'the rules and principles of international law'.[308] An important question seems to be whether the Tribunal will be compelled to apply or at least to consider, the application of the principle of *uti possidetis*. The answer seems to be positive for the following reasons.

First, the applicable law in Article 4(1) applies both to the determination of the land and maritime boundary alike, and at least with regard to the land boundary there cannot be any doubt that the tribunal will be compelled to apply the principle of *uti possidetis*. This follows both from the Constitutional documents of both States[309] and from Opinion No. 3 of the Badinter Commission. These documents, as mentioned earlier, do not differentiate between the boundary on land and at sea.[310] From the previous discussions it may be recalled that the principle of *uti possidetis* has acquired the status of a 'generally recognized rule of (customary) international law' and accordingly reference to 'rules and principles of international law', in the absence of an express or implied exclusion,[311] includes also a reference to the (potential) application of *uti possidetis*. The relevance of the latter may be furthermore implied by Article 5 of the Agreement setting the 'critical date' for the dispute. According to the latter:

> No document or action undertaken unilaterally by either side after 25 June 1991 shall be accorded legal significance the tasks of the Arbitral Tribunal or commit either side of the dispute and cannot, in any way, prejudge the award.

As both the proclamation of the Croatian EFPZ and of the Slovenian ZEP may be interpreted also as 'unilateral actions' undertaken after 25 June 1991, it is interesting to see how the tribunal will tackle this issue.[312]

4.8.4 Territorial contact of Slovenia with the high seas and zones of sovereign rights and jurisdictions

Taking into account that the 'territorial contact to the high seas' has been throughout the past 20 years characterized by Slovenia as its 'vital interest', it is noteworthy that request for the latter has not been expressly mentioned in the draft agreement prepared by Slovenia and submitted within the framework of the Joint Commission of International Law Experts. That request was however implied in Article 3 of the Slovenian Draft which provided as one of the tasks of the tribunal/court the determination 'of the lateral boundary of the

308 Article 4(1).
309 Cf fn 29.
310 See section 4.3.2.
311 Cf fn 32.
312 See sections 3.3.4 and 3.3.6.

Maritime boundaries in the (Eastern) Adriatic 187

areas of sovereign rights between the two States'.[313] When it comes to applicable law, Article 6 of the Slovenian draft provided that the Court/Tribunal would have to rule the dispute *primarily* on the basis of Article 38(2) of the ICJ's Statute, therefore *ex aqueo et bono*.[314] The application of *ex aqueo et bono* has in fact been seen by Slovenia as a safeguard against the prevalent views within the recent jurisprudence of the ICJ and/or arbitral tribunals which at least since 1992 seem to favour the application of the 'equidistance/relevant circumstances rule' with regard to the delimitation of shelf/EEZ and the 'equidistance/special circumstances rule' regarding the delimitation of the territorial sea.[315] *Prima facie* it seems that the application of (modified) equidistant line, particularly due to the specific characteristics of the Slovenian coastline, could not result in a line which would grant to Slovenia 'territorial contact to the high seas'.

The solution adopted by the 2009 Agreement is indeed also original and by all means *sui generis*, because it provides different criteria for different sets of questions. While 'the course of the maritime and land boundary between the Republic of Croatia and the Republic of Slovenia'[316] has to be decided on the basis of 'the rules and principles of international law', the determination of the 'Slovenian junction to the high seas'[317] and for the determination of 'the regime for the use of the relevant maritime areas',[318] the Arbitral Tribunal has to apply 'international law, equity and the *principle of good neighbourly relations* in order to achieve a *fair and just result* by taking into account all relevant circumstances'.[319] The latter formulation, although not expressly mentioning *ex aqueo et bono* seems to contain important elements of the latter[320] and may be associated at least with *equity praeter legem*.[321] Additionally, the various provisions

---

313 Cf fn 292, Art. 3. According to the Croatian negotiators such formulation would prejudice the decision of the Court/Tribunal. Personal notes of the author.

314 Ibid. The word 'primarily' was included in the draft in order to emphasis the position of Slovenia according to which a decision *ex aqueo et bono* may in certain cases represent an upgrading of international law and not its exclusion. Some experts have, however, expressed doubts whether such conditional application would be understood by the ICJ as an express agreement to adjudicate the dispute *ex aqueo et bono*. See S. Drenik, '*Arbitražni sporazum: potek pogajanj in dosežene rešitve*', Pravna praksa, No. 45, Ljubljana, 2009, Appendix. See also V.D. Degan, '*Pravičnost i medunarodno pravo u razgraničenjima morskih prostora*', PPP, Vol. 49, No. 164, Zagreb, 2010, p. 139 at p. 142.

315 For a general discussion, see Y. Tanaka, *Predictability and Flexibility in the Law of Maritime Delimitations, Studies in International Law*, Vol. 8, Oxford and Portland, OR: Hart Publishing, 2006 (particularly Chapters 4–6).

316 Article 3(1)(a).

317 Article 3(1)(b).

318 Article 3(1)(c).

319 Article 4(2).

320 A decision *ex aqueo et bono* must according to Sohn '[t]o the extent that it goes outside the applicable law, or acts where no law is applicable … proceed upon objective considerations of what is *fair and just*'. Emphasis added. See L.B. Sohn, 'Arbitration of International Disputes *ex aqueo et bono*', in P. Sanders (ed.), *Liber Amicorum for Martin Domke*, The Leiden, Netherlands: Martinus Nijhoff, 1957, p. 330 at p. 331.

321 According to Sohn '… Equity is applied *praeter legem*, in addition to law, whenever a tribunal is specifically empowered to decide in accordance with international law *and* equity.…'. Ibid, p. 332. Cf fn 314 (Degan), pp. 141 and 153.

188   *Extension of Coastal State Jurisdiction in Enclosed or Semi-enclosed Seas*

of the Arbitration Agreement have to be read in the light of its Preamble which in paragraph 4 expressly makes reference to the commitment of the two States to a peaceful settlement of disputes 'in the spirit of good neighbourly relations, reflecting *their vital interests*'.[322]

The first potential problem seems to relate to the relation between the 'definition of the course of the maritime boundary' which has to be determined on the basis of the rules and principles of international law, and the 'Slovenian junction to the high seas' which on the other hand has to be decided in line with the provision of Article 4(b) (*'quasi' ex aqueo et bono*). The two sets of tasks are, however, closely linked, as Slovenian 'junction' to the high seas can only be achieved by establishing a 'kind' of borderline with Croatia up to or close to point T5.[323] That in turn raises the question whether the tribunal will interpret 'junction to the high sea' as referring to a 'territorial contact of Slovenia to the high seas' or less likely, just to a specific functional regime of navigation and/or of overflight to the high seas.[324] The dilemma seems to be accentuated by the fact that although the expression 'junction to the high seas' has been used in some delimitation agreements,[325] it does not have a commonly understood legal meaning and has not been judicially tested.

Furthermore, unlike the draft special agreement submitted by Slovenia within the 'mixed commission', the 2009 Arbitral Agreement does not expressly mention the task of the Arbitral Tribunal to delimit for example the continental shelf and zones of sovereign rights. Mention should also be made of the fact that on the critical date of 25 June 1991 the former SFRY had a territorial sea and *ipso facto* a continental shelf, but it did not exercise sovereign rights and jurisdiction on superjacent waters beyond its territorial sea (EEZ).

However, it seems unlikely that the Arbitral Tribunal will just disregard the actual extension of jurisdiction (proclamation of an EFPZ and ZEP) by both Slovenia and Croatia, although they might be both characterized by the parties as 'actions undertaken unilaterally after the 25 June 1991'. It seems that the Arbitral Tribunal would at least have to decide on the apportionment and/or the right of

---

322 See also Art. 31 of VCLT.

323 See, however, the 'corridor' solution adopted by the Drnovšek-Račan draft Treaty (section 4.7.3), and the discussion in 4.7.2.2. See also Rudolf and Kardum, op. cit., 13–14.

324 The two States disagree on this point. At the moment of the ratification of the Arbitration Agreement (9 November 2009) Croatia issued a unilateral declaration stating that 'nothing in the Agreement shall be understood as an acquiescence of Croatia to the Slovenian claim regarding its territorial junction with the high seas' (author's translation). Slovenia, on the other hand, in its law on the ratification of the Arbitration Agreement (19 April 2010) included a declaration (Art. 3) expressly stating *inter alia* that the task of the Arbitral Tribunal is to determine the territorial junction of the territorial sea of Slovenia with the high seas. See OGRS, No. 57/2010, 16 July 2010. It is suggested that both statements have the nature of 'unilateral interpretative declarations'. See Sancin, op. cit., p. 101 and fn 238.

325 See Art. 4 of the Drnovšek-Račan draft treaty. The Term 'junction' seems to imply a narrow territorial contact. In the Land, Island and Maritime Frontier Dispute (*El Salvador/Honduras: Nicaragua intervening*) Case it was used in relation to a point of contact of two rivers or watersheds. Cf fn 5, paras 99, 112. See also Case Concerning Kasikili/Sedudu Island (*Botswana/Namibia*), ICJ Reports 1999, p. 1045, para. 21.

Slovenia to a continental shelf and/or on which State has the right to extend its 'sovereign rights' and jurisdiction over the disputed area of superjacent waters (i.e. delimitation of potential zones). Furthermore, as already suggested, the term 'maritime boundary', *ipso facto* includes, if applicable, also the delimitation of the continental shelf and zones of sovereign rights and jurisdictions.[326]

Although it is impossible to predict the outcome of the arbitral proceedings, it seems possible to conclude that the provisions of the 2009 Agreement, which require the tribunal to determine the 'regime of the relevant areas' (seemingly also of the internal waters and territorial sea) and the Slovenian 'junction' to the high seas, in addition to the sole determination of the (maritime) boundary; all this in a spirit of good neighbourly relations by taking into account vital interests of both States, reflecting the spirit of Part IX of UNCLOS and hopefully representing an important precedent for the resolution of similar disputes in the (sub)region.

4.9 Concluding remarks

As explained above, there seems to be enough evidence that (at least) the judicial opinion has been in favour of the application of the principle of *uti possidetis (juris)* to maritime delimitations. Further, there seems to be a tendency in the recent jurisprudence of international courts and tribunals towards the presumption that 'internal maritime lines' between various administrative (federal) entities may become international boundaries (*effectivités, uti possidetis de facto*) or at least that they will be taken into account as special or relevant circumstance in the definition of the latter. There seems also to be no valid reason why two or more States could not at least by agreement retain the 'internal waters status' within a 'border bay', particularly if the rights of third States are not affected.

Particularly, the 2002 Protocol concluded between Croatia and Serbia and Montenegro seems to be a clear proof of the fact that even in the most geographically and/or politically complicated situations it is possible to conclude an agreement on 'provisional arrangements of a practical nature', applicable (also) to internal waters and/or territorial sea. It seems also possible to assert that the 'two-tier' system created by the 2009 Arbitration Agreement between Slovenia and Croatia wherein the resolution of the maritime boundary between an EU Member State and a candidate Member State is linked to the pre-accession negotiations of the latter, may represent a powerful precedent also for other Adriatic States aspiring to join the EU (Albania, Bosnia and Herzegovina and Montenegro), and eventually for other Mediterranean States, including Turkey and Greece. Overall, it seems possible to conclude that all three discussed cases highlight the importance of an agreement on the regime of the disputed areas (co-operation) in addition to the sole questions of sovereignty and call for an innovative solution in the spirit of Part IX of UNCLOS.

---

326 Cf fn 17.

5 Present and future co-operation of Adriatic States: Has Part IX of UNCLOS been implemented in the Adriatic?

This chapter aims to determine whether the provisions of Part IX of UNCLOS have been applied in the Adriatic Sea and whether co-operation has been limited to the three areas expressly listed by Article 123. Special attention is devoted to the legal basis of co-operation and to some areas in which sub-regional Adriatic co-operation is required in addition to regional Mediterranean co-operation. Emphasis is also placed on the potential benefit of the extension of coastal State jurisdiction by Adriatic States. The current and potential co-operation between Adriatic States will be assessed against two backgrounds: the Mediterranean region and the EU. Furthermore, this chapter aims to suggest to Adriatic States some additional areas in which they should strengthen their co-operation in line with the provisions of Part IX of UNCLOS, and proposes possible alternatives to the unilateral extension of coastal State jurisdiction and delimitation of maritime zones in the Adriatic Sea.

5.1 Existing forms of co-operation at Mediterranean level: an Adriatic Sea perspective

This section offers an analysis of the most relevant existing institutional co-operative arrangements at Mediterranean level which involve the participation of Adriatic States. The discussion broadly follows the structure of Article 123 of UNCLOS, analyzing first the co-operation in the field of protection and preservation of the marine environment, followed by a discussion of the areas of fisheries, marine scientific research and other areas of actual or potential co-operation.

5.1.1 Protection and preservation of the marine environment

The main instrument for the Mediterranean environmental protection is the Barcelona Convention with its Protocols (Barcelona System) originally adopted under the auspices of the UNEP MAP in 1976.[1] The Barcelona Convention

---

1 For a general discussion, see E. Raftopoulos, 'The Mediterranean Response to Global Challenges: Environmental Governance and the Barcelona Convention System', in D. Vidas and P.J. Schei (eds),

Part IX of UNCLOS and the Adriatic Sea 191

represents a flexible system which has been constantly updated and which allows for adequate and relatively prompt legislative response to new threats to the Mediterranean environment and prompt adjustments to new emerging principles in the field of marine environmental law and sustainable development in general. With the adoption of the 1995 amendments, the Barcelona Convention extended its scope of application, and was renamed as the Convention for the Protection of the Marine Environment and the Coastal Regions of the Mediterranean.[2]

However, as emphasized by Raftopoulos:

> International environmental governance cannot be fully understood if it is not approached simultaneously as a multiplicity of conventional regimes of governance and as a process of continuous and structured negotiation.[3]

It is accordingly suggested that the Barcelona System has to be read and applied together with different conventional regimes managing the protection of the environment and sustainable development, both at regional and global levels.[4] The relation between the Barcelona system and the various IMO Conventions related to ship source pollution represents a prime example in this regard.[5]

It is noteworthy that all Adriatic States are parties to the 'framework' Barcelona Convention and that only Bosnia and Herzegovina has not ratified the 1995 amendments.[6] It is also important to note that the amended Barcelona Convention and the Protocols which have been so far acceded to by the EU are forming part of the EU legal order.[7] This, however, does not necessarily eliminate the need for additional sub-regional co-operation in the Adriatic Sea, although such co-operation may have different forms and extents. The two main forms seem to be co-operation in the implementation of a certain Protocol to the Barcelona Convention or co-operation in a field which has not been directly addressed by the Barcelona System, for example ship safety or prevention of operational

---

The World Ocean in Globalisation: Climate Change, Sustainable Fisheries, Biodiversity, Shipping, Regional Issues, Leiden and Boston, MA: Martinus Nijhoff Publishers, 2011, pp. 507–532.

2 Amendments adopted on 10 June 1995. The Convention was originally known as the 'Convention for the Protection of the Mediterranean Sea against Pollution'. The amendments incorporated within the Barcelona Convention and its Protocols include some emerging principles of environmental law adopted at the 1992 Rio Conference (UNCED), e.g. the precautionary principle, the 'polluter pays' principle and the principle of sustainable development. See section 5.1.3.

3 See Raftopoulos, op. cit., p. 509.

4 Ibid, p. 508.

5 See for example the discussion on the 'Prevention and Emergency Protocol' in section 5.1.3.2 and the 'Regional Strategy for Prevention Off and Response to Marine Pollution from Ships' prepared by REMPEC in 2005. The first specific objective of the 'regional strategy' relates to the 'ratification of relevant IMO Conventions' (vessel source pollution) by Mediterranean States. See UNEP(DEC)/MED IG. 16/10, 30 September 2005, Annex 1, p. 1.

6 See H. Slim and T. Scovazzi, 'Study of the current status of ratification, implementation and compliance with maritime agreements and conventions applicable to the Mediterranean Sea Basin: With a specific focus on the ENPI South Partner Countries', Part II: Regional Report, AGRECO Consortium, 2009, pp. 132–133.

7 See sections 3.5.1 and 5.1.3.

192 *Extension of Coastal State Jurisdiction in Enclosed or Semi-enclosed Seas*

pollution.[8] This work's assertion is that such co-operation can be undertaken in the Adriatic primarily in the context, or at least by taking into account relevant EU policies and regulations.[9]

5.1.2 The Barcelona System

The Barcelona System currently includes the amended framework Convention and the following protocols:[10]

(a) Protocol for the Prevention and Elimination of Pollution of the Mediterranean Sea by Dumping from Ships and Aircraft or Incineration at Sea,[11] as amended in Barcelona on 10 June 1995 (amendments not yet in force);

(b) Protocol Concerning Co-operation in Preventing Pollution from Ships and, in Cases of Emergency, Combating Pollution of the Mediterranean Sea,[12] signed in Valletta on 25 January 2002 (in force since 17 March 2004);

(c) Protocol for the Protection of the Mediterranean Sea against Pollution from Land-Based Sources and Activities,[13] as amended in Syracuse on 7 March 1996 (amendments in force since 11 May 2008);

(d) Protocol Concerning Specially Protected Areas and Biological Diversity in the Mediterranean,[14] signed in Barcelona on 10 June 1995 (in force since 12 December 1999);

(e) Protocol for the Protection of the Mediterranean Sea against Pollution Resulting from Exploration and Exploitation of the Continental Shelf and the Sea-Bed and its Subsoil,[15] signed in Madrid on 14 October 1994 (in force since 24 March 2011);

(f) Protocol on the Prevention of Pollution of the Mediterranean Sea by Transboundary Movements of Hazardous Wastes and their Disposal,[16] signed in Izmir on 1 October 1996 (not yet in force); and

(g) Protocol on Integrated Coastal Zone Management,[17] signed in Madrid on 21 January 2008 (in force since 24 March 2011).

---

8 See section 5.4.1.1. The main source of regulation of ship source pollution in the Mediterranean is not the Barcelona System, but the global instruments adopted under the auspices of IMO (e.g. MARPOL, SOLAS, COLREG, etc.). Cf fn 4.

9 See for example the discussion on the Implementation of the EU Integrated Maritime Policy in the Mediterranean and Adriatic in sections 3.5.2.2 and 5.6.

10 The amended Convention entered into force on 9 June 2004. See T. Scovazzi, 'The 2008 Mediterranean Protocol on Integrated Coastal Zone Management and the European Community', in A. Del Vecchio (ed.), *La Politica Marittima Comunitaria*, Rome: Aracne, 2009, p. 159 at pp. 161–162.

11 Dumping Protocol.

12 Prevention and Emergency Protocol.

13 Land-Based Protocol.

14 Biodiversity Protocol. See also section 3.3.3.

15 Offshore Protocol.

16 Waste Protocol.

17 ICZM Protocol.

One of the improvements of the amended Barcelona Convention is that its geographical scope of application has been extended to 'all maritime waters of the Mediterranean Sea'.[18] At least from a legal standpoint the geographical scope of application of the Barcelona Convention is not dependent on the extension of coastal States' jurisdiction in the Adriatic Sea.[19] Two observations should, however, be made in this regard. The first is that the geographical scope of application of certain Protocols differs from that of the framework Convention, depending on the subject matter regulated (e.g. continental shelf, coastal zones, etc.).[20] Second, reference should also be made to the fact that not all Protocols to the Barcelona Convention are in force and that not all Mediterranean and/or Adriatic States are parties to those Protocols[21] which are currently in force; and to the potential problems related with the enforcement of the provisions of certain Protocols against non-parties, particularly on the Adriatic and Mediterranean high seas.[22]

5.1.2.1 Enforcement of the Barcelona system on the high seas: How much added value would bring the extension of coastal State jurisdiction?

Taking into account that the Barcelona System in principle applies also to the high seas, and having in mind its evolving character, the question arises as to how much would the extension of jurisdiction by Mediterranean coastal States actually increase their prescriptive and enforcement powers in the field of the protection and preservation of the marine environment, particularly in light of the already existing continental shelf regime[23] and of the limitations provided by UNCLOS on the regulation of navigation by a coastal State in its EEZ. Reference should be made to the fact that certain sources of pollution would not be affected for purely geographical reasons (e.g. land-based pollution) while, as stated, with regard to pollution from sea-bed activities, the prescriptive and enforcement powers of the Mediterranean coastal States are already available under the continental shelf regime.[24] Ruiz ultimately argues that the added value of establishing an EEZ or ecological zones in the Mediterranean would mainly relate to the protection and preservation of wildlife and biodiversity, a matter regulated by UNCLOS.[25]

18 The original Barcelona Convention does not apply to internal waters. See Art. 1(2).
19 See sections 3.3.4–3.3.6.
20 See the Biodiversity Protocol (Art. 2), the Offshore Protocol (Art. 2), the Prevention and Emergency Protocol (Art. 2) and the ICZM Protocol (Art. 3).
21 See section 5.1.3.
22 See J. Ruiz, 'Mediterranean Cooperation and Third States', paper delivered at the 11th Mediterranean Research Meeting Florence and Montecatini Terme, 24–27 March 2010, pp. 9–13.
23 See section 3.1.
24 Articles 208(1) and 214 of UNCLOS.
25 See Ruiz, op. cit., p. 20. Article 194(5) of UNCLOS provides that '[t]he measures taken in accordance with this Part [Part XII] shall include those necessary to protect and preserve rare or fragile ecosystems as well as the habitat of depleted, threatened or endangered species and other forms of marine life'. Regarding the protection of biodiversity see also Art. 61(4) of UNCLOS.

194 *Extension of Coastal State Jurisdiction in Enclosed or Semi-enclosed Seas*

It seems however necessary not to underestimate the limited but nonetheless important 'functional jurisdiction', including both prescriptive and enforcement rights, that the coastal State can exercise in its EEZ in the field of protection and preservation of the marine environment, including in the field of prevention of ship source pollution and preservation of biodiversity. The coastal State's powers in this respect include the right to 'permit, regulate and control dumping including the right to enforce such provisions,[26] although, it may be argued that Mediterranean States are also entitled to exercise equivalent powers on the basis of the existing continental shelf regime.[27] Another important power given to the coastal State in its EEZ is provided by Article 211(6) of UNCLOS which provides that a coastal State may, where existing international rules are inadequate and subject to the approval by the IMO, establish an area within its EEZ for which it may prescribe laws for the prevention of pollution from vessels 'implementing such international rules and standards or navigational practices as are made applicable, through the [IMO] for special areas', or in certain cases even other national measures approved by the IMO.[28] It should be noted, however, that there seem to be no cases of 'specially protected areas' established solely under the complicated provisions of Article 211(6) of UNCLOS. A better option in the Adriatic and Mediterranean seems to include, as discussed in this work, the designation of one or more PSSA[29] and/or SPAMI, based on relevant IMO Guidelines[30] and/or on the relevant provisions of the Biodiversity Protocol to the Barcelona Convention.[31] Reference should, however, be made to the fact that neither the designation nor the implementation of the regime of a potential PSSA or that of a SPAMI is directly dependent upon the extension of coastal State jurisdiction, therefore upon the proclamation of an EEZ or *sui generis* zone of jurisdiction.[32]

Notwithstanding the above, and outside the context of 'specially protected areas', worthy of mention are the enforcement powers provided to the coastal State by Article 220 of UNCLOS in cases where there is 'serious damage or threat of serious damage' to the marine environment by a vessel navigating in the coastal States' EEZ (or alternatively ZEP). Such powers may include measures such as 'physical inspection' and ultimately the 'institution of proceedings' and/or 'detention' of such violating vessel.[33] Reference should be furthermore made to the second paragraph of Article 111 of UNCLOS which provides:

> The right of hot pursuit shall apply *mutatis mutandis* to violations in the exclusive economic zone ..., of the laws and regulations of the coastal State

---

26 See Arts 210(5) and 216 of UNCLOS.
27 See Art. 210(5) of UNCLOS, and Ruiz, op. cit., p. 20.
28 See R. Churchill and V. Lowe, *The Law of the Sea*, 3rd edn, Manchester: Manchester University Press, 1999, p. 395.
29 See the discussion in section 5.5.
30 Ibid.
31 See the discussion on the Biodiversity Protocol in section 5.1.3.1.
32 Ibid.
33 See Art. 220 of UNCLOS, paras 3–6.

applicable in accordance with this Convention to the exclusive economic zone or the continental shelf ....

It follows therefore that 'hot pursuit' may be in such cases commenced also within an EEZ or ZEP for relevant violations within such zones, and may be continued without interruption outside such zone.[34] Reference should also be made to the fact that the extension of jurisdiction by an EU Member State (e.g. Italy) automatically entails the extension of the EU legal order in that part of the Sea,[35] which seems to be particularly relevant for current and future EU Member States in the Adriatic.[36]

Far from unimportant is also the fact that the various international conventions regulating liability and compensation for oil and HNS pollution damage (e.g. 1992 CLC and FUND, 2003 Supplementary Fund Protocol, Bunkers Convention, the HNS and 2010 HNS Conventions)[37] are, or will be after their entry into force (e.g. 2010 HNS), applicable not only to pollution damage caused within the territory or territorial sea of a contracting State, but also to pollution damage which occurs:

> ... in the exclusive economic zone of a contracting State, established [proclaimed] in accordance with international law, *or, if a contracting State has not established such zone, in an area beyond and adjacent to the territorial sea of that State determined by that State in accordance with international law and extending not more than 200 nautical miles from the baselines from which the breadth of its territorial sea is measures.*[38]

A Mediterranean ZEP in this regard seems to be a clear example of an 'area beyond and adjacent to the territorial sea' mentioned in the second part of the previous paragraph. Noteworthy is the fact that the geographical scope of application of the various international conventions, which directly or indirectly

---

34 See in this regard V. Ibler, 'The Importance of the Exclusive Economic Zone as a Non-Resource Zone', in B. Vukas (ed.), *Essays on the New Law of the Sea*, Prinosi za poredbeno proučavanje prava i međunarodno pravo, Vol. 18, No. 21, Zagreb, 1985, p. 118 at 134.

35 See section 3.5.1, and R. Churchill, 'The European Union and the Challenges of Marine Governance: From Sectoral Response to Integrated Policy?' in Vidas and Schei (eds), op. cit., p. 395 at pp. 412–413. The precise extent of such powers depends, however, on the nature of the proclaimed zone (e.g. EEZ, FPZ, ZEP).

36 Adriatic States may in this regard be conveniently divided between EU Member States (Italy, Slovenia and Greece), acceding State (Croatia) candidate States (Montenegro) and potential candidate States (Albania and Bosnia and Herzegovina). See the discussion in section 3.5.

37 For a 'List of State Parties to the relevant CLC and FUND Conventions', see <http://www.iopcfunds.org/about-us/membership/map/>. See also IOPC Funds, 'Montenegro becomes 109th 1992 Fund Member State', 30 November 2012. Available at <http://www.iopcfunds.org/news-events/detail/item/91/>.

38 Emphasis added. Article II(a)(ii) of the 1992 CLC, Art. 3(a)(ii) of the 1992 Fund, Art. 3(a)(ii) of the 2003 Supplementary Fund Protocol, Art. 2(a)(ii) of the Bunkers Convention, and Art. 3(b) of the 1996 and 2010 HNS Convention. See also definition of a 'Convention area' in Art. 1(1) of the Nairobi International Convention on the Removal of Wrecks, 2007.

196 *Extension of Coastal State Jurisdiction in Enclosed or Semi-enclosed Seas*

represent the basis on which victims of oil pollution from Member States can claim compensation for damage caused by spills of persistent and oil bunkers (and HNS), does not cover the traditional high seas. An exception is represented by the cost of preventive measures, which may be undertaken also within the adjacent high seas (e.g. potential EEZs) with the aim of preventing or minimizing damage within the territory or a territorial sea of a State Party.[39] It is therefore submitted that the impact of the extension of coastal State jurisdiction in the Adriatic Sea, particularly when it comes to the protection and preservation of the marine environment, should not be underestimated.

The States parties to the Barcelona Convention impliedly recognized this during their 16th Ordinary Meeting held in Marrakesh in November 2009. The Marrakesh Declaration straightforwardly invites State Parties:

> ... to extend, in accordance with international law, the areas under their jurisdiction ... recalling *that the right to do so can be used to achieve the protection of the marine environment.*[40]

This passage seems to be a confirmation of the belief, among Adriatic and Mediterranean States, that the extension of jurisdiction (e.g. proclamation of EEZs or ZEPs) over the nowadays Mediterranean high seas, may, particularly in the field of the protection and preservation of the marine environment, improve the implementation and/or enforcement not only of the Barcelona System,[41] but as emphasized by Raftopoulos, also of the related '... multiplicity of conventional regimes managing the protection of the environment and sustainable development at interacting regional and global levels ...'.[42]

5.1.2.2 EEZs or ZEPs?

An interesting question is whether the above cited passage from the Marrakesh Declaration promotes the proclamation of full EEZs or just an *in plus stat minus* ZEPs. In this regard it may be stated that the adoption of the 2005 Mediterranean Strategy for Sustainable Development[43] and of the ICZM Protocol[44] confirm the fact that the scope of application of the Barcelona System has been expanding

---

39 Article II(b) of the 1992 CLC, Art. 3(b) of the 1992 Fund, Art. 3(b) of the 2003 Supplementary Fund Protocol, Art. 2(b) of the Bunkers Convention, Art. 3(d) of the 2010 HNS Convention. Nonetheless, the 2010 HNS Convention covers, in addition to pollution damage and cost of preventive measures, also loss of life or personal injury on board or outside the ship (except where this relates to a 'passenger'), and property damage outside the ship. See Arts 1(6)(a) and (b), 4(1) and 3(c) of the 2010 HNS Convention. See also N.A. Martinez Gutiérrez, *Limitation of Liability in International Maritime Conventions: The Relationship between Global Limitation Conventions and Particular Liability Regimes*, London and New York, NY: Routledge, 2011, p. 154.

40 Emphasis added. See UNEP MAP; UNEP (DEPI) MED IG.19/8, Annex I, p. 4, 24 November 2009.

41 See section 5.1.2.3.

42 See Raftopoulos, op. cit., p. 508. An example being the 1992 CBD Convention.

43 See UNEP MAP; UN (DEC)/MED WG. 277/4, Annex 1, 27 June 2005 and UNEP(DEC)/MED IG. 16/7, 8–11 November 2005.

44 See section 5.1.3.5.

from the sole protection of the marine environment towards a holistic sustainable governance of the Mediterranean Sea and its coastal zones. This is evidenced in the Marrakesh Declaration,[45] in the Preamble of which the State Parties to the Barcelona Convention declared themselves to be:

> *Concerned* by the serious threats to the environment that are confronting the Mediterranean, including the *destruction of its biodiversity*, adverse effects on the countryside, coastline and water resources, soil degradation, desertification, coastal erosion, eutrophication, pollution from land-based sources, *negative impact related to the growth of maritime traffic, the over-exploitation of natural resources, the harmful proliferation of algae, or other organism, and the unsustainable exploitation of marine resources.*[46]

The Preamble to the Marrakesh Declaration points therefore to the implied wish of State Parties to extend the scope of application of the Barcelona System to areas not directly addressed (e.g. destruction of biodiversity, negative impact related to the growth of maritime traffic) or not addressed at all (the over-exploitation of natural resources, the harmful proliferation of algae, or other organism, and the unsustainable exploitation of marine resources).[47] The entry into force of the ICZM Protocol in 2011 represents in this regard a revolutionary development, as it advocates the establishment of an integrated coastal zone management regime in the Mediterranean, focused primarily on the management of coastal zones and on its relation with 'coastal waters' (inc. territorial waters) and thus departing from the traditional concept of 'marine environmental protection'.[48] The fact that co-operation in some of the mentioned fields (e.g. in the field of ship safety) has been already addressed at the Adriatic level,[49] seems on the other hand to point at the prospective need for better co-ordination between the regional and sub-regional co-operative arrangements.

The ultimate evidence of a shift towards a holistic sustainable governance of the Mediterranean Sea is provided in the substantive part of the Marrakesh Declaration, by means of which the parties declared that they are resolved to promote better regional environmental governance in the Mediterranean, *inter alia*, by:

> … *Confirming* the need for an integrated approach that guarantees coherence between the various sectoral strategies and takes into consideration their impact on ecosystems;

---

45 See section 5.1.2.1.
46 Emphasis added. Preamble, para. 2.
47 Among other activities not directly covered by the Barcelona System Scovazzi mentioned some activities that may take place in the future, such as carbon sequestration in the sea-bed. See T. Scovazzi, 'The Mediterranean Guidelines for the Determination of Environmental Liability and Compensation: The Negotiations for the Instrument and the Question of Damage that can be Compensated', in A. Von Bogdandy and R. Wolfrum (eds), *Max Planck Yearbook of United Nations Law*, Vol. 13, The Netherlands: Koninklijke Brill, 2009, p. 183 at p. 201.
48 See the discussion on the ICZM Protocol in section 5.1.3.5.
49 See section 5.4.1.

198 *Extension of Coastal State Jurisdiction in Enclosed or Semi-enclosed Seas*

...

Enhancing collaboration with regional fisheries management organisations and others ... *on issues relating to the conservation and sustainable management of the Mediterranean Sea and its resources and to achieve better protection of the most endangered species and their habitats in the Mediterranean.*[50]

The 2009 Marrakesh Declaration seems to additionally point to the fact that, as in the case of the EU,[51] preference may be given by Mediterranean States to 'holistic EEZs' over 'sectoral ZEPs'.[52] It is nonetheless suggested that all mentioned benefits deriving from the extension of coastal State jurisdiction in the environmental field and/or relating to the protection of biodiversity, may be achieved by the coastal State also with the sole proclamation of a 'Mediterranean' ZEP.[53]

5.1.2.3 Compliance with the Barcelona Convention

One of the main defects of the Barcelona system is that it is a 'pick up' system where State Parties choose first of all one of the two versions of the framework Convention and the Protocols which they wish to join. This has resulted in a situation where participation in the Protocols varies – some of the new Protocols took too long to enter into force; some are not yet in force; and to situations where some States are parties to newer drafts, while other remain parties to older versions.[54]

An equally important problem is the non-implementation by certain States of their existing obligations, including obligations from Protocols already in force and binding on such States. This may be due to different reasons (including political reasons),[55] although it is suggested that the main reason is lack of capacity for proper implementation, either human, financial, or both. Furthermore, particularly in the past, the proper implementation of the Convention and its Protocols was difficult to follow, as the information provided in the Reports submitted by State Parties on the basis of Article 26 of the (amended) framework Convention have varied substantially both in form and extent, with certain States not submitting any report at all.[56] Obviously, States were only required to report on Protocols to which they were parties and which entered into force. The non-implementation of existing obligations has been a serious problem felt also in the Adriatic Sea.

---

50 Emphasis added. Cf fn 40.
51 See the discussion in section 3.5 of the recent positions of the EU (Commission) regarding the extension of coastal State jurisdiction in the Mediterranean Sea.
52 See, however, the discussion in section 3.6 (Concluding Remarks).
53 See the discussion in sections 3.3 and 3.6.
54 See section 5.1.2. See also I. Papanicolopulu, 'Tools for the Governance of Regional Seas: A Comparative Study of the Mediterranean and the Caribbean', paper delivered at the 11th Mediterranean Research Meeting Florence and Montecatini Terme, 24–27 March 2010, pp. 7–8.
55 Ibid, p. 20 and Slim and Scovazzi, op. cit. (Part II), p. 73.
56 See UNEP/MAP, 'Report of the Compliance Committee to the 16th Meeting of the Contracting Parties', UNEP (DEPI)/MED IG 19/7, 24 October 2009, p. 3.

Part IX of UNCLOS and the Adriatic Sea 199

A breakthrough in this regard seems to have occurred at the 15th Meeting of the State Parties to the Barcelona Convention held in Almeria in January 2008. At that meeting the State Parties adopted the Procedures and Mechanism on Compliance[57] and set up a Compliance Committee[58] with a view to promote compliance and implementation with the Barcelona Convention and its Protocols. The role of the Compliance Committee representing all State Parties seems to be well thought through and may be decisive in the improvement of the compliance and implementation of the Barcelona System. Taking into account the complexities of the Mediterranean area[59] it is reasonable to agree with the drafters of the *Report of the Compliance Committee to the 16th Meeting of the Contracting Parties* that:

> … It is in fact essential that the Compliance Committee's role should not be seen and experienced by the Contracting parties as a punitive or coercive one, but on the contrary as one of giving advice assistance, if the Committee is to work in a constructive climate of trust and in close cooperation with the Contracting Parties.[60]

One of the three cases in which the Compliance Committee is entitled to act (and ultimately the most important from the standpoint of future implementation of the Convention) is where the 'case of non-compliance may be referred to it by a party which, despite its best efforts, considers that it is not in a position to meet its obligations'.[61] The 'services' of the Compliance Committee may be therefore requested by a considerable number of States, including some Adriatic (particularly non-EU) States. Considering the present and/or future EU perspective of all Adriatic States, it can be suggested that an equally important role with regard to the membership and compliance to the Barcelona System by Adriatic States may be played by the EU, particularly through its accession to a specific protocol within the Barcelona System (e.g. Offshore Protocol).[62]

Nonetheless, it seems possible to envisage that the advisory role of the Compliance Committee may improve compliance with the existing obligations under the Barcelona Convention and represent an additional argument for the ratification of additional Protocols by Mediterranean and Adriatic States, particularly for those with currently less experience and administrative capacity (e.g. Bosnia and Herzegovina and Albania). In the Adriatic context it would be particularly welcomed if Bosnia and Herzegovina, following other Adriatic States,

---

57 Decision IG 17/2. See UNEP (DEPI)/MED IG.17/10, Annex V, 15–18 January 2008, pp. 23–27.
58 Ibid. The Committee comprises seven Members and seven alternate Members, elected by the Meeting of State Parties on the basis of a balanced geographical distribution. Cf fn 56, p. 1.
59 See section 1.1.
60 Cf fn 56, p. 4.
61 The Compliance Committee may also intervene if there is a request by the party affected by the non-compliance or upon the request of the Secretariat. Ibid, p. 1.
62 See the discussion of the Offshore Protocol to the Barcelona Convention in section 5.1.3.4.

200 *Extension of Coastal State Jurisdiction in Enclosed or Semi-enclosed Seas*

ratifies the 1995 amendments to the Barcelona Convention and considers the ratification of the amended and/or new Protocols.[63]

5.1.3 Implementation of the Barcelona System by Adriatic States

The previous section illustrates the fact that the Barcelona system, particularly due to its flexibility, evolving character and linkages to other conventional regimes seems to represent an adequate legal framework for the protection and preservation of the Mediterranean Sea and its coastal zones in general. The purpose of the following discussion is to analyze the level of Adriatic co-operation in relation to particular Protocols, and to determine if and how these Protocols have been implemented in the Adriatic Sea. Special attention is devoted to Protocols or to areas regulated by existing Protocols to the Barcelona Convention which require particular co-operation of Adriatic States in their sub-regional implementation.[64]

5.1.3.1 The Biodiversity Protocol

One of the most important Protocols from the standpoint of this work is the Biodiversity Protocol.[65] This Protocol obliges State Parties to identify activities which have or are likely to have significant adverse impacts on the conservation and sustainable use of biological diversity in the Mediterranean Sea; monitor their effects; and provide for relevant protection measures.[66] The Biodiversity Protocol is different to that adopted to the 'original' Barcelona Convention in 1982,[67] and it replaces the latter in relations between the parties to both Protocols. It has been in force since 1999 and all Adriatic States (with the exception of Bosnia and Herzegovina) and the EU are parties to it.[68] It should be emphasized that the geographical scope of application of the Biodiversity Protocol is not limited any more to internal waters and territorial seas, as was the case with the 1982 Protocol,[69] but includes all maritime waters (including the high seas), the

---

63 See 'Signatures and Ratifications of the Barcelona Convention for the Protection of the Marine Environment and the Coastal Region of the Mediterranean and its Protocols as at 29th November 2012'. Available at <http://www.unepmap.org/index.php?module=content2&catid=001001004>.

64 Due to space restriction, the analysis omits the implementation of the Dumping and the Waste Protocols in the Adriatic Sea. These Protocols, however, prevalently aim to implement at the regional Mediterranean level two global Conventions, i.e. the 1996 Protocol to the 1972 London Convention and the Basel Convention. Particularly the latter has been widely ratified by Adriatic States. See Slim and Scovazzi, op. cit., pp. 43–44 and 92–94. Cf fn 63.

65 See section 3.3.3, and M. Pavliha, '*Mednarodnopravni argumenti v luči prava EU zoper plinske terminale v Tržaškem zalivu*', Podjetje in delo, No. 8, Ljubljana, 2010, section 4.4.

66 See Art. 3(5) of the Protocol, and Raftopoulos, op. cit., p. 521. Emphasis added.

67 Protocol Concerning Mediterranean Specially Protected Areas (in force from 23 March 1986). Among Adriatic States only Bosnia and Herzegovina remains a party to that Protocol.

68 Cf fn 63.

69 Cf fn 67, Art. 2.

sea-bed and subsoil and the terrestrial coastal areas designated by each of the parties, including wetlands.[70]

An important achievement of the Biodiversity Protocol is the establishment of a List of SPAMIs which may contain sites which 'are of importance for conserving the components of biological diversity in the Mediterranean – therefore sites which contain ecosystems specific to the Mediterranean area or the habitats of endangered species; are of special interest at the scientific, aesthetic or educational levels'[71] and which may be located wholly or partially on the high seas.[72] The importance of proclaiming a SPAMI lies also in the fact that within such an area State Parties may adopt and enforce even such protective measures as for example the 'regulation of the passage of ships' and/or 'the regulation or prohibition of fishing, hunting, taking of animals and harvesting of plants or their destruction'.[73] This is particularly noteworthy as in certain cases such protective measures even exceed the competences which a coastal State is entitled to exercise in its EEZ.[74] Reference should also be made to the fact that the regime of a SPAMI may be similar to that of a PSSA and as suggested, it should also preferably work together with a PSSA[75] or with some other IMO-approved measures (e.g. routeing measures, vessel traffic service systems, etc.).[76] Taking into account the geographical and political complexities of both the Mediterranean and Adriatic Seas, it seems in fact perfectly possible to agree with Scovazzi that independently of the applicable legal framework:

> It would be practically impossible to get general acceptance of any measure affecting shipping in an MPA beyond national jurisdiction or in areas where the limits of national sovereignty or jurisdiction have not yet been defined without previous endorsement at the world level within IMO in any forms provided under the relevant IMO instruments (establishment of a PSSA, ship routeing systems, including areas to be avoided, compulsory pilotage schemes, vessel traffic management systems).[77]

---

70 See Art. 2(1). See also Churchill and Lowe, op. cit., p. 393.

71 Article 4.

72 Article 9(2). For a detailed discussion, see T. Scovazzi, 'Note on the establishment of marine protected areas beyond national jurisdiction or in areas where the limits of national sovereignty or jurisdiction have not been defined in the Mediterranean Sea', UNEP(DEPI)/MED WG.359/Inf. 3 rev.1, Tunis: RAC/SPA, 10 June 2011.

73 Article 6(c)(g). See also T. Scovazzi, 'Marine Protected Areas and Navigation', *Il Journadas Internacionales de Seguridad Maritima y Medio Ambiente*, IUEM, 2006, pp. 77–86.

74 See Art. 56 of UNCLOS, and Art. 6 of the Biodiversity Protocol. According to Art. 6(i) '[t]he parties, in conformity with international law and taking into account the characteristics of each specially protected area, shall take ... any other measure aimed at safeguarding ecological and biological processes and the landscape'. See also the 'omnibus' clause in Art. 6(h).

75 See section 5.5. States parties to the Barcelona Convention decided at their 14th Meeting in 2005 '[t]o assess and identify those SPAMIs which are exposed to environmental risks by international shipping activities and could be proposed for designation as PSSAs by the IMO'. See Report of the 14th Ordinary Meeting of the Contracting Parties, Annex III, II.B.2(4), UNEP(DEPI)/MED IG.16/13, Portorož, 2005, p. 22. See also Raftopoulos, op. cit., p. 522.

76 See section 5.4.

77 Scovazzi, 'Note of the establishment of marine protected areas ...', op. cit., pp. 47–48.

202 *Extension of Coastal State Jurisdiction in Enclosed or Semi-enclosed Seas*

That expert additionally opines that in the light of the close link between the protection of the marine environment and the sustainable exploitation of marine living resources, proposals for (tranboundary) SPAMIs affecting also the protection of living resources '... should include a reference to the measures adopted or to be adopted in the future by GFCM, also considering that this institution has already made use of area-based management tools by establishing fisheries restricted areas in order to protect the deep sea sensitive habitats'.[78] From an extensive interpretation of the provisions of the Biodiversity Protocol it would furthermore appear that the coastal State(s) may be entitled within the SPAMI to adopt also some measures regarding the protection of underwater cultural heritage located in that area.[79]

Proposals for the inclusion in the SPAMI List may however be submitted by a State Party alone only 'if the area is situated in *a zone already delimited*, over which *it exercises sovereignty and jurisdiction*'.[80] Alternatively, if the area is located 'partly or wholly on the high seas' or in a disputed area 'where the limits of national sovereignty and jurisdiction have not yet been defined', the proposal has to be submitted by 'the neighbouring parties concerned'.[81] These provisions, particularly if read together with the detailed 'disclaimer' provision embodied in Article 2(2) of the Biodiversity Protocol,[82] seem to provide Adriatic and Mediterranean States with an important practical tool, enabling them to immediately protect areas of particular natural and/or cultural value also in the absence of a delimitation agreement and/or unilateral extension of jurisdiction.

Moreover, as pointed out by Scovazzi, and as confirmed by many recent (unilateral) extension of coastal State jurisdictions discussed in this work, a SPAMI cannot be a 'paper area'. States have an obligation to agree at an early stage and reach consensus on the different measures with regard to planning, management, supervision and monitoring to be included in their (transboundary) SPAMI proposal. These should be later followed by the elaboration of a detailed management plan and by the establishment of a 'management body'.[83] Noteworthy is the fact that once an area is included in the SPAMI list, all State Parties are bound 'to comply with the measures applicable to the SPAMI and not to authorize or undertake any activities that may be contrary to the objectives for which the SPAMI was established'.[84]

---

78 Ibid, p. 48. See also the discussion in section 5.2.

79 See Arts 8(2) and 6(e).

80 Article 9(2)(a).

81 Article 9(2)(b).

82 'Nothing in this Protocol ... shall prejudice the rights, the present or future claims or legal views of any state relating to the law of the sea, in particular, the nature and the extent of maritime areas, the delimitation of maritime areas between states ... as well as the nature and extent of the jurisdiction of the coastal State, the flag State and the port state'. See the discussion in Scovazzi, 'Marine Protected Areas and Navigation', op. cit., pp. 83–84.

83 See the detailed discussion in Scovazzi, 'Note of the establishment of marine protected areas ...', op. cit., Part III, pp. 32–51.

84 Article 8(3) of the Protocol. For a broad analysis of the various problems and suggested solutions with regard to the enforcement of the regime of the SPAMI on the high seas (e.g. against 'Third

Part IX of UNCLOS and the Adriatic Sea 203

For the time being the only SPAMI encompassing areas of high seas is the already discussed 'Mediterranean Sanctuary' in the Ligurian Sea.[85] However, the EU has been recently funding a project implemented by the (UNEP) RAC/SPA[86] which aims to identify areas of 'conservation interest' on the Mediterranean high seas for potential inclusion in the SPAMI List. The first phase of the project was implemented in the period 2008–2009 and was aimed at the identification of 'priority conservation areas' on the Mediterranean high seas, while the second phase undertaken in the period 2010–2012 involves the drafting of presentation reports (proposals) for the areas to be identified as candidates for the SPAMI List.[87] Obviously, as the report may be submitted only by consensus, the drafting of a presentation report and ultimately the presentation of a 'joint' SPAMI proposal for a certain area requires an advanced level of co-operation between the States concerned.

An important outcome of the first part of the project was the compilation of the list of priority conservation areas located (partly or wholly) on the high seas, and likely to include sites that could be candidates for the SPAMI List. It is particularly important that the list includes also the Central and Northern Adriatic as a possible area for the proclamation of a SPAMI.[88] The report makes express reference to the ecological value of the area (biological productivity, importance for life history, importance for threatened species), and to the fact that '... establishing a protected area in this site would require significant marine restoration effort'.

It seems important in this regard that at the Extraordinary Meeting of the Focal Points for SPAs, held in Istambul on 1 June 2010, the Slovenian representative invited all Adriatic States to participate at a conference entitled 'Towards a representative MPAs network in the Adriatic',[89] which was held at the end of October 2010 in Slovenia, *inter alia* with the specific aim to progress towards co-ordinated measures for establishing a SPAMI in this 'high-seas' region.[90] The next steps for Adriatic States seem to be, therefore, to co-operate in the detailed 'geographical identification' of the area to be covered by such SPAMI and the selection of the most appropriate 'protection measures' to be applied within it,[91] taking obviously into account already existing regimes addressing the safety of international navigation[92] and the historical patterns

---

States'), see the discussion of the 'Mediterranean Sanctuary' in section 3.3.3 and Chapter 6 (Conclusions).

85 See section 3.3.3.

86 See <http://www.rac-spa.org/>.

87 UNEP MAP, Report of the Extraordinary Meeting of the Focal Points for SPAs, UNEP (DEPI)/MED WG.348/5, 4 June 2010, p. 4, fn. 30.

88 Ibid. Annex II, Item 5.

89 Cf fn 87, p. 7, para. 52.

90 See 'Workshop's Conclusions'. Available at <http://www.zrsvn.si/dokumenti/73/2/2010/ConclRec_Final_2120.pdf>.

91 See Art. 6 of the Biodiversity Protocol.

92 See section 5.4.1.1.

204 *Extension of Coastal State Jurisdiction in Enclosed or Semi-enclosed Seas*

of local fishermen.[93] An important precedent in this context could be represented by France and Spain which expressed, in 2010, its intention to co-operate in the preparation of a SPAMI proposal for the Gulf of Lions, including the adjacent high-seas area, and by the example of Spain which envisages a similar co-operation with Morocco and Algeria regarding the Alboran Sea.[94] In this respect it would seem that the establishment of such SPAMI may represent a viable alternative to the extension of coastal State jurisdiction and/or to alleviate the difficulties arising from overlapping jurisdictional claims and unsettled maritime boundaries in that area.[95]

5.1.3.2 The Prevention and Emergency Protocol

The Prevention and Emergency Protocol, which replaces between the parties to both Protocols the 'original' 1976 Protocol,[96] has seen specific sub-regional implementation at the Adriatic level. On the basis of both Protocols, the parties undertake to co-operate in cases of pollution of the Mediterranean Sea by oil and other harmful substances and to promote contingency plans and means for combating pollution of the sea.

The difference is, however, that the Prevention and Emergency Protocol which entered into force in 2004, further reinforced such co-operation with reporting obligations and the designation of ports of refuge for ships in distress.[97] In the Adriatic, Croatia, Italy, Montenegro and Slovenia are State Parties to the Prevention and Emergency Protocol, while Albania and Bosnia Herzegovina are still parties to the 'original' 1976 Protocol. Independently of the version of the Protocol, regional co-operation in the Mediterranean has been co-ordinated by the REMPEC,[98] whose tasks, pursuant to the Prevention and Emergency Protocol, are no longer limited to intervention in emergency situations, but also envisage a more general co-operation in the field of protection and preservation of marine pollution, particularly from ship-source pollution. REMPEC is an interesting case of a hybrid international organization. Despite the fact that it has been established within the framework of the Barcelona Convention with the aim to facilitate the implementation of the Prevention and Emergency Protocol, it is administered by IMO and also works closely with the EU.[99] The main goals of REMPEC are to '… assist the Mediterranean coastal States in ratifying, transposing, implementing and enforcing international maritime conventions

---

93 See the discussion in section 4.7.4.
94 Cf fn 87, paras 50–51.
95 See sections 3.3.4–3.3.6. See also the discussion in Chapter 6 (Conclusions).
96 Protocol Concerning Co-operation in Combating Pollution of the Mediterranean Sea by Oil and other Harmful Substances in Cases of Emergency (in force from 12 February 1976).
97 See Slim and Scovazzi, op. cit. (Part I), p. 136, and Pavliha, op. cit., section 4.6.
98 REMPEC is administered by IMO and UNEP and has its headquarters in Malta.
99 REMPEC is for example in charge of the EU-funded SafeMed Projects, which aims at developing Euro-Mediterranean co-operation in the field of maritime safety and security, prevention of pollution from ships and marine environmental issues particularly by providing technical advice and support to the non-EU Mediterranean countries.

related to the prevention of, preparedness for and response to marine pollution from ships'.[100] As such, it represents a formidable link between IMO and the Barcelona System, or in other words between a global and regional governance regime relating to ship source pollution. As pointed out by Raftopolous:

> The contextualising effect of the [Prevention and Emergency] Protocol, does not, in any way, 'regionalise' the substance of the relevant global conventional regimes governing vessel-source pollution; instead it 'regionalises' their implementation and enforcement in the framework of the Barcelona Convention System.[101]

An important landmark in this process is represented by the adoption in 2005 of a Regional Strategy for Prevention of and Response to Marine Pollution from Ships, prepared by REMPEC and adopted at the 14th Meeting of Contracting Parties to the Barcelona Convention in Portorož (Slovenia).[102] The Strategy was adopted for a period of ten year and it stipulates, although in rather declaratory language, the main implementation goals and related commitments of the contracting States, together with a detailed timetable. Not surprisingly, the first specific objective of the Regional Strategy is the ratification, transposition and full compliance with the relevant (IMO) conventions with a specific emphasis on the MARPOL Convention.[103] In the context of our discussion it is particularly noteworthy that the mentioned (regional) Strategy calls upon member States to the Barcelona Convention to:

> ... establish, when and where possible, and without prejudice to the sovereign right of the States, areas under their jurisdiction *enabling the implementation of the MARPOL Convention in term of prosecution of offenders*. Such areas can be developed on a regional or sub-regional basis, in a coordinated way and in compliance with international law as defined by UNCLOS.[104]

It is asserted that examples of such areas could be both the EEZ and the *sui generis* Mediterranean ZEP, established on the basis of UNCLOS.

A noteworthy 'sub-regional' implementation of the Prevention and Emergency Protocol occurred in 2005 with the conclusion by Italy, Slovenia and Croatia of the Agreement on the Sub-Regional Contingency Plan for Prevention of, Preparedness for, and Response to Major Marine Pollution Incidents in the

---

100 See <http://www.rempec.org>.
101 See Raftopoulos, op. cit., p. 511.
102 UNEP(DEC)/MED IG. 16/10, 30 September 2005. The Regional Strategy was prepared and endorsed by the 7th Meeting of REMPEC's Focal Points (REMPEC/WG.26/9/2).
103 Ibid, Annex 1, p. 1.
104 Emphasis added. Ibid, section 4.7.(d), p. 11. See also A. Khee-Jin Tan, 'The EU Ship-Source Pollution Directive and Recent Expansion of Coastal State Jurisdiction', in D. Vidas (ed.), *Law, Technology and Science for Oceans in Globalisation: IUU Fishing, Oil Pollution, Bioprospecting, Outer Continental Shelf*, Leiden and Boston, MA: Martinus Nijhoff Publishers, 2010, p. 291 at pp. 296–300.

206 Extension of Coastal State Jurisdiction in Enclosed or Semi-enclosed Seas

Adriatic Sea.[105] This Sub-Regional Contingency Plan was adopted within the framework of the Barcelona Convention and in conformity with Article 17 of the Prevention and Emergency Protocol. The reasoning for the adoption of an Adriatic contingency plan is clearly explained in the Preamble to the 2005 Agreement, which provides that the:

> … Mediterranean Sea in general and the Adriatic Sea in particular, *is the major route for transporting of oil and that there is a permanent risk of pollution*, which imposes on the Mediterranean coastal States in the Adriatic sub-region an obligation to constantly develop measures for preventing pollution from ships and to organize and prepare responses to marine pollution incidents, and that such permanent efforts have to be made at national, sub-regional and regional levels.[106]

The approach adopted by the 2005 Agreement is indeed noteworthy. This sub-regional Agreement was initially concluded only by the three most developed Adriatic States (Italy, Slovenia and Croatia), which were at the time already parties to the Prevention and Emergency Protocol and supposedly capable of implementing it. The Agreement however left the door open and envisaged the successive accession by the remaining Adriatic States. Article 4 provides that:

> Other Parties to the Barcelona Convention and its Prevention and Emergency Protocol, in the Adriatic sub-region, may join this Agreement subject to the consent of the Signatories of the Agreement.

Such geographical 'build-up' approach may represent a useful precedent also for the Adriatic implementation of some other Protocols to the Barcelona Convention and co-operation in other fields. There are good perspectives that the 2005 Agreement will be, in the near future, extended to other Adriatic States, particularly to Montenegro and Albania.[107]

5.1.3.3 The Land-Based Protocol

All Adriatic States (with the exception of Bosnia and Herzegovina) are Parties to the amended Land-Based Protocol. The amended Protocol applies to the entire 'Mediterranean Hydrological Basin', including obviously the Adriatic

---

105 Concluded on 9 November 2005 in Portorož, Slovenia. See OGRS, No. 61/2008, 16 June 2008.
106 Emphasis added.
107 Section 17 of the 2010 Ancona Declaration adopted at the 12th Adriatic and Ionian Council (AII), 5 May 2010:

> … encourage the application of the criteria foreseen by the 'Sub-Regional Contingency Plan for Prevention of, Preparedness for, and Response to Major Marine Pollution Incidents in the Adriatic Sea' by all Participating [Adriatic] States ….

See also section 5.4.1.

Part IX of UNCLOS and the Adriatic Sea 207

Hydrological Basin. This brings along an accentuated duty of co-operation regarding the environmental protection of the Adriatic coastal zones with particular emphasis on the protection of waterways, estuaries and/or ground water draining the Adriatic Sea.

One of the most important requirements of the amended Land-Based Protocol is embodied in Article 5, according to which, States with the aim to eliminate 'land-based' pollution:

> ... shall elaborate and implement, individually and jointly, as appropriate, national and regional action plans and programmes, containing measures and timetables for their implementation.

Such regional plans, which have to be adopted at the meeting of State Parties,[108] were adopted for the first time in 2009 (e.g. in the field of reduction of BOD2 from urban waste).[109] The adoption of the mentioned measures was based on Article 15 of the Land Based Protocol, which provides that specific emphasis when preparing 'short and long-term regional plans and programmes, containing measures and timetables for their implementation' should be placed on the phasing out of inputs and substances (from land-based sources) that are 'toxic, persistent and liable to bioacumulate'.

Although a comprehensive discussion of the Land Based Protocol is beyond the scope of this work, it is nonetheless suggested, also due to the importance of this source of pollution, that Adriatic States should not be satisfied with the 'lowest Mediterranean common denominator approach', but instead they should endeavour to co-operate in the preparation of specific sub-regional plans and programmes which should either contain 'stricter provisions' or require the 'phasing out' of inputs of certain substances for which no agreement could be reached on the regional Mediterranean level.

It is asserted again that a precious guidance and lowest common denominator should, taking into account the present or future EU perspective of all Adriatic States, be represented by applicable EU standards related to emissions or water quality. The central role has been played by the Water Framework Directive[110] adopted in 2000. Noteworthy is the fact that the 2000 Directive applies not only to fresh water, but also to coastal waters (internal waters or territorial seas), up to one nmi seaward, measured from the baseline.[111] This Directive, similarly to the Land Based Protocol, requires member States to manage water resources and

---

108 See Art. 15.
109 See Slim and Scovazzi, op. cit. (Part II), p. 17.
110 Directive 2000/60/EC of the European Parliament and of the Council of 23 October 2000 establishing a framework for Community action in the field of water policy, OJ L327, 22 December 2000, p. 1.
111 See definition of 'coastal water' in Art. 2(7). It should be noted, however, that since the mid-1970s, the EU has adopted various directives related to emissions of various kinds including dangerous substances, titanium dioxide, urban waste water, nitrates and waste from industrial installations. Some of these have been repealed as a result of the adoption of the Water Framework Directive. See Churchill, op. cit., pp. 410–411.

208 *Extension of Coastal State Jurisdiction in Enclosed or Semi-enclosed Seas*

control emissions, based where appropriate on a 'river basin principle'. Member States, including Adriatic ones (Italy, Slovenia), have been required to adopt programmes with measures and specific targets to be achieved in the period 2009–2015.[112]

Reference should also be made to the fact that the Water Framework Directive provides a direct link to other 'relevant international agreements'. The measures envisaged by the Directive should in fact contribute, among others, to:

> … achieving the *objectives of relevant international agreements*, including those which *aim to prevent and eliminate pollution of the marine environment* … with the ultimate aim of achieving concentrations in the marine environment near background values for naturally occurring substances and close to zero for man-made synthetic substances.[113]

In this regard a relevant question could be whether there is a need for an additional set of EU legislation between a regional treaty to which both the EU and the majority of its Member States are State Parties (e.g. Land Based Protocol), and the legislations of EU Member States. It would seem possible to endorse Churchill's view that the benefits of such an action may be primarily the imposition by the EU of higher standards than those incorporated in a regional treaty (e.g. Land-Based Protocol). Additionally, the EU can enforce pollution standards more effectively *vis-à-vis* both Member States and individuals, if a certain measure forms part of the EU *acquis*.[114] It may be accordingly concluded that the effective application of the provisions of the Land Based Protocol and/or the implementation of relevant EU standards over the entire Adriatic Sea basin (whichever is the higher), should represent the minimum criteria to be pursued at the sub-regional (Adriatic) level.

5.1.3.4 The Offshore Protocol

Another area regulated by a separate Protocol to the Barcelona Convention but which seems to require specific Adriatic sub-regional co-operation is the prevention of pollution resulting from exploration and exploitation of the continental shelf and the sea-bed and its subsoil. This is regulated by the Offshore Protocol. The Offshore Protocol entered into force on 24 March 2011, but it has not been ratified by the EU nor by its Member States, with the

---

112 See Commission Staff Working Documents, Member State: Slovenia and Member State: Italy; River Basin Management Plans (17/30 and 27/30), Accompanying the document Report from the Commission to the European Parliament and the Council on the Implementation of the Water Framework Directive (2000/60/EC), River Basin Management Plans, COM(2012)670 final, Brussels, 14 November 2012. For more information, see <http://ec.europa.eu/environment/water/participation/map_mc/map.htm>.
113 Article 1(e).
114 See Churchill, op. cit., p. 411.

exception of Cyprus.[115] Among the Adriatic States only Albania has ratified it so far.[116]

It is interesting to note that despite past declared opposition by the EU and some of its Member States (France),[117] the European Commission has recently prepared a proposal on the accession of the EU to the Offshore Protocol, which may after its eventual adoption, pave the way to the subsequent accession of Mediterranean EU Member States (Italy, Greece, France, Slovenia, Malta) and other (including Adriatic) States to the Protocol.[118] It should not come as a surprise that these legislative and policy actions at EU level have been triggered by the tremendous consequences of the Deepwater Horizon accident which occurred in 2010 in the Gulf of Mexico area.[119]

Reference should be made to the fact that the Offshore Protocol is a comprehensive document covering areas such as licensing of operators, contingency planning, mutual assistance in cases of emergency, transboundary pollution and monitoring within the entire Mediterranean Sea, including the continental shelf.[120] It seems therefore surprising, that the most criticized provision of the Offshore Protocol has been the 'channelling of liability' on operators and the requirement for them to 'have and maintain insurance cover or other financial security in order to ensure compensation for damages caused by the activities covered by the Protocol'.[121] As this provision reflects one of the basic principles of contemporary environmental law, (the 'polluter pays principle'), it is peculiar that the delegations of the EU and France at the time of the adoption of the Offshore Protocol expressed a 'reservation pending consideration' centred exactly on Article 27(2) of the Protocol imposing those two requirements upon operators.[122] No doubt Scovazzi was right when he claimed that such a 'lowest-common-denominator' attitude by the EU does not help in the protection and preservation of the Mediterranean and Adriatic marine environment.[123]

---

115 Cf fn 63. Member States to the Protocol include (as per 29 November 2012) Albania, Cyprus, Libya, Morocco, Syria and Tunisia.

116 Ibid.

117 See Scovazzi, 'The 2008 Mediterranean Protocol ...', op. cit., p. 168.

118 European Commission, 'Proposal for a Council Decision on the accession of the European Union to the Protocol for the Protection of the Mediterranean Sea against pollution resulting from exploration and exploitation of the continental shelf and the sea-bed and its subsoil', 27 October 2011. It is expected that the EU will accede to the Offshore Protocol in 2013.

119 Following the Deep Water Horizon accident the EU Commission adopted a Communication 'Facing the challenge of the safety of offshore oil and gas activities' COM(2010)560 final, Brussels, 12 October 2010. The 2010 Directive calls also upon the 're-launching, in close cooperation with the Member States concerned the process toward bringing into force the Protocol combating pollution from offshore activities in the Mediterranean'. Section 5.1.

120 Article 2 (Geographical coverage).

121 Article 27(2).

122 See Scovazzi, 'The 2008 Mediterranean Protocol ...', op. cit., p. 168.

123 Scovazzi questioned: 'Would it not be better if the European Community had remained absent from a negotiation rather than distinguishing itself for taking such poor positions?', ibid, pp. 168–169.

210 *Extension of Coastal State Jurisdiction in Enclosed or Semi-enclosed Seas*

Particularly the recent 'environmental tragedy' in the Gulf of Mexico seems to point at the pressing need for Adriatic States to further regulate (stringent safety requirements) and monitor the operators exploiting the Adriatic continental shelf. In order to protect the potential victims of oil pollution deriving from offshore drilling in the Adriatic (including for example the vital tourism sector), it would seem imperative for all Adriatic States to channel the liability on operators and particularly to ensure that they have adequate insurance cover.

Due to the geographical characteristics of the Northern and Central Adriatic and the Mediterranean in general, it is almost certain that even an incident of much lower proportions than the one experienced in the Gulf of Mexico would have a devastating effect on the Adriatic marine environment and its coastal zones, and would most likely affect the territories and/or zones of jurisdiction of more than one Adriatic State.[124] It is therefore suggested that Adriatic States should ratify the Offshore Protocol and endeavour to co-operate in the implementation of its provisions, with a special emphasis on Article 27(2) regulating liability and compensation.

A particularly important development within the framework of the Barcelona System in the field of liability and compensation has been the adoption at the 15th Meeting of the State Parties to the Barcelona Convention in 2008 of the Guidelines for the Determination of Liability and Compensation for Damage Resulting from Pollution of the Marine Environment in the Mediterranean Sea Area.[125] The latter were adopted as a first-step in the implementation of Article 16 of the Barcelona Convention according to which:

> The Contracting Parties undertake to cooperate in the formulation and adoption of appropriate rules and procedures for the determination of liability and compensation for damage resulting from the pollution of the marine environment in the Mediterranean Sea Area.

Such Guidelines are obviously not mandatory for State Parties. However, as pointed out by Guideline A, paragraph 3:

> While not having a legally binding character *per se,* these Guidelines are intended to strengthen cooperation among the Contracting Parties for the development of a regime of liability and compensation for damage resulting

---

124 See the 'Recommendations by the IUCN Mediterranean Sea Expert Group concerning the Protocol for the Protection of the Mediterranean Sea Against Pollution Resulting from Exploration and Exploitation of the Continental Shelf and the Seabed and its Subsoil', Procida/Naples, 1 October 2010. The experts expressed themselves '[c]onscious that such accident [as the Deep Water Horizon accident] could have irreversible and adverse consequences for the fragile ecosystem and biodiversity of the Mediterranean Sea' and '[w]orried about the adverse transboundary consequences of a similar accident in the Mediterranean Sea. On that occasion they urged all Mediterranean States who have not done so, including the EU, to consider ratifying the Offshore Protocol. Copy on file with the author.

125 UNEP(DEPI)/MED.IG.17/10, 18 January 2008, p. 133.

Part IX of UNCLOS and the Adriatic Sea 211

from pollution of the marine environment in the Mediterranean Sea Area *and to facilitate the adoption by the Contracting Parties of relevant legislation.*

The Parties opted for a soft-law instrument, therefore, for the voluntary unification of their provision in the field of liability and compensation through the incorporation into their national legislation of a set of provisions for damage resulting from pollution of the Mediterranean, based as much as possible on the provisions of the Guidelines. The latter are of general nature and may be applied to all areas of marine pollution covered by the Barcelona System, with the exception of those which have been already regulated at the international level (e.g. by the CLC and FUNDS Conventions, the Bunkers Convention, HNS, etc.).[126] It should be noted that liability for damage covered by the Guidelines, which covers also environmental damage,[127] attaches to the operator. The liability of the latter is strict,[128] although States may establish limits of liability on the basis of international treaties or relevant domestic legislation. The parties to the Barcelona Convention for the time being could not however agree to the inclusion in the Guidelines of a set of provisions regarding the requirement of a compulsory insurance,[129] nor on the establishment of a 'Mediterranean Compensation Fund',[130] but instead left this question open for the future.

As the majority of Adriatic States have joined, or are expected to join in the near future the existing conventions regulating the liability and compensation for accidental ship source pollution (e.g. the 1992 CLC and Fund Conventions, the Supplementary Fund Protocol, the Bunkers Convention, the 2010 HNS)[131] it follows that the regulation of liability and compensation for damage resulting from 'offshore activities'[132] represents a missing link in the 'International Compensation System for Oil Pollution Damage' in the Adriatic Sea. It seems therefore advisable for Adriatic States to endeavour to co-operate in the drafting of a unified set of provisions channelling the liability for such types of pollution on the operator (strict liability)[133] and providing furthermore for exceptions and limits of liability and the requirement for compulsory insurance on offshore operators exploiting the Adriatic sea-bed and subsoil. The need for such co-operation seems to be accentuated by the recent entry into operation of some new gas platforms in the Adriatic Sea exploiting 'transboundary

---

126 See Scovazzi, 'The Mediterranean Guidelines ...', op. cit., p. 17.
127 'For the purposes of these Guidelines "environmental damage" means a [measurable] adverse change in a natural or biological resource or [measurable] impairment of a natural or biological resource service which may occur directly or indirectly'. (Guideline D9).
128 See Pavliha and Grbec, op. cit., pp. 312–313.
129 According to Guideline K, para. 18: 'The Contracting Parties, after a period of five years from the adoption of these Guidelines, may, on the basis of an assessment of the products available on the insurance market, envisage the establishment of a compulsory insurance regime'. Note the difference with Art. 27(2) of the 1994 Offshore Protocol.
130 Guideline L, para. 29.
131 See Slim and Scovazzi, op. cit. (Part I), pp. 110–111, 115–116.
132 See Art. 208 of UNCLOS.
133 See Guidelines F and G.

212   *Extension of Coastal State Jurisdiction in Enclosed or Semi-enclosed Seas*

fields', i.e. fields straddling the continental shelf of two Adriatic States (e.g. Italy-Croatia).[134]

In this context, considering the EU dimension of all Adriatic States, the publication by the European Commission in October 2011 of a Proposal by the Commission for a Regulation on safety of offshore oil and gas prospecting, exploration and production activities is of great importance.[135] This proposal may, if finally endorsed by EU legislators, provide at least a partial solution to EU member States with regard to the (strict) liability of operators of offshore operations, and with regard to related payment of compensation. It is suggested that the solutions envisaged by the proposed Regulation may, after entry into force, represent an important guidance and/or policy signal to other Adriatic and Mediterranean States, particularly to those aspiring to join the EU in a not to distant future. Noteworthy is that this legislative proposal (Regulation) was issued by the Commission simultaneously with the proposal for the accession of the EU to the Offshore Protocol to the Barcelona Convention. It may be also clearly noted from the explanatory notes attached to the two proposals, that the forthcoming EU Regulation has been meant to complement, and in certain cases implement in practice (e.g. strict liability of operators) the relevant provisions of the Off-Shore Protocol.[136]

It may be asserted that one of the main improvements of the proposed Regulation will, after its eventual entry into force, be the extension of the geographical scope of application of the EU Environmental Liability Directive,[137] from coastal waters and territorial sea as is currently the case, to all marine waters under the jurisdiction of member States.[138] This directive already provides the strict liability of the operator for damage arising out from oil and gas activities which causes or may cause significant environmental damage to protected species and natural habitats and for related payment of compensation. Despite the fact that the discussed extension of the geographical scope of application of the Environmental Liability Directive has met with resistance by industry and insurers, it is hoped that the proposed Regulation and related amendments to the Directive will enter into force shortly.[139]

---

134 See Rigzone; 'Eni Starts Up Gas Production in Adriatic Sea', 7 April 2010. Available at <http://www.rigzone.com/news/article.asp?a_id=90663>.

135 See European Commission, 'Proposal for a Regulation of the European Parliament and of the Council on safety of offshore oil and gas prospecting, exploration and production activities', COM(2011)688 final, 2011/0309(COD), Brussels, 27 October 2011.

136 Cf fn 118, section 14.

137 Directive 2004/35/CE of the European Parliament and of the Council of 21 April 2004 on environmental liability with regard to the prevention and remedying of environmental damage, OJ EU L 143, 30 April 2004, p. 56

138 Cf fn 135. Article 37 replaces the definition in Art. 2(1)(b) of the Environmental Liability Directive and defines 'water damage' as including damage that significantly adversely affects: '(ii) the environmental status of the marine waters concerned, as defined in Directive 2008/56/EC [Marine Strategy Directive] [...]'. See Environmental Liability Directive, p. 56.

139 An indication in this direction could be the adoption by the EU Commission of 'Commission Decision of 19 January 2012 on setting up of the European Union Offshore Oil and Gas Authorities Group', which should *inter alia* 'facilitate the transfer of knowledge among stakeholders

Reference should be also made to the fact that the contracting States to the Barcelona Convention, including all Adriatic States, adopted at its 17th Meeting in February 2012, a Decision which calls upon contracting States to ratify the Offshore Protocol as soon as possible, and preferably before the next annual meeting. The contracting States requested the Co-ordinating Unit (MAP) to prepare an Action Plan for a ten-year period, stating the main objectives, key activities, priorities, timeframe and resources needed for the effective implementation of the Offshore Protocol in the Mediterranean Sea.[140]

Despite these developments, it is nonetheless suggested that a set of provisions (model law), based primarily on the '2008 Guidelines' and relevant EU standards, could be elaborated within the framework of Adriatic co-operation and simultaneously included in the domestic legislation of Adriatic States. If this were to prove too ambitious, then a 'build-up' approach, similar to that of the 2005 Sub-Regional Contingency Plan[141] with, for example Italy, Slovenia and Croatia taking the lead, and other Adriatic States following in the near future, could be envisaged.

5.1.3.5 The ICZM Protocol

The most recent Protocol to the Barcelona Convention is the ICZM Protocol, adopted in 2008, which entered into force on 24 March 2011.[142] This Protocol represents an important break-through in the evolution of the Barcelona system. Unlike other Protocols, the ICZM Protocol addresses primarily the management and/or sustainable development of coastal zones and its interface with adjacent coastal waters and also aims to mitigate the present and future effects of climate change.[143] The maritime and land part are accordingly treated as a single entity although the particularities of both the 'landward and seaward' side are taken into account. Article 2(g) explains 'integrated coastal management':

> ... as a dynamic process for the sustainable management and use of coastal zones, taking into account at the same time the fragility of coastal ecosystems and landscapes, the diversity of activities and uses, their intereactions, the maritime orientations of certain activities and uses, and their impact on both the marine and land parts.

---

and assist in the production of formal guidelines relating to best practices'. See OJ EU C 18, 21 January 2012, p. 8.

140 UNEP/MAP, 'Report of the 17th ordinary meeting of the contracting parties to the Convention for the protection of the marine environment and the coastal region of the Mediterranean and its protocols', Decision IG 20/12, UNEP(DEPI)/MED IG.20/8, 14 February 2012.

141 See section 5.1.3.2.

142 Cf fn 63. Contracting States include (as per 29 November 2012) Albania, the EU, France, Montenegro, Morocco, Slovenia, Spain, Syria. Croatia ratified the ICZM Protocol on 12 October 2012.

143 See Art. 5(e) of the 2008 ICZM Protocol.

ICZM, therefore, is not to be understood exclusively as an instrument of environmental governance, since natural, socio-economic and cultural elements should also be taken into account in an integrated manner.[144] Its should be achieved primarily through the adoption of policies, strategies, plans and programmes, with an active involvement of all relevant stakeholders, on national, local and (sub) regional levels.

The ICZM Protocol is therefore an upgrade of the existing Protocols to the Barcelona Convention as it enters into fields such as 'land use strategies, plans and programmes covering urban development', set-back zones, co-ordination of economic activities both on sea and on land, as well as other sectoral policies. It balances allocations of use, whereby priority should be given to public services and activities requiring sea proximity.[145] The flexible geographical scope of application of the Protocol is regulated by Article 3, which provides that:

> The seaward limit of the coastal zone is the external limit of the territorial sea and the landward limit of the coastal zone is the limit of the competent coastal units as defined by parties.

A State Party therefore has the discretion to opt for different limits if certain conditions are fulfilled.[146] Consequently the geographical scope of application of the Protocol is limited to areas of sovereignty (internal waters, territorial sea and/or coastal territory) and not to zones of sovereign rights and jurisdiction (e.g. EEZ, EFZ, ZEPs, etc). These may be explained firstly by highlighting the emphasis that the Protocol and ICZM in general give to the sea–land interface. Additionally, reference should be made to the different types of rights that the coastal State is entitled to exercise within its territory and territorial sea (sovereignty), in comparison to zones of sovereign rights and jurisdictions. The ICZM Protocol is currently in force in all Adriatic States, with the exception of Italy and the EU.[147]

From the standpoint of potential Adriatic co-operation the provisions of Articles 17 and 18 of the ICZM Protocol seem particularly important. Article 17 requires the Parties to the Protocol to 'elaborate' on a 'common regional framework for integrated coastal zone management in the Mediterranean'.[148] Article 18 in turn provides that '[t]he Parties are bound to formulate a national strategy for integrated coastal zone management and coastal implementation

---

144 See Art. 5(1) of the Protocol.
145 See M. Prem, 'MSP and ICZM Implementation in the Mediterranean Sea', ppt. presentation, International Conference on ICZM and MSP, Venice, 4–5 June 2012.
146 Article 3.
147 Cf fn 63.
148 The 'Action Plan for the implementation of the ICZM Protocol for the Mediterranean (2012–2019)' adopted at the 17 Meeting of the Contracting States to the Barcelona Convention (February 2012), envisages as one of its main objectives the preparation of a 'Common Regional Framework for ICZM'. The latter should include 'Regional policies, guidelines and plans necessary for the effective implementation of the Convention, protocols, and strategies, adopted, updated and implemented'. Cf fn 140, Annex II, p. 26.

Part IX of UNCLOS and the Adriatic Sea 215

plans and programmes consistent with the Regional Framework'. Also in this case it would seem advisable for Adriatic States, *inter alia* in the light of the relevant EU guidelines and policies[149] to co-operate in the elaboration of a common sub-regional (Adriatic) framework regarding integrated coastal zone management (ICZM). The preparation by Slovenia, Croatia and Italy of a common framework for the Northern Adriatic could represent an important first step in this direction. Such 'obligation' seems to derive also from Article 1 of the ICZM Protocol which provides that: '... the Parties shall establish a common framework for the integrated management of the Mediterranean coastal zone *and shall take the necessary measures to strengthen regional co-operation for this purpose*'.[150]

The need for such sub-regional co-operation regarding ICZM (and related maritime spatial planning)[151] has been identified during the last couple of years in many *foras*, including within the EU and Adriatic Ionian initiative.[152] Noteworthy is the fact that a case study was recently prepared on behalf of the European Commission which focused on the potential of maritime spatial planning (MSP) in the Mediterranean, with a specific emphasis on (case study of) the Adriatic Sea.[153] When trying to distinguish MSP and ICZM, reference should be made to the fact that MSP aims at a more co-ordinated management of maritime space, and that as such it does not directly address the sea–land interface nor the management of coastal zones, as is the case with ICZM.[154] MSP may accordingly be understood as an integral part or at least as closely interrelated with ICZM. An important difference is, however, that MSP is not limited only to the territorial sea. The main practical difference lies in the fact that while ICZM is focused on the sustainable management of coastal zones (with an emphasis on the coastal zone/sea interface), MSP deals with the sustainable management of maritime areas, including areas where the coastal State exercises sovereign rights and/or jurisdiction (continental shelf, EEZs and/or *sui generis* zones of jurisdiction). It is

---

149 See for example the Recommendation adopted on 30 May 2002 by the European Parliament and the Council concerning the implementation of integrated coastal zone management in Europe, OJ L 148 of 6 June 2002, as well as the Communication from the Commission of 7 June 2007, An Evaluation of Integrated Coastal Zone Management, COM(2007)308 final, particularly para. 3.4. See also Scovazzi, 'The 2008 Mediterranean Protocol ...', op. cit., p. 169, and Pavliha, op. cit., section 4.5.

150 Emphasis added.

151 Hereinafter MSP.

152 See section 5.4.1. See also 'Communication from the Commission 'Roadmap for Maritime Spatial Planning: Achieving Common Principles in the EU', COM(2008)791 final, Brussels, 25 November 2008, and 'Maritime Spatial Planning in the EU   Achievements and Future Development', COM (2010)771 final, Brussels, 17 December 2010.

153 Policy Research Corporation, 'The potential of Maritime Spatial Planning in the Mediterranean Sea. Case Study Report: The Adriatic Sea', Study carried out on behalf of the European Commission, January 2011. Available at <http://ec.europa.eu/maritimeaffairs/documentation/studies/documents/case_study_adriatic_sea_en.pd>.

154 According to the EU Commission Study: 'Maritime Spatial Planning is a process of analysing and allocating parts of three-dimensional marine space (ecosystems) to specific uses, to achieve ecological, economic and social objectives that are usually specified through a political process. It is a tool for improved decision-making and provides a framework for arbitrating between competing human activities and managing their impact on the marine environment....'. Ibid, p. 1.

216 *Extension of Coastal State Jurisdiction in Enclosed or Semi-enclosed Seas*

nonetheless suggested that MSP may be, at least in the Adriatic context, undertaken also on the (nearby) high seas, within areas of 'potential EEZs'.[155]

Noteworthy is the fact that the EU Commission's study identifies the Northern Adriatic, including adjacent areas of high seas, as having 'more potential for the application of MSP than other parts of the Adriatic'. The study interestingly mentions that:

> … [g]iven the crowdedness of the area and the involvement of several countries in the region [Slovenia, Italy and Croatia], *cross-border/international MSP* could be considered a more efficient tool in order to resolve competition in terms of maritime space compared to National Maritime Spatial Planning.

It is suggested that the reasons for such position are due to the narrowness of the Northern Adriatic and/or of the 'border-bay' Gulf of Trieste,[156] where the majority of activities undertaken on a national or local level by one of the bordering States will, in the great majority of cases, have transboundary implications'.[157]

It may be accordingly concluded that the evolving Barcelona system is a prime example of a proper application of Part IX of UNCLOS in enclosed or semi-enclosed seas. An appropriate functioning of the system in the Adriatic requires however specific sub-regional co-operation both in the implementation of the Protocols which are already in force and, even more so in areas covered by (amended or new Protocols) which have not entered into force or have not been widely ratified at the wider Mediterranean level (Offshore, ICZM). In particular, the 2009 Marrakesh Declaration seems to point at co-operation in the field of mitigation and/or adaptation to climate change as another area whereby Mediterranean States should endeavour to co-operate, and where most likely specific sub-regional (Adriatic Sea) co-operation will be required.[158] It is however suggested that such type of co-operation could also be undertaken within the framework of the ICZM Protocol. One of the objectives of integrated coastal management is according to the ICZM Protocol also to 'prevent and/or reduce the effect of natural hazards and in particular of climate change, which can be induced by natural or human activities'.[159]

---

155 See also the discussion in section 3.3.

156 Ibid, pp. 47–48.

157 Ibid, p. 19. Among potential competitive activities in the Northern Adriatic the study makes reference to port operations, intense maritime traffic, fishing, LNG/gas platforms, sand extraction activities and coastal and marine tourism'. Ibid.

158 On 22 October 2010 representatives of 18 Mediterranean States (including Albania, Croatia, Italy and Slovenia) signed in Athens a 'Joint Declaration: On the Establishment of The Mediterranean Climate Change Initiative'. See <http://www.medclimatechangeinitiative.org/content/signing-ceremony-led-deputy-foreign-minister-hellenic-republic-spyros-kouvelis-concluded-18->.

159 See Art. 5(e) in relation to Art. 22 of the ICZM Protocol. For a discussion of potential effects of climate change in the Mediterranean, see M. Markovic, 'Mediterranean Instrument to Combat Climate Change: Protocol on Integrated Coastal Zone Management in the Mediterranean', Barcelona: IEMed, 2010.

5.2 Management and conservation of living resources

Regional institutional co-operation in the field of fisheries in the Mediterranean, which for this specific purpose includes the Black Sea and connecting waters, is primarily undertaken (outside the framework of the EU CFP)[160] through the GFCM. Reference should, however, be made also to the ICCAT which has competence over all tuna and tuna-like species in the Convention area including in the waters of the Mediterranean.[161] As the scope of application of the two regional organizations overlaps (the GFCM being in charge of marine living resources in general), the two organizations adopted a practical *modus vivendi* according to which the GFCM 'confirms' the ICCAT decision regarding 'tuna quotas' and 'tuna-like-fishes' in general.[162] An increasingly important actor in the field of management and conservation of living resources both in the Mediterranean and particularly in the Adriatic Sea is the EU with its CFP.[163] The EU is, however, also a party to the GFCM and participates actively in its deliberations.[164]

The GFCM was established in 1949 under the auspices of the FAO in order to co-ordinate activities related to fisheries management, regulation and research in the Mediterranean, the Black Sea and connected waters. This section, however, focuses primarily on the GFCM Agreement as amended in 1997, which entered into force in 2004.[165] The latter substantially increased the powers of the GFCM and imposed some new obligations on State Parties, including the obligation to contribute to the autonomous budget of the GFCM.[166] It should be noted that all Adriatic States (with the exception of Bosnia and Herzegovina) are parties to the 'new' GFCM Agreement[167] and that its geographical scope of application includes both the high seas and/or areas under national sovereignty and/or

---

160 For the objectives of the EU CFP in the Mediterranean and Adriatic Sea, see 'Communication by the Commission laying down a Community Action Plan for the conservation and sustainable exploitation of fisheries resources in the Mediterranean Sea under the Common Fisheries Policy', COM(2002)535 final, Brussels, 09.10.2002. See also 'Council Regulation (EC) No. 1967/2006 of 21 December 2006 concerning management measures for the sustainable exploitation of fishery resources in the Mediterranean Sea', OJ L 409 of 30.12.2006; corrigendum: OJ L 36 of 8.2.2007.

161 See Slim and Scovazzi, op. cit. (Part II), pp. 31–33.

162 Another agreement whose geographical scope of application includes also the Mediterranean Sea is the 1996 Agreement on the Conservation of Cetaceans of the Black Sea, Mediterranean and Contiguous Atlantic Area (the so-called ACCOBAMS Agreement). Ibid, pp. 26–29.

163 See Ruiz, op. cit., p. 14. Article II(4) of the (consolidated) GFCM Treaty provides:

> A Regional Economic Integration Organization that is a Member of the Commission [GFCM] shall exercise its membership rights at an alternative basis with its Member States that are Members of the Commission in the areas of their respective competences. Whenever a Regional Economic Integration Organization [EU] that is a Member of the Commission exercises its right to vote, its Member States shall not exercise theirs, and conversely.

164 According to Art. 3(1)(d) of the TFEU the EU shall have exclusive competences with regard to 'the conservation of marine biological resources under the common fisheries policy'. See also the discussion in section 3.5.2.1.

165 See Slim and Scovazzi, op. cit. (Part 1), p. 130.

166 Article IX.

167 See Slim and Scovazzi, op. cit. (Part I), pp. 130–131.

218 *Extension of Coastal State Jurisdiction in Enclosed or Semi-enclosed Seas*

jurisdiction.[168] From the legal standpoint, therefore, the actual and/or potential extension of coastal States jurisdiction by Adriatic and Mediterranean States should not affect the competences of the GFCM.

It is particularly important that the GFCM is entitled, by a two-thirds majority, to adopt binding recommendations on conservation and rational measurements of the resources of the Mediterranean Sea, and this may include the adoption of measures relating to fishing methods and gear, minimum size of species to be fished, fishing areas, minimum landing size, fishing seasons, and even the regulation of fishing effort and its allocation among Member States.[169] Of particular importance are the powers of the GFCM regarding the establishment of fisheries restricted areas on the high seas which have been so far primarily adopted with the aim to protect Mediterranean deep sea habitats. A notable example is Recommendation 30/2006/3[170] through which the GFCM, upon the recommendation of its Scientific Advisory Committee, prohibited fishing with towed dredges and bottom trawl nets in three Mediterranean high seas areas: the 'Eratosthemes Seamount Area' (Eastern Mediterranean); the Nile Delta Area cold hydrocarbon seeps; and the deep water coral reefs (referred to as the 'Lophelia reef off Capo Santa Maria di Leuca'). The latter is particularly interesting as it is located in front of the Strait of Otranto in the immediate vicinity of the Adriatic Sea.

There is, however, an 'opt-out' clause for Member States, as the recommendations of the GFCM are binding for a certain Member State only if it does not object to it within 120 days from its notification.[171] Furthermore, Article V(4) of the GFCM Agreement provides that '[i]f objections to a recommendation are made by more than one-third of the Members to the Commission, the other Members shall be relieved forthwith of any obligation to give effect to that recommendation ...'. Taking this into account, coupled with the difficult procedure for the adoption of such measures and the potential problems with their enforcement against third States on the high seas, it is reasonable to agree with Ruiz that:

> ... the further establishment of EEZ or fishing protection zone by coastal States can certainly increase their regulatory and enforcement powers with respect to third states' fishing vessels, and contribute to halt IUU fishing in the Mediterranean.[172]

---

168 The Agreement applies to the 'Region' which includes the entire Mediterranean, Black Sea and connecting waters. See Preamble.

169 See Art. III (b)(i).

170 See GFCM, 'Compendium of Decisions of the GFCM', Scientific Advisory Committee, Twelfth Section, Budva, Montenegro, 25–29 January 2010, pp. 9–10.

171 Article V.3.

172 Ruiz, op. cit., p. 16. See also Art. 56(1)(a) of UNCLOS. It is argued that if fisheries jurisdiction were extended by for example all Adriatic States, many fish stocks would become shared fish stocks, and consequently, their management subject to a duty of co-operation under Art. 63(1) of UNCLOS. See also relevant provisions of the 1994 'Fish Stocks Agreement'.

Part IX of UNCLOS and the Adriatic Sea   219

So far, no resolutions on fisheries-restricted areas have been adopted in the Adriatic Sea.[173] It would seem, however, that a similar effect could be achieved through the proclamation of SPAMIs.[174] The potential overlap and the need for a co-ordinated approach seems to have been recognized also by the GFCM and (UNEP) RAC/SPA. The two institutions in 2008 signed a Memorandum of Understanding through which they agreed to co-operate *inter alia* with regard to the '[d]evelopment and participation in the implementation of the Ecosystem Approach to Fisheries in the Mediterranean Region'.[175]

It is therefore suggested that the establishment of one or more Adriatic cross-border SPAMIs or marine protected areas may foster Adriatic co-operation also in the field of conservation and management of marine living resources, particularly in the Northern Adriatic.

Reference should also be made to the fact that the EU Commission's study on the application of maritime spatial planning in the Adriatic makes reference to the 'fish migration loop' between Italy, Croatia and Slovenia in the Northern Adriatic, and emphasizes that protection by one country alone cannot be effective, given the trans boundary nature of such stocks.[176] The study ultimately points out that maritime spatial planning '… can provide the process that may lead to an agreement between the stakeholders and the participating countries with regard to the establishment of [cross-border] marine protected areas'.[177] In the Adriatic context this seems to require further sub-regional co-ordination and co-operation in stock assessment and management, the establishment of a common database as a source of data for stock assessment, and ultimately the harmonisation of management plans between the relevant States (e.g. Italy, Slovenia and Croatia).[178]

Taking into account the exclusive competences of the EU in this field (currently on behalf of Slovenia, Italy), and the imminent accession of Croatia to the EU, coupled with the candidate status of Montenegro and the potential candidate status of Albania and Bosnia and Herzegovina, it seems that the main role in the conservation and management of the living resources of the Adriatic

---

173 No measures have been adopted specifically for the Adriatic Sea. However, in 2005, the GFCM, with its Recommendation (REC.CM-GFCM/29/2005/1) prohibited the use of towed dredges and trawl nets fisheries at depths beyond 1000 meters. The prohibition applies to the entire Convention area, including the Adriatic Sea. It is noteworthy that the Adriatic Sea is on the basis of Resolution GFCM/33/2009/2 (Establishment of Geographical Sub-Areas in the GFCM Area Amending the Resolution GFCM/31/2007/2), is subdivided into two sub-areas: the Northern and the Southern Adriatic. See Annex 1.

174 See section 5.1.3.1, and Art. 6(g) of the Biodiversity Protocol.

175 See Slim and Scovazzi, op. cit. (Part II), p. 33.

176 According to the study, fish migrate in a loop following the currents in the Northern Adriatic. Reference is made to (past) overfishing in the area and to the fact that '… if important spots along this cross-border loop are protected, these species may regenerate. …'. Cf fn 153 (Research Co-operation), p. 48.

177 Ibid.

178 See European Commission: 'Third Stakeholders' Workshop on Maritime Affairs; Towards a strategy for the Adriatic Ionian Macro-Region', Portorož/Portorose, Slovenia, 17 September 2012 (Round Table on Healthier Marine Environment and Sustainable Fishery).

220   *Extension of Coastal State Jurisdiction in Enclosed or Semi-enclosed Seas*

Sea will be played, in the years to come, by the EU and its CFP. The latter position has been recently reflected also in the EU Communication 'A Maritime Strategy for the Adriatic and Ionian Seas', adopted at the end of November 2012, which identifies as one of the main goals of the Strategy the effective implementation of the principles of the EU CFP in the Adriatic and Ionian Seas.[179] Priority areas to be developed within the 'Adriatic-Ionian Strategy' should according to the 2012 Communication include the achievement of sustainable management of fisheries, including the development of multiannual plans and measures such as MPAs in their wider sense.[180]

Notwithstanding the above, the full application of the EU CFP over the current Adriatic high seas is, and will be also after the (theoretical) membership of all Adriatic States to the EU, still dependent on the extension of coastal State jurisdiction for fisheries purposes (proclamation of EEZ, EFZ) by Adriatic States.[181]

5.3 Co-operation in the field of marine scientific research

The only international organization which has specific competence in the field of marine scientific research in the Mediterranean is the CIESM with its seat in Monaco. It was established in 1919 and under the current statutes (CIESM Agreement), as revised on 8 April 1997, its aim is to promote research in co-operation with other similar national and international organisations, to foster multilateral programmes for the monitoring of the marine environment and to facilitate the exchange of data in the field of oceanography, marine biology, geology and chemistry. The CIESM is, however, involved only in the promotion of 'pure or fundamental scientific research', i.e. research which is in principle not of direct relevance to the exploitation of living and non-living natural resources.[182] Slovenia, Croatia and Italy are parties to CIESM, although there are no obstacles for scientists from non-State Parties to participate in CIESM projects.[183]

It is indeed regrettable that there are no specialised institutional forms of co-operation between Adriatic States, nor a forum for the exchange of data in the field of marine scientific research. It is important to note, however, that such a need was identified and proposals made in this regard at the already discussed (Adriatic-Ionian) stakeholders' meeting in Portorož, held in September 2012 under the auspices of the EU. [184] The Workshop's Conclusions put forward a proposal 'to collect existing data and organise a common (regional) database for

---

179 European Commission, 'Communication from the Commission: A Maritime Strategy for the Adriatic and Ionian Seas', COM(2012)713 final, 30.11.2012, p. 11. See the discussion in section 5.6.

180 Ibid.

181 See section 3.5.1. The CFP nonetheless applies to vessels flying an EU flag and fishing on the (Adriatic) high seas.

182 See Slim and Scovazzi, op. cit. (Part II), pp. 38–39.

183 Ibid, (Part I), p. 126.

184 Cf fn 178 (Round Table on Healthier Marine Environment and Sustainable Fishery).

data on status, impact, pressures and human activities', centred on the Adriatic and Ionian seas.

Nonetheless, reference should be made to the fact that particularly marine scientific institutions from Adriatic States often co-operate in the undertaking of joint scientific programmes. An example has been the ADRIACOMS[185] which builds upon the Italian–Slovenian–Croatian agreement for scientific and technological collaboration in the Adriatic Sea and aimed at establishing an integrated management model for Adriatic and river basins coasts. Partners to the Project included originally the three competent ministries and 19 marine scientific organizations from Croatia, Italy and Slovenia. During its most recent phase (2007–2009), the Project was also expanded to Montenegro.

When it comes to research in the field of fisheries, reference should be made to the increasingly important role of the GFCM. Among its functions there is in fact also the duty 'to encourage, recommend, coordinate and, as appropriate, undertake research and development activities, including cooperative projects in the areas of fisheries and the protection of living marine resources ...'.[186] On the sub-regional, including Adriatic, level the various projects undertaken under the auspices of FAO are particularly important, as for example the COPEMED (Western Mediterranean), the EASTMED (Eastern Mediterranean) and in the Adriatic the ADRIAMED Projects. The latter project has been implemented since 1999 and aims to promote scientific co-operation among Adriatic countries, in line with the (FAO) Code of Conduct for Responsible Fisheries. The Project, which also aims at enlarging the scope of information on the Adriatic Sea related to shared fishery resources, involves all Adriatic States.[187] Nonetheless, as properly pointed out in the 2012 EU Communication 'A Maritime Strategy for the Adriatic and Ionian Seas', there is a need for further scientific co-operation between the region's countries in order to better link scientific research with the needs of fisheries and aquaculture,[188] and ultimately with the needs of a 'holistic' maritime spatial planning and/or ICZM in the Adriatic Sea.[189]

When it comes to the potential benefits of the extension of coastal State jurisdiction in the field of marine scientific research, reference should be made primarily to Article 56(1)(b)(ii) of UNCLOS which provides coastal States with jurisdiction for this purpose. As pointed out by Ruiz:

> ... the [Mediterranean] coastal State will be in a better position to control marine scientific research conducted by Third States when it has declared an EEZ.[190]

---

185 More information available at <http://213.174.143.38/download/adriacosm-0-pdf-13477691.html#>.
186 See Art. III (ii)(e) of the GFCM Agreement.
187 The Project has been funded by the Italian Ministry of Agriculture, Food and Forestry Policies and since 2007 by the European Commission.
188 Cf fn 179, p. 11.
189 See the discussion in sections 5.1.3.5 and 5.4.
190 See Ruiz, op. cit., pp. 24–25.

This is a result of the fact that a coastal State has, in the exercise of its jurisdiction granted by Article 56 of UNCLOS and governed by Part XIII of UNCLOS, the right to regulate, authorize and conduct marine scientific research[191] within its EEZ or relevant *sui generis* zone.[192] Noteworthy is the fact that marine scientific research in the EEZ and on the continental shelf can be conducted only with the consent of the coastal State.[193] Although a coastal State shall 'in normal circumstances' grant its consent for marine scientific research projects by third States or competent international organizations, such a duty is substantially diluted by a list of circumstances, where a coastal State may at its discretion[194] withhold its consent to the conduct of marine scientific projects by other States or international organizations. Such cases include *inter alia* instances where a certain research project is of direct significance to the exploration and exploitation of natural resources, whether living or non-living.[195] This basically means that despite the formal obligation for the coastal State to grant consent, such consent may be withheld if the research is related to the economic exploitation of the EEZ.

It is nonetheless asserted that such exercise of jurisdiction should be exercised by Adriatic coastal States in the spirit of Part IX of UNCLOS while taking into account their obligation of co-operation deriving from Article 123(c) of UNCLOS. It is furthermore suggested that particularly current and future EU Member States may have an interest in extending fully the EU competences on marine scientific research (including policies, programmes, specific funding, etc.)[196] also to their 'potential EEZs'. Nonetheless, EU Programmes in this field should up to the maximum extent possible involve all Adriatic States, and not only EU members and/or formal candidate States.

5.4 Other co-operative arrangements between Adriatic States

Adriatic sub-regional co-operation has in the past been particularly accentuated in the field of protection and preservation of the marine environment. Prior to 1990, however, this had been particularly due to the isolationistic policy of Albania understood as a *de facto* co-operation between Italy and the SFRY.[197]

---

191 Article 246(1) of UNCLOS. See the general discussion in D. Attard, *Exclusive Economic Zone in International Law*, Oxford: Clarendon Press, 1987, pp. 106–117.
192 See for example the discussion of the French and Slovenian ZEP in sections 3.3.2 and 3.3.6.
193 Article 246(2) of UNCLOS.
194 Emphasis added. See also M. Pavliha and N.A. Martínez Gutiérrez, 'Marine Scientific Research and the 1982 United Nations Convention on the Law of the Sea', Ocean and Coastal Law Journal, Vol. 16, No. 1, Maine: University of Maine, School of Law, 2010, p. 115 at 121–123.
195 Article 246 (5)(a) of UNCLOS.
196 See for example Regulation (EU) No. 1255/2011 of the European Parliament and of the Council of 30 November 2011 establishing a Programme to support the further development of an Integrated Maritime Policy, OJ EU, L 321, 5.11.2011, p. 1. See also European Commission, 'Marine Knowledge 2020 from seabed mapping to ocean forecasting (Green Paper)', COM(2012)473 final, Brussels, 29.8.2012.
197 Albania acceded to the Barcelona Convention in 1990. See Slim and Scovazzi, op. cit. (Part I), p. 132.

Part IX of UNCLOS and the Adriatic Sea 223

The two States took an active part in the existing Mediterranean co-operative arrangements which included the Barcelona system, GFCM and CIESM, while specific sub-regional forms of co-operation were primarily aimed at supplementing those already existing at the regional (Mediterranean) level.

An important milestone in the environmental protection of the Adriatic which preceded the adoption of MAP and/or the Barcelona Convention was the conclusion in 1974 of the Italy–SFRY Belgrade Agreement.[198] The latter, however, did not contain specific provisions regarding the protection of the Adriatic marine environment and was more intended as a framework for the identification of various problems and the conclusion of additional agreements in this field.[199] Its main achievement was the establishment of a joint 'Italo–Yugoslav' Commission which did not have decision-making powers and whose goals were primarily to carry out research activities, and to advise the two governments on any question relating to marine pollution. It should be noted that the scope of application of the 1974 Belgrade Agreement extended to all Adriatic waters, including therefore the high seas.[200]

It is, to a certain extent, ironic that the next important document relating to the environmental protection of the Adriatic Sea was signed less than three weeks after the proclamation of independence of Slovenia and Croatia (25 June 1991) and after the breaking up of the war on the territories of the former SFRY. Reference is made here to the Declaration on the Adriatic Sea, signed in Ancona on 13 July 1991.[201] The importance of the 1991 Declaration derives from the fact that it was the first multilateral document aimed at the protection of the Adriatic Sea, signed not just by Italy and the SFRY, but also by Albania, Greece and the European Commission. The adopted document was therefore a political declaration with, however, strong wording and clear commitments. The signatories declared their firm intention to co-operate in the environmental protection of the Adriatic Sea and the preservation of its ecological balance and to undertake joint comprehensive regional programmes in this regard.[202]

The importance given to the close interrelation between the Adriatic and the Ionian can be clearly implied from the participation at the conference and the signature of the Declaration also by Greece. Although the war on the territories of the former SFRY stopped for almost ten years a comprehensive Adriatic multilateral (sub-regional) co-operation, continued during the 1990s between Italy, Slovenia and Croatia within the framework of the Commission for

---

198 OGRI of 22 February 1977. The Agreement entered into force on 20 April 1977.
199 M. Gestri, '*I rapporti di vicinato marittimo tra l'Italia e gli Stati nati dalla dissoluzione della Iugoslavia*', in N. Ronzitti (ed.), *I rapporti di vicinato dell'Italia con Croazia, Serbia-Montenegro e Slovenia*, Rome: Luiss University Press-Giuffrè, 2005, p. 177 at pp. 207–208.
200 See Art. 1.
201 At that time it was disputed whether the SFRY still also represented the Republic of Slovenia and the Republic of Croatia which formally proclaimed independence on 25 June 1991.
202 Scovazzi mentioned that the 'Adriatic Sea Declaration' has been listed as a Treaty by the official Italian publication on Treaties in force. See T. Scovazzi, 'Regional Cooperation in the Field of the Environment', in T. Scovazzi (ed.), *Marine Specially Protected Areas*, The Netherlands: Kluwer Law International, 1999, p. 81 at p. 97.

224 *Extension of Coastal State Jurisdiction in Enclosed or Semi-enclosed Seas*

the protection of the Adriatic Sea and coastal area from pollution, usually referred to as the 'Trilateral Commission'. The latter replaced the mixed Italo–Yugoslav Commission established on the basis of the Belgrade Agreement and achieved substantial results, also due to the work of its sub-commissions first among which was the 'Working Group for environmentally safe-sea traffic'.[203] The latter has been instigated the preparation of important agreements between the three States particularly in the field of safety of navigation and prevention of ship-source pollution, therefore in areas not directly addressed by existing regional co-operative arrangements (The Barcelona System).[204]

The next important milestone in the Adriatic sub-regional co-operation was the launching of the Adriatic–Ionian Initiative (AII)[205] and the signature of the Ancona Declaration in 2000. The latter was adopted at the Conference on Development and Security in the Adriatic and Ionian; held on 19 and 20 May 2000 and signed by all Adriatic States (with the exclusion at that time of Serbia and Montenegro)[206] and the EU. The AII is, however, formally a distinct co-operative arrangement from that of the Trilateral Commission. The Ancona Declaration builds on the structure and content of the (1991) 'Adriatic Sea Declaration' although it is broader in its scope of application. The aim of the Ancona Declaration (and of AII in general) is in fact not only to achieve the protection and preservation of the Adriatic Sea and its ecological balance, but instead:

> … to foster peace and security in the Adriatic and Ionian Region by promoting sustainable economic growth and *environmental protection* and by *exploiting cultural heritage* that the countries in this region share ….[207]

Areas of co-operation include, without prejudice to other areas of co-operation which may be selected in the future, economics, transport and tourism co-operation, sustainable development and protection of the environment, co-operation in the fields of culture, science and education; and co-operation in the fight against illegal activities.[208] If transferred to the maritime context it would seem that the emphasis is placed on the protection and preservation of the marine environment, with additional emphasis on maritime safety and security, and impliedly also to the protection of underwater cultural heritage and the fight against illegal activities.

The second important difference between the two initiatives is represented by the geographical scope of application. The Ancona Declaration is not focused

---

203 See Gestri, op. cit., p. 208.
204 See the discussion in section 5.4.
205 'AII'.
206 Serbia and Montenegro joined the AII in 2002. After the dissolution of the Union in 2006, both Serbia and Montenegro retained their membership.
207 Emphasis added. Preamble, para. 4.
208 Ibid, para. 3.

Part IX of UNCLOS and the Adriatic Sea 225

only on the Adriatic Sea, but on the *Adriatic and Ionian region*.[209] An interesting question is accordingly whether the Ancona Declaration treats the Adriatic and Ionian as a separate marine region and/or sub-region of the wider Mediterranean Sea? It would seem however that the expression 'Adriatic and Ionian region' refers to the overall territories of all the signatories and not specifically to the Adriatic and Ionian seas. This can be implied from Article 1 of the Declaration where emphasis is placed on the Adriatic and Ionian as an 'area of peace, stability and increasing prosperity', while the ultimate answer seems to be provided by the Preamble to the Ancona Declaration according to which the aim of the Declaration is to foster '... synergies, coordination and complementarities between the Adriatic and the Ionian cooperation network launched at the Conference ...'. The aim of the 'Ancona Process' is therefore to better co-ordinate and to foster synergies between two distinct co-operation networks, the Adriatic and Ionian. Such interpretation seems confirmed also in the (2008) Marine Strategy Directive which defines the Adriatic and Ionian as two separate sub-regions of the Mediterranean Sea[210] and seems to be ultimately confirmed also by the concluded agreements within the framework of the AII.

It is also noteworthy that the Ancona Declaration provides an express link to the Barcelona Convention. Article 5 of the Declaration in fact stresses '... the need to take into account the Adriatic and Ionian dimension within the Convention for the Protection of the Mediterranean Sea against pollution ...'. This reinforces the assertion that co-operation undertaken within the framework of AII is not intended to conflict with that directly undertaken within the framework of the Barcelona Convention. Nonetheless, due to the expanding scope of application of the Barcelona system,[211] there seems to be a need for better co-ordination between the two and other co-operative arrangements in the Adriatic (e.g. Trilateral Commission).

5.4.1 Agreements concluded within the AII framework

It is important to emphasize that the majority of the agreements in the maritime field concluded within the framework of the AII, and particularly those from the field of safety of navigation in the Adriatic Sea, were prepared by the Trilateral Commission despite the fact that some were signed on the occasion of the launching of the AII in Ancona in 2000. The common characteristic of such agreements is that they apply either to the Adriatic (e.g. Northern Adriatic) or to the Ionian, and not to the Adriatic and Ionian basin. The goals of the Ancona Declaration have therefore been achieved through a co-ordinated network of bilateral and/or trilateral binding agreements on a certain topic and not, generally

---

209 See the recent proposals regarding the establishment of an 'Adriatic-Ionian' (EU) macro region. Available at <http://www.aii-ps.org/index.php/adriatic-ionian-macroregion>.
210 See Art. 4(2) of the Marine Strategy Directive.
211 See sections 5.1.2.1–5.1.2.2.

226 *Extension of Coastal State Jurisdiction in Enclosed or Semi-enclosed Seas*

speaking, through a single multilateral convention involving all Adriatic States and/or the EU.

Such a build-up approach can be implied also from paragraph 7 of the Preamble, which provides that States build:

> … upon a multifaceted network of bilateral relations that they intend to further strengthen by promoting new bilateral agreements, such as those signed in the framework of the present Conference, which can create a homogeneous, multilateral pattern of cooperation through shared content and objectives ….

The organizational structure of the AII is therefore in many respects similar to that of the Union for the Mediterranean[212] and its predecessor Euro-Mediterranean Partnership (Barcelona Process),[213] with the notable difference that the process is not directly driven by the EU. There are also clear signs that the AII is, after the first decade of its existence, broadening its activities to other areas, of which particularly noteworthy is the protection and preservation of Adriatic underwater cultural heritage.[214] It is nonetheless suggested that the recently adopted Communication of the European Commission on 'A Maritime Strategy for the Adriatic and Ionian Seas'[215] represents additional evidence of the forthcoming leading role of the EU in the field of Adriatic (and Ionian) co-operation.

5.4.1.1 Safety of navigation

Concluded agreements in the field of safety of navigation in the Adriatic may be broadly divided into three groups. The first group relates to the establishment of a joint system of vessel traffic service in the Adriatic Sea. A network of bilateral agreements was concluded in the period 2000–2001 between Italy on one side and Slovenia, Croatia, Albania and (Serbia) Montenegro for the Adriatic and between Italy and Greece regarding the Ionian.[216]

A second group of agreements, based obviously on the successful conclusion of the first group of agreements, related to the establishment of a mandatory ship reporting system in the Adriatic (Adriatic Traffic). A trilateral Memorandum of Understanding was concluded between Italy, Slovenia and Croatia,[217] supplemented by two bilateral agreements concluded between Italy and Albania,

---

212 'UFM'.
213 The UFM was launched (on a French initiative) on 13 July 2008 at the Paris Summit for the Mediterranean as a partnership of 27 EU States and 16 States located in the Southern Mediterranean and Middle East. It upgrades the previously existing Euro-Mediterranean Partnership (Barcelona Process).
214 See section 5.7.
215 Cf fn 179.
216 See Gestri, op. cit., p. 209, fn 117–119.
217 See Memorandum of Understanding between the Government of the Republic of Slovenia, the Government of the Republic of Croatia and the Government of the Italian Republic on Mandatory Ship Reporting System in the Adriatic Sea, OGRS 96/2000, 19 October 2000.

Part IX of UNCLOS and the Adriatic Sea 227

and Italy and (Serbia) Montenegro.[218] In December 2002 the IMO, upon a joint proposal by all Adriatic States, also formally confirmed the 'Adriatic Traffic' with its entry into force as of 1 July 2003.[219] Since then, all oil tankers of 150 gross tonnage and above and all ships exceeding 300 gross tonnage and carrying dangerous or polluting goods as cargo, need to report to the designated Adriatic coastal authorities their entry into the Adriatic, their position at certain points and their departure from the Adriatic Sea.[220] In the elaboration of a comprehensive 'Adriatic system' the Adriatic States opted therefore for a two-tier approach. The first step was a conclusion of a series of bilateral and trilateral binding agreements between themselves, while the second was the submission of a joint proposal to the IMO.

The same approach has been followed with the third group of agreements which relate to the establishment of a common routeing system and traffic separation schemes in the Adriatic. A Memorandum of Understanding has been concluded between Italy, Croatia and Slovenia relating to the Northern Adriatic;[221] coupled with bilateral agreements between Italy and (Serbia) Montenegro and Albania regarding routeing measures in parts of the central and southern Adriatic.[222] Although the agreed 'traffic separation schemes' did not cover the entire Adriatic, in 2003 the Adriatic States concerned jointly proposed to the IMO the adoption (confirmation) of the agreed measures.[223] These measures were then confirmed on 28 May 2004.[224]

It is therefoer important to highlight that since 1 December 2004 there has been in force a system of traffic separation schemes in the Northern Adriatic regulating navigation to and from the ports of Koper (Slovenia) and Trieste and Monfalcone (Italy) crossing the maritime areas of Croatia, Slovenia and Italy (see Figure 5.1).

There seems to be an agreement among users and policymakers alike, that the (Northern) Adriatic is, particularly with regard to maritime safety and prevention of marine pollution, a 'high risk area'. This is not only due to the extremely dense traffic of cargo ships and tankers, but also to the increasing number of yachts and

---

218 See Gestri, op. cit., pp. 210–211, fnn 120–123.
219 Resolution MSC.139(76), Mandatory Ship Reporting Systems, 5 December 2002. See also 'Establishment of a Mandatory Ship Reporting System in the Adriatic Sea known as "ADRIATIC TRAFFIC": Submitted by Albania, Croatia, Italy, Slovenia and Yugoslavia, NAV 47/3/4, 30 March 2001'.
220 Cf fn 217, articles 3.2.1–3.2.3.
221 Memorandum of Understanding between the Government of the Republic of Slovenia, the Government of the Republic of Croatia and the Government of the Italian Republic on the Establishment of a Common Routeing System and Traffic Separation Scheme in the Northern Part of the Northern Adriatic, OGRS No. 96/2000, 19 October 2000.
222 See Gestri, op. cit., p. 210, fnn 123–126.
223 See Albania, Croatia, Italy, Slovenia, (Serbia) Montenegro, 'Establishment of new recommended Traffic Separations Schemes and other new Routeing Measures in the Adriatic Sea', IMO Doc. NAV 49/3/07, 23 March 2003.
224 See IMO, Report of the Maritime Safety Committee on its Seventy-Eight Session, MSC 78/26 of 28 May 2004, p. 86 and Annex 21, and 'New and Amended Traffic Separation Schemes', COLREG.2/Circ. 54 of 28 May 2004.

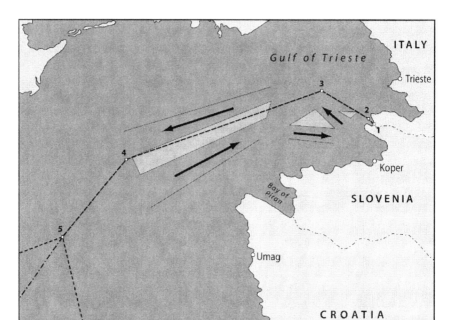

Figure 5.1 Traffic separation schemes in the Northern Adriatic (Port of Koper)

pleasure boats in the area.[225] It may be asserted that further (Northern) Adriatic co-operation in this field should focus on upgrading and further integration of the already existing measures (vessel traffic services, Adriatic Traffic, routing measures). The need for further standardisation and exchange of maritime traffic information between national maritime authorities, ensuring consistency with the applicable EU systems (e.g. SafeSeaNet), has been perceived by stakeholders and policymakers as the next area for which Adriatic (Ionian) co-operation is needed.[226] Proposals have also been echoed for the extension of existing (compulsory) routeing measures applicable to the Northern Adriatic to other parts of the Adriatic Sea.[227] It is suggested that the designation of an 'Adriatic PSSA', endorsed by IMO, would represent an appropriate framework for such upgrading and/or further integration of existing measures relating to ship safety and ship source pollution in the Adriatic Sea.[228]

---

225 Cf fn 178, Conclusions (Round Table on Competitive and Sustainable Transport and a Safer and More Secure Marine Space).
226 Cf fn 178, p. 10. See also European Commission, High level stakeholders conference 'Setting an Agenda for Smart, Sustainable and Inclusive Growth from the Adriatic and Ionian Seas', Zagreb Conclusions, Zagreb, 6 December 2012.
227 See H. Kačić, 'Traffic Separation Schemes in the Adriatic Sea', paper delivered at the roundtable 'EU Maritime Policy and the (Northern) Adriatic', organized by the Maritime Law Association of Slovenia (MLAS), Portorož, Slovenia, 20 May 2011.
228 See general discussion in section 5.5.

Part IX of UNCLOS and the Adriatic Sea 229

5.5 Adriatic PSSA: Added value to the protection of the Adriatic marine environment?

Notwithstanding the Adriatic's 'Special Area' status under Annex I of MARPOL, as part of the wider Mediterranean where all operational discharges of oily waters from ships are prohibited,[229] one of the main problems in the Adriatic Sea is still operational pollution, or in other words 'illegal discharges' from ships. It has been estimated that an annual average of 250 illegal oil spills occurred in the Adriatic in early 2000 and there are indicators that the situation has not substantially improved since then.[230] Additionally, an increasingly important problem in the Adriatic Sea is the occurrence of discharges of ballast waters, particularly from ships having their port of departure outside the Mediterranean. The of ballast waters released in 2003 in the Adriatic ports of Croatia, Italy and Slovenia amounted to 8 million tonnes, although less that 10 per cent of that quantity originated outside the Mediterranean.[231] With the expected increase in maritime traffic in the Adriatic, particularly after the completion of the envisaged new oil and LNG terminals in the Adriatic ports of Vlore, Ploče, Omišalj and Trieste which will open new 'export routes' of (Caspian) oil and gas,[232] it would seem that the quantity of discharged ballast water in the Adriatic Sea, particularly that originating outside the Mediterranean, may increase dramatically.

A logical consolidation of the existing measures in the field of safety of navigation and prevention of ship-source pollution could be the designation of the entire Adriatic waters (by the IMO) as a PSSA. Such course of action has been followed also by many other EU States, including those bordering the semi-enclosed Baltic Sea.[233] The possibility of the 'proclamation' of PSSAs in the Adriatic has already been raised by the '2005 Agreement on the Sub-regional Contingency Plan' with which Slovenia, Croatia and Italy agreed to co-operate in the designation of PSSAs in the area covered by the Plan.[234] It is important to note that the PSSA may be located within or beyond the limits of the territorial sea, and as pointed out by Slim and Scovazzi it '... offers the opportunity to enable the development of common

---

229 Regulations for the Prevention of Pollution by Oil. The entire Mediterranean has also a 'Special Area Status' under Annex V of MARPOL (Regulations for the Prevention of Pollution from Garbage from Ships). Annex VI (Regulations for the Prevention of Air Pollution from Ships) on the other hand allows for the establishment of special emission control areas.

230 See D. Vidas, 'Particularly Sensitive Sea Areas: The Need for Regional Cooperation in the Adriatic Sea', in K. Ott (ed.), *Croatian Accession to the European Union: Institutional Challenges*, Vol. 4, Zagreb: Institute of Public Finance, 2006, p. 347 at pp. 364–365.

231 Ibid.

232 Ibid, pp. 361–363.

233 In 2004 the IMO confirmed a joint proposal by Belgium, France, Ireland, Portugal, Spain and the UK, the *Western European Atlantic Waters* as a PSSA (IMO Doc. MEPC 49/8/1, 11 April 2003). The same occurred in 2005 with the *Baltic Sea area* (with the exception of Russian waters) based on the joint proposal by Denmark, Estonia, Finland, Germany, Latvia, Lithuania, Poland and Sweden (IMO Doc. MEPC 51/8/1, 19 December 2003).

234 See section 5.1.3.2.

230　*Extension of Coastal State Jurisdiction in Enclosed or Semi-enclosed Seas*

jurisdictional and enforcement regimes for environmentally significant marine areas …'.[235]

At this point it may be useful to refer to the definition of a PSSA which, according to Vidas, can be defined as '… a marine area that needs special protection through action by the IMO because of its significance for recognized ecological or socio-economic or scientific reasons, and because it may be vulnerable to damage by international shipping activities'.[236] The three general requirements which are further elaborated in the Revised Guidelines for the Identification and Designation of Particularly Sensitive Sea Areas[237] are, however, not cumulative, as one criteria must be fulfilled. Furthermore, as provided by Article 1.5 of the 2005 PSSA Guidelines:

> Identification and designation of any PSSA and the adoption of any associated protective measures requires consideration of three integral components: *the particular attributes of the proposed area [Adriatic], the vulnerability of such an area to damage by international shipping activities, and the availability of associated protective measures within the competences of IMO to prevent, reduce, or eliminate risks from these shipping activities.*[238]

Therefore, it follows that to the extent approved by the IMO, the PSSA status allows coastal State(s) to enforce specific associated measures (within the competence of IMO), e.g. compulsory reporting systems and/or pilotage, routeing measures, Special Area Status under MARPOL and/or application of discharge restrictions. Taking into account that three of the said protective measures are already in force in the Adriatic (the Special Area Status on the basis of Annexes I and V of MARPOL, the reporting system on the basis of SOLAS (Adriatic Traffic), and a system of routeing measures in the Northern Adriatic on the basis of COLREG), what would be the added value of proclaiming an Adriatic PSSA? It is important to note in this regard that the proposed associated measures may have 'an identified legal basis' also in IMO conventions and/or codes which are not yet in force. A clear example in this regard is represented by the 2004 Ballast Water Convention which, however, is unlikely to enter into force in the near future.[239]

5.5.1 Work undertaken in relation to the proclamation of an Adriatic PSSA

The idea to proclaim an Adriatic PSSA originates from a Croatian proposal and was based on studies carried out in the period 2004–2006. In 2006, a Joint Expert

---

235　See Slim and Scovazzi, op. cit. (Part II), p. 36.
236　Emphasis added. See Vidas, op. cit., p. 349.
237　IMO Assembly Resolution A. 982(24), 1 December 2005, para. 4. Hereinafter, 2005 PSSA Guidelines.
238　Emphasis added.
239　See Slim and Scovazzi, op. cit. (Part I), pp. 120–122.

Part IX of UNCLOS and the Adriatic Sea 231

Group on the PSSA comprising representatives of all Adriatic States (later replaced by the Correspondence Group) was established upon the Croatian initiative and held several meetings including the meetings in Opatija (April 2006) and Portorož (October 2006).[240] According to the prepared draft text of the Proposal[241] the associated protection measures applicable in the Adriatic PSSA would in addition to the strengthening of the already existing measures (e.g. the extension of the existing routeing measures to other parts of the Adriatic) include also some associated protective measures having its identifiable legal basis in the 2004 Ballast Water Convention. That would include the designation of the Adriatic Sea as a No-Ballast-Water in the Adriatic in ships from other seas (including from the Mediterranean) and secondly on the extension of the existing mandatory ship reporting system also on ballast waters entering the Adriatic.[242] Other associated measures proposed in the future could include, for example, the 'Special Area Status' on the basis of Annexes II and VI of the MARPOL Convention and/or other measures embodied in present or potential future IMO Guidelines and Codes; and this even before their entry into force.

It is accordingly regrettable that despite an ambitious timetable for the submission of the joint proposal to the IMO (end of 2007) the work on the proposal stopped. It is hoped that the proposal will eventually be realized and submitted to the IMO and that the entire waters of the Adriatic will be, like those of the Western European Atlantic Waters (2004) and the Baltic in 2005 (without Russian waters),[243] proclaimed a PSSA. It is at least encouraging that authorities and stakeholders from all Adriatic States (and the EU) participating at the high level stakeholder conference 'Setting an Agenda for Smart, Sustainable and Inclusive Growth from the Adriatic and Ionian Sea' held in Zagreb on 6 December 2012, '… express readiness to continue the joint efforts towards the designation of the Adriatic Sea as a Particularly Sensitive Sea Area (PSSA), in accordance with the IMO Guidelines.'[244]

It is suggested that an Adriatic PSSA would represent a flexible tool, a potential forum and a main incentive for Adriatic States for discussing the management

---

240 See Vidas, op. cit., p. 370.
241 Designation of the Adriatic Sea as a Particularly Sensitive Area (draft). On file with the author.
242 See Vidas, op. cit., p. 369. Noteworthy is the fact that the contracting parties to the Barcelona Convention adopted in 2011, through the assistance of REMPEC, a Harmonized Voluntary Arrangements for Ballast Water Management in the Mediterranean Region. The Guidelines provide guidance and options to vessels transitting the Mediterranean with regard to ballast water management and exchange, although presently only on a voluntary basis. The Guidelines have been 'in force' since 1 January 2012 and will be applicable up to the time the 2004 Ballast Water Convention enters into force. See IMO, 'International Convention for the Control and Management of Ship's Ballast Water and Sediments. Communication received from the Regional Marine Pollution Emergency Response Centre for the Mediterranean Sea', BWM.2/Circ.35, 15 August 2011, Annex 1.
243 Cf fn 233.
244 Cf fn 226 (Zagreb Conclusions).

232 Extension of Coastal State Jurisdiction in Enclosed or Semi-enclosed Seas

of the risks posed by international shipping,[245] including by operational pollution. Furthermore, as pointed out by Vidas:

> ... the designation of a PSSA in the Adriatic Sea can provide a significant regional cooperative framework, in line with the EU policy, and also highlight the awareness of the vulnerability of the Adriatic Sea environment.[246]

It seems possible to conclude that the proclamation of the Adriatic PSSA, in addition to the proclamation of SPAMIs over the most vulnerable Adriatic Sea areas, may substantially contribute to the protection of the Adriatic marine environment from shipping activities, including from operational pollution (including ballast water).[247]

5.6 Role of the EU in the protection and preservation of the Adriatic marine environment[248]

The EU competences in the field of protection and preservation of the marine environment are shared,[249] unlike in the field of 'conservation and management of living resources', where these competences are exclusive. Nonetheless, the (external) competences may be also exclusive, if this affects common EU rules.[250] Both in the case of exclusive or shared competence, the EU may decide to exercise its competences *internally* by adopting EU legislation, or *externally* by entering into binding international agreements on the subject.

An important breakthrough in the field of the protection and preservation of the (EU) marine environment occurred with the adoption of the 2007 Communication of the Commission regarding an Integrated Maritime Policy for the European Union (*the Blue Book*)[251] which advocates the exploitation of the potential of the sea in order to achieve growth in an environmentally sustainable manner, and furthermore with the adoption of the Marine Strategy Directive[252]

---

245 See Vidas, op. cit., p. 348.
246 Ibid.
247 See the discussion in D. Vidas. and M. Kostelac Markovčić, 'Ballast Water and Alien Species: Regulating Global Transfers and Regional Consequences', in Vidas and Schei (eds), *The World Ocean in Globalisation*, op. cit., p. 371 at pp. 390–392.
248 For a discussion of the recent initiatives of the EU regarding *inter alia* the conservation and management of the living resources and/or the application of its CFP in the Mediterranean, see fn 160 and section 3.5.2.
249 Article 4(2)(e) of the TFEU.
250 See 'Declaration concerning the competence of the European Community with regard to matters governed by the United Nations Convention on the Law of the Sea of 10 December 1982 and the Agreement of 28 July 1994 relating to the implementation of Part XI of the Convention', OJ L 179 of 23 June 1998, and Art. 3(2) of the TFEU. See also Art. 2(2) of the TFEU regulating the competences at the 'internal' (EU) level.
251 COM(2007)575 final of 10 October 2007. See also the Communication 'Progress Report on the EU's Integrated Maritime Policy', COM (2009)540 final of 15 October 2009.
252 OJ EU L 164 of 25 June 2008. See also L. Juda, 'The European Union and Ocean Use Management: The Marine Strategy and the Maritime Policy', ODIL, Vol. 38, No. 3, 2007, pp. 259–281. The de-pollution of the Mediterranean Sea by the year 2020 is also one of the priority projects of the UFM.

Part IX of UNCLOS and the Adriatic Sea   233

in 2008 which aims at providing '… a framework within which Member States shall take the necessary measures to achieve or maintain good environmental status in the marine environment by the year 2020 at latest'.[253]

Of particular importance in the Mediterranean and Adriatic context are the efforts of the EU to promote an Integrated Maritime Policy for better Governance of the Mediterranean.[254] The latter are also reflected in the recently adopted Communication by the Commission on 'A Maritime Strategy for the Adriatic and Ionian Seas',[255] which sets out the framework for the elaboration of a 'coherent maritime strategy and corresponding Action Plan by the end of 2013'. The Communication aims to provide a framework for the adaptation of the Integrated Maritime Policy to the needs and potential of the Adriatic and Ionian Seas and coastal areas, and reflects the established EU's position that 'sea-basin cooperation is a milestone in the development and implementation of the EU's Integrated Maritime Policy'.[256] The Maritime Strategy Directive is perceived to be the 'environmental pillar' of the EU integrated maritime policy.[257]

One of the overriding principles of the 2008 Marine Strategy Directive is that '[t]he diverse conditions, problems and needs of the various marine region or sub-regions making up the marine environment in the Community [EU] require different and specific solutions'.[258] Member States are therefore required to develop a marine strategy for their own marine waters in accordance with a plan of action set up by the Directive which should however reflect the overall perspective of the regions or sub-regions involved.[259] 'Community [EU] waters' are, for the purposes of the 2008 Directive, divided into four regions (the Baltic Sea, the North-East Atlantic Ocean, the Mediterranean Sea and the Black Sea). The Mediterranean Sea is then on the basis of Article 4(2)(b) subdivided into four sub-regions, namely: (a) the Western Mediterranean Sea; (b) the Adriatic Sea; (c) the Ionian and Central Mediterranean Sea; and (d) the Aegean-Levantine Sea.[260] The Directive, therefore, clearly identifies the Adriatic Sea as a separate management sub-region within the wider Mediterranean region. It should be noted, however, that the

---

253 Article 1(1). See also Communication from the Commission to the Council and the European Parliament Establishing an Environmental Strategy for the Mediterranean, COM(2006)475 final, 5.9.2006.

254 See section 3.5.2.2.

255 Cf fn 179.

256 Ibid, p. 3.

257 See for example Cyprus Presidency of the Council of the European Union, 'Declaration of the European Ministers responsible for the Integrated Maritime Policy and the European Commission, on a Marine and Maritime Agenda for growth and jobs (the "Limassol Declaration")', 8 October 2012, Limassol, para. 24.

258 Preamble, section 10.

259 Preamble, section 11. See also Art. 5. For a further discussion see T. Markus *et al.*, 'Legal Implementation of Integrated Ocean Policies: The EU's Marine Strategy Framework Directive', IJMCL, Vol. 26, 2011, pp. 59–90.

260 Article 3(2) provides that maritime regions and sub-regions are designed for the purpose of facilitating the implementation of this Directive and are determined by taking into account *hydrological, oceanographic and biogeographic features*. Emphasis added.

234 Extension of Coastal State Jurisdiction in Enclosed or Semi-enclosed Seas

geographical scope of the Directive is limited to waters over which Member States and/or third States in the same region or sub-region exercise sovereignty or jurisdiction rights in accordance with UNCLOS,[261] and not on the high seas. It is suggested that this is an important consideration and should be taken into account by present and future EU Member States in the Adriatic and Mediterranean, when considering their options with regard to the extension of coastal state jurisdiction beyond the limits of their territorial sea.

The Directive also has an *external dimension* as it calls upon Member States to 'make every effort to ensure a close co-ordination not only with all Member States, but also with 'concerned third countries in a particular region or sub-region' and in this regard, 'where practical and appropriate', to make use of 'existing institutional structures established in marine regions or sub-regions, in particular Regional Seas Conventions [e.g. Barcelona Convention]'.[262] The concerned 'third countries' in the Adriatic are currently Croatia, Bosnia and Herzegovina, Montenegro and Albania. Obviously, a 'non EU Member State' cannot be legally bound to co-operate with EU Member States in the implementation of the provisions of an EU Directive. Nonetheless, the Marine Strategy Directive obliges EU Member States to '... consider the implications of their programmes of measures on waters beyond their marine waters in order to minimise the risk of damage to, and if possible have a positive impact on, those waters'.[263] This provision, read in the light of the relevant UNCLOS provisions, seems to require Member States, as emphasized by Markus *et al.*, to ensure at least '... that they do not cause damage or threats of damage, or transfer damage to areas in the high seas'.[264]

It is therefore particularly important that on 16 June 2008, on the occasion of the Meeting of the Trilateral Commission attended for the first time by all Adriatic States and the EU,[265] all Adriatic States signed a Joint Statement on the Environmental Protection of the Adriatic Sea.[266] With the latter they 'declared themselves committed to endeavour to cooperate towards a common operative approach in order to achieve the goals of the Marine Strategy Directive'. Slovenia went even further when, on 17 December 2009, its Parliament adopted a Resolution on the Strategy for the Adriatic Sea.[267] The latter directly exhorts the preparation of a Marine Strategy for the Adriatic in line with the Marine Strategy Directive, and calls upon the Slovenian Government to start the necessary procedure regarding the convening of a multilateral diplomatic conference.

---

261 Article 3(1)(a). See also Markus *et al.*, op. cit., p. 70.
262 Preamble, section 13 and Art. 6(1).
263 Article 13(8).
264 Markus et al., op. cit., p. 70.
265 The extension of the Trilateral Commission to all Adriatic States was one of goals of the Slovenian initiative named the 'Adriatic Sea Partnership' launched at the MAP sub-regional conference on the Sustainable Development Strategy for the Adriatic in Portorož, Slovenia, 5–6 June, 2006. Montenegro became a full member of the 'Trilateral Commission' on 25 May 2010.
266 *Skupna izjava o okoljski zaščiti Jadranskega morja*, 16 June 2008, Portorož, Slovenija.
267 *Resolucija o strategiji za Jadran (ReSJad)*, OGRS, No.106/2009, 22 December 2009.

Part IX of UNCLOS and the Adriatic Sea 235

The Resolution further expressly calls for the establishment of a SPA (SPAMI) over the waters of the Northern Adriatic[268] and emphasizes that the proclamation of the Slovenian ZEP in 2005 was crucial from the standpoint of the protection of the marine environment of the Northern Adriatic.[269] Both the 2008 (Portorož) Joint Statement and the 2009 Resolution by the Slovenian Parliament seem to confirm the commitment of Adriatic States to endeavour to co-operate in the achievements of the goals of the 2008 Directive. The latter therefore represents another important co-operative framework with regard to the environmental governance of the Adriatic Sea.

Noteworthy is the fact that the Trilateral Commission, which was joined by Montenegro in 2010, currently undertakes its work in four sub-commissions, each covering 'priority areas' of Adriatic co-operation.[270] In addition to the sub-commission for ballast water management[271] and the sub-commission for the preparation of amendments to the sub-regional (Adriatic) contingency plan,[272] reference should be made to the sub-commission for the unification of methods of assessment and development of indicators to assess the state of the marine environment. The latter was established with the specific aim of co-ordinating activities and exchanging information regarding the implementation of the EU Marine Strategy Directive among Adriatic States. These sub-commissions were joined in 2010 by the sub-commission on integrated coastal zone management in the Adriatic.[273] It is suggested accordingly that the Trilateral Commission may be nowadays regarded as one of the most important institutional frameworks for the co-operation of Adriatic States. Its activities, in fact, do not just cover the field of marine environmental protection, but relate to the holistic governance of the Adriatic Sea and its coastal zones. Its potential, however, has yet to be fully exploited, particularly through an enhanced co-ordination with other regional (Mediterranean) and sub-regional (Adriatic and/or Ionian) co-operative frameworks.

5.7 Other areas of co-operation

It is lastly suggested that another area which calls for enhanced Adriatic co-operation is the protection of underwater cultural heritage. There are in fact numerous underwater archaeological sites located just along the coasts of Croatia, both within the internal and/or territorial waters and beyond.[274] A substantial number of underwater archaeological sites can also be found in the Northern Adriatic, particularly along the coast of the Istria Peninsula, and

268 Article 7.
269 See section 3.3.6.
270 Presentation of the 'Trilateral Commission' and of its current work. Available at <http://www.mzoip.hr/default.aspx?id=10251>.
271 See section 5.5.
272 See section 5.1.3.2.
273 See section 5.1.3.5.
274 For a partial list, see <http://icua.hr/en/underwatersitesandmuseums>.

236 Extension of Coastal State Jurisdiction in Enclosed or Semi-enclosed Seas

obviously also along the Italian Adriatic coast, and relevant coasts of Albania and Montenegro.

Although certain (limited) protective measures may be undertaken both under the regime of a SPAMI[275] and that of a PSSA,[276] it would seem that a comprehensive legal basis for sub-regional Adriatic co-operation in this field has been finally provided for with the entry into force in 2009 of the UNESCO Convention to which all Adriatic States are parties.[277] The Convention encourages States parties to enter into regional and/or sub-regional agreements and/or to develop existing agreements with which States may adopt rules and regulations which ensure better protection of underwater cultural heritage than those adopted by the framework UNESCO Convention.[278] Reference to Adriatic co-operation in this particular area has been recently emphasized by the 2010 Ancona Declaration,[279] although ultimately such obligations derive from the ICZM Protocol.[280]

In the light of the foregoing, it would seem advisable for Adriatic States to endeavour to co-operate in the formulation of a Sub-Regional Adriatic Convention on the Protection and Preservation of Underwater Cultural Heritage. This could be the result of a process which may be driven together with or separately from efforts to adopt a similar regional convention at the Mediterranean level.[281] Furthermore, the adoption of specific protection measures in this regard should be considered also when submitting relevant proposals for the proclamation of SPAMI and/or of the Adriatic PSSA. It is suggested that Adriatic States could also explore the possibilities for the proclamation (and delimitation) of specific 'archaeological zones' which could be modelled on the Italian example of 2004.[282] The eventual regime of such zones will have to be fully compliant with the relevant provisions of UNCLOS and/or the 2009 UNESCO Convention.[283]

Lastly, another area where additional Adriatic sub-regional co-operation should be sought relates to safety of navigation and prevention of pollution from pleasure yachts and boats. It is this author's assertion that these activities nowadays represent an important risk to safety of navigation and protection of biodiversity in the (Northern) Adriatic.[284]

---

275 See section 5.1.3.1.
276 See Art. 4.4.1 of the 2005 PSSA Guidelines.
277 See Slim and Scovazzi, op. cit. (Part I), p. 120.
278 See Art. 6.
279 AII, '2010 Ancona Declaration', 12th Adriatic and Ionian Council, Ancona, 5 May 2010.
280 See para. 8. Article 13(1) of the ICZM Protocol provides that: 'The Parties shall adopt, individually or collectively, all appropriate measures to preserve and protect ... the underwater cultural heritage, in conformity with the applicable national and international instruments'. It should be noted, however, that the geographical scope of application of the ICZM Protocol does not include the EEZ and/or the high seas. See section 5.1.3.5.
281 T. Scovazzi, *L'approche régionale à la protection du patrimoine culturel sous-marin: Le cas de la Méditerranée*, AFDI, LV, 2009, p. 577 at p. 583.
282 See the discussion in section 3.3.5.
283 Ibid.
284 The adoption by the contracting states of the Barcelona Convention in 2008 of a voluntary set of 'Guidelines concerning pleasure craft activities and the protection of the marine environment in the Mediterranean' may represent an important aid and a starting point for such co-operation. See UNEP, Report of the 15th Ordinary Meeting of the Contracting Parties to the Convention

5.8 Concluding remarks

As discussed throughout this chapter, the provisions of Part IX of UNCLOS are being increasingly implemented in the Adriatic Sea. Moreover, during the last decade the areas of co-operation have not been limited to those listed in the second part of Article 123 of UNCLOS. However, we recall that important forms of Adriatic co-operation have their origins and existed even before the adoption of UNCLOS in 1982 (e.g. the Barcelona System, GFCM, CIESM, 1974 Belgrade Agreement). It is suggested that Adriatic and Mediterranean co-operation have been influenced, but that on the other hand had also influenced the inclusion and content of Article 123 (Part IX) of UNCLOS.[285]

In the field of the protection and preservation of the Adriatic marine environment and its coastal zones, the two main forms of co-operation have been, in addition to the recent co-operative framework established through the EU Marine Strategy Directive,[286] the implementation of a certain Protocol to the Barcelona Convention or co-operation in an area not directly addressed by the mentioned Convention (e.g. safety of navigation). It is suggested that the designation of an Adriatic PSSA and/or SPAMIs, coupled with the strengthening of port State control in the Adriatic (e.g. with the accession of all Adriatic States to the Paris MOU),[287] may substantially contribute to the reduction of operational pollution, including illegal discharges in the Adriatic Sea.

Furthermore, it is foreseeable that, although all Adriatic States actively participate in the work of the GFCM, the main future actor (and/or co-ordinator) in the field of conservation and management of the Adriatic living resources will be the EU through its CFP. This, however, subject to the extension of fisheries jurisdiction in the Adriatic by EU Member States. Regarding co-operation in the field of marine scientific research, it seems that there is a need in the Adriatic for a more institutionalized co-operation (e.g. through a specific co-operation body or a 'clearing house') in addition to the co-operation undertaken through CIESM in the field of pure scientific research and through FAO with regard to fisheries. The scientific co-operation undertaken within the framework of the EU Marine Strategy Directive with an active involvement of the expanded 'Trilateral Commission and its Sub-commission for the unification of methods of assessment and development of indicators to assess the state of the marine environment' seem to represent an important step forward in the right direction.[288]

---

for the Protection of the Marine Environment and the Coastal Region of the Mediterranean and its Protocols, Decision IG 17/9, UNEP(DEPI)/MED IG.17/10, Annex V., Almeria, 2008, p. 225.

285 See the discussion in section 2.3.
286 See section 5.6.
287 See Ruiz, op. cit., p. 21.
288 See the discussion in section 5.6

238 *Extension of Coastal State Jurisdiction in Enclosed or Semi-enclosed Seas*

There also seems to be the need for the expansion of the scope of application of undertaken projects and co-operation in general to some other areas also (e.g. the exploitation of renewable energies (hydro, wind, waves), potential genetic resources of the Adriatic sea-bed, deep-water canyons,[289] the effect of underwater noise, integrated coastal zone management and maritime spatial planning, including climate change and/or early warnings against catastrophic events).[290]

In this respect, it must be recognized that in all the areas discussed above and generally in all areas directly or indirectly addressed by UNCLOS, Part IX (Article 123) of UNCLOS represents a sound, although in most cases not the only, nor as explained on the case in the Adriatic Sea, primary, legal basis for such co-operation.

---

289 One of the recommendations of the IUCN Group of Expert on Mediterranean Governance adopted at their meeting in Procida/Naples (1 October 2010) was: '*De faire reconnaitre l'importance fondamentale des trois sous ensembles de canyons du golfe du Lion*, de l'Adriatique, *et de la mer Egèe-Levantine dens le fonctionnement hydrodynamique et biologique de la Méditerranèe*'. Emphasis added. 'Recommandation pour la protection des canyons de la Méditerranèe'. Cf fn 124.

290 Cf fn 196 (EU Communication), particularly 'List of major research topics requiring a cross-thematic approach', pp. 9–10.

6 Current state and possible way forward

When discussing the recent progress of extension of coastal State jurisdiction in the Adriatic Sea from a wider Mediterranean perspective it seems necessary to distinguish between four different scenarios. The first is the adoption of a framework law (e.g. the 1994 Maritime Code of Croatia, Italy's Law No. 61)[1] where the proclamation of an EEZ or of an *in plus stat minus* zone is subject to an additional act by the Head of State and/or of the Government. The second is the formal proclamation of an EEZ (or of a *de facto* EEZ) whereby the entry into force of its regime is subject to a moratorium (e.g. the 2003 proclamation by Croatia) or subject to the adoption of additional implementing legislation (e.g. the 2005 EEZ proclamation by Tunisia).[2] The third scenario is represented by an 'unconditional proclamation' of an EEZ and of its regime. In the few cases where Mediterranean States have adopted this third approach (e.g. Cyprus, Egypt, Morocco, Syria, Lebanon)[3] there is evidence that the regime of the EEZ has not been, or at least has not been fully, implemented in practice. The proclamation of the Slovenian ZEP seems to represent a fourth scenario. Slovenia adopted in 2005 a law proclaiming a ZEP in the Northern Adriatic[4] without enforcing its regime in practice. It therefore follows, as a fourth scenario, that particularly in the Adriatic Sea, the formal proclamation of an EEZ (or even of a *sui generis* zone) does not automatically entail the entry into force of its regime.

An interesting tendency in the wider Mediterranean Sea has been the adoption of 'framework laws' which allow for the proclamation and/or flexible application of various elements of the EEZ regime along different segments of the coast in a way which takes into account the specific geographical, and sometimes even political, characteristics of the (Central) Mediterranean region (e.g. Malta, Tunisia, Libya).[5] The 2009 EEZ proclamation by Libya,[6] coupled with the recent transformation of the French Mediterranean ZEP into a full EEZ and

---

1 Sections 3.3.4–3.3.5.
2 Sections 3.3.4 and 3.4.4.
3 Sections 3.1, 3.2, 3.4.1 and 3.4.2.
4 Section 3.3.6.
5 Sections 3.4.3–3.4.5.
6 Section 3.4.3.2.

240 *Extension of Coastal State Jurisdiction in Enclosed or Semi-enclosed Seas*

the recent initiatives of the EU,[7] seem to point to the fact that the favour has been, at least in the wider Mediterranean Sea, shifting from sectoral EFZs and/or ZEPs to holistic EEZs. Such an assertion seems to ultimately find support in the 2009 Marrakesh Declaration adopted at the 16th meeting of the State Parties to the Barcelona Convention.[8]

6.1 Extension of coastal State jurisdiction in the Adriatic: 'Mini EEZs' or real *sui generis* zones?

As discussed in Chapter 3, the current practice of Adriatic States, except for Albania and Montenegro, is still based on the proclamation of *sui generis* (*in plus stat minus*) zones.[9] It is, however, expected that Albania and Montenegro will also follow the example of other Adriatic States and that they will be ultimately influenced by the future positions of the EU in this regard.[10] As the admissibility of the proclamation of *sui generis* zones is addressed in Chapter 3,[11] this section focuses on the legal nature of the two identified sub-groups of maritime zones: *in plus stat minus* (derived) zones and (real) *sui generis* zones. Reference will be made to the rights of third States in such zones and to some potential benefits and/or problems with their proclamation from the standpoint of the overall governance of the Adriatic and the Mediterranean Seas.

6.1.1 In plus stat minus?

A useful starting point for this discussion is the 2004 Report of the United Nations Secretary-General on *Oceans and the Law of the Sea*[12] which seems to have impliedly alluded to the specific jurisdictional situation in the Adriatic Sea. According to the UN Secretary-General:

> … Regarding implementation at the national level, another disturbing element of state practice was to proclaim a *de facto* exclusive economic zone under various other denominations. Although the legal regime of such zones may be well identical to the regime of an exclusive economic zone or at least not in contravention to it, the introduction of new denominations is bound to create confusion or uncertainty, especially as to the rights and obligations of other States.

---

7 Section 3.5.2.
8 Section 5.1.2.2.
9 Sections 3.3.4–3.3.6.
10 Sections 3.1 and 3.5.
11 See Concluding Remarks.
12 UN, 'Oceans and the Law of the Sea: Report of the Secretary-General', Doc.A/59/62 of 4 March 2004, para. 42. Quoted also in T. Scovazzi, 'Recent Developments as regards Maritime Delimitation in the Adriatic Sea', in R. Lagoni and D. Vignes (eds), *Maritime Delimitation*, Leiden and Boston, MA: Martinus Nijhoff Publishers, 2006, p. 189 at p. 202.

Current state and possible way forward   241

Although it seems possible to agree that the proclamation of *de facto* EEZ under other denominations is undesirable,[13] it should be reiterated that nothing in UNCLOS or customary international law prevents the proclamations of narrower zones of jurisdiction where the coastal State is entitled to exercise only some of the competences under the EEZ regime. The general rule in this regard has been conveniently stated by Treves as follows: '... Zones that incorporated claims that are included in those contained in the notion of a recognized zone can be considered as compatible with UNCLOS, and in general with international law'.[14]

It may also be noted that while the (unco-ordinated) proclamation of *in plus stat minus* zones may indeed create some inconveniences for third States,[15] these zones may — alone or in combination with some other 'Mediterranean' legal instruments (e.g. proclamation of SPAMI)[16] — represent a useful tool for addressing some specific problems (e.g. protection of biodiversity, marine mammals, etc.) in some geographically and/or politically complicated areas as indeed found in certain parts of the Adriatic and Mediterranean. It is therefore suggested that the proclamation of *in plus stat minus* zones may help Adriatic States in their quest for solutions, reflecting the spirit of Part IX of UNCLOS. Particularly the ZEP which has at least in the Adriatic context (Slovenia and Italy)[17] proved to be something more than a simple 'zone of ecological protection', seems to represent an extremely useful tool for the protection of the Adriatic marine environment in line with the 'ecosystem' and the 'sustainable development' approach.[18] Also in political terms the proclamation of ZEPs may represent a common denominator and an acceptable transition between the high seas and the full EEZ regime for all Adriatic States.[19] A co-ordinated approach by all Adriatic States seems, however, to be crucial. This seems to have also been the position of the EU at least since 2002.[20]

Also in cases of the proclamation of ZEPs there would still be a need for Adriatic States to agree on a delimitation line or to enter into 'provisional agreements of a practical nature' in line with Articles 74(3) and 83(3) of

---

13 See the discussion of the Croatian EFPZ (a *de facto* EEZ) in section 3.3.4. Scovazzi opined that '... it cannot be denied that the risk of "confusion and uncertainty" exists, unless Mediterranean [or Adriatic] States can reach a general understanding on a unitary "presential" scheme based on the general interests as of their common sea as a whole.' See Scovazzi, op. cit., p. 203.

14 T. Treves, 'Potential Exclusive Economic Zones in the Mediterranean', paper delivered at the 11th Mediterranean Research Meeting Florence and Montecatini Terme, 24–27 March 2010, p. 3. See also Concluding Remarks in Chapter 3.

15 See I. Papanicolopulu, 'A Note on Maritime Delimitation in a Multizonal Context: The Case of the Mediterranean', ODIL, Vol. 38, No. 4, 2007, p. 381. Cf fn 13.

16 Section 5.1.3.1.

17 Sections 3.3.5–3.3.6.

18 It is suggested that a more appropriate denomination which would better reflect the functional jurisdictions that a coastal State is entitled to exercise in such zone, could be a 'Zone of *Environmental* Protection'.

19 See the discussion of the French ZEP in section 3.3.2.

20 Section 3.5.

242 *Extension of Coastal State Jurisdiction in Enclosed or Semi-enclosed Seas*

UNCLOS.[21] An interesting precedent and possible solution in certain vulnerable trans-boundary areas (e.g. Northern Adriatic) seems to be pointed out by the 'Mediterranean (Pelagos) Sanctuary' proclaimed by France, Italy and Monaco which has been partially located on the high seas of the Ligurian and Tyrrhenian.[22] The 'Mediterranean Sanctuary' in fact highlights a possible link between an *in plus stat minus* zone (e.g. ZEP) and the proclamation of a 'transboundary' SPAMI on the basis of the Biodiversity Protocol to the Barcelona Convention.[23] Although reference is made in Chapter 5 to the fact that the proclamation of a SPAMI may in certain specific cases in itself represent a viable alternative to the unilateral extension of jurisdiction by coastal States (at least in the SPAMI area),[24] it is suggested that the previous and/or contemporary extension of jurisdiction, particularly for environmental purposes (e.g. proclamation of ZEPs), may solve the main problem in relation to the implementation of the regime of the SPAMI on the high seas: which appears to be its enforcement against States non-Parties to the Protocol (third States). Such a course of action seems ultimately to be in line with Article 28(2) of the Biodiversity Protocol which provides as follows:

> The Parties undertake to adopt appropriate measures, consistent with international law, to ensure that no one engages in any activity contrary to the principles or purposes of this Protocol.[25]

The inclusion of a certain 'transboundary area' into the SPAMI List[26] (coupled with the co-ordinated extension of jurisdiction for the purposes of the protection of biodiversity) may at least with regard to the part of the SPAMI located on the high seas temporarily, or in certain cases even permanently, override not only the potential problems related to the unilateral extension of jurisdiction by coastal States, but also the various problems involved with the delimitation of zones of sovereign rights and jurisdiction (overlapping claims) in the SPAMI area, and may furthermore substantially improve the protection and preservation of areas of particular natural and/or cultural importance in the Mediterranean.[27] Such a

---

21 Section 2.4.2.5.
22 Section 3.3.3.
23 Section 5.1.3.1.
24 Ibid.
25 See sections 5.1.3.1 and 3.3.3.
26 It should be noted, however, that '[t]he decision to include the area in the SPAMI list shall be taken by consensus by the Contracting Parties, which shall also approve the management measures applicable to the area'. See Art. 9(3)(c) of the Biodiversity Protocol.
27 See Art. 3(1)(a) of the Biodiversity Protocol. Efforts regarding the establishment of the Northern Adriatic SPAMI may be undermined by the intention of Italy to allow the construction, despite strong objections by Slovenia, of two LNG terminals one on the shore and another in the middle of the ecologically vulnerable Gulf of Trieste in the immediate proximity of the Italy–Slovenia territorial sea boundary (see Figure 4.4). See Malačič *et al.*, 'Environmental Impact of LNG Terminals in the Gulf of Trieste (Northern Adriatic)', Integration of Information for Environmental Security, Vol. 3, Springer, 2008, pp. 361–381, and M. Pavliha, '*Mednarodnopravni argumenti v luči prava EU zoper plinske terminale v Tržaškem zalivu*', Podjetje in delo, No. 8, Ljubljana, 2010.

Current state and possible way forward 243

solution, which may in some cases be deemed to be the equivalent of a joint management zone, seems to be completely in line with Articles 74(3) and 83(3) and will no doubt represent a solution in the spirit of Part IX of UNCLOS.[28] Reference should finally be made to the fact that the three Northern Adriatic coastal States have already adopted framework laws and/or actually extended their jurisdiction in the environmental field (including in the field of the protection of biodiversity),[29] and that the area of the Northern Adriatic high seas has also been identified by the recent UNEP RAC/SPAs report as a candidate site to be included in the SPAMI List.[30]

6.1.2 Real sui generis *zones or mini EEZs?*

A different question is posed by the legal nature of some Adriatic zones, particularly *sui generis* ZEPs (Slovenia and Italy) which on the one hand represent a *minus* with regard to the overall regime of the EEZ, while at the same time they provide to the coastal State also some rights and/or jurisdictions which do not form part of the concept of the EEZ. Reference is made here particularly to the various rights which the two coastal States are or were, prior to the adoption of relevant national legislation, entitled to exercise within our zones discussed here in the field of the protection of underwater cultural heritage. Although the included rights undoubtedly exist under other parts of UNCLOS, customary international law and/or a separate multilateral treaties (e.g. the 2001 UNESCO Convention) – the fact remains that the creation of such mixed *sui generis* zones, unlike previously discussed *in plus stat minus* zones (e.g. French ZEP) are first of all questionable from the standpoint of international law while it is suggested that due to its mixed nature they do not help legal predictability.[31]

When discussing the admissibility of the proclamation of such 'real' *sui generis* zones reference should also be made to what was stated by ITLOS in the MV Saiga No. 2 Case Judgment with regard to Guinea's 150 km customs zone. According to the Tribunal:

> In the exclusive economic zone, the coastal State has jurisdiction to apply customs laws and regulations in respect of artificial islands, installations and structures (article 60, paragraph 2). In the view of the Tribunal, the Convention does not empower a coastal State to apply its customs laws in respect of any other parts of the exclusive economic zone not mentioned above.[32]

---

28 Section 2.4.2.5.
29 Sections 3.3.4–3.3.6.
30 Section 5.1.3.1.
31 In the group of 'real' *sui generis* zones it is possible to include also the two *20 nmi non-sailing (closed) zones* along the Gaza Strip, in which navigation is restricted to the activities of the Israeli Navy. See Art. XI of Annex I of the Agreement between Israel and the Palestine Liberation Organization on the Gaza Strip and the Jericho Area, Cairo, 4 May 1994.
32 The M/V 'SAIGA' (No. 2) Case (*Saint Vincent and the Grenadines v Guinea*), ITLOS Reports, 1999, para. 127. See also Separate Opinion of Judge Vukas, para. 20.

244 *Extension of Coastal State Jurisdiction in Enclosed or Semi-enclosed Seas*

As the 'archaeological zone' is according to UNCLOS linked to the geographical extent of the contiguous zone,[33] it seems that the above *dictum* should represent guidance for Adriatic States when proclaiming *in plus stat minus* zones based on the concept of the EEZ. As discussed, Adriatic States may avail themselves of a wide array of tools and/or co-operative arrangements in the field of the protection and preservation of the Adriatic's underwater cultural heritage including the proclamation of archaeological-contiguous zones up to 24 nmi, cooperation within the framework of the UNESCO Convention, while certain preventive measures may be envisaged also within the future SPAMI's and/or Adriatic PSSA.[34] Such regime(s) should, however, exist alongside[35] and not as a part of the EEZ regime. It may be thus concluded that *in plus stat minus* zones are compatible with international law as long as (and up to the extent that) the rights claimed by the coastal State do not go beyond those envisaged by Part V of UNCLOS.[36]

6.1.3 Rights of third States and the relation of sui generis zones with the high seas

A further important question relates to the rights of third States in the *sui generis* zones discussed throughout this work and to the relation of these zones with the high seas. In this regard it is possible to support Treves' assertion that:

> … the establishment of a zone in which less rights are claimed than those set out for the EEZ should not be seen as an excuse for not recognizing to third States at least the same freedoms of the high seas that UNCLOS recognizes them in the EEZ under Article 58.[37]

This means that independently of the nature of the *sui generis* zone, the communication freedoms and other rights of third States which would exist in the case of a proclamation of a full EEZ are 'untouchable' and represent the minimum rights for all States in all cases.[38] Beyond those provided in Article 58 of UNCLOS the exact number[39] and/or the quality of the various 'freedoms of the high seas' applicable in a *sui generis* zone depend first of all on the proclaimed elements of an EEZ and are in the Adriatic and Mediterranean subject to the *ipso facto* existing continental shelf regime.[40]

An interesting question is also whether the proclaimed 'derived' zones (e.g. the Croatian EFPZ) and/or *sui generis* zones (e.g. Slovenian ZEP) proclaimed in

---

33 See Art. 303(2) in relation with Art. 33 of UNCLOS.
34 Section 5.6.2.
35 As for example the case with the regime of the contiguous zone.
36 See also Treves, op. cit., p. 3.
37 Ibid.
38 Such freedoms may be restricted and/or regulated for e.g. through the proclamation of a SPA, SPAMI and/or PSSA in the mentioned area. See sections 5.1.3.1 and 5.6.
39 See Art. 87 of UNCLOS.
40 Section 3.1.

the Adriatic and Mediterranean still forming part of the high seas. Reference should be made in this regard to the (implied) definition of the 'high seas' found in Article 86 of UNCLOS, according to which:

> The provisions of this Part [Part VII of UNCLOS] apply to all parts of the sea *that are not included in the exclusive economic zone*, in the territorial sea or in the internal waters of a State, or in the archipelagic waters of an archipelagic State ....[41]

Although the question would deserve further scholarly attention, it seems not too hazardous to suggest that the dividing element is represented by the provision of Article 56(1)(a) of UNCLOS, referring to the exercise of 'sovereign rights for the purpose of exploring and *exploiting*, conserving and managing the natural resources, whether living or non-living, of the waters superjacent to the sea-bed ... by the coastal State'. In the case of the Adriatic Sea, also taking into account the *ipso facto* existing shelf regime, the dividing element seems to be the criteria of the exercise of sovereign rights regarding the exploitation of the living resources of such a zone. Such an explanation seems to follow from the main *raison d'être* of the introduction of the concept of the EEZ in international law which is the exercise by coastal States of sovereign rights regarding the exploitation and management of living resources located in front of its coast.[42]

According to the suggested interpretation, the Croatian EFPZ may be associated with an EEZ, while the Italian and Slovenian ZEPs (as previously in the wider Mediterranean the French) would still be deemed to form part of the high seas. The division is however not completely 'problem-free' as within the Italian and/or the Slovenian ZEPs the two coastal States are (or will be) entitled to exercise some important elements of an FPZ,[43] particularly in the field of the protection of biodiversity and/or marine mammals. It is nonetheless suggested that the decisive factor is that within the mentioned zones the two States are not entitled to exercise 'sovereign rights regarding the exploitation of living resources'. This in turn seems to suggest that legally speaking the two zones still form part of the high seas.

Obviously, for a certain area to be legally deprived of its high seas status it is not enough to adopt a framework law representing the legal basis for the subsequent proclamation of a *de facto* EEZ or of its regime, but the actual proclamation of its regime. The current situation with the Croatian EFPZ is peculiar, as its regime is formally in force, although not for States parties to the EU.[44] From the legal

---

41 Emphasis added.
42 See D. Attard, *Exclusive Economic Zone in International Law*, Oxford: Clarendon Press, 1987, p. 1. See also M. Škrk, 'Exclusive Economic Zones in Enclosed or Semi-Enclosed Seas', in B. Vukas (ed.) *The Legal Regime of Enclosed or Semi-Enclosed Seas: The Particular Case of the Mediterranean, Prinosi za poredbeno proučavanje prava i međunarodno pravo*, Vol. 19, No. 22, Zagreb, 1988, p. 159 at pp. 166–167.
43 See sections 3.3.5–3.3.6.
44 See section 3.3.4.

246 Extension of Coastal State Jurisdiction in Enclosed or Semi-enclosed Seas

standpoint it would however seem difficult to defend the position that the area included in the Croatian *de facto* EEZ is due to the temporary non-implementation of its regime to a (limited) number of States, still forming part of the high seas.

6.2 Delimitation of zones of sovereign rights and jurisdiction

Regarding the delimitation of zones of sovereign rights or jurisdictions (EEZs, *sui generis* zones), it would appear from the reactions to the unilateral delimitation of the Croatian EFPZ[45] that it is not very likely for the few Adriatic and Mediterranean States who have already concluded shelf agreements, to agree to an automatic conversion of the shelf line into an 'all purpose' single maritime boundary. On the contrary, from the recent State practice in the Mediterranean involving *inter alia* Italy, Cyprus, Spain and most recently Lebanon,[46] it may be concluded that there is a tendency by Mediterranean States to unilaterally provide for the provisional limits of the various zones of jurisdiction by using the method of equidistance. Such a practice seems however to contradict the express provision of Article 74 of UNCLOS, particularly its third paragraph.[47]

Leanza interestingly opines that the unilateral setting of the median line as the provisional delimitation line, may represent an 'arrangement of a practical nature'[48] on the basis of Article 74(3) of UNCLOS. It is, however, doubtful whether a unilaterally set median line fulfils the clear multilateral and/or bilateral requirements for co-operation embodied in Articles 74(3) and 83(3) of UNCLOS.[49] It thus seems safer to agree with Andreone who suggests that particularly States bordering enclosed or semi-enclosed seas should reach an agreement also on the provisional delimitation of their maritime areas or alternatively they should refrain from extending their zones up to the median line.[50]

It should also be noted that the question of whether existing shelf agreements should be automatically applied to superjacent waters has been answered negatively both by prevailing State practice in the Mediterranean and ultimately by the ICJ in the 2009 Romania-Ukraine Judgment.[51] This implies by analogy that boundaries delimiting exclusively *sui generis* zones of jurisdiction, subject to an agreement to the contrary, shall not be automatically applicable when such zone will be 'upgraded' with other elements and/or transformed

---

45 Ibid.
46 See section 3.1, and the overall discussion in Chapter 3.
47 See section 2.4.2.5.
48 U. Leanza, '*L'italia e la scelta di rafforzare la tutela del ambiente marino: L'istituzione di zone di protezione ecologica*', *Rivista di diritto internazionale*, Vol. LXXXIX, No. 2, Milano: Giuffrè, 2006, p. 314 at pp. 331–333.
49 See section 2.4.2.5.
50 See G. Andreone, '*La Zona Ecologica Italiana*', Il Diritto Marittimo, Anno CIX-Terza Serie, Vol. I, January–March, Genova, 2007, p. 1 at p. 22.
51 See Maritime Delimitation in the Black Sea (*Romania v Ukraine*), ICJ Reports 2009, para. 69.

Current state and possible way forward 247

into a full EEZ. It is suggested accordingly that the recent practice of some Mediterranean States (including Albania and Greece), which have concluded agreements delimiting all their maritime areas, both present and future (potential zones) seems to represent a proper way ahead also in the Adriatic context. The discussion in Chapter 4 highlights the importance in the Adriatic Sea of the conclusion of agreements on the 'regime of the disputed areas' (e.g. preservation of historic fishing rights of local fishermen, navigation, etc.) in addition to the sole (final) delimitation and the fact that such a consideration should be taken into account by Adriatic States also when submitting their (maritime) delimitation dispute to a third party adjudication (ICJ, *Ad Hoc* Arbitral Tribunal).[52]

6.3 A possible way forward in the Adriatic Sea

Chapters 3 and 5 illustrate the fact that the co-ordinated extension of coastal State jurisdiction by Adriatic States would be beneficial to the overall governance of the Adriatic Sea. This seems to be the case particularly in the light of new trends which advocate for a holistic approach to maritime affairs (integrated maritime policy) for the Mediterranean and/or the Adriatic. The advantages of the extension of coastal State jurisdiction in the environmental field are not only related to the (limited) enforcement powers which the coastal State is entitled to exercise in its EEZ in the field of prevention of ship source pollution, but are instead related to the overall preservation of biodiversity and/or sustainable governance of the Adriatic.[53] The extension of jurisdiction would furthermore strengthen the implementation and would eliminate the various dilemmas regarding the enforcement of certain Mediterranean legal instruments (e.g. Barcelona System) against third States on the Adriatic's high seas. It is far from unimportant that the extension of jurisdiction by an EU Member State in a particular field automatically entails a concurrent extension of the EU *aquis* to that particular zone depending on the nature of the proclaimed area (EEZ, FPZ, ZEP, etc.). For example, the extension of jurisdiction by an EU Member State in the environmental field (e.g. proclamation of ZEPs) in the Adriatic would automatically extend the geographical scope of application of the Marine Strategy Directive[54] and the Habitats Directive[55] to the newly pro-claimed zone, while in the field of conservation and management of living resources this would trigger the automatic application of the EU CFP to that area.[56]

Taking into account the (actual or potential) overlapping claims of Italy, Slovenia and Croatia over the superjacent waters of the Northern Adriatic, and

---

52 Sections 4.8.2–4.8.4.
53 Section 5.1.2.1.
54 See Art. 3(1).
55 See Case C-6/04, *Commission v UK*, Judgment of 20 October 2005 [2005] ECR I-9017, paras. 115–117.
56 Section 3.5.1.

of Slovenia and Croatia regarding the continental shelf,[57] it seems, that a possible practical solution to both problems of delimitation of the superjacent waters and/or the continental shelf could be to temporarily (e.g. until the award of the Arbitral Tribunal in the Slovenia/Croatia Arbitration),[58] or even permanently, overcome through the submission of a joint proposal and the actual designation of a SPAMI which would include also the high seas of the Northern Adriatic. It is important to reiterate that such a SPAMI may include both the superjacent waters and/or the continental shelf, and that the protective measures adopted within it may be directed both at the protection of the marine environment, its living resources and in certain cases even at the protection of the underwater cultural heritage.[59] The regime of the already proclaimed ZEPs (and the Croatian EFPZ) in the Northern Adriatic may, on the other hand, complement the existing SPAMI and represent the legal basis for the enforcement of its regime against States non-Parties to the Biodiversity Protocol (e.g. vessels sailing to the Northern Adriatic ports and flying a flag of convenience).

The Adriatic States could obviously agree also on some other 'provisional arrangements of a practical nature' in line with Article 74(3) of UNCLOS which should ideally address co-operation in various fields and where particular emphasis should be given to co-operation in the field of the protection and preservation of the marine environment. The two *interim* agreements concluded in 2002 between Tunisia and Algeria[60] and Croatia and (Serbia) Montenegro[61] are good examples in this regard.

It should also be noted that if the envisaged SPAMI is implemented, it will cover less than half of the Adriatic high seas (Northern and eventually Central Adriatic) and, accordingly, it could not represent a comprehensive solution. Despite the fact that the approval by the IMO of the Adriatic PSSA may extend some of the potential protective measures applicable in a SPAMI (e.g. the non-ballast discharge zone) also to other parts of the Adriatic,[62] it is suggested that such measures would be more effective if complemented by a co-ordinated extension of jurisdiction by Adriatic coastal States.

The first step in this regard could be the co-ordinated implementation of the regime of the existing zones in the field of the protection and preservation of the marine environment (ZEPs) by Italy, Slovenia and Croatia in the (Northern and Central) Adriatic.[63] Ideally, Montenegro and Albania should also follow suit. As there are indicators that both Montenegro and Albania may accept the median

---

57 Sections 3.3.4–3.3.6.
58 Section 4.8.
59 The submission of a SPAMI joint proposal may be facilitated by the already existing system of traffic separation schemes in the Northern Adriatic straddling the territorial seas of Italy, Slovenia and Croatia. See section 5.4.1.1.
60 Section 2.4.2.5.1.
61 The Croatia-(Serbia) Montenegro agreement is, however, applicable only to internal waters and/ or territorial sea of the two States. See section 4.6.1.
62 Section 3.1.
63 Sections 3.3.4–3.3.6.

Current state and possible way forward 249

line as a provisional delimitation line with Italy,[64] it seems possible to predict that the provisional delimitation of zones of jurisdiction (e.g. ZEPs) between those three States should not represent an insurmountable obstacle. The next step could then be the co-ordinated extension of jurisdiction also for fisheries (or ultimately the proclamation of full EEZs).

It is suggested that such a step will now be easier/is now even more desirable now that Croatia has joined the EU. The practical effect of the second step would be the automatic extension of the EU CFP to almost three-quarters of the present Adriatic high seas, while from the practical point of view the benefit would then be the most likely preservation of the 'historical catch share' of the three States within the EU CFP beyond the limits of their territorial seas,[65] based on the principle of 'relative stability'.[66] Such extension of jurisdiction could then be accompanied by a simultaneous extension of jurisdiction for fisheries purposes by Montenegro and Albania, which should ideally follow the conclusion of a 'bilateral fisheries agreement' between the EU and the two States regulating the fishing of EU vessels within the mentioned two zones. The latter agreement would obviously cease being in force at the moment of the accession of Albania and Montenegro to the EU.

Although the proposals may be described as *de lege ferenda* and might ultimately be seen to be overly optimistic, reference should be made to the fact that they are based also on this work's assertion, according to which States bordering enclosed and semi-enclosed seas have a *bona fide* obligation to exercise all their rights and perform all their duties under UNCLOS, including those regulating the extension of coastal State jurisdiction and/or delimitation of maritime zones, in the light of the general duty (policy) of co-operation embodied in Part IX of UNCLOS.[67] As suggested in Chapter 2, such 'duty of co-operation' is legally more stringent if an (e.g. unilateral) extension of jurisdiction affects or is likely to affect the management of living resources, protection and preservation of the marine environment and/or marine scientific research.[68]

In the light of the foregoing it may be concluded that the Adriatic Sea is in need of protection, both with regard to the protection and preservation of the marine environment and/or conservation of its living resources; and that the proclamation of ZEPs and/or PFZs, and ultimately full EEZs may be a useful tool in this regard. It is suggested however that such a goal would be best achieved by co-ordinated action by all Adriatic States and not by unilateral extensions of jurisdiction by particular States. As pointed out by the EU Commission in its 2009

---

64 Section 3.1, fn 30 and section 4.6.1.

65 S. Boelaert Suominen, 'The European Community, the European Court of Justice and the Law of the Sea', IJMCL, Vol. 23, No. 4, 2008, p. 643 at pp. 655–656. See also the discussion in section 4.7.4.

66 Member States are granted, by the EU Council, an immutable percentage of fishery quotas (fishery opportunities) in certain waters (e.g. the Adriatic), based also on their historic catch in that area. What is fixed is the percentage, while the amount of the catch depends on the availability of stocks (total available catch) for a certain year. Ibid.

67 See introductory statement of Art. 123 of UNCLOS, and section 2.3.4.3.

68 See second element of Art. 123, and section 2.3.4.4.

Communication, Towards an Integrated Maritime Policy for Better Governance of the Mediterranean:

> ... Given disparities in the political and economic situation, improvement of the governance of the maritime space at sub-regional level could be encouraged. Progress in this respect is achieved in particular when adjacent States agree to delimit a common maritime border or *effectively jointly manage their living and non-living resources* ....[69]

It is thus submitted that the proposed co-ordinated action should also include an agreement regarding the final or temporary borders of the relevant zones, or where this is not possible, an agreement on 'provisional arrangement of a practical nature', for example joint zones of jurisdiction (and/or SPAMIs) or at least joint development covering the disputed areas.[70] Such co-ordinated extension of jurisdiction should, however, be seen as a tool for achieving an even higher degree of co-operation among Adriatic States in their quest for a sustainable (holistic) governance of the Adriatic Sea and not as a substitute for such enhanced co-operation. Chapter 2 in this regard illustrated that Part IX of UNCLOS represents a basic legal cornerstone on which Adriatic and Mediterranean States could build their present and future co-operation in order to achieve such a goal.

---

69 Communication from the European Commission, Towards an Integrated Maritime Policy for better governance in the Mediterranean, COM(2009) 466, 11 September 2009.
70 M. Grbec, '*Problematika morskih pasov v Severnem Jadranu*', *Podjetje in delo*, No. 6–7, Year 23, Ljubljana, 2007, p. 1439, at pp. 1449–1450.

Select bibliography[1]

Books

Anish, F.A., *The International Law of Maritime Boundaries and the Practice of States in the Mediterranean*, Oxford: Clarendon Press, 1993

Attard, D., *Exclusive Economic Zone in International Law*, Oxford: Clarendon Press, 1987

Bradford, E., *Mediterranean: Portrait of a Sea*, London: Penguin Books, 2000

Brownlie, I., *African Boundaries, Legal and Diplomatic Encyclopedia*, Royal Institute of International Law, Guildford, London and Worchester: Billing & Sons Limited, 1979

Brownlie, I., *Principles of Public International Law*, 7th edn, Oxford: Oxford University Press, 2008

Churchill, R. and Owen, D., *The EU Common Fisheries Policy*, Oxford: Oxford University Press, 2010

Churchill, R. and Lowe V., *The Law of the Sea*, 3rd edn, Manchester: Manchester University Press, 1999

Charney, J.I. and Alexander L.M. (eds), *International Maritime Boundaries*, Vol. II, ASIL, Dordrecht, Boston, MA and London: Martinus Nijhoff Publishers, 1989

Charney, J.I. and Alexander L.M. (eds), *International Maritime Boundaries*, Vol. I, ASIL, Dordrecht and Boston, MA: Martinus Nijhoff Publishers, 1993

Charney, J.I. and Smith, R.W. (eds), *International Maritime Boundaries*, Vol. IV, The Hague, Boston, MA and London: Martinus Nijhoff Publishers, 2002

Charney, J.I. and Alexander L.M. (eds), *International Maritime Boundaries*, ASIL, Vol. III, The Hague, Boston, MA and London: Martinus Nijhoff Publishers, 2004

Colson, D.A. and Smith, R.W. (eds), *International Maritime Boundaries*, Vol. V, ASIL, Leiden and Boston, MA: Martinus Nijhoff Publishers, 2005

Colson, D.A. and Smith, R.W. (eds), *International Maritime Boundaries*, Vol. VI, ASIL, Leiden and Boston, MA: Martinus Nijhoff Publishers, 2011

Cordona Llorens, J. (ed.), *Cursos Euromediterráneos Bancaja de Derecho Internacional*, Vol. VIII/IX, Castellón, 2004/2005

Del Vecchio, A. (ed.), *La Politica Marittima Comunitaria*, Aracne, 2009

DOALOS, *Handbook on the Delimitation of Maritime Boundaries*, New York, NY: UN, 2000

DOALOS, *The Law of the Sea: Enforcement by Coastal States, Legislative History of Article 220 of UNCLOS*, United Nations Publications, New York, NY: UN, 2005

Francalanci, G. and Presciuttini, P., *A History of the Treaties and Negotiations for the Delimitation of the Continental Shelf and Territorial Waters between Italy and the Nations of the Mediterranean (1966–1992)*, Genova: Istituto Idrografico della Marina, 2000

---

1 All website references correct as at 1 December 2012.

252 *Extension of Coastal State Jurisdiction in Enclosed or Semi-enclosed Seas*

Francalanci, G. and Scovazzi, T. (eds), *The Mediterranean: Selected Maps*, Genova: Istituto Idrografico della Marina, 1992

Garabello, R. and Scovazzi, T. (eds), *The Protection of the Underwater Cultural Heritage Before and After the 2001 UNESCO Convention*, Leiden and Boston, MA: Martinus Nijhoff Publishers, 2003

Gavouneli, M., *Functional Jurisdiction in the Law of the Sea*, Publication on Ocean Development, Vol. 62, Leiden and Boston, MA: Martinus Nijhoff Publishers, 2007

Gudmundur, A. *et al.* (eds), *The Yearbook of Polar Law*, Vol. 1, The Netherlands: Brill, 2009

Ibler, V., *Medunarodno pravo mora i Hrvatska*, Zagreb: Barbat, 2001

Kim, S.P., *Maritime Delimitation and Interim Arrangements in North East Asia*, Leiden and Boston, MA: Martinus Nijhoff Publishers, 2004

Kohen, M.G. (ed.), *Secession: International Law Perspectives*, Cambridge and New York, NY: Cambridge University Press, 2006

Lagoni, R. and Vignes, D. (eds), *Maritime Delimitation*, Leiden and Boston, MA: Martinus Nijhoff Publishers, 2006

Leanza, U., *Il nuovo diritto del mare e la sua applicazione nel Mediterraneo*, Torino: G. Giappicheli Editore, 1993

Leanza, U., *Il regime giuridico internazionale del mare Mediterraneo*, Studi e documenti di diritto internazionale e comunitario, No. 44, Napoli: Editioriale Scientifica, 2008

Martínez Gutiérrez, N.A., *Limitation of Liability in International Maritime Conventions: The Relationship between Global Limitation Conventions and Particular Liability Regimes*, London and New York, NY: Routledge, 2011

Martínez Gutiérrez, N.A. (ed.), *Serving the Rule of International Maritime Law: Essays in Honour of Professor David Joseph Attard*, London and New York, NY: Routledge, 2010

Mihelič, D., *Ribič, kje zdaj tvoja barka plava? Piransko ribolovno območje skozi čas*, Koper: Založba Annales, 2007

Ministry of Foreign Affairs (Slovenia), *Pariška mirovna pogodba*, Ljubljana, 1997

Ministry of Foreign Affairs (Slovenia), *White Paper on the Border between the Republic of Slovenia and the Republic of Croatia*, Ljubljana: Delo, 2006

Ndiaye, M.T. and Wolfrum, R. (eds), *Law of the Sea, Environmental Law and Settlement of Disputes: Liber Amicorum Judge Thomas A. Mensah*, Leiden and Boston, MA: Martinus Nijhoff Publishers, 2007

Nordquist, M.H. *et al.* (eds), *United Nations Convention on the Law of the Sea 1982: A Commentary*, six volumes, Dordrecht, Boston, MA and London: Martinus Nijhoff Publishers, 1985, 1989, 1991, 1993, 1995, 2002

Prescott, V. and Schofield, C., *The Maritime Political Boundaries of the World*, 2nd edn, Leiden and Boston, MA: Martinus Nijhoff Publishers, 2005

Ramphal, S., *Triumph for UNCLOS; The Guyana-Suriname Maritime Arbitration*, London: Hansib Publications, 2008

Ronzitti, N. (ed.), *I raporti di vicinato dell'Italia con Croazia, Serbia-Montenegro e Slovenia*, Rome: Luiss University Press-Giuffrè, 2005

Sanders, P. (ed.), *Liber Amicorum for Martin Domke*, The Leiden, Netherlands: Martinus Nijhoff, 1957

Scovazzi, T. (ed.), *Marine Specially Protected Areas*, The Netherlands: Kluwer Law International, 1999

Shaw, M., *International Law*, 6th edn, Cambridge: Cambridge University Press, 2008

Symmons, C.R., *Historic Waters in the Law of the Sea: A Modern Re-appraisal*, Publications on Ocean Development, Leiden and Boston, MA: Martinus Nijhoff Publishers, 2008

Bibliography   253

Tanaka, Y., *Predictability and Flexibility in the Law of Maritime Delimitation*, Oxford: Hart Publishing, 2006

Turcho Bulgherini, E. (ed.), *Studi in onore di Antonio Lefebvre D'Ovidio*, Milano: Giufré Editore, 1995

Turkalj, T., *Piranski zaljev: Razgraničenje teritorijalnog mora između Hrvatske i Slovenije*, Pravo 29, Zagreb: Organizator, 2001

Vasciannie, S.C., *Land-Locked States and Geographically Disadvantaged States in the International Law of the Sea*, Oxford: Clarendon Press, 1990

Vidas, D., *Hrvatsko-slovensko razgraničenje*, Zagreb: Školska knjiga, 2009

Vidas, D. (ed.), *Protecting the Polar Marine Environment; Law and Policy for Pollution Prevention*, Cambridge: Cambridge University Press, 2000

Vidas, D. (ed.), *Law, Technology and Science for Oceans in Globalisation: IUU Fishing, Oil Pollution, Bioprospecting, Outer Continental Shelf*, Leiden and Boston, MA: Martinus Nijhoff Publishers, 2010

Vidas, D. and Schei, P.J. (eds), *The World Ocean in Globalisation: Climate Change, Sustainable Fisheries, Biodiversity, Shipping, Regional Issues*, Leiden and Boston, MA: Martinus Nijhoff Publishers, 2011

Von Bogdandy, A. and Wolfrum, R. (eds), *Max Planck Yearbook of United Nations Law*, Vol. 13, The Netherlands: Koninklijke Brill, 2009

Vukas, B. (ed.), *Essays on the New Law of the Sea, Prinosi za poredbeno proučavanje prava i međunarodno pravo*, Vol. 18, No. 21, Zagreb, 1985

Vukas, B. (ed.), *The Legal Regime of Enclosed or Semi-Enclosed Seas: The Particular Case of the Mediterranean*, Prinosi za poredbeno proučavanje prava i međunarodno pravo, Vol. 19, No. 22, Zagreb, 1988

Vukas, B., *The Law of the Sea: Selected Writings*, Publications on Ocean Development, Leiden and Boston, MA: Martinus Nijhoff Publishers, 2004

Weil, P., *The Law of Maritime Delimitations–Reflections*, Cambridge: Grotius Publications Limited, 1989

Westerman, S., *The Juridical Bay*, Oxford: Clarendon Press, 1987

Chapters in books

Boyle, A., 'Globalism and Regionalism in the Protection of the Marine Environment', in D. Vidas (ed.), *Protecting the Polar Marine Environment; Law and Policy for Pollution Prevention*, Cambridge: Cambridge University Press, 2000, p. 19

Carleton, M., 'Red Sea/Persian Gulf Maritime Boundaries', in D.A. Colson and R.W. Smith (eds), *International Maritime Boundaries*, Vol. V, Leiden and Boston, MA: Martinus Nijhoff Publishers, ASIL, 2005, p. 3467

Churchill, R., 'The European Union and the Challenges of Marine Governance: From Sectoral Response to Integrated Policy?', in D. Vidas and P.J. Schei (eds), *The World Ocean in Globalisation: Climate Change, Sustainable Fisheries, Biodiversity, Shipping, Regional Issues*, Leiden and Boston, MA: Martinus Nijhoff Publishers, 2011, p. 395

Gestri, M., '*I rapporti di vicinato marittimo tra l'Italia e gli Stati nati dalla dissoluzione della Iugoslavia*', in N. Ronzitti (ed.), *I raporti di vicinato dell'Italia con Croazia, Serbia-Montenegro e Slovenia*, Rome: Luiss University Press-Giuffrè, 2005, p. 177

Grbec, M., 'Extension of Coastal State Jurisdiction in the Mediterranean: Quasi EEZs or real *sui-generis* zones?', in N.A. Martínez Gutiérrez (ed.), *Serving the Rule of International Maritime Law: Essays in Honour of Professor David Joseph Attard*, London and New York, NY: Routledge, 2010, p. 181.

Ibler, V., 'The Importance of the Exclusive Economic Zone as a Non-Resource Zone', in B. Vukas (ed.), *Essays on the New Law of the Sea, Prinosi za poredbeno proučavanje prava i međunarodno pravo*, Vol. 18, No. 21, Zagreb, 1985, p. 118

Kanehara, A., 'A legal and practical arrangements of disputes concerning maritime boundaries pending their final solution and law enforcement: from a Japanese perspective', in N.A. Martinez Gutiérrez (ed.), *Serving the Rule of International Maritime Law: Essays in Honour of Professor David Joseph Attard*, London and New York, NY: Routledge, 2010, p. 95

Khee-Jin Tan, A., 'The EU Ship-Source Pollution Directive and Recent Expansion of Coastal State Jurisdiction', in D. Vidas (ed.), *Law, Technology and Science for Oceans in Globalisation: IUU Fishing, Oil Pollution, Bioprospecting, Outer Continental Shelf*, Leiden and Boston, MA: Martinus Nijhoff Publishers, 2010, p. 291

Leanza, U., '*La zona economica esclusiva nella evoluzione del diritto del mare*', in E. Turcho Bulgherini (ed.), *Studi in onore di Antonio Lefebvre D'Ovidio*, Tomo I, Milano: Giufré Editore, 1995, p. 541

Mensah, T.A., 'Joint Development Zones as an Alternative Dispute Settlement Approach in Maritime Boundary Delimitation', in R. Lagoni and D. Vignes (eds), *Maritime Delimitation*, Leiden and Boston, MA: Martinus Nijhoff Publishers, 2006, p. 143

Pazartis, P., 'Secession and International Law: the European dimension', in M.G. Kohen (ed.), *Secession: International Law Perspectives*, Cambridge and New York, NY: Cambridge University Press, 2006, p. 355

Raftopoulos, E., 'The Mediterranean Response to Global Challenges: Environmental Governance and the Barcelona Convention System', in D. Vidas and P.J. Schei (eds), *The World Ocean in Globalisation: Climate Change, Sustainable Fisheries, Biodiversity, Shipping, Regional Issues*, Leiden and Boston, MA: Martinus Nijhoff Publishers, 2011, p. 507

Reisman, M. and Arsanjani, M.H., 'Some Reflections on the Effect of Artisanal Fishing on Maritime Boundary Delimitation', in M.T. Ndiaye and R. Wolfrum (eds), *Law of the Sea, Environmental Law and Settlement of Disputes: Liber Amicorum Judge Thomas A. Mensah*, Leiden and Boston, MA: Martinus Nijhoff Publishers, 2007, p. 629

Scovazzi, T., 'Maritime Delimitations in the Mediterranean Sea', in J. Cordona Llorens (ed.), *Cursos Euromediterráneos Bancaja de Derecho Internacional*, Vol. VIII/IX, Castellón, 2004/2005, p. 357

Scovazzi, T., 'Legal Issues Relating to Navigation through Arctic Waters', in A. Gudmundur *et al.* (eds), *The Yearbook of Polar Law*, Vol. 1, The Netherlands: Brill, 2009, p. 371

Scovazzi, T., 'Recent Developments as regards Maritime Delimitation in the Adriatic Sea', in R. Lagoni and D. Vignes (eds), *Maritime Delimitation*, Leiden and Boston, MA: Martinus Nijhoff Publishers, 2006, p. 189

Scovazzi, T., 'Regional Cooperation in the Field of the Environment', in T. Scovazzi (ed.), *Marine Specially Protected Areas*, The Netherlands: Kluwer Law International, 1999, p. 81

Scovazzi, T., 'The Mediterranean Guidelines for the Determination of Environmental Liability and Compensation: The Negotiations for the Instrument and the Question of Damage that can be Compensated', in A. Von Bogdandy and R. Wolfrum (eds), *Max Planck Yearbook of United Nations Law*, Vol. 13, The Netherlands: Koninklijke Brill, 2009, p. 183

Scovazzi, T., 'The 2008 Mediterranean Protocol on Integrated Coastal Zone Management and the European Community', in A. Del Vecchio (ed.), *La Politica Marittima Comunitaria*, Rome: Aracne, 2009, p. 159

Scovazzi, T. and Francalanci, G., 'Bosnia and Herzegovina-Croatia (Report Number 8-14)', in J.I. Charney and R.W. Smith (eds), *International Maritime Boundaries*, Vol. IV, 2002, p. 2887

Bibliography 255

Scovazzi, T. and Francalanci, G., 'Italy-Yugoslavia (Territorial Sea)', in J.I. Charney and L.M. Alexander (eds), *International Maritime Boundaries*, Vol. II, ASIL, Dordrecht, Boston, MA and London: Martinus Nijhoff Publishers, 1989, p. 1639

Scovazzi, T. and Papanicolopulu, I., 'Albania/Greece (Report Number 8-21)', in D.A. Colson and R.W. Smith (eds), *International Maritime Boundaries*, Vol. VI, ASIL, Leiden and Boston, MA: Martinus Nijhoff Publishers, 2011, p. 4462

Scovazzi, T. and Papanicolopulu, I., 'Cyprus Lebanon (Report Number 8-19)', in D.A. Colson and R.W. Smith (eds), *International Maritime Boundaries*, Vol. VI, ASIL, Leiden and Boston, MA: Martinus Nijhoff Publishers, 2011, p. 4445

Škrk, M., 'Exclusive Economic Zones in Enclosed or Semi-Enclosed Seas', in B. Vukas (ed.), *The Legal Regime of Enclosed or Semi-Enclosed Seas: The Particular Case of the Mediterranean, Prinosi za poredbeno proučavanje prava i medunarodno pravo*, Vol. 19, No. 22, Zagreb, 1988, p. 159

Sohn, L.B., 'Arbitration of International Disputes *ex aqueo et bono*', in P. Sanders (ed.), *Liber Amicorum for Martin Domke*, The Leiden, Netherlands: Martinus Nijhoff, 1957, p. 330

Vella, I., 'A new advent for renewable offshore resources', in N.A. Martínez Gutiérrez (ed.), *Serving the Rule of International Maritime Law: Essays in Honour of Professor David Joseph Attard*, London and New York, NY: Routledge, 2010, p. 136

Vidas, D., 'Particularly Sensitive Sea Areas: The Need for Regional Cooperation in the Adriatic Sea', in K. Ott (ed.), *Croatian Accession to the European Union: Institutional Challenges*, Vol. 4, Zagreb: Institute of Public Finance, 2006, p. 347

Vidas, D. and Kostelac Markovčić, M., 'Ballast Water and Alien Species: Regulating Global Transfers and Regional Consequences', in D. Vidas and P.J. Schei (eds), *The World Ocean in Globalisation: Climate Change, Sustainable Fisheries, Biodiversity, Shipping, Regional Issues*, Leiden and Boston, MA: Martinus Nijhoff Publishers, 2011, p. 371

Vukas, B., 'Enclosed and Semi-Enclosed Seas', in B. Vukas, *The Law of the Sea: Selected Writings*, Publications on Ocean Development, Leiden and Boston, MA: Martinus Nijhoff Publishers, 2004, p. 263.

Vukas, B., 'The Mediterranean: An Enclosed or Semi-Enclosed Sea?', in B. Vukas, *The Law of the Sea: Selected Writings*, Publications on Ocean Development, Leiden and Boston, MA: Martinus Nijhoff Publishers, 2004, p. 284

Vukas, B., 'The extension of the jurisdiction of the coastal States in the Adriatic Sea', in N. Ronzitti (ed.), *I rapporti di vicinato dell' Italia con Croazia, Serbia-Montenegro e Slovenia*, Rome: Luiss University Press-Giuffrè, 2005, p. 251

Vukas, B., 'Sea Boundary Delimitation and Internal Waters', in M.T. Ndiaye and R. Wolfrum (eds), *Law of the Sea, Environmental Law and Settlement of Disputes: Liber Amicorum Judge Thomas A. Mensah*, Leiden and Boston, MA: Martinus Nijhoff Publishers, 2007, p. 553

Theses

Attard, D., *The Mediterranean as an 'Enclosed Sea' in the New Law of the Sea*, Doctoral Thesis, Faculty of Laws, Malta: University of Malta, 1977

Grbec, M., *Delimitation of the Maritime Boundary between the Republic of Slovenia and the Republic of Croatia*, LL.M. Thesis, Malta: IMO IMLI, 2001

Grbec, M., *Extension of Coastal State Jurisdiction in Enclosed or Semi-Enclosed Sea: An Adriatic Sea Perspective*, Ph.D. Thesis, Malta: IMO IMLI, 2011

Gutiérez Fons, C.M., *The Legal Status of the Gulf of Fonseca: Is a condominium of the enclosed waters possible?*, LL.M. Thesis, Malta: IMO IMLI, 2004

Articles

Allen, S., 'Case Concerning the Frontier Dispute (Benin/Niger)', ICLQ, Vol. 55, 2006, p. 729

Alexander, L.M., 'Regionalism and the Law of the Sea: The case of semi-enclosed seas', ODIL, Vol. 2, Issue 2, 1974, p. 151

Alexander, L.M., 'Regional Arrangements in the Oceans', AJIL, Vol. 71, No. 1, 1977, p. 84

Andreone, G., '*La Zona Ecologica Italiana*', *Il Diritto Marittimo, Anno CIX-Terza Serie*, Vol. I, January–March, Genova, 2007, p. 1

Avbelj, M. and Letnar Černič, M., 'The Conundrum of the Piran Bay. *Slovenia v. Croatia* – The Case of Maritime Delimitation', *Journal of International Law and Policy, The University of Pennsylvania Journal of International Law & Policy*, Vol. 5, No. 2, 2007

Boelaert Suominen, S., 'The European Community, the European Court of Justice and the Law of the Sea', IJMCL, Vol. 23, No. 4, 2008, p. 643

Chevalier, C., 'Governance of the Mediterranean Sea: Outlook for the Legal Regime', IUCN Malaga: Centre for Mediterranean Cooperation, 2005

Churchill, R., 'Dispute Settlement under the UN Convention on the Law of the Sea: Survey for 2007', IJMCL, Vol. 23, No. 4, 2008, p. 601

Churchill, R., 'Dispute Settlement under the UN Convention on the Law of the Sea: Survey for 2009', IJMCL, Vol. 25, No. 4, 2010, p. 458

Craven, M., 'The EC Arbitration Commission on Yugoslavia', BYIL, Vol. 66, 1995, p. 388

Degan, V.Đ., 'Consolidation of Legal Principles on Maritime Delimitation: Implications for the Dispute between Slovenia and Croatia in the North Adriatic', CJIL, Vol. 6, No. 3, 2007, p. 601

Degan, V.Đ., '*Pravni naslov i efektivnost kao osnove suverenosti*', PPP, Vol. 47, No. 162, Zagreb, 2008, p. 1

Degan, V.D., '*Pravičnost i međunarodno pravo u razgraničenjima morskih prostora*', PPP, Vol. 49, No. 164, Zagreb, 2010, p. 139

De La Fayette, L., 'The Award in the Canada-France Maritime Boundary Arbitration', IJMCL, Vol. 8, No. 1, 1993, p. 77

Del Vecchio Capotosti, A., '*In Maiore Stat Minus*: A Note on the EEZ and the Zones of Ecological Protection in the Mediterranean Sea', ODIL, Vol. 39, No. 3, 2008, p. 287

DOALOS, 'The United Nations Convention on the Law of the Sea: A historical perspective'. Available at <http://www.un.org/Depts/los/convention_agreements/convention_historical_perspective.htm>

Drenik, S., '*Arbitražni sporazum: potek pogajanj in dosežene rešitve*', Pravna praksa, No. 45, Ljubljana, 2009, Appendix, p. I

Grbec, M., '*Razmejitev morskih pasov v mednarodnem pravu*', Pravnik, Vol. 57, No. 4–5, Ljubljana, 2002, p. 255

Grbec, M., '*Problematika morskih pasov v (severnem) Jadranu*', Podjetje in delo, No. 6/7, Year 23, Ljubljana, 2007, p. 1439

Gržetić, Z. *et al.*, '*O granicama u sjevernom Jadranu (1948–2009) s posebnim osvrtom na kronološki kartografski prikaz*', PPP, Vol. 49, No. 164, Zagreb, 2010, p. 19

Harrison, J., 'Judicial Law-Making and the Developing Order for the Oceans', IJMCL, Vol. 22, No. 2, 2007, p. 283

Juda, L., 'The European Union and Ocean Use Management: The Marine Strategy and the Maritime Policy', ODIL, Vol. 38, No. 3, 2007, p. 259

Bibliography 257

Klemenčič, M., 'The Border Agreement between Croatia and Bosnia and Herzegovina: The first, but not the last', *IBRU Boundary and Security Bulletin*, Winter, 1999–2000, p. 96

Kunič, J., 'The Slovenian-Croatian Border Question', IFIMES, Ljubljana, 2007

Kvinikhidze, S., 'Contemporary Exclusive Fishery Zones or Why Some States Still Claim an EFZ', IJMCL, No. 23, 2008, p. 271

Leanza, U., '*L'Italia e la scelta di rafforzare la tutela del ambiente marino: L'istituzione di zone di protezione ecologica*', *Rivista di diritto internazionale*, Vol. LXXXIX, No. 2, Milano: Giuffrè, 2006, p. 309

Malačič *et al.*, 'Environmental Impact of LNG Terminals in the Gulf of Trieste (Northern Adriatic)', Integration of Information for Environmental Security, Vol. 3, Springer, 2008, p. 361

Markovič, M., 'Mediterranean Instrument to Combat Climate Change: Protocol on Integrated Coastal Zone Management in the Mediterranean', Barcelona: IEMed, 2010

Markus, T. *et al.*, 'Legal Implementation of Integrated Ocean Policies: The EU's Marine Strategy Framework Directive', IJMCL, Vol. 26, 2011, p. 59

Notarnartolo-Di-Schiara *et al.*, 'The Pelagos Sanctuary for the Mediterranean Marine Mammals', Aquatic Conservation: Marine and Freshwater Ecosystems, No. 18, Issue 4, Willey InterScience, 2008, p. 367

Papanicolopulu, I., 'A Note on Maritime Delimitation in a Multizonal Context: The Case of the Mediterranean', ODIL, Vol. 38, No. 4, 2007, p. 381

Pellet, A., 'The Opinions of the Badinter Arbitration Committee: A Second Breath for the Self-Determination of Peoples', EJIL, No. 3, 1992, p. 178

Pavliha, M., '*To morje je vse, kar imam*', Pravna praksa, No. 5, Ljubljana, 2001, p. 33

Pavliha, M. and Grbec, M., 'The 2003 Supplementary Fund Protocol: An Important Improvement to the International Compensation System for Oil Pollution Damage', *Zbornik Pravnog Fakulteta u Zagrebu*, Year 58, Vol. 1–2, Zagreb, 2008, p. 307

Pavliha, M., '*Mednarodnopravni argumenti v luči prava EU zoper plinske terminale v Tržaškem zalivu*', Podjetje in delo, No. 8, Ljubljana, 2010, p. 1537

Pavliha, M., 'Essay on Ethics in International Maritime Law', *European Transport Law*, Vol. XLVII, No. 5, 2012, p. 461

Pavliha, M. and Martínez Gutiérrez, N.A., 'Marine Scientific Research and the 1982 United Nations Convention on the Law of the Sea', *Ocean and Coastal Law Journal*, Vol. 16, No. 1, Maine: University of Maine, School of Law, 2010, p. 115

Politakis, G.P., 'The French-Canadian Arbitration around St. Pierre and Miquelon: Unmasked Opportunism and the Triumph of the Unexpected', IJMCL, Vol. 8, No. 1, 1993, p. 105

Radan, P., 'Post-Secession International Borders: A Critical Analysis of the Opinions of the Badinter Arbitration Commission', *Melbourne University Law Review*, Vol. 24, No. 3, Melbourne, 2000, p. 50

Ratner, S., 'Drawing a better line: Uti possidetis and the border of new States', AJIL, Vol. 90, No. 4, 1996, p. 590

Rudolf, D. ml. and Kardum, I., '*Sporazum o arbitraži između Hrvatske i Slovenije*', PPP, Vol. 49, No. 164, Zagreb, 2010, p. 3

Sancin, V., 'Slovenia-Croatia Border Dispute: From "Drnovšek-Račan" to "Pahor-Kosor" Agreement', European Perspectives – *Journal of European Perspectives of the Western Balkans*, Vol. 2, No. 2, 2010, p. 93

Scovazzi, T., 'Implications of the new Law of the Sea for the Mediterranean', Marine Policy, Vol. 5, Issue 4, 1981, p. 302

Scovazzi, T., 'The Declaration of a Sanctuary for the Protection of Marine Mammals in the Mediterranean', IJMCL, Vol. 8, No. 4, 1993, p. 510

Scovazzi, T., 'The Mediterranean Marine Mammals Sanctuary: The Signature of an Agreement Establishing a Sanctuary for Marine Mammals', IJMCL, Vol. 16, No. 1, 2001, p. 132

Scovazzi, T., 'Marine Protected Areas and Navigation', *Il Journadas Internacionales de Seguridad Maritima y Medio Ambiente*, IUEM, 2006, p. 77

Scovazzi, T., 'The entry into force of the 2001 UNESCO Convention on the Protection of the Underwater Cultural Heritage', *Aegean Rev Law Sea*, Vol. 1, No. 1, Berlin and Heildeberg: Springer, 2009, p. 19

Scovazzi, T., 'Maritime Boundaries in the Eastern Mediterranean Sea', Policy Brief, Mediterranean Policy Program, Washington, DC: The German Marshal Fund of the United States, June 2012, p. 1

Šebenik, N., '*Teritorialni dostop do odprtega morja v mednarodni sodni in arbitražni praksi*', Pravna Praksa, Vol. 28, No. 49–50, Ljubljana, 2009, Appendix, p. I

Seršič, M., 'The Crisis in the Eastern Adriatic and the Law of the Sea', ODIL, Vol. 24, No. 3, 1993, p. 291

Shaw, M., 'The Heritage of States: The Principle of Uti Possidetis Juris Today', BYIL, Vol. 67, 1996, p. 75

Shaw, M., 'People, Territorialism and Boundaries', EJIL, No. 8, 1997, p. 497

Smith, J.J., 'An independent Quèbec's Maritime Claims in the Gulf of St Lawrence and Beyond', Can.Y.B. Int'l L., 1997, p. 113

Symmons, C.R., 'The Maritime Border Areas of Ireland, North and South', IJMC, Vol. 24, No. 3, 2009, p. 457

Stelekatos-Loverdos, M.C., 'The Contributions of Channels to the Definition of Straits Used for International Navigation', IJMCL, Vol. 13, No. 1, 1998, p. 71

Tanaka, Y., 'Reflections on Maritime Delimitation in the *Nicaragua/Honduras* Case', *Zeitschrift für ausländisches öffentliches Recht und Völkerrecht*, Vol. 68. No. 4, Max Planck Institute, 2009, p. 903

Topalović, D. and Blake, G.H., 'The Maritime Boundaries of the Adriatic Sea', Maritime Briefing, Vol. 1, No. 8, University of Durham, 1996, p. 36

Türk, D., 'Recognition of States: A Comment', EJIL, Vol. 4, 1993, p. 66

Vidas, D., 'Global Trends in Use of the Seas and the Legitimacy of Croatia's Extension of Jurisdiction in the Adriatic Sea', *Zagreb: Croatian International Relations Review*, Vol. 9, No. 32, 2003, p. 8

Vidas, D., 'The UN Convention on the Law of the Sea, the European Union and the Rule of Law: What is going on in the Adriatic', IJMCL, Vol. 24. No. 1, 2009, p. 1

Studies, reports and guidelines

Charney, J.I., 'The Maritime Boundaries of Quebéc', Report, March 9, 1992 as amended by the '2001 Update of the Maritime Boundaries of Québec (Updated and Complementary Texts of 2001)', November 14, 2001

Joint Expert Group of the Adriatic States on the PSSA, 'Designation of the Adriatic Sea as a Particularly Sensitive Area', draft proposal, 2007

Oral, N. *et al.*, 'The Role of Maritime Zones in Promoting Effective Governance for the Protection of the Mediterranean', Report of the Expert Group on Governance of the Mediterranean Sea, Prepared for the European Commission, Directorate General for Maritime Affairs and Fisheries: Mediterranean and Black Sea, 2009

Bibliography 259

Pellet, A. *et al.*, 'The Territorial Integrity of Québec in the Event of the Attainment of Sovereignty', Report prepared for the Québec's Ministére des relations internationals (Translation by William Boulet), 1992

Policy Research Corporation, 'The potential of Maritime Spatial Planning in the Mediterranean Sea. Case Study Report: The Adriatic Sea', Study carried out on behalf of the European Commission, Brussels, January 2011

Scovazzi, T. (ed.), 'Note on the establishment of marine protected areas beyond national jurisdiction or in areas where the limits of national sovereignty or jurisdiction have not yet been defined in the Mediterranean Sea', UNEP, UNEP(DEPI)/MED WG.359/ Inf.3 rev. 1, Tunis: RAC/SPA, 10 June 2011, pp. 32–37

Slim, H. and Scovazzi, T., 'Study of the current status of ratification, implementation and compliance with maritime agreements and conventions applicable to the Mediterranean Sea Basin: With a specific focus on the ENPI South Partner Countries', Parts I and II, Tables of Participation to the Relevant Treaties, AGRECO Consortium, 2009

UN Secretariat, 'Study of the juridical regime of the historic waters, including historic bays', UN Doc. A/CN.4/143, 9 March 1962

UN, 'Oceans and the Law of the Sea: Report of the Secretary-General', Doc.A/59/62 of 4 March 2004

Lectures, addresses and papers delivered at seminars and conferences

Attard, D., 'The Delimitation of Maritime Zones: Some Mediterranean Experiences', Proceedings of the 5th International Conference on Traffic Science, Portorož, University of Ljubljana, Faculty of Maritime Studies and Transportation & Slovenian Society for Traffic Science, 27–30 October 2001, p. 1

Juste Ruiz, J., 'Mediterranean Cooperation and Third States', paper delivered at the 11th Mediterranean Research Meeting, Florence and Montecatini Terme, 24–27 March 2010

Kačić, H. 'Traffic Separation Schemes in the Adriatic Sea', paper delivered at the round-table 'EU Maritime Policy and the (Northern) Adriatic', organized by the Maritime Law Association of Slovenia (MLAS), Portorož, Slovenia, 20 May 2011

Koh, T., 'The Negotiating Process of the Third United Nations Conference on the Law of the Sea', UN, Audiovisual Library of International Law, Lecture Series

Kohen, M., '*Uti Possidetis* and Maritime Delimitations', UN, Audiovisual Library of International Law, Lecture Series

Kohen, M., '*Uti possidetis* and Maritime Delimitation', ppt presentation, Geneva: The Graduate Institute, 2009. Available at <http://untreaty.un.org/cod/avl/pdf/ls/ Kohen_UtiPossidetis-MaritimeDelimit.pdf>

Oral, N., 'Governance for the Protection of the Mediterranean Sea Marine Environment and the Role of Maritime Zones', paper delivered at the 11th Mediterranean Research Meeting Florence and Montecatini Terme, 24–27 March 2010

Papanicolopulu, I., 'Tools for the Governance of Regional Seas: A Comparative Study of the Mediterranean and the Caribbean', paper delivered at the 11th Mediterranean Research Meeting Florence and Montecatini Terme, 24–27 March 2010

Schiano di Pepe, L., 'Towards a "New" International Role of the EU in Protecting the Marine Environment? The Mediterranean Sea as a Case Study', paper delivered at the 11th Mediterranean Research Meeting, Florence & Montecatini Terme, 24–27 March 2010

Scovazzi, T., 'The Delimitation of National Coastal Zones: The Agreements Concluded by Italy', paper delivered at the 11th Mediterranean Research Meeting Florence and Montecatini Terme, 24–27 March 2010

Škrk, M., '*Pomorski zakonik Republike Slovenije v luči mednarodnega prava*', *X. Dnevi javnega prava*, Proceedings, Portorož, 2004, p. 493

Treves, T., 'Potential Exclusive Economic Zones in the Mediterranean', paper delivered at the 11th Mediterranean Research Meeting, Florence and Montecatini Terme, 24–27 March 2010

Vidas, D., 'The Adriatic Sea Governance and Maritime Delimitation Issue: The Case of Croatia's EEZ', paper delivered at the 11th Mediterranean Research Meeting Florence and Montecatini Terme, 24–27 March 2010

Index

'access regime' 181
access to high seas 157, 160–62
Act No. 15 (1978) (Spain) 76
ad hoc arbitration 182, 185, 247
added value to protection 193–6, 229–32
adoption of UNCLOS III 17–21;
    inclusion of specific rules 20–21;
    position of states at UNCLOS III
    19–20; pre-UNCLOS III period 18–19
ADRIACOMS 221
ADRIAMED 221
Adriatic Ionian Initiative 215–17, 220–26,
    231–3
Adriatic PSSA 229–32, 236–8, 248; *see also*
    PSSA
Adriatic Sea 1–2, 6–16, 229–32; Adriatic
    PSSA 229–32; as (semi-)enclosed sea
    6–16
Adriatic Traffic 227–8
Aegean Sea 19
Agreement between [...] Cyprus and [...]
    Egypt on the Delimitation of the EEZ
    106–7
agreements concluded within AII
    framework 225–8; safety of navigation
    226–8
AII framework 225–8; *see also* Adriatic
    Ionian Initiative
Albania 1–2, 71–3, 75, 124, 222–3
Alboran Sea 204
Algeria 51–2, 64–7, 72, 75, 78–80, 117,
    121; Tunisia/Algeria Agreement 64–7
alternative joint zones 131
Ancona Agreement 224–5, 236
'Ancona Process' 225
Andreone, G. 79, 100
applicability of *effectivités* 141–8; in conflict
    with international law 144–8
application of Article 74(3) 64–7

application of conventional rules 67
Arab Jamahiriya 116, 118–19
archaeological zones 96–101, 103, 236,
    244
areas of co-operation 38–9, 235–6
arms trafficking 67
Article 56(1) 77–8, 81, 85, 96, 121–2
Article 56(3) 69
Article 57 56
Article 65 85–6
Article 74(3) 58, 61–7, 92, 246; 2002
    Tunisia/Algeria Agreement 64–7
Article 77(3) 69
Article 80 88
Article 83(3) 58, 61–2, 64–7
Article 89 72–3
Article 122 22–30; connection to another
    sea 26–7; evolution of 22–5;
    proclaimed EEZ 29–30; territorial seas
    and EEZs of coastal states 28–9; two
    state requirements 25–6
Article 123 2, 30, 35–46, 57–8, 190–216;
    areas of co-operation 38–9; effect on
    other users of enclosed seas 45–6;
    institutional vs non-institutional
    co-operation 44–5; interrelation
    between first and second elements
    42–3; introductory statement of 39–42;
    obligation to co-operate 36–8
Article 134 37
Article 300 41–2
artificial islands 54, 70, 77, 81, 88, 102–3,
    123, 243
artificial outlets 26–9
Atlantic tuna 77
Attard, D. 18–19
automatic application of *uti possidetis*
    135
autonomy 14–15

262 *Extension of Coastal State Jurisdiction in Enclosed or Semi-enclosed Seas*

Award of the Arbitral Tribunal of 31 July 1989 90–91
Award of the Arbitral Tribunal in the Matter of an Arbitration between Barbados and Trinidad & Tobago (2006) 69
Award of the Arbitral Tribunal in the Matter of an Arbitration between Guyana and Suriname (2007) 61–2
Award of the Arbitral Tribunal in the ST Pierre et Miquelon Case 147

Badinter Commission 135–8, 158, 186
Bahrain 53
Balkans wars 162, 223–4
Ballast Water Convention (2004) 230–31
Baltic Sea 50
Bangladesh 60, 62–3
Barcelona Convention 85, 115, 190–91, 196–200, 209–210, 223–6, 234–8
Barcelona System 44, 190–200, 223–6; compliance with Barcelona Convention 198–200; EEZs vs. ZEPs 196–8; enforcement on high seas 193–6; Protocols included 192–200
Bay of Bengal 151
Bay of Biscay 76
Bay of Boka Kotorska 138, 145, 148–9, 152, 162–5
Bay of Piran 138, 145, 148–9, 152, 167, 169–73, 185
Belfast Agreement (1999) 149
Belgrade Agreement 223–4, 237–8
Benin v Niger 141–4
better governance of Mediterranean 130–32
bilateral fisheries agreement 249
binding recommendations 41, 218
bioaccumulation 207
Biodiversity Protocol 83, 85, 115, 200–204, 248
Black Sea 27, 217
Blue Book on an Integrated Maritime Policy for the EU 130, 232
BOD2 207
Boelaert-Suominem, S. 125
bona fide obligation 38, 67, 91, 105, 249
border bays 134–89; Bay of Piran 169–72; in international law 148–53
Border Treaty (1999) 154–5, 158–60
Bosnia and Herzegovina 124, 153–62, 191, 199–200; access to high seas 160–62; legality on enclosure 155–7; solution in line with Part IX UNCLOS

153–62; treaty with Croatia on state border 158–60
bottom trawl nets 218
boundaries on land 136–7
boundary agreement 139
breach of duty of co-operation 91, 93–4; *see also* duty of co-operation
Bunkers Convention 195–6, 211
Burkina Faso v Mali 134, 141–3

Case Concerning the Arbitral Award of 31 July 1989 90–91
Case Concerning the Frontier Dispute (2005) 141
Central American Court of Arbitration 151
channelling of liability 209
Charney, J.I. 146–7, 160–61
Churchill, R. 62, 148–9, 156, 208
CIESM Agreement 220, 223
CLC 211
clearing houses 237–8
climate change 213, 216, 238
'closed' seas 150–52
co-agent Lowe 40–42; *see also* Mox Plant Case
co-operation of Adriatic States 190–238; Adriatic PSSA 229–32; conclusion 237–8; existing forms at Mediterranean level 190–216; management and conservation of living resources 217–20; marine scientific research 220–22; other areas of co-operation 235–6; other co-operative arrangements 222–8; protection and preservation role of EU 232–5
co-ordination of activities 43–5, 57, 65–6, 97
coastal state jurisdiction by EU member states 125–6
Code of Conduct for Responsible Fisheries 221
colonial *effectivités* 143–4
COLREG 230
Common Fisheries Policy 180
common zones *see* alternative joint zones
Compensation Fund 211–12
compliance with Barcelona Convention 198–200
Compliance Committee 199
concept of (semi-)enclosed sea 17–67
concerned 'third' countries 234, 244

Index 263

concerted action 126, 128–30, 132
conclusion of provisional arrangements pending delimitation 61–7
condominium solution 172
Conference Communiqué 130–31
configuration of the Mediterranean 6–9
conflict with international law 144–8
connection to another sea/ocean by narrow outlet 26–7
conservation interest lists 203
conservation of living resources 43, 53–4, 217–20
Constitution of Ireland 149–50
Constitutional Act 1867 (Canada) 146
contact with high seas 186–9
contemporary law of the sea 17–67
contiguous zones 96–9, 146–7, 244
continental shelf 9, 68–74, 172–4; delimitation of 71–4; Slovenian claim to its own 172–4
contingency 229–32
COPEMED 221
coral reefs 218
corridor of undivided EEZs 51, 100
Counter-Memorial of the United Kingdom 36, 42
critical dates 144, 171, 182, 186, 188
Croatia 1–2, 76, 87–94, 101–5, 124, 153–89; 2009 Arbitral Agreement with Slovenia 134, 181–9; delimitation of boundary with Montenegro 162–6; ecological and fisheries protection zone 87–94; maritime delimitation dispute with Slovenia 166–81; solution in line with Part IX UNCLOS 153–62
Croatian Maritime Code (1994) 87–8, 95, 161
customs zones 243–4
Cypriot Proclamation to Provide for an EEZ (2004) 105–8
Cyprus 50, 72, 105–112, 119, 157

Dayton Agreement 158
de facto EEZs 105–124
de facto implementation of ZEP regime 100–101
de lege ferenda proposals 249
Decision on Amending the Decision on the Extension of the Republic of Croatia in the Adriatic Sea (2004) 93
decolonization 135–6, 140, 143–4
deep sea sensitive habitats 202, 218
Deepwater Horizon 209
definition of *uti possidetis* 134–5

Degan, Đ.V. 151
degree of uniformity 56
delimitation of EEZs 52–3, 58–60
delimitation of historic waters 151–3
delimitation of maritime boundaries 134–89; between Croatia and Montenegro 162–6; border bays in international law 148–53; conclusion 189; Croatia/Bosnia and Herzegovina 153–62; dissolution of former SFRY 135–9; Slovenia/Croatia 2009 Arbitral Agreement 181–9; Slovenia–Croatia dispute 166–81; *uti possidetis* 134–5, 139–48
delimitation of Mediterranean continental shelf 71–4
delimitation of zones of sovereign rights 246–7
Denmark 51, 53
derived zones 244–5
destruction of biodiversity 197–8, 200–201
development of concept of (semi-)enclosed sea 17–67
discharges 229, 237–8, 248
discretion 222
'Disegno di Legge' 101
dissolution 145
dissolution of former SFRY 135–9
doctrine of effective control 141–8
driftnets 83–4, 180
drilling platforms 123, 210–212
Drnovšek-Račan Treaty 174–9, 182
Dubrovnik 162
duty of co-operation 33–5, 58–9, 61–3, 91–3
duty of maximum extent permitted by international law 48–9

Eastern Adriatic 134–89
EASTMED 221
ecological and fisheries protection zone (Croatia) 87–94, 100
Ecosystem Approach to Fisheries 219
EEZs 51–67, 196–8; vs. ZEPs 196–8
effect of Art. 123 on other users of enclosed seas 45–6
effective control 145, 172–3
effectivités 141–8, 169–75; *see also uti possidetis*
Egypt 72, 75, 105–9
El Salvador v Honduras 134–5, 139–40, 142, 147
enclavement 172, 175

enclosed or semi-enclosed seas 6–16;
Adriatic 9–13; conclusion 15–16;
Mediterranean 6–9; Mediterranean
and/or Adriatic 13–15
enclosure of MZs of Bosnia/Herzegovina
within SFRY system of straight
baselines 155–7
end of *sui generis* zones era in
Mediterranean 122–4
energy production 77, 88, 123
enforcement of Barcelona System on high
seas 193–6
enforcement powers 194–5
environmental tragedies 210
equidistance 79, 170, 187–8
equitable compromise 174
equity *praeter legem* 187–8
Eratosthemes Seamount Area 218
Erika disaster 80
Estonia 50
EU *see* European Union
European *acquis* 180–81
European Union 44–5, 124–32, 182–4,
213–16, 232–5; *Blue Book* 130;
involvement of 183–4; recent
positions regarding extension of coastal
state jurisdiction 124–32; role in
preservation of marine environment
232–5
evolution of Article 122 22–5; ISNT and
RSNT 24–5
ex aqueo et bono 182, 187–8
Exchange of Notes 50
exercise of rights and duties 42–3
exhortation to co-operate 36–8
existing forms of co-operation 190–216;
Barcelona System 192–200;
implementation of Barcelona System
200–216; preservation of marine
environment 190–92
exploitability 18, 43, 53, 63, 78, 86, 102,
123, 197, 211–12, 222, 238
export routes 229
extension of breadth of territorial seas
47–51; maximum permitted by
international law 48–9; practice of
states bordering (semi-)enclosed seas
50–51; proposals at UNCLOS III and
within SBC 47–8
extension of coastal state jurisdiction
68–133, 193–6; added value 193–6;
conclusion 133; continental shelf
68–74; Mediterranean *status quo* 74–6;
recent positions of EU 124–32;

recently proclaimed EEZs 105–124; *sui
generis* zones 76–105
external limits of Libyan EEZ 116–18

federal territorial sea 137–8, 148
Finland 50–51
first Mediterranean *sui generis* zone
83–7
First World War 167
fish migration loop 219–20
fisheries protection zone (Libya) 114–19
fisheries protection zone (Spain) 76–80
fisheries restricted areas 218–20
Fishing Waters (Designation) and
Extended Maritime Jurisdiction Act
(2005) 121–2
fixing external limits of EEZs 56–8
flag State jurisdiction 1–5, 97; current
jurisdictional landscape 1–2; Part IX
UNCLOS 2
flags of convenience 94, 248
flying other nations' flags 77, 93, 151
former SFRY *see* Bosnia and Herzegovina;
Croatia; Montenegro; Slovenia
former USSR 14
framework laws 80, 87, 94–5, 99, 101,
105–124, 239–50; delimitation of
zones of sovereign rights 246–7; mini
EEZs 240–46; possible way forward
247–50
France 20, 71, 75–6, 78–83, 85–6, 90, 94,
122–4; EEZs 122–4
France v Canada (1992) 147
Franck, T.M. 146
free access to fisheries 74
freedoms of the seas 18, 50–51, 99
Frontier Case (1986) 134, 141
functional jurisdiction 92, 194
FUNDS Convention 211

gas prospecting 211–12
general policy of co-operation 40, 49, 65,
74
general rules of UNCLOS 39–42
Geneva Convention 17–19
geographical characteristics of Slovenian
coastline 167
geographical identification 203, 212
German Democratic Republic 52
Gestri, M. 56
GFCM 202, 217, 223, 237–8
global norms 32, 53
good faith 41–2, 45, 49, 58, 61–3
Greece 19, 50, 71–3

Index 265

'grey areas' 178–9
ground water draining 207
Guidelines of PSSA 230
Guillaume, Gilbert 183
Guinea Bissau v Senegal (ICJ 1989) 90–91,
    140
Gulf of Finland 51
Gulf of Fonseca Judgment 140, 147,
    151–2
Gulf of Lions 204
Gulf of Mexico 209–210
Gulf of Sidra 117
Gulf of Trieste 216
Guyana 61–2

Habitats Directive 247
*Handbook on the Delimitation of Maritime
    Boundaries* 174–5
harvesting of plants 201
Higgins, R. 146
high seas 1–2, 26–9, 69, 73, 80, 85, 90,
    100, 133, 160–62, 172–4, 193–6, 199–
    200, 244–5; access to 160–62;
    definition of 244–5; enforcement of
    Barcelona System on 193–6
'historic bay' status 117, 152
historic fishing rights 53–4, 128, 177–81,
    203–4
historical background of Slovenian
    coastline 167
historical catch share 249
HNS pollution damage 195, 211
holistic approach to protection 99, 124,
    130, 250
holistic EEZs 132–3
hortatory provision 41–2, 45
'hot pursuit' 194–5
Hudson Bay 146–7
hybrid zones 114

Ibler, V. 54
ICCAT 217
ICZM Protocol 213–16, 236
*Identification and Designation of Particularly
    Sensitive Seas Areas* 230
illegal activities 224
illegal discharges 229, 237–8
illegal immigration 67
IMO 11, 179, 191, 194, 201, 204–5,
    226–32, 248–9
implementation of Barcelona System 200–
    216; Biodiversity Protocol 200–204;
    ICZM Protocol 213–16; Land-Based
    Protocol 206–8; Offshore Protocol

208–213; Prevention and Emergency
    Protocol 204–6
implementation of Part IX of UNCLOS
    190–238
implementing orders 120; *see also*
    framework laws
in plus stat minus zone 81–2, 86–8, 94–101,
    105, 122, 129–30, 133, 196, 239–43;
    see also real *sui generis* zones
inclusion of specific rules in UNCLOS
    20–21
inconveniences 126–7
independence 135–45, 151, 155, 162,
    169–73
India–Sri Lanka Agreement 151–3
influence of Part IX UNCLOS
    46–67; extension of breadth of
    territorial sea 47–51; proclamation
    of EEZs 51–67
initiatives from EU re extension of coastal
    jurisdiction 126–32; integrated
    maritime policy for better governance
    130–32; Venice Declaration (2003)
    127–30
inland water *see* 'closed' seas
institution of proceedings 194–5
institutional co-operation 44–5,
    237–8
integrated maritime policy for better
    governance 130–32, 213–16, 232–3
interdependence 35
interim co-operation 162–3
Interim Delimitation Agreement (2002)
    89–90
internal maritime lines 189
internal waters arrangements 159,
    163–6
international community 176
International Court of Justice 53, 59–60,
    69, 72, 90, 134, 139–44, 150–51,
    182–7, 247
international law 78, 144–53, 187
interrelation between first and second
    elements Art. 123 42–3
introductory statement of Art. 123
    39–42
Iran 21–4, 31–4, 53; Iranian proposal
    31–3
Iraq 32, 47, 52
ISNT 24–5, 33–4, 54
isolationist policies 222–3
Israel 52, 72–3, 105, 109, 111–12
Italian Draft Law on Establishment of a
    ZEP 94–5, 98, 101

266 *Extension of Coastal State Jurisdiction in Enclosed or Semi-enclosed Seas*

Italy 1–2, 20, 65, 71, 75–6, 79, 81, 83, 85–6, 90–105, 121, 124
ITLOS 44, 243–4
IUU fishing *see* unregulated fishing

Janša, Janez 182
Japan 51, 77
Joint Declaration for the Establishment of a Sanctuary for the Protection of Marine Mammals in the Mediterranean (1993) 82–6
joint fishing zones 63, 177–81
joint management 150–51
joint sovereignty 142
Judge Andersen 44
junction of the high seas 186–9
juridical status 175
jurisdiction delimitation 246–7
jurisdictional maritime landscapes 1–2, 74–6
'jurisdictional move' 123
jus cogens 139, 148

Klek-Neum Corridor 153, 155
Klemenčič, M. 160
Korea 51, 53, 77
Kunič, J. 137

Land, Island and Maritime Frontier Case (1992) 134–5, 139–40, 147, 152
land and maritime boundary delimitation 162–6; 2002 Protocol 163–6
Land-Based Protocol 206–8
Law on the Exclusive Economic Zone and the Zone of Ecological Protection (2003) 81
law of maritime delimitation 58
law of the sea 144–8
Leanza, U. 15, 18, 25, 30, 36, 71, 100, 246
Lebanon 72–3, 105, 109, 112, 122–4; EEZs 122–4
legal definition of (semi-)enclosed sea 23–30; Article 122 25–30; Article 123 35–46; evolution of Article 122 22–5; Iranian proposal 31–3; ISNT 33–4; RSNT 34–5
legal obligation 40
legal predictability 243
legal status of waters 15–16
legal validity of letters 140
legality of enclosure 154–7
legitimate interests of states 121, 174
Libya 72, 114–21; Libyan FPZ (2009) 118–19; limits of FPZ 116–18

Libya/Malta Case 60, 69
Lophelia reef 218
low water mark 117
Lowe, V. 148–9, 156, 183

Malta 72, 75, 119, 121–2
Maltese Fisheries Conservation and Management Act (2001) 122
management of living resources 37, 43, 78, 217–20
mandatory co-ordination 37–8
MAP 213, 223
Mare Clausum 6
Mare Nostrum 6, 106, 122
marine mammal conservation 83–6, 99, 101
marine pollution 205–6, 210–211, 227–9; *see also* pollution
marine scientific research 220–22
Marine Strategy Directive 130, 225, 232–5, 237, 247
maritime boundary between Croatia and Slovenia 168–74; border Bay of Piran 169–72; territorial contact of Slovenia with high seas 172–4
Maritime Code of Croatia 239
maritime delimitations 139–48; conflict with international law 144–8; *effectivités* 141–4; pre-2007 jurisprudence on *uti possidetis* 140–41; *see also* delimitation of maritime boundaries
maritime policy for better governance 130–32
Maritime Strategy Directive (2008) 232–3
Markus, T. 234
MARPOL Convention 205, 229–32
Marrakesh Declaration 196–8, 216
maximum extent permitted by international law 48–9
median line 109, 246, 248–9
Mediterranean Hydrological Basin 206–7
Mediterranean Sea 1–2, 6–16, 68–76; configuration of 6–9; and the continental shelf 68–74; as (semi-) enclosed sea 6–16; *status quo* of 74–6
Mediterranean Strategy for Sustainable Development (2005) 196–7
Mediterranean-level co-operation 190–216
Memorial of Ireland 32, 39–40
Mexico 34
mini EEZs 240–46; vs. real *sui generis* zones 243–4; *see also* real *sui generis* zones
minimum landing sizes 218
mobility of shipping 74

modus vivendi line 142–3
Monaco 71, 83, 86
Montenegro 1–2, 89, 124, 138, 162–6; delimitation of boundary with Croatia 162–6
moral obligation 40
Morocco 75, 78–9
Mox Plant Case 32–4, 36, 39–42, 44
Mozambique–Tanzania Agreement 151–3
MSP 215–16
Myanmar 60, 62–3

narrow outlets 26–9
navigation 50–51, 54–5, 113, 147, 155–61, 179, 201, 203–4, 224–8, 236
Nicaragua v Honduras 139, 143
Nile Delta 218
non-enclavement 175
non-institutional co-operation 44–5
non-living resources 63
non-riparian states *see* riparian states
North Sea Continental Shelf Case 53
Note Verbale 79–80, 91–3, 173

OAU Cairo Resolution 140
obligation to co-operate 36–8, 58, 68, 92–3, 105, 117, 121, 216; relevance of chairman's statement 37–8
Oceans and Laws of the Sea (UN) 240–41
'offshore activities' 211
Offshore Protocol 199, 208–213
open seas *see* high seas
operational pollution 237–8
operative modalities 101
'opt-out' clauses 218–19
Osimo Treaty 179
OSPAR Commission 44
other areas of co-operation 38–9, 235–6
other co-operative arrangements between Adriatic States 222–8; agreements within AII framework 225–8
overexploitation of fisheries resources 77, 87
overflight 113

Palagruža threshold 13
Paris MOU 237–8
Part IX UNCLOS 2–3
Pavliha, M. 41
Pelagos sanctuary 83–7, 95, 203
Pellet, A. 135, 146
Perry, William 181–2
physical inspection 194–5
'pick up' system 198

police authority 175
pollution 29, 32, 84, 193–5, 199–201, 205–6, 210–211, 227–8, 236–8
pollution damage 195, 210
ports of refuge 204
position of border bays in international law 148–53; state practice re border bays 148–53
position of states at UNCLOS III 19–20, 51–5; conservation of living resources 53–4; delimitation of EEZs 52–3; navigation 54–5; right to proclaim EEZ 52
positions of the EU 124–32; extension/delimitation by EU member states 125–6; recent EU initiatives 126–32
possible way forward 247–50
post-colonial *effectivités* 143–4
potential vs. proclaimed EEZ 29–30
practice of states bordering (semi-)enclosed sea 50–51
pre-UNCLOS III period 18–19
Prescott, V. 156–7
preservation of Adriatic marine environment 37, 43, 129–30, 138, 190–92, 232–5
preservation of historic fishing rights 53–4, 177–81
Presidential Decree (2011) 99–101
Prestige disaster 80
Prevention and Emergency Protocol 204–6
Prevlaka peninsula 162, 164
primarily territorial seas requirement 28–9
principle of reciprocity 177–8
principle of *uri possidetis* in areas of conflict 144–8
priority conservation areas 203, 235
Procedures and Mechanism on Compliance 199
proclamation of Adriatic PSSA 230–32
proclamation of EEZs 1–2, 29–30, 51–67; Article 74(3) 61–7; delimitation of EEZs 58–60; fixing external limits of EEZs 56–8; *ipso facto* existence 55–6; positions of states at UNCLOS III 51–5
prohibition of fishing 114
proliferation of algae 197, 201
proposals by states at UNCLOS III 47–8
protection of Adriatic marine environment 37, 43, 99, 129–30, 138, 190–92, 229–35; proclamation of Adriatic PSSA 230–32

268 *Extension of Coastal State Jurisdiction in Enclosed or Semi-enclosed Seas*

protection of biodiversity 99–100, 236
provision for (semi-)enclosed seas 13–15
provisional arrangements applicable to
  internal waters 63–4, 163–6
provisional practical arrangements
  pending delimitation 61–7
PSSA 194, 201, 228–32, 236; Guidelines
  230
psychotropic substances 67
punishment 67

quasi EEZs 76–105; *see also sui generis* zones
'quasi' *ex aqueo et bono* 188; *see also ex aqueo et
  bono*

Raftopoulos, E. 191, 196, 205
ratione materiae 132
Ratner, S. 134
real *sui generis* zones 94–101, 240–46; *in plus
  stat minus* 240–43; rights of third States
  244–6; vs. mini EEZs 242–4; vs mini
  EEZs 243–4; *see also sui generis* zones
reasons for inclusion of specific rules in
  UNCLOS III 20–21
rebutable presumption 147
recently proclaimed EEZs 105–124;
  Cyprus 105–112; France and the
  Lebanon 122–4; Libya 114–19; Malta
  121–2; Syria 112–14; Tunisia 119–21
reciprocity 177–8
Recommended Routes System 11
recreational fishing 165–6
reflecting spirit of Part IX 181–9
regime of navigation 179
regulation of passage of ships 201
relation of *sui generis* zones with high seas
  244–6
relative stability 249
relevance of chairman's statement 37–8
'relevant circumstances' 142
REMPEC 204–5
Report of the Compliance Committee 199
Report of the Role of Maritime Zones… 131
Reserved Fishing Zone 75, 80
right of access 180
right of innocent passage 175–6
right to maximum extent permitted by
  international law 48–9
right to proclaim an EEZ 52
rights of abuse 41
rights of third states 244–6
riparian states 43, 45–6, 149, 151, 153
river basin principle 208
roadmap for accession negotiations 184

role of EU in preservation of marine
  environment 232–5
Romania/Ukraine Case (2009) 59–60, 91
routing measures 227–8
Royal Decree No. 1315/1997 (Spain)
  76–7
RSNT 24–5, 34–5
Ruiz, J. Juste 193–4, 218–19, 221–2

SafeSeaNet 228
safety of navigation 50–51, 203–4, 224–8,
  236
salvage operations 165–6
Sanader, Ivo 182
Sanctuary Agreement (2002) 84–6
SBC 20, 46–8
Schofield, C. 156–7
Scovazzi, T. 36, 38, 56, 58, 202, 209,
  229–30
Sea of Azov 150–51, 171
seabed and its subsoil 69–70, 123, 138,
  200–201, 238
search and rescue 66–7
secession 145–6
Second World War 167
sectoral zones 132–3, 138, 198
security threats 67
Sekolec, Jernej 184
self-restraint 78
Serbia 89–90, 162–3
serious damage 194
set back zones 214
Shaw, M. 135, 146
Shelf Agreements 90, 101, 120–21
ships in distress 204
Simma, Bruno 183
Slim, H. 229–30
Slovenia 1–2, 76, 90, 93–4, 101–5, 124,
  138, 166–89; 2009 Arbitral Agreement
  with Croatia 181–9; maritime
  delimitation dispute with Croatia
  166–81; territorial contact with high
  seas 186–9
Slovenian continental shelf 90
solution in line with Part IX UNCLOS
  64–7, 86, 92, 148–62, 166–89, 216,
  222, 237–8, 249–50; access of Bosnia
  and Herzegovina to high seas 160–62;
  boundary between Croatia and
  Slovenia 168–74; Drnovšek-Račan
  Treaty 2001 174–7; geographical
  characteristics 167; joint fishing zones
  177–81; legality of enclosure 155–7;
  reflecting spirit of Part IX 181–9;

treaty between Croatia and Bosnia/
Herzegovina 158–60
SOPS 177–81
sovereignty 49–50, 65, 73, 77, 88, 99,
114–15, 171, 186–9, 246–7
Spain 71, 75–82, 90, 157; fisheries
protection zone 76–80
SPAMI 83, 194, 201–4, 219, 232, 235–8,
243–4, 248, 250
'special agreements' 139
special fishing zones 114–20
specially protected areas 194–5
specific geography of Mediterranean 121
specific rules on (semi-)enclosed seas 20–21
spills 194–6; *see also* pollution
spirit of understanding and co-operation.
63–4
Škrk, M. 30, 36, 39, 177
state practice re border bays 148–53;
delimitation of historic waters 151–3;
Sea of Azov, Strait of Kerch 150–51
status quo of Mediterranean 74–6
straight baselines 117–18, 150, 153,
155–7, 171
Strait of Gibraltar 26–7
Strait of Kerch 150–51
Strait of Otranto 11–13, 72
strict liability 211–12
Sub-Regional Adriatic Convention 236
sui generis zones 76–105; ecological and
fisheries PZ (Croatia) 87–94; fisheries
PZ (Spain) 76–80; Pelagos sanctuary
83–7; relation with high seas 244–6;
zone of ecological protection (France)
80–83; zone of ecological protection
(Italy) 94–101; zone of ecological
protection (Slovenia) 101–5
superjacent waters 63–5, 68–72, 86,
89–91, 98, 121–3, 188–9, 245–8
Suriname 61–2
sustainable exploitation 86–7, 127,
179–80, 224
Sweden 51
Symmons, C.R. 149, 152
Syria 105, 112–14, 119
system of straight baselines 155–7

tabula rasa rule 140
temporary line of delimitation 80,
89–90
termination of *status quo* 76
territorial access 174
territorial contact of Slovenia with high
seas 172–4, 186–9

Territorial Waters and Contiguous Zone
Act (1971) 122
Tomuscat, T. 146
tourism 210
toward integrated maritime policy 130–32
towed dredge nets 218
traditional freedoms of the seas 18, 54–5
Traffic Separation Schemes 11, 227
transboundary oilfields 211–12
transition from *sui generis* zone to full EEZ
114–19
travaux préparatoires 27, 29, 37, 40–42, 57
trawl nets 180
treaty on state border between Croatia and
Bosnia/Herzegovina 158–60
Treves, T. 2, 70, 241, 244
Trilateral Commission 224–8, 234–5,
237–8
tuna quotas 217–20
Tunisia 34, 64–5, 71–2, 75, 119–21;
Tunisia/Algeria Agreement 64–7
Tunisia–Italy Shelf Delimitation
Agreement (1971) 65
Türk, D. 136–7
Turkey 19, 25, 31–4, 47–51, 105, 109
two state requirements 24–6
2002 Protocol 163–6
2002 Tunisia/Algeria Agreement 64–7
2009 Arbitral Agreement between
Slovenia and Croatia 134, 181–9; Bay
of Piran 185; EU element 183–4;
principle of *uti possidetis* 186; zones of
sovereign rights 186–9
2009 Declaration of Libyan EEZ 118–19

UNCLOS III 17–67; adoption of 17–21;
conclusion 67; establishment of 17–21;
influences of Part IX of UNCLOS
46–67; legal definition of (semi-)
enclosed sea 22–30; rights and duties
of States 30–46
underwater cultural object protection
96–101, 103, 236
underwater noise 238
UNEP MAP 190–92
UNESCO Convention 236, 243–4
unilateral delimitation 79, 246
United Nations convention on the Law of
the Sea 87–8
UNPROFOR 162–3
unregulated fishing 126, 129
unsettled maritime boundaries 204
untouchable rights 244
urban development 214

urban waste 207–8
Uruguay 47–8, 51
uti possidetis 134–89; and conflict with
  international law 144–8; definition
  134–5; pre-2007 jurisprudence on
  140–41; *see also* delimitation of
  maritime boundaries
uti possidetis de facto see effectivités
uti possidetis (juris) 134–5, 138–44, 189; *see
  also* independence

VCLT 74
Venice Declaration (2003) 127–30, 132
Vidas, D. 9–10, 230, 232
Vienna Convention (1978) 140
violations of protocols 194–5
Virginia Commentary 27, 35–6, 41, 46
virtual EEZs 105–124
'vision documents' 130

Vukas, B. 23, 26, 36, 39, 165, 184
Water Framework Directive 207–8
wildlife preservation 193–4
wind turbines 123
work undertaken re Adriatic PSSA
  230–32

Yugoslavia 138

ZEPs 94, 196–8
zone of ecological protection (France)
  80–83
zone of ecological protection (Italy)
  94–101
zone of ecological protection (Slovenia)
  101–5
zones similar to EEZs 51–67
zones of sovereign rights 65, 73–4, 77, 88,
  99, 114–15, 186–9, 246–7

Taylor & Francis
eBooks
FOR LIBRARIES

ORDER YOUR FREE 30 DAY INSTITUTIONAL TRIAL TODAY!

Over 23,000 eBook titles in the Humanities, Social Sciences, STM and Law from some of the world's leading imprints.

Choose from a range of subject packages or create your own!

- ▶ Free MARC records
- ▶ COUNTER-compliant usage statistics
- ▶ Flexible purchase and pricing options

- ▶ Off-site, anytime access via Athens or referring URL
- ▶ Print or copy pages or chapters
- ▶ Full content search
- ▶ Bookmark, highlight and annotate text
- ▶ Access to thousands of pages of quality research at the click of a button

For more information, pricing enquiries or to order a free trial, contact your local online sales team.

UK and Rest of World: **online.sales@tandf.co.uk**
US, Canada and Latin America:
e-reference@taylorandfrancis.com

www.ebooksubscriptions.com

Taylor & Francis eBooks
Taylor & Francis Group

A flexible and dynamic resource for teaching, learning and research.